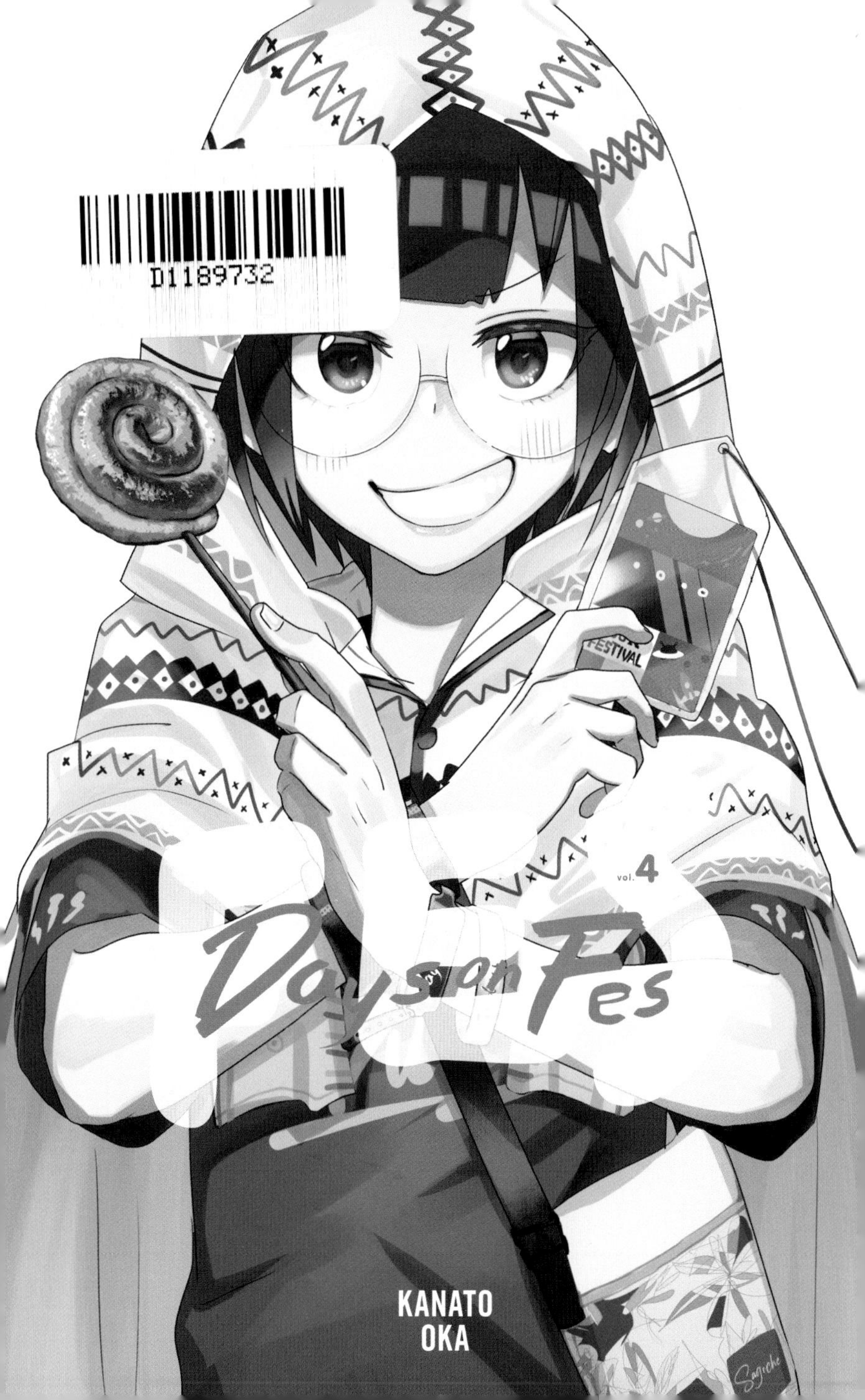
vol. 4
Days on Fes
FESTIVAL
KANATO
OKA

Days on Fes

contents

FES 14

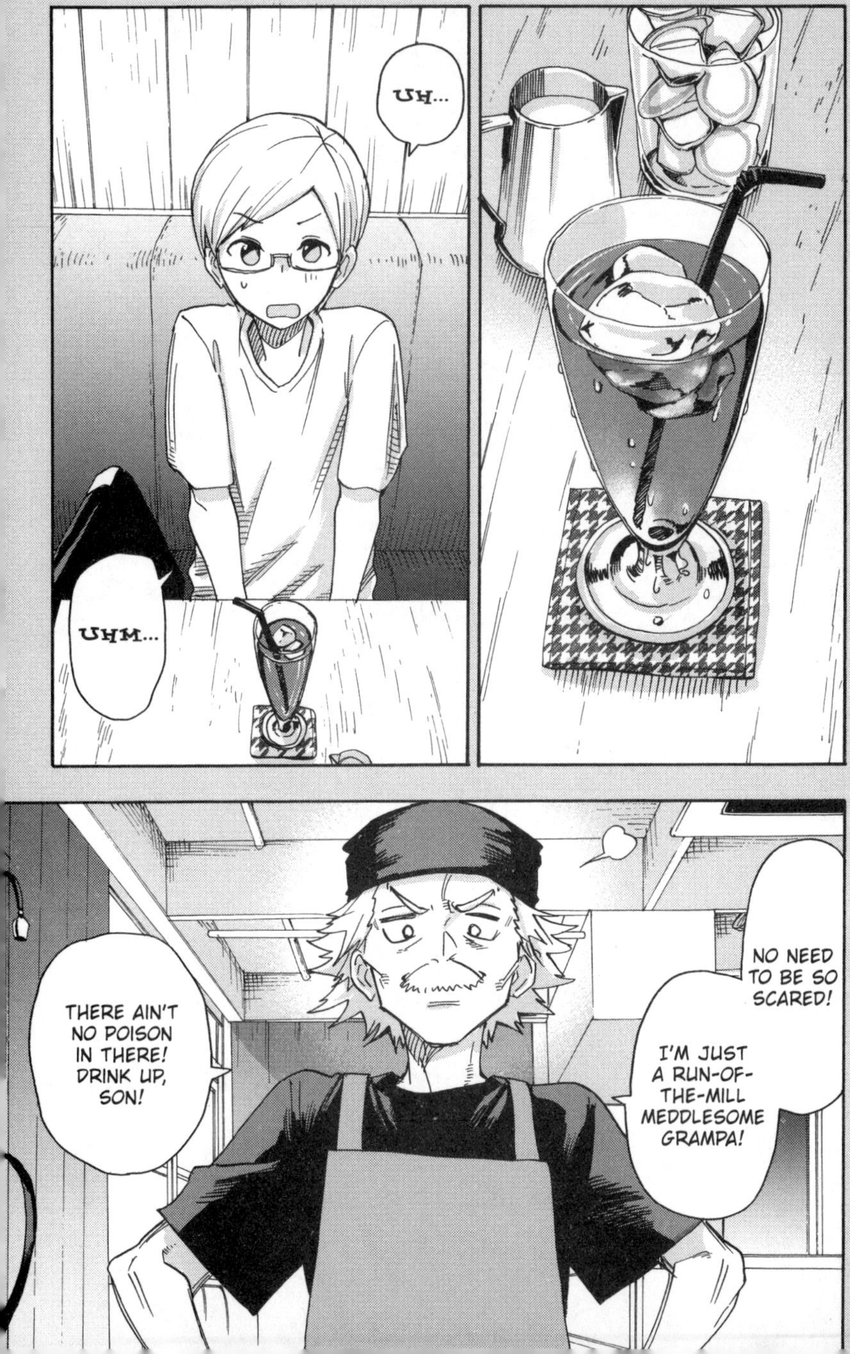
UH...
UHM...
NO NEED TO BE SO SCARED!
I'M JUST A RUN-OF-THE-MILL MEDDLESOME GRAMPA!
THERE AIN'T NO POISON IN THERE! DRINK UP, SON!

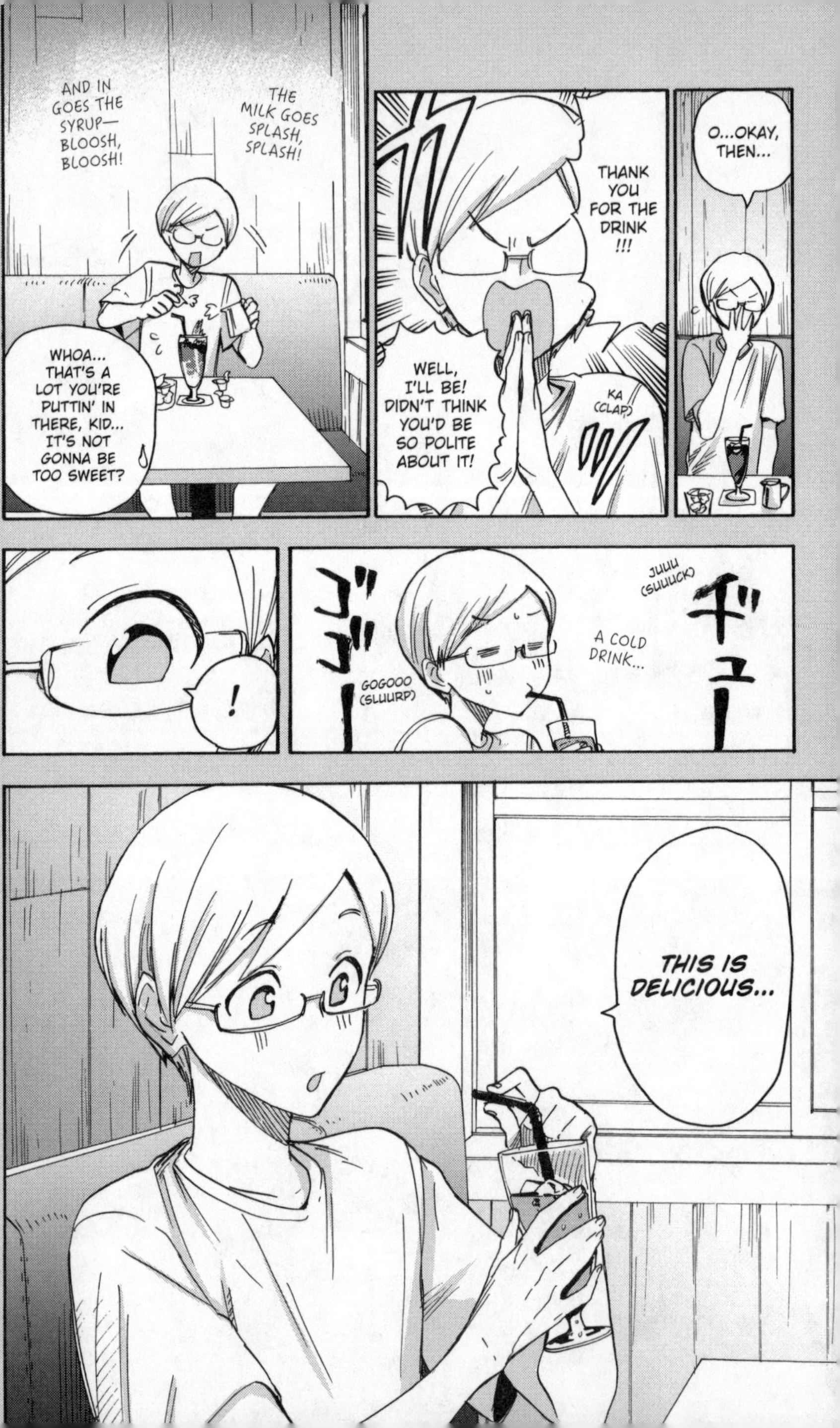
O...OKAY, THEN...
THANK YOU FOR THE DRINK!!!
WELL, I'LL BE! DIDN'T THINK YOU'D BE SO POLITE ABOUT IT!
KA (CLAP)
THE MILK GOES SPLASH, SPLASH!
AND IN GOES THE SYRUP—BLOOSH, BLOOSH!
WHOA... THAT'S A LOT YOU'RE PUTTIN' IN THERE, KID... IT'S NOT GONNA BE TOO SWEET?
ギュー
JUUU (SUUUCK)
A COLD DRINK...
GOGOOO (SLUURP)
ゴゴー
!
THIS IS DELICIOUS...

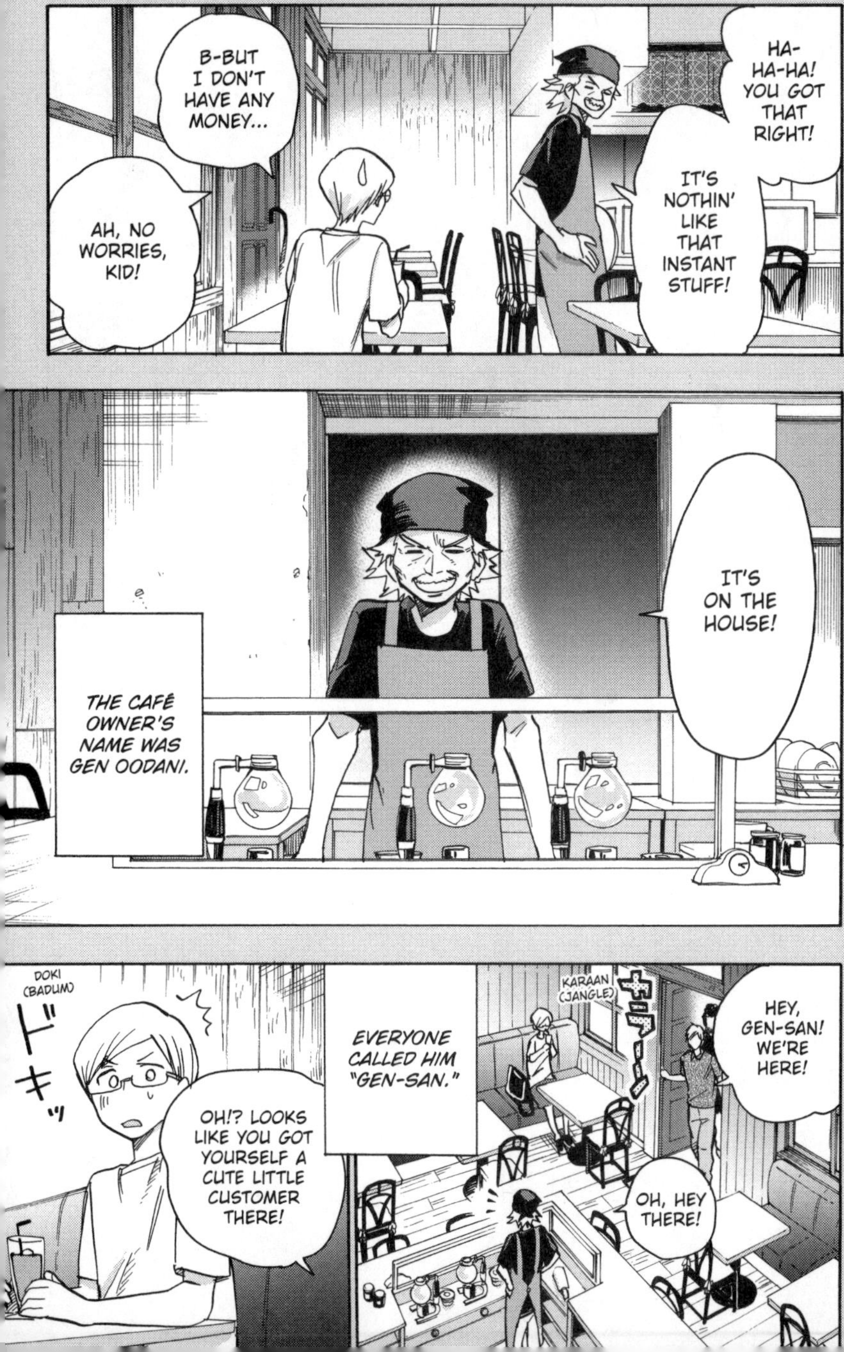
HA-HA-HA! YOU GOT THAT RIGHT!
IT'S NOTHIN' LIKE THAT INSTANT STUFF!
B-BUT I DON'T HAVE ANY MONEY...
AH, NO WORRIES, KID!
IT'S ON THE HOUSE!
THE CAFÉ OWNER'S NAME WAS GEN OODANI.
KARAAN (JANGLE)
HEY, GEN-SAN! WE'RE HERE!
OH, HEY THERE!
EVERYONE CALLED HIM "GEN-SAN."
DOKI (BADUM)
OH!? LOOKS LIKE YOU GOT YOURSELF A CUTE LITTLE CUSTOMER THERE!

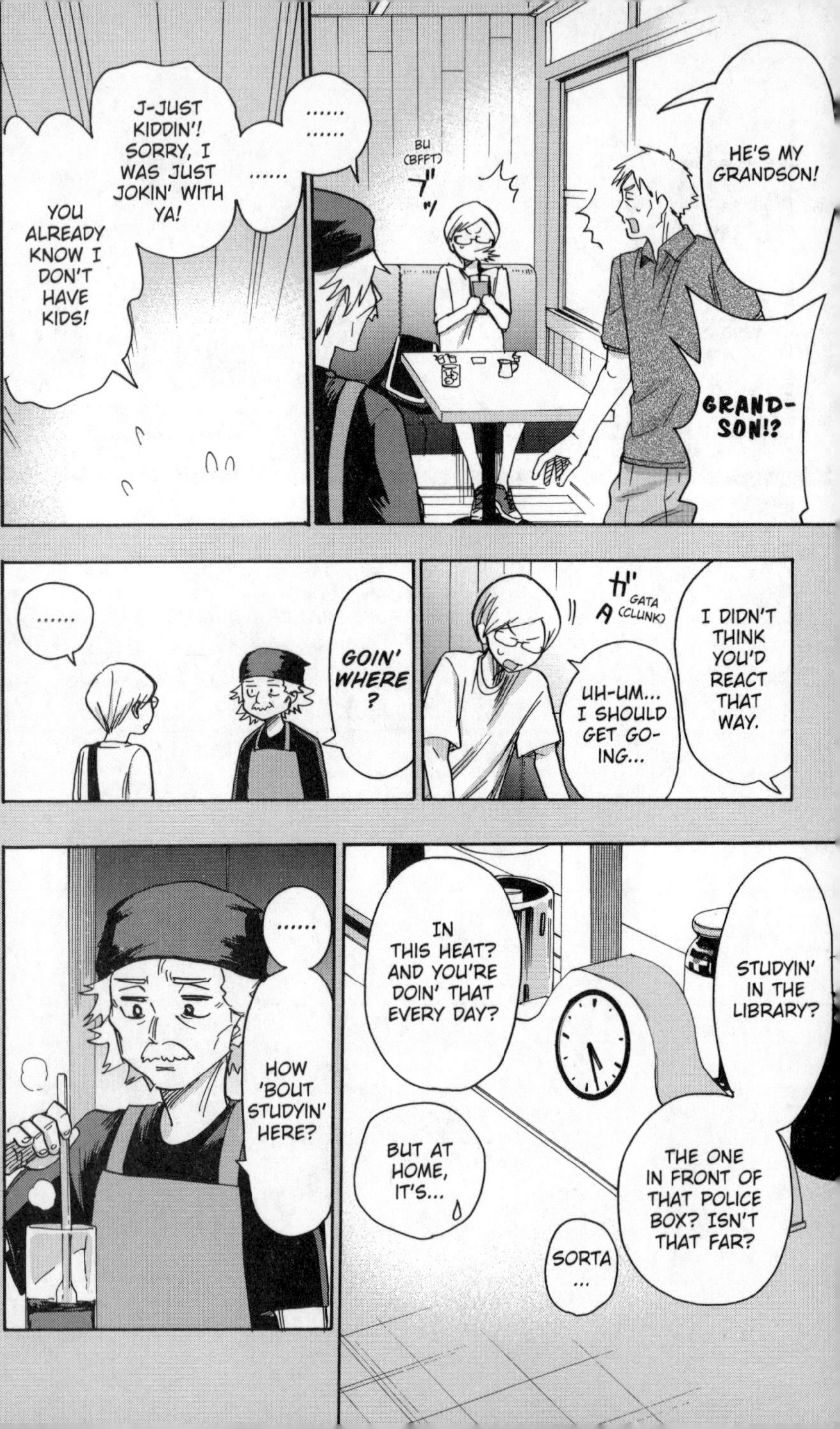
HE'S MY GRANDSON!
BU (BFFT)
GRAND-SON!?
......
......
......
J-JUST KIDDIN'! SORRY, I WAS JUST JOKIN' WITH YA!
YOU ALREADY KNOW I DON'T HAVE KIDS!
I DIDN'T THINK YOU'D REACT THAT WAY.
GATA (CLUNK)
UH-UM... I SHOULD GET GO-ING...
GOIN' WHERE?
......
STUDYIN' IN THE LIBRARY?
IN THIS HEAT? AND YOU'RE DOIN' THAT EVERY DAY?
THE ONE IN FRONT OF THAT POLICE BOX? ISN'T THAT FAR?
BUT AT HOME, IT'S...
SORTA ...
......
HOW 'BOUT STUDYIN' HERE?

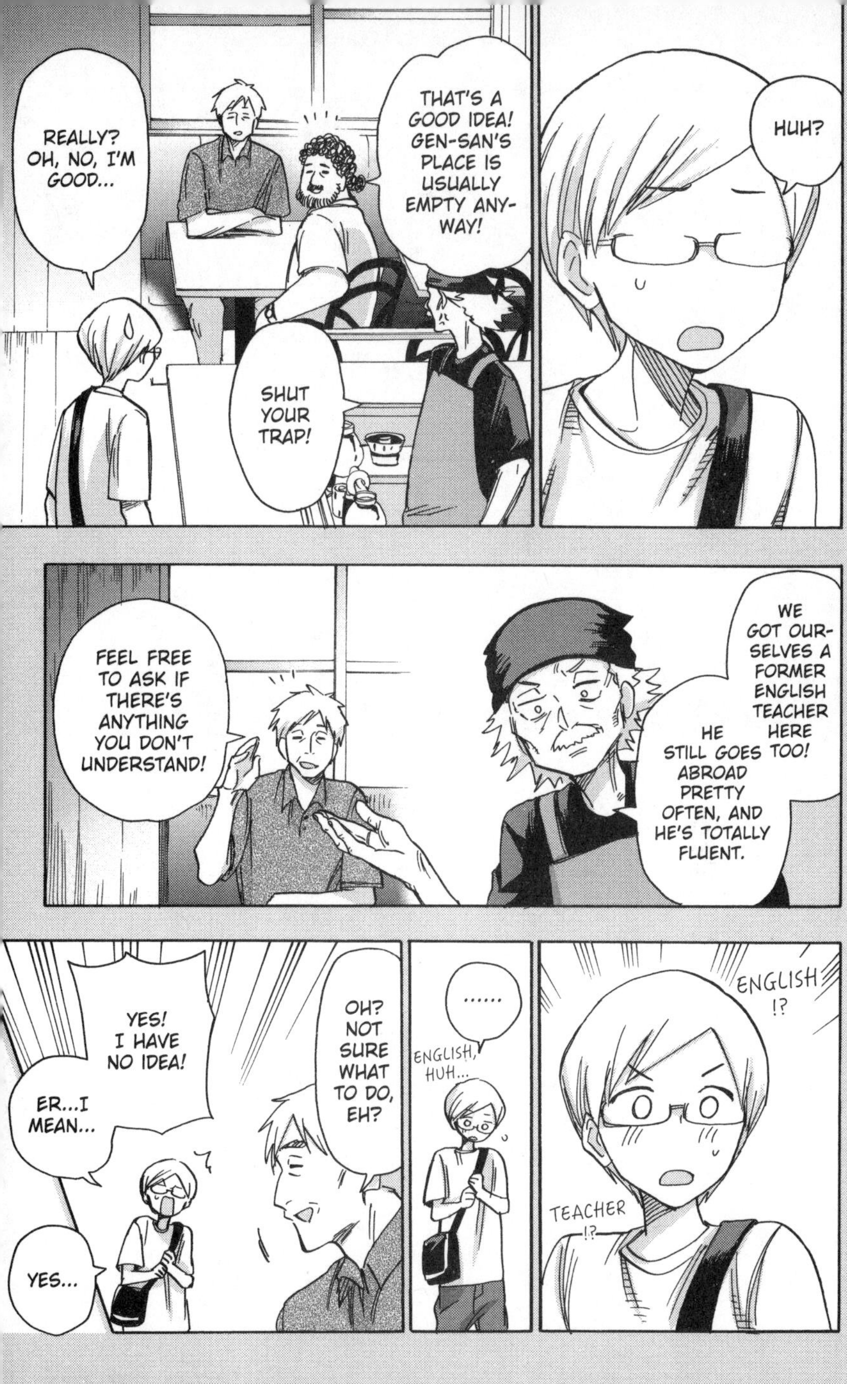
HUH?
THAT'S A GOOD IDEA! GEN-SAN'S PLACE IS USUALLY EMPTY ANYWAY!
REALLY? OH, NO, I'M GOOD...
SHUT YOUR TRAP!
WE GOT OURSELVES A FORMER ENGLISH TEACHER HERE TOO!
HE STILL GOES ABROAD PRETTY OFTEN, AND HE'S TOTALLY FLUENT.
FEEL FREE TO ASK IF THERE'S ANYTHING YOU DON'T UNDERSTAND!
ENGLISH !?
TEACHER !?
......
ENGLISH, HUH...
OH? NOT SURE WHAT TO DO, EH?
YES! I HAVE NO IDEA!
ER...I MEAN...
YES...

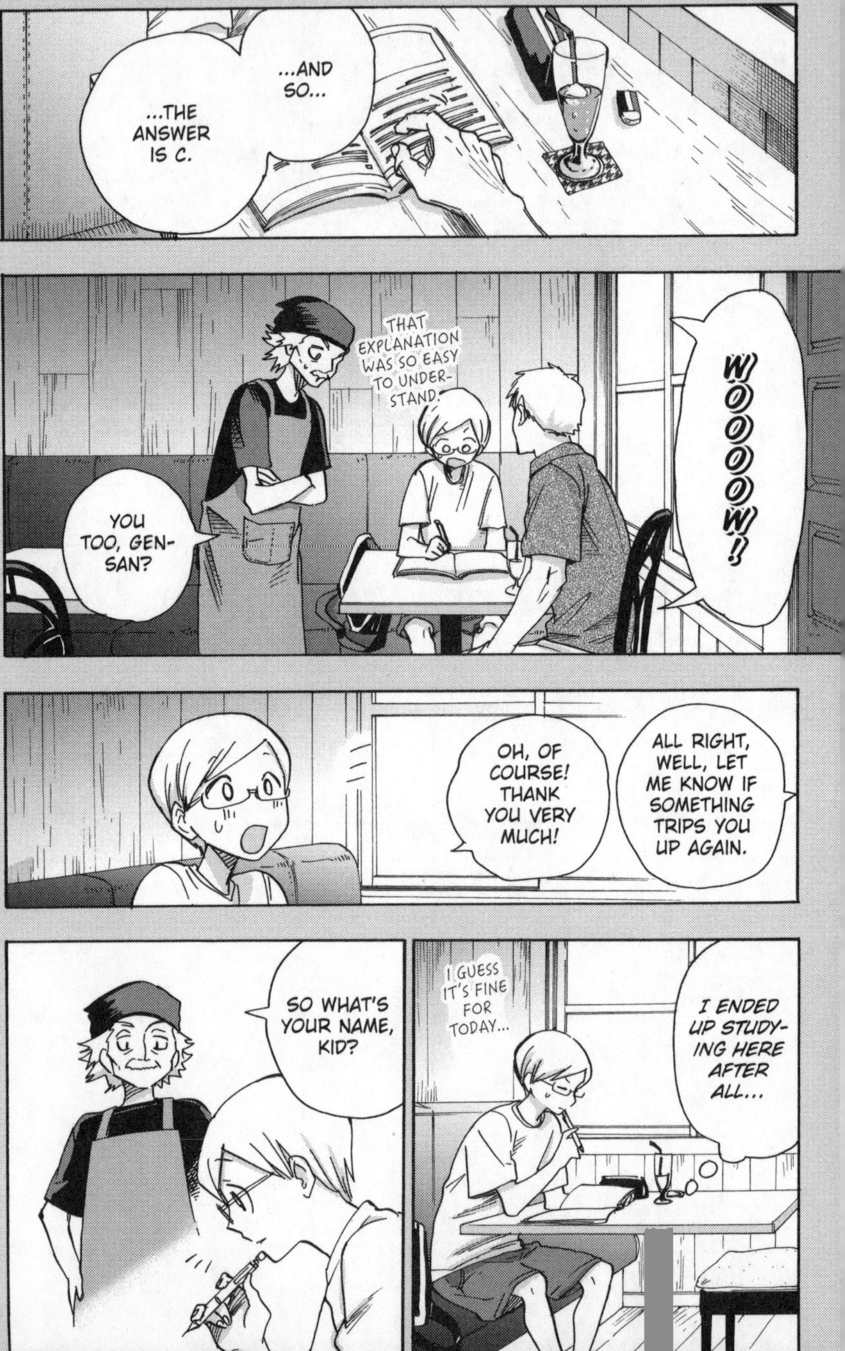
...AND SO...
...THE ANSWER IS C.
WOOOOOW!!
THAT EXPLANATION WAS SO EASY TO UNDER-STAND.
YOU TOO, GEN-SAN?
ALL RIGHT, WELL, LET ME KNOW IF SOMETHING TRIPS YOU UP AGAIN.
OH, OF COURSE! THANK YOU VERY MUCH!
I ENDED UP STUDY-ING HERE AFTER ALL...
I GUESS IT'S FINE FOR TODAY...
SO WHAT'S YOUR NAME, KID?

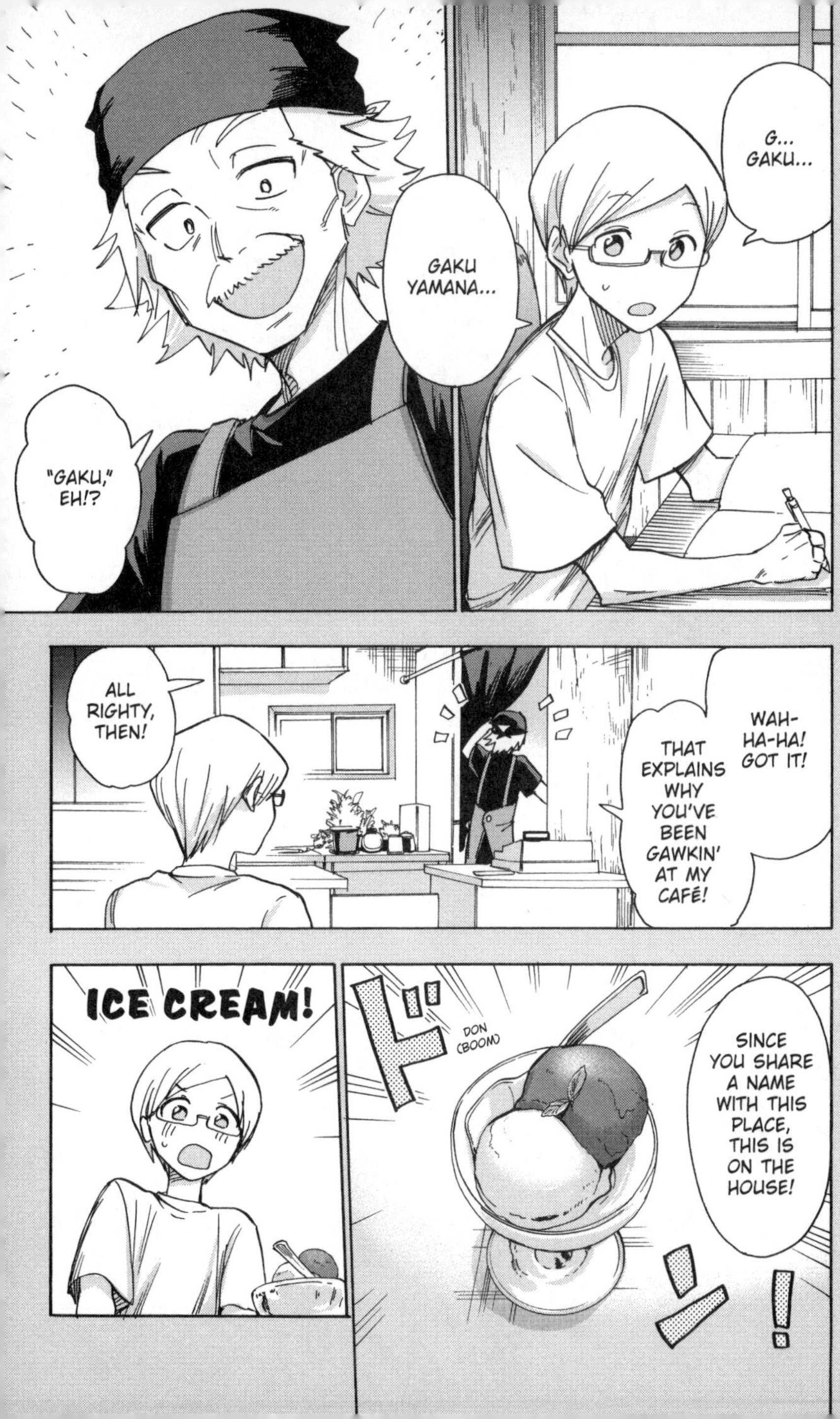
G... GAKU...
GAKU YAMANA...
"GAKU," EH!?
WAH-HA-HA! GOT IT!
THAT EXPLAINS WHY YOU'VE BEEN GAWKIN' AT MY CAFÉ!
ALL RIGHTY, THEN!
DON (BOOM)
SINCE YOU SHARE A NAME WITH THIS PLACE, THIS IS ON THE HOUSE!
ICE CREAM!

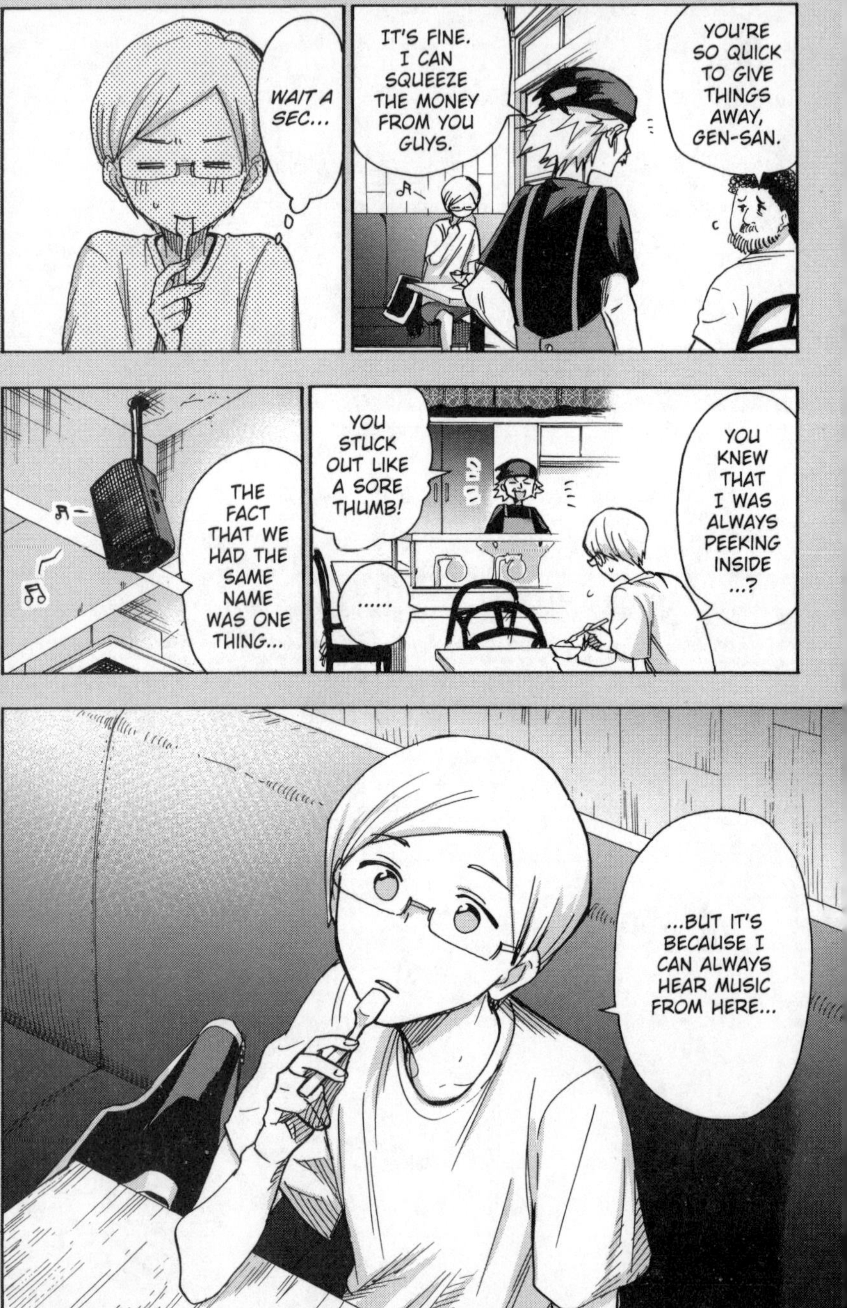
YOU'RE SO QUICK TO GIVE THINGS AWAY, GEN-SAN.
IT'S FINE. I CAN SQUEEZE THE MONEY FROM YOU GUYS.
WAIT A SEC...
YOU KNEW THAT I WAS ALWAYS PEEKING INSIDE ...?
YOU STUCK OUT LIKE A SORE THUMB!
......
THE FACT THAT WE HAD THE SAME NAME WAS ONE THING...
...BUT IT'S BECAUSE I CAN ALWAYS HEAR MUSIC FROM HERE...

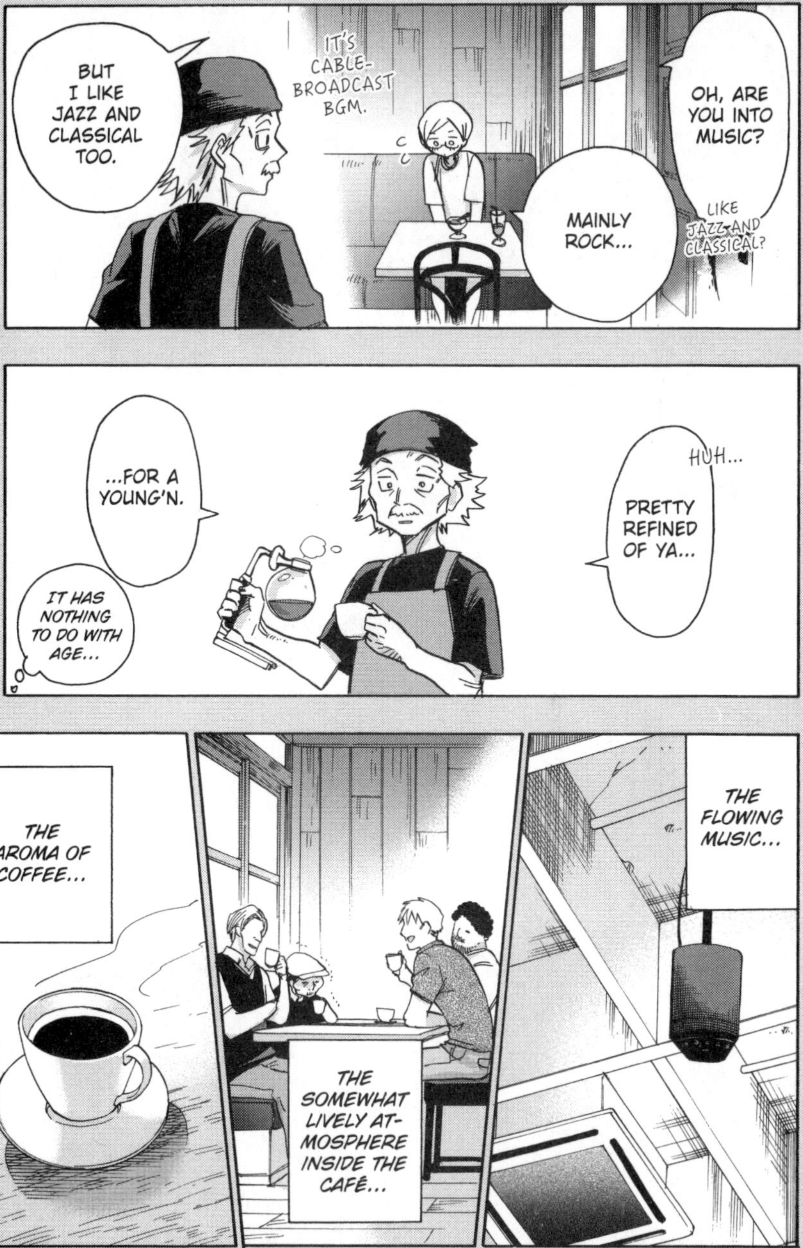
OH, ARE YOU INTO MUSIC?
LIKE JAZZ AND CLASSICAL?
MAINLY ROCK...
IT'S CABLE-BROADCAST BGM.
BUT I LIKE JAZZ AND CLASSICAL TOO.
HUH...
PRETTY REFINED OF YA...
...FOR A YOUNG'N.
IT HAS NOTHING TO DO WITH AGE...
THE FLOWING MUSIC...
THE SOMEWHAT LIVELY AT-MOSPHERE INSIDE THE CAFÉ...
THE AROMA OF COFFEE...

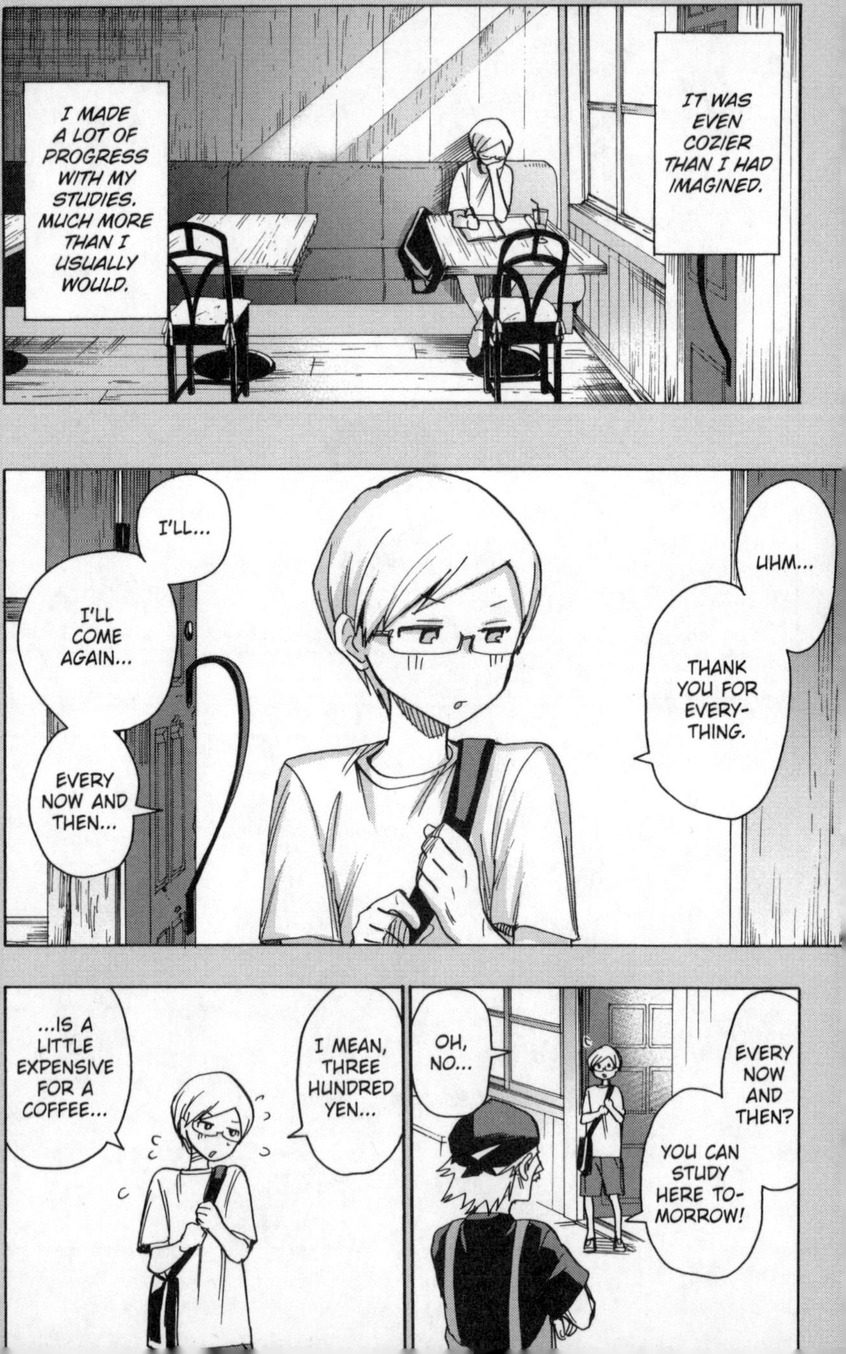
IT WAS EVEN COZIER THAN I HAD IMAGINED.
I MADE A LOT OF PROGRESS WITH MY STUDIES. MUCH MORE THAN I USUALLY WOULD.
UHM...
THANK YOU FOR EVERYTHING.
I'LL...
I'LL COME AGAIN...
EVERY NOW AND THEN...
EVERY NOW AND THEN?
YOU CAN STUDY HERE TOMORROW!
OH, NO...
I MEAN, THREE HUNDRED YEN...
...IS A LITTLE EXPENSIVE FOR A COFFEE...

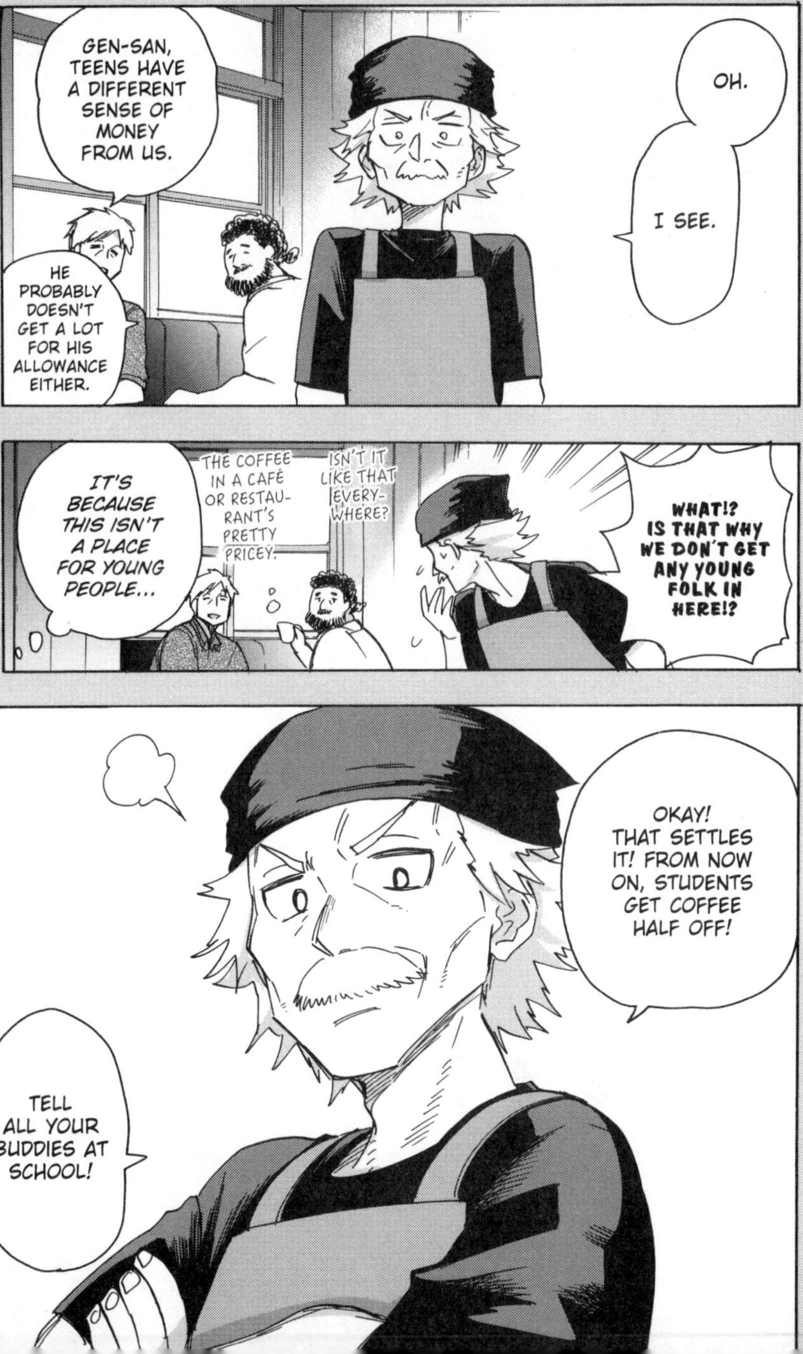
OH.
I SEE.
GEN-SAN, TEENS HAVE A DIFFERENT SENSE OF MONEY FROM US.
HE PROBABLY DOESN'T GET A LOT FOR HIS ALLOWANCE EITHER.
WHAT!? IS THAT WHY WE DON'T GET ANY YOUNG FOLK IN HERE!?
ISN'T IT LIKE THAT EVERY-WHERE?
THE COFFEE IN A CAFÉ OR RESTAU-RANT'S PRETTY PRICEY.
IT'S BECAUSE THIS ISN'T A PLACE FOR YOUNG PEOPLE...
OKAY! THAT SETTLES IT! FROM NOW ON, STUDENTS GET COFFEE HALF OFF!
TELL ALL YOUR BUDDIES AT SCHOOL!

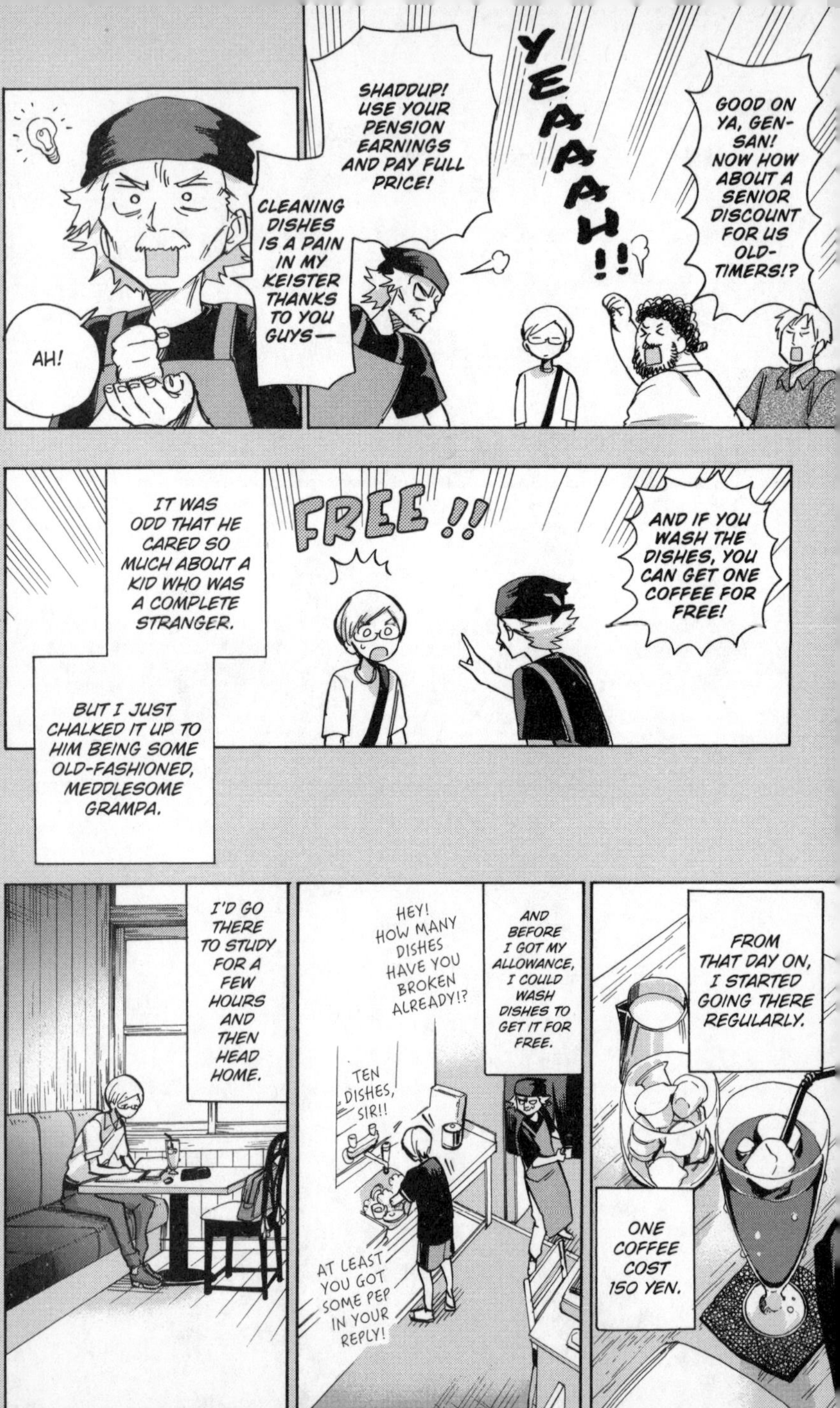
GOOD ON YA, GEN-SAN! NOW HOW ABOUT A SENIOR DISCOUNT FOR US OLD-TIMERS!?
YEAAAH!!
SHADDUP! USE YOUR PENSION EARNINGS AND PAY FULL PRICE!
CLEANING DISHES IS A PAIN IN MY KEISTER THANKS TO YOU GUYS—
AH!
AND IF YOU WASH THE DISHES, YOU CAN GET ONE COFFEE FOR FREE!
FREE!!
IT WAS ODD THAT HE CARED SO MUCH ABOUT A KID WHO WAS A COMPLETE STRANGER.
BUT I JUST CHALKED IT UP TO HIM BEING SOME OLD-FASHIONED, MEDDLESOME GRAMPA.
FROM THAT DAY ON, I STARTED GOING THERE REGULARLY.
ONE COFFEE COST 150 YEN.
AND BEFORE I GOT MY ALLOWANCE, I COULD WASH DISHES TO GET IT FOR FREE.
HEY! HOW MANY DISHES HAVE YOU BROKEN ALREADY!?
TEN DISHES, SIR!!
AT LEAST YOU GOT SOME PEP IN YOUR REPLY!
I'D GO THERE TO STUDY FOR A FEW HOURS AND THEN HEAD HOME.

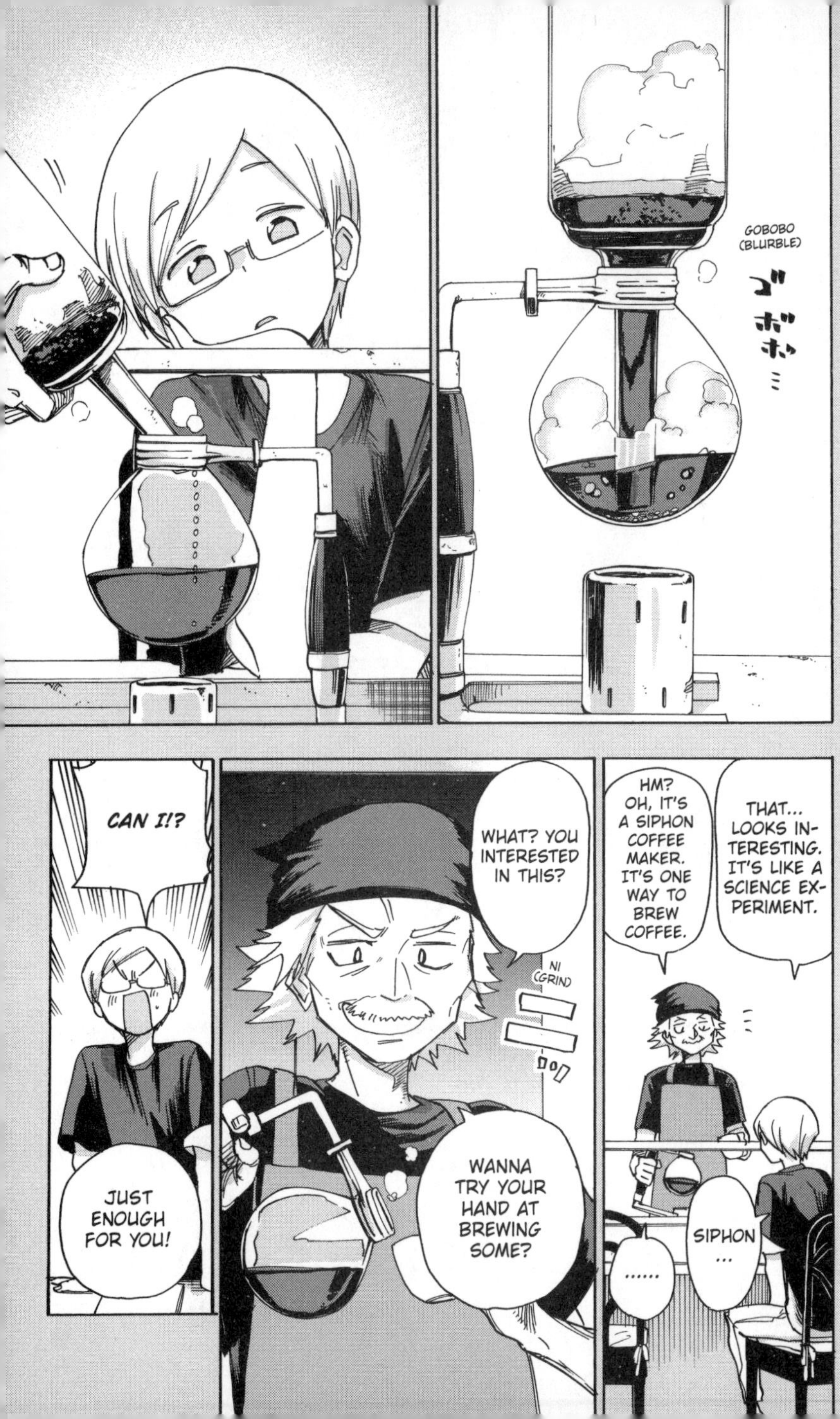
GOBOBO
(BLURBLE)
ゴボボッ
THAT... LOOKS INTERESTING. IT'S LIKE A SCIENCE EXPERIMENT.
HM? OH, IT'S A SIPHON COFFEE MAKER. IT'S ONE WAY TO BREW COFFEE.
SIPHON ...
......
WHAT? YOU INTERESTED IN THIS?
NI
(GRIN)
WANNA TRY YOUR HAND AT BREWING SOME?
CAN I!?
JUST ENOUGH FOR YOU!

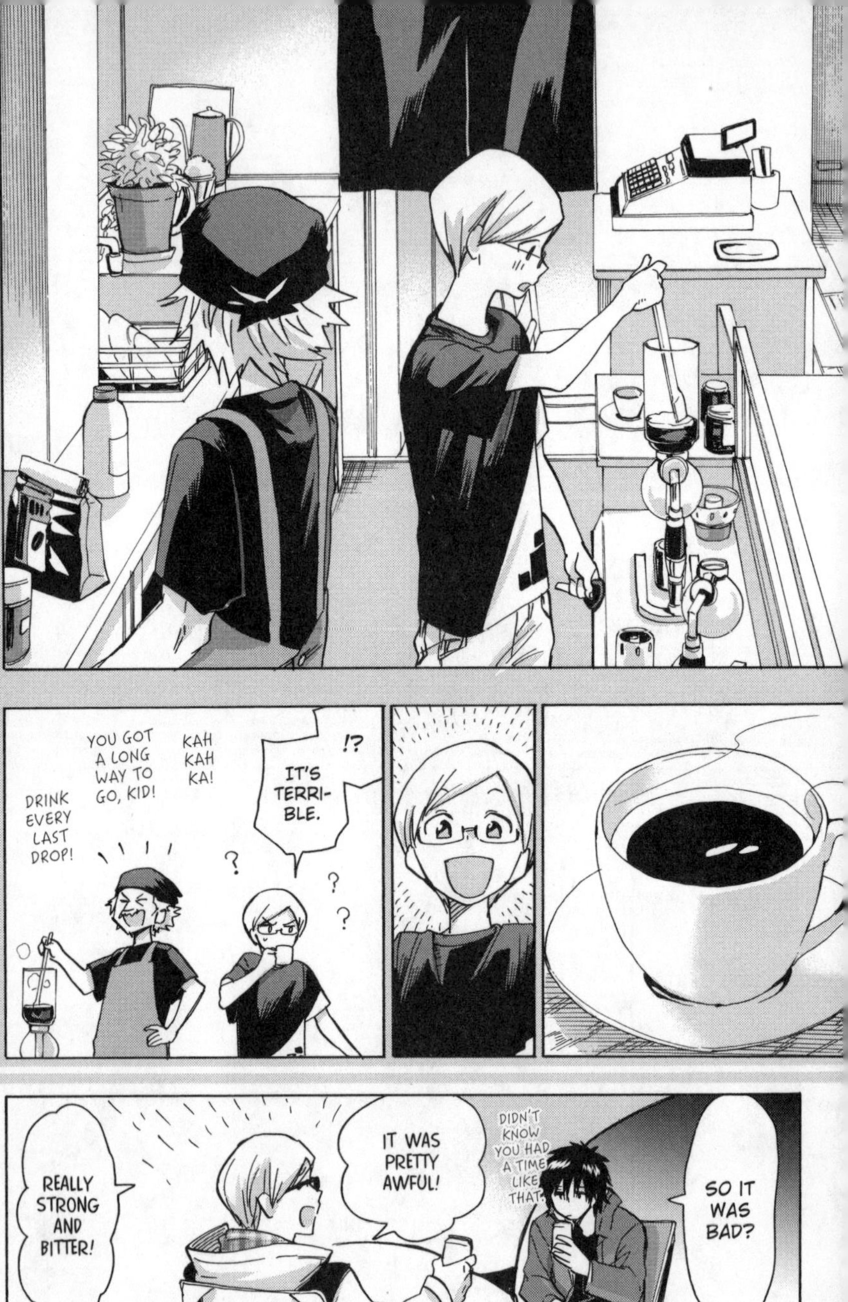
!?
IT'S TERRI-BLE.
KAH KAH KA!
YOU GOT A LONG WAY TO GO, KID!
DRINK EVERY LAST DROP!
SO IT WAS BAD?
DIDN'T KNOW YOU HAD A TIME LIKE THAT.
IT WAS PRETTY AWFUL!
REALLY STRONG AND BITTER!

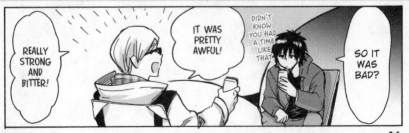

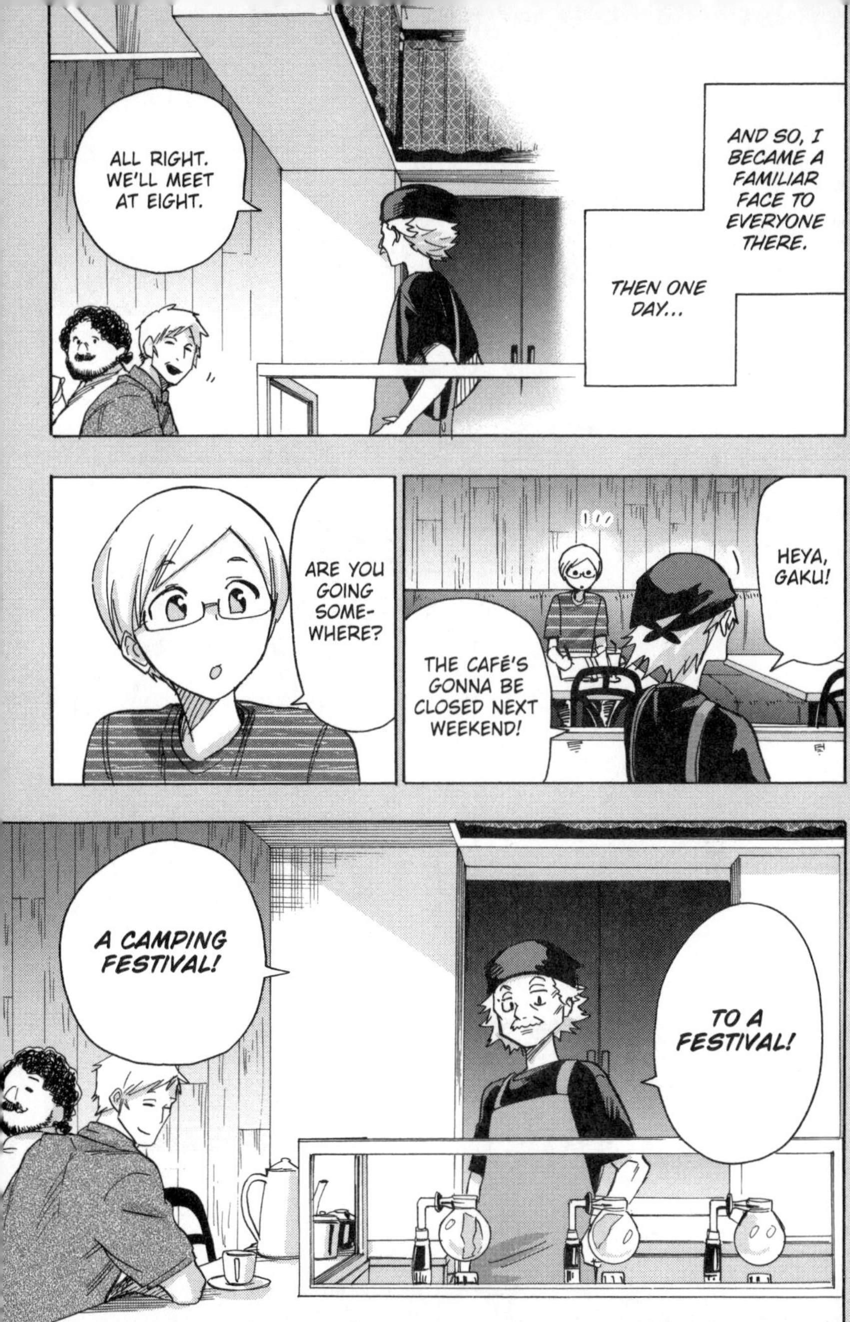
AND SO, I BECAME A FAMILIAR FACE TO EVERYONE THERE.
THEN ONE DAY...
ALL RIGHT. WE'LL MEET AT EIGHT.
HEYA, GAKU!
THE CAFÉ'S GONNA BE CLOSED NEXT WEEKEND!
ARE YOU GOING SOME-WHERE?
TO A FESTIVAL!
A CAMPING FESTIVAL!

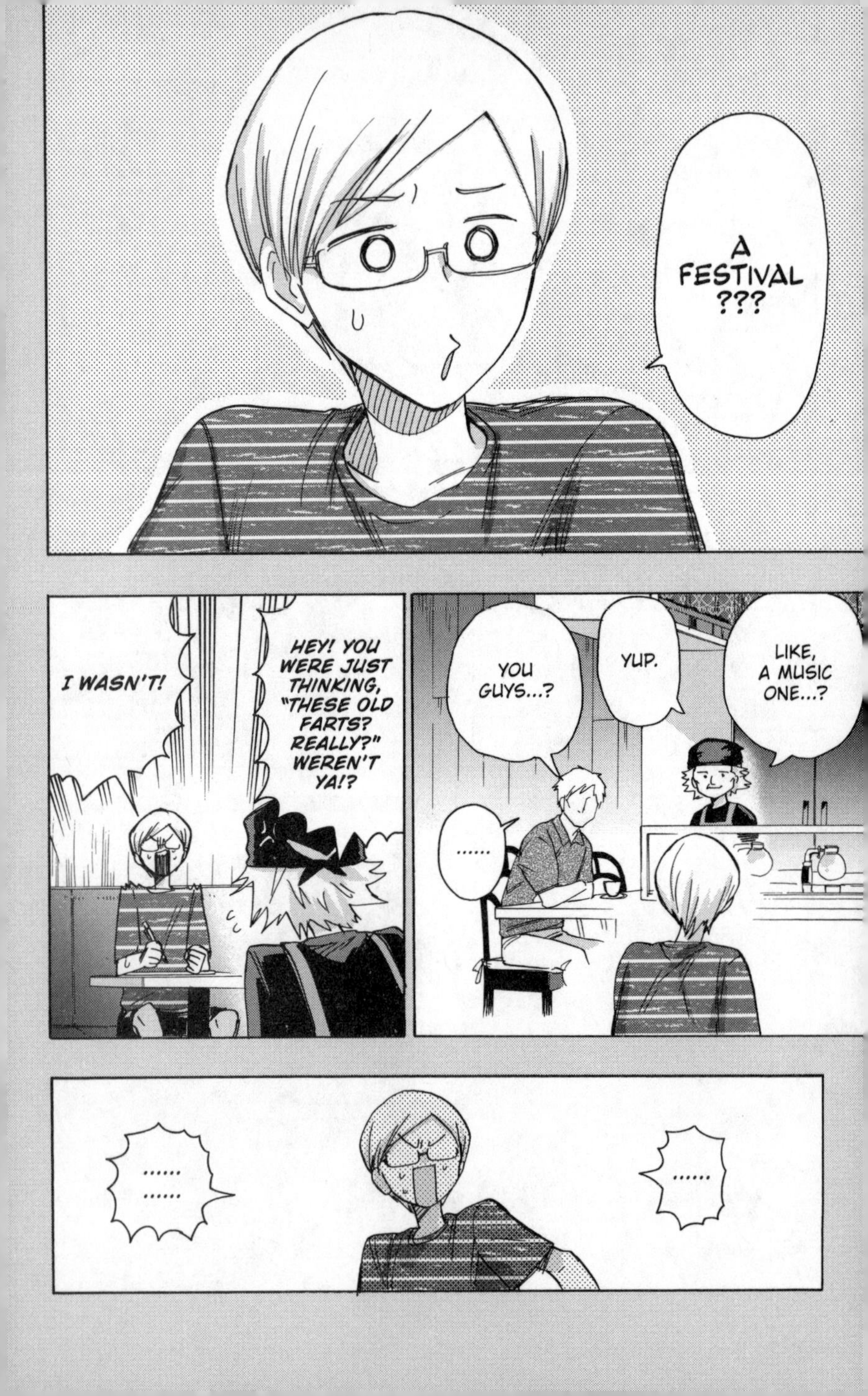
A FESTIVAL ???
LIKE, A MUSIC ONE...?
YUP.
YOU GUYS...?
......
HEY! YOU WERE JUST THINKING, "THESE OLD FARTS? REALLY?" WEREN'T YA!?
I WASN'T!
......
....

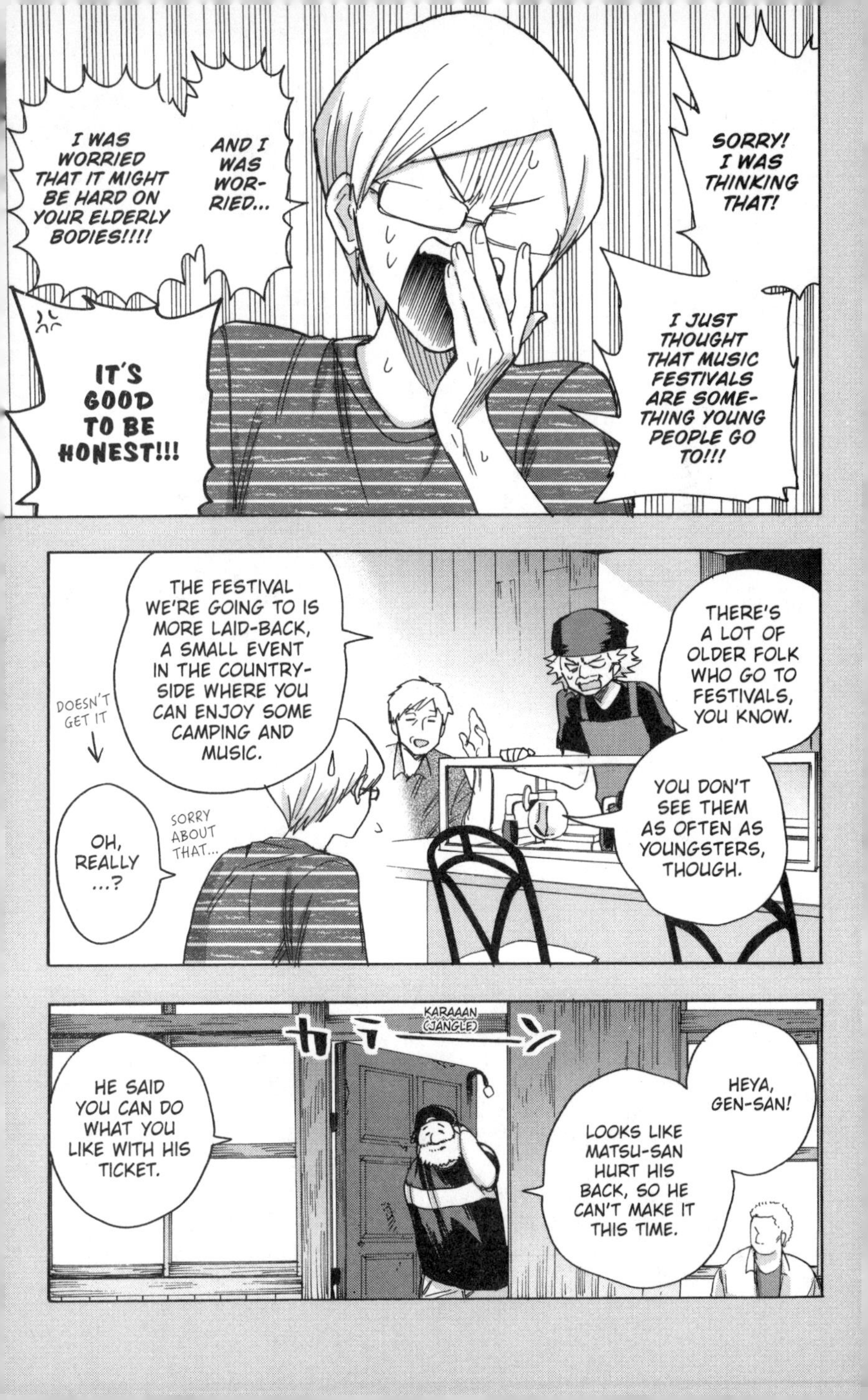
SORRY! I WAS THINKING THAT!
I JUST THOUGHT THAT MUSIC FESTIVALS ARE SOME-THING YOUNG PEOPLE GO TO!!!
AND I WAS WOR-RIED...
I WAS WORRIED THAT IT MIGHT BE HARD ON YOUR ELDERLY BODIES!!!!
IT'S GOOD TO BE HONEST!!!
THERE'S A LOT OF OLDER FOLK WHO GO TO FESTIVALS, YOU KNOW.
YOU DON'T SEE THEM AS OFTEN AS YOUNGSTERS, THOUGH.
THE FESTIVAL WE'RE GOING TO IS MORE LAID-BACK, A SMALL EVENT IN THE COUNTRY-SIDE WHERE YOU CAN ENJOY SOME CAMPING AND MUSIC.
DOESN'T GET IT
SORRY ABOUT THAT...
OH, REALLY ...?
KARAAAN (JANGLE)
HEYA, GEN-SAN!
LOOKS LIKE MATSU-SAN HURT HIS BACK, SO HE CAN'T MAKE IT THIS TIME.
HE SAID YOU CAN DO WHAT YOU LIKE WITH HIS TICKET.

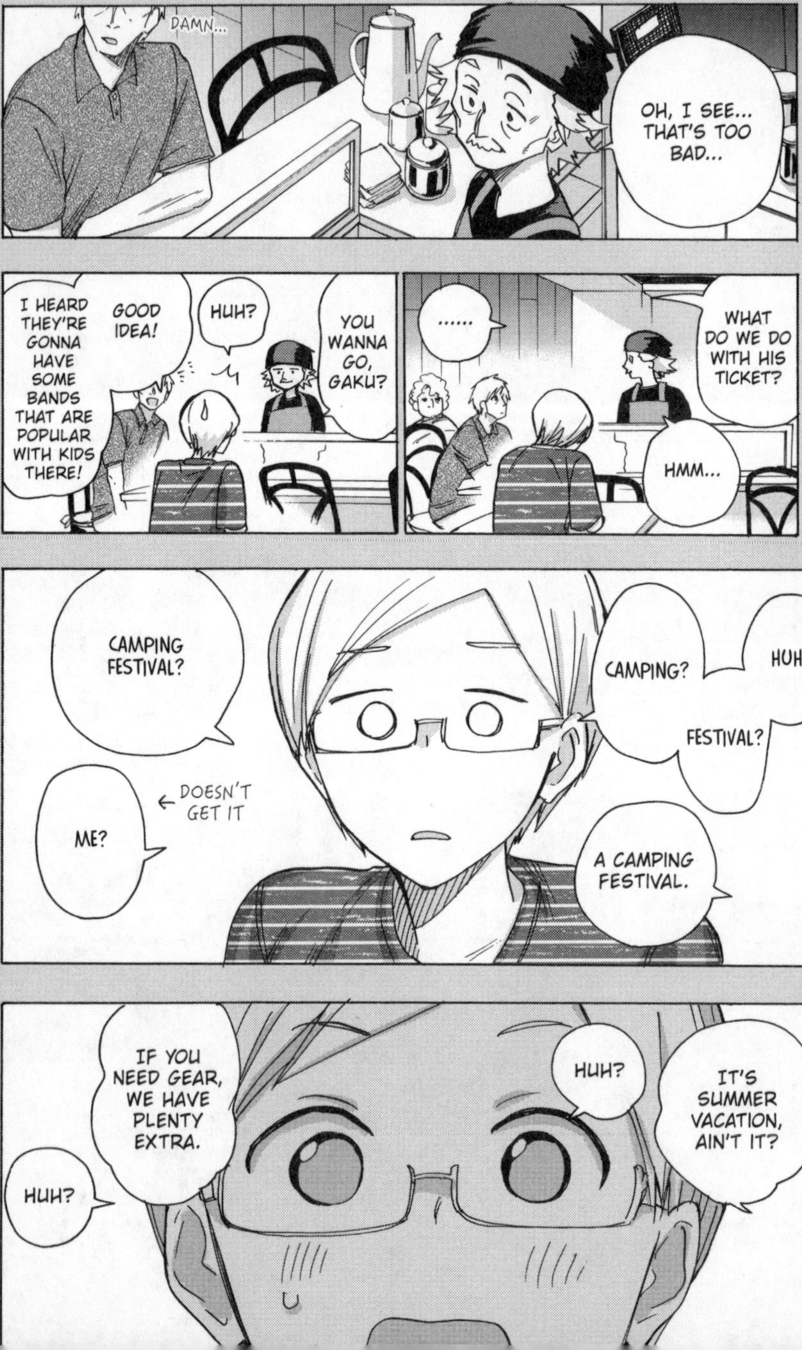
OH, I SEE... THAT'S TOO BAD...
DAMN...
WHAT DO WE DO WITH HIS TICKET?
......
HMM...
YOU WANNA GO, GAKU?
HUH?
GOOD IDEA!
I HEARD THEY'RE GONNA HAVE SOME BANDS THAT ARE POPULAR WITH KIDS THERE!
HUH?
CAMPING?
FESTIVAL?
CAMPING FESTIVAL?
A CAMPING FESTIVAL.
ME?
← DOESN'T GET IT
IT'S SUMMER VACATION, AIN'T IT?
HUH?
IF YOU NEED GEAR, WE HAVE PLENTY EXTRA.
HUH?

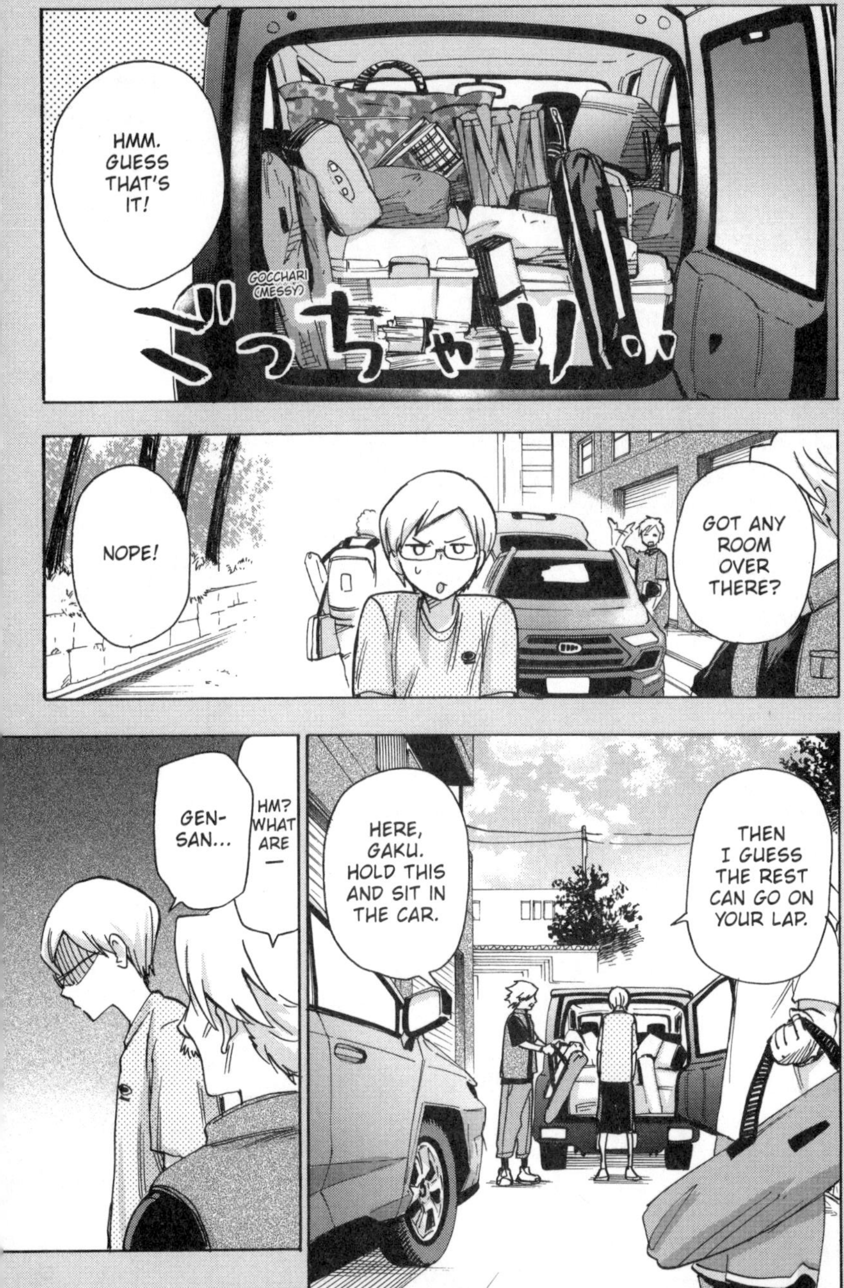
HMM. GUESS THAT'S IT!
ごっちゃり
GOCCHARI (MESSY)
GOT ANY ROOM OVER THERE?
NOPE!
THEN I GUESS THE REST CAN GO ON YOUR LAP.
HERE, GAKU. HOLD THIS AND SIT IN THE CAR.
HM? WHAT ARE—
GEN-SAN...

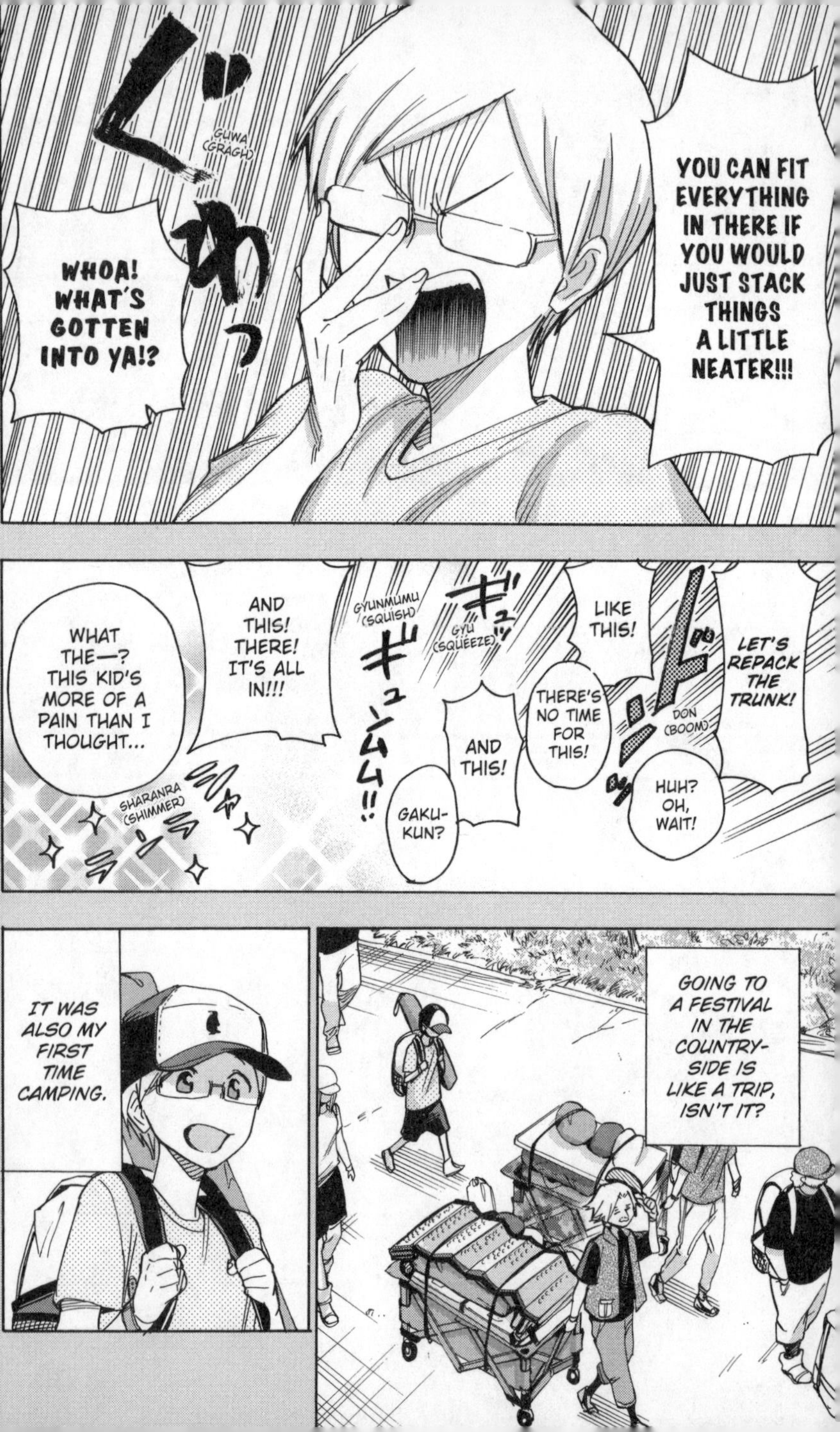
YOU CAN FIT EVERYTHING IN THERE IF YOU WOULD JUST STACK THINGS A LITTLE NEATER!!!
GUWA (GRAGH)
WHOA! WHAT'S GOTTEN INTO YA!?
LET'S REPACK THE TRUNK!
DON (BOOM)
HUH? OH, WAIT!
LIKE THIS!
THERE'S NO TIME FOR THIS!
GYU (SQUEEZE)
AND THIS!
GAKU-KUN?
GYUNMUMU (SQUISH)
AND THIS! THERE! IT'S ALL IN!!!
WHAT THE—? THIS KID'S MORE OF A PAIN THAN I THOUGHT...
SHARANRA (SHIMMER)
GOING TO A FESTIVAL IN THE COUNTRYSIDE IS LIKE A TRIP, ISN'T IT?
IT WAS ALSO MY FIRST TIME CAMPING.

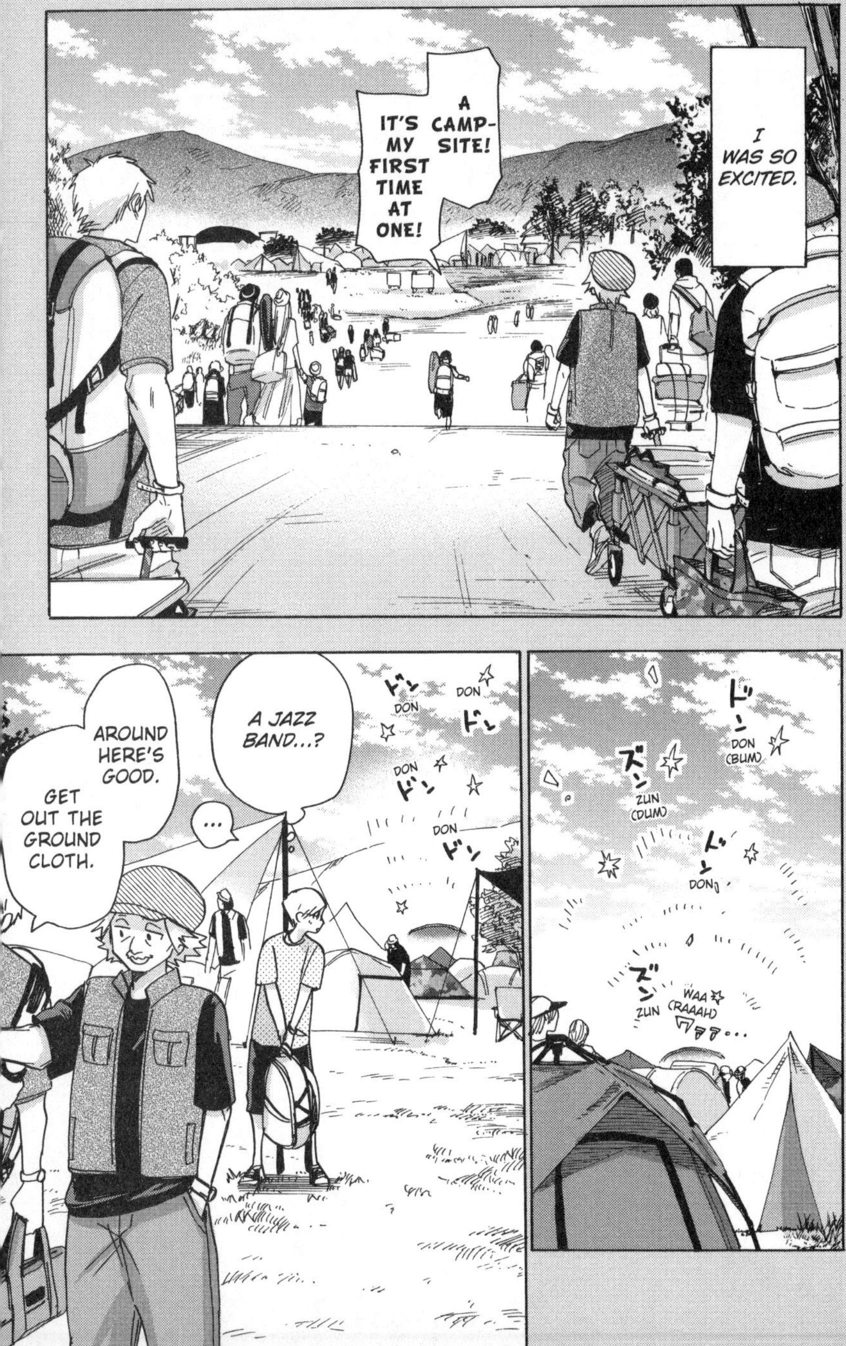
I WAS SO EXCITED.
A CAMPSITE! IT'S MY FIRST TIME AT ONE!
ドーン DON (BUM)
ズン ZUN (DUM)
ドーン DON
ズン ZUN
WAA (RAAAH) ワァァ…
ドン DON
ドン DON
ドン DON
ドン DON
A JAZZ BAND...?
AROUND HERE'S GOOD.
GET OUT THE GROUND CLOTH.
...

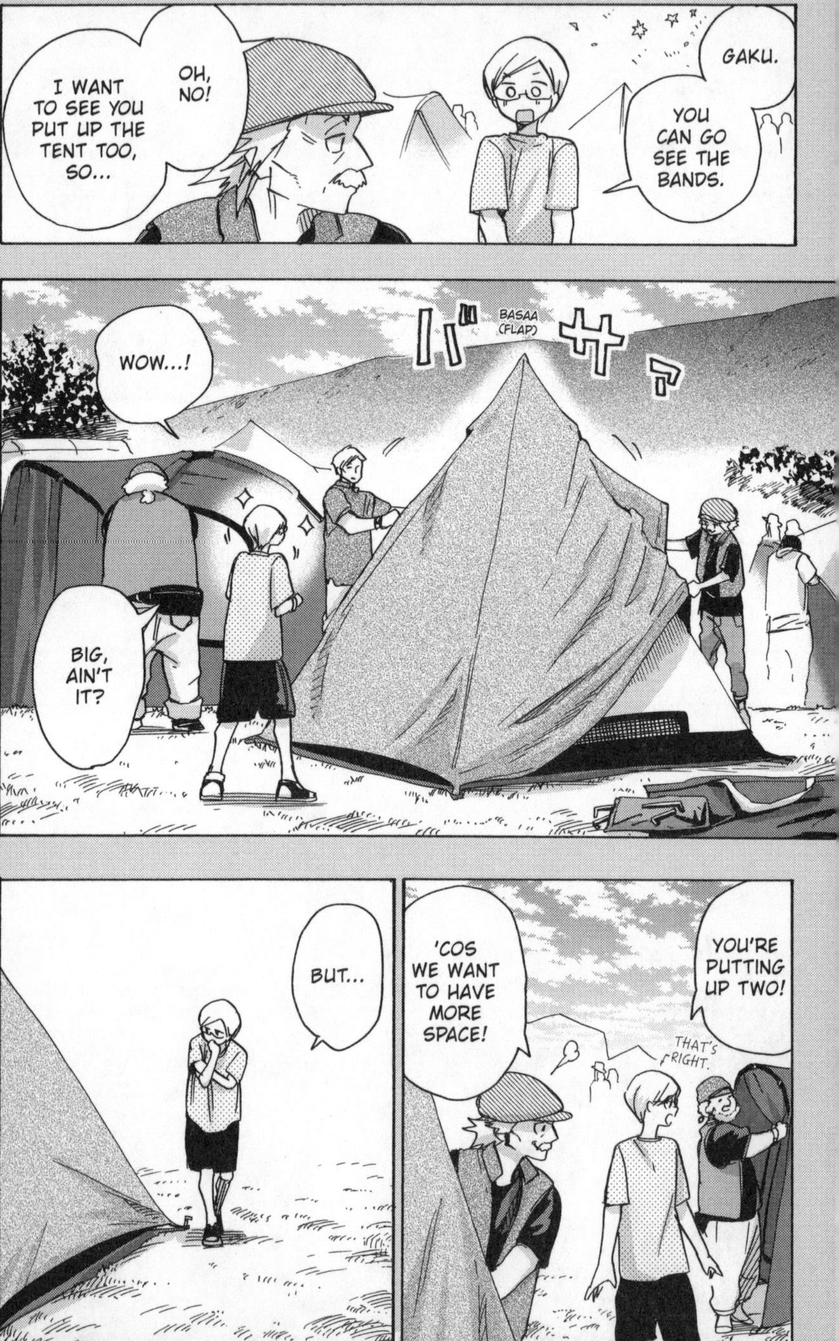
GAKU.
YOU CAN GO SEE THE BANDS.
OH, NO!
I WANT TO SEE YOU PUT UP THE TENT TOO, SO...
バサァ
BASAA (FLAP)
WOW...!
BIG, AIN'T IT?
YOU'RE PUTTING UP TWO!
THAT'S RIGHT.
'COS WE WANT TO HAVE MORE SPACE!
BUT...

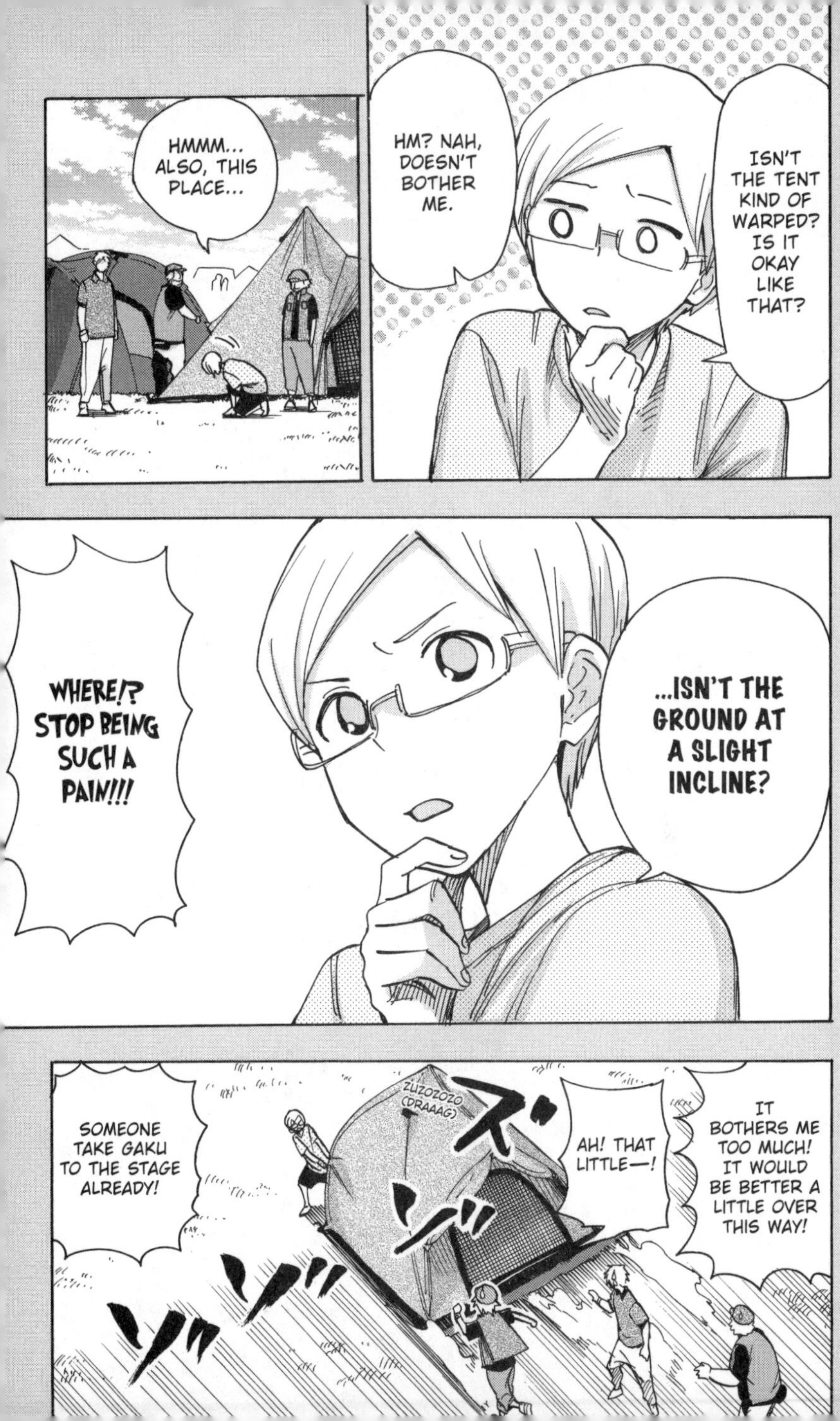
ISN'T THE TENT KIND OF WARPED? IS IT OKAY LIKE THAT?
HM? NAH, DOESN'T BOTHER ME.
HMMM... ALSO, THIS PLACE...
...ISN'T THE GROUND AT A SLIGHT INCLINE?
WHERE!? STOP BEING SUCH A PAIN!!!
IT BOTHERS ME TOO MUCH! IT WOULD BE BETTER A LITTLE OVER THIS WAY!
AH! THAT LITTLE—!
ZUZOZOZO (DRAAAG)
SOMEONE TAKE GAKU TO THE STAGE ALREADY!

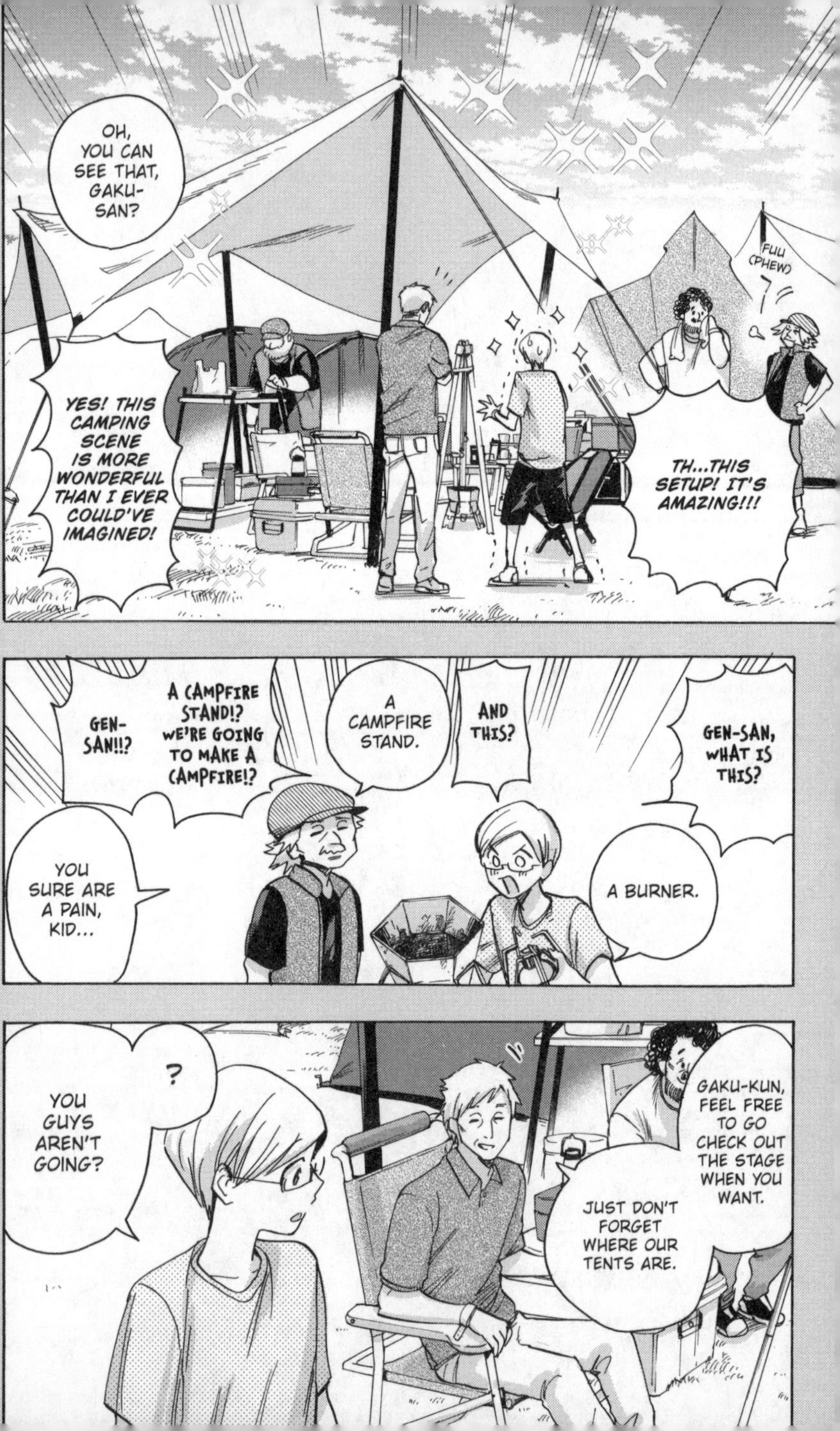
FUU (PHEW)
TH...THIS SETUP! IT'S AMAZING!!!
OH, YOU CAN SEE THAT, GAKU-SAN?
YES! THIS CAMPING SCENE IS MORE WONDERFUL THAN I EVER COULD'VE IMAGINED!
GEN-SAN, WHAT IS THIS?
A BURNER.
AND THIS?
A CAMPFIRE STAND.
A CAMPFIRE STAND!? WE'RE GOING TO MAKE A CAMPFIRE!?
GEN-SAN!!?
YOU SURE ARE A PAIN, KID...
GAKU-KUN, FEEL FREE TO GO CHECK OUT THE STAGE WHEN YOU WANT.
JUST DON'T FORGET WHERE OUR TENTS ARE.
?
YOU GUYS AREN'T GOING?

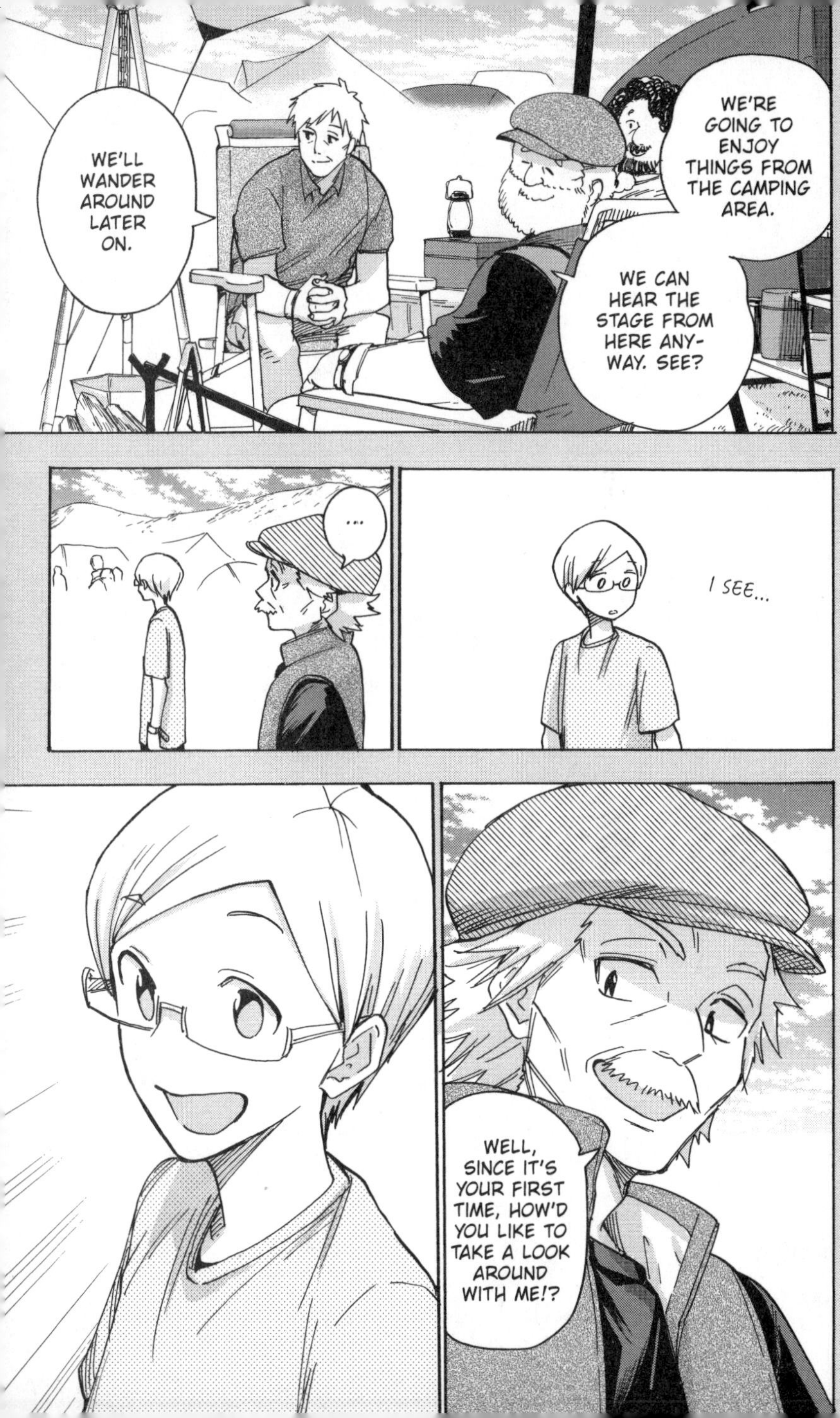
WE'RE GOING TO ENJOY THINGS FROM THE CAMPING AREA.
WE CAN HEAR THE STAGE FROM HERE ANY-WAY. SEE?
WE'LL WANDER AROUND LATER ON.
I SEE...
...
WELL, SINCE IT'S YOUR FIRST TIME, HOW'D YOU LIKE TO TAKE A LOOK AROUND WITH ME!?

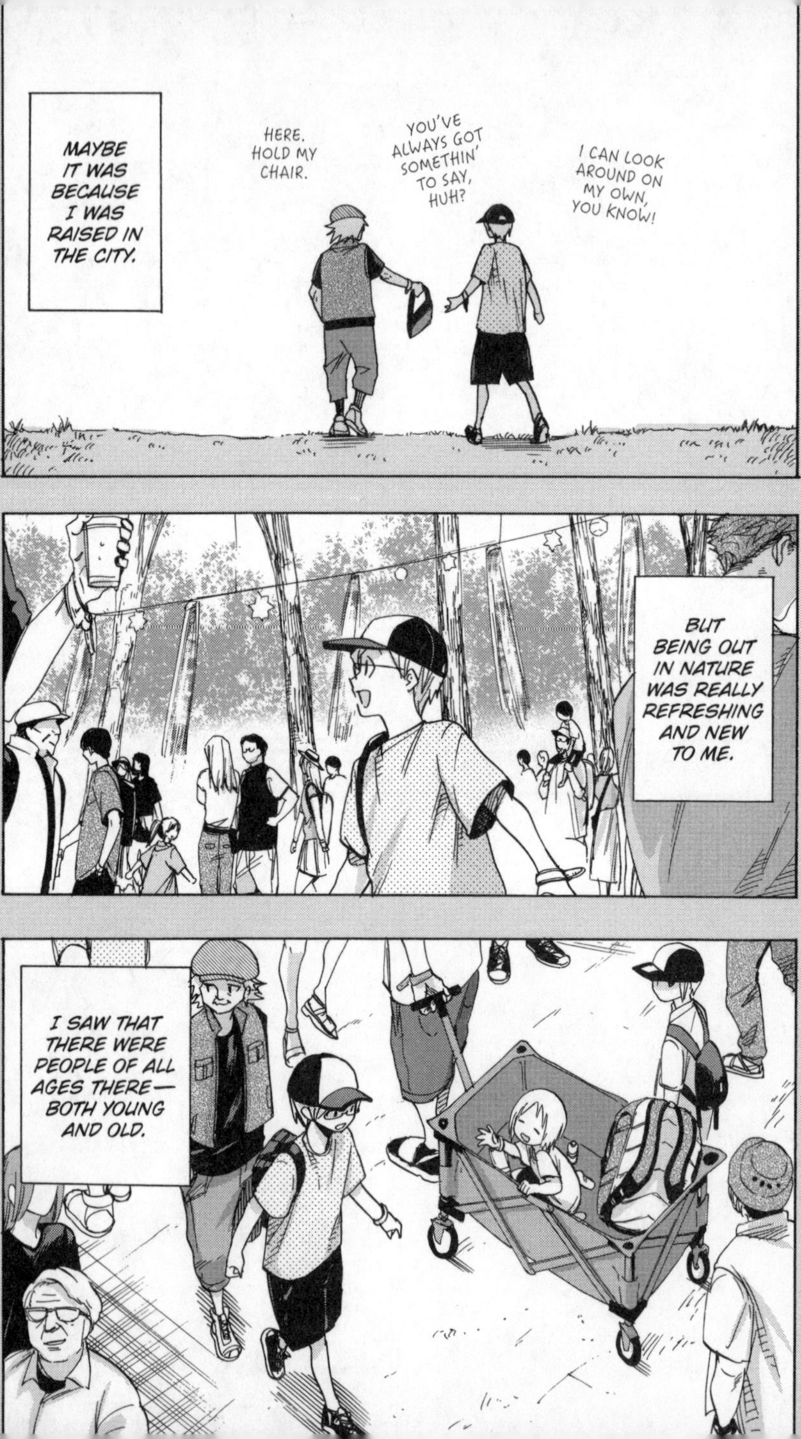
I CAN LOOK AROUND ON MY OWN, YOU KNOW!
YOU'VE ALWAYS GOT SOMETHIN' TO SAY, HUH?
HERE. HOLD MY CHAIR.
MAYBE IT WAS BECAUSE I WAS RAISED IN THE CITY.
BUT BEING OUT IN NATURE WAS REALLY REFRESHING AND NEW TO ME.
I SAW THAT THERE WERE PEOPLE OF ALL AGES THERE—BOTH YOUNG AND OLD.

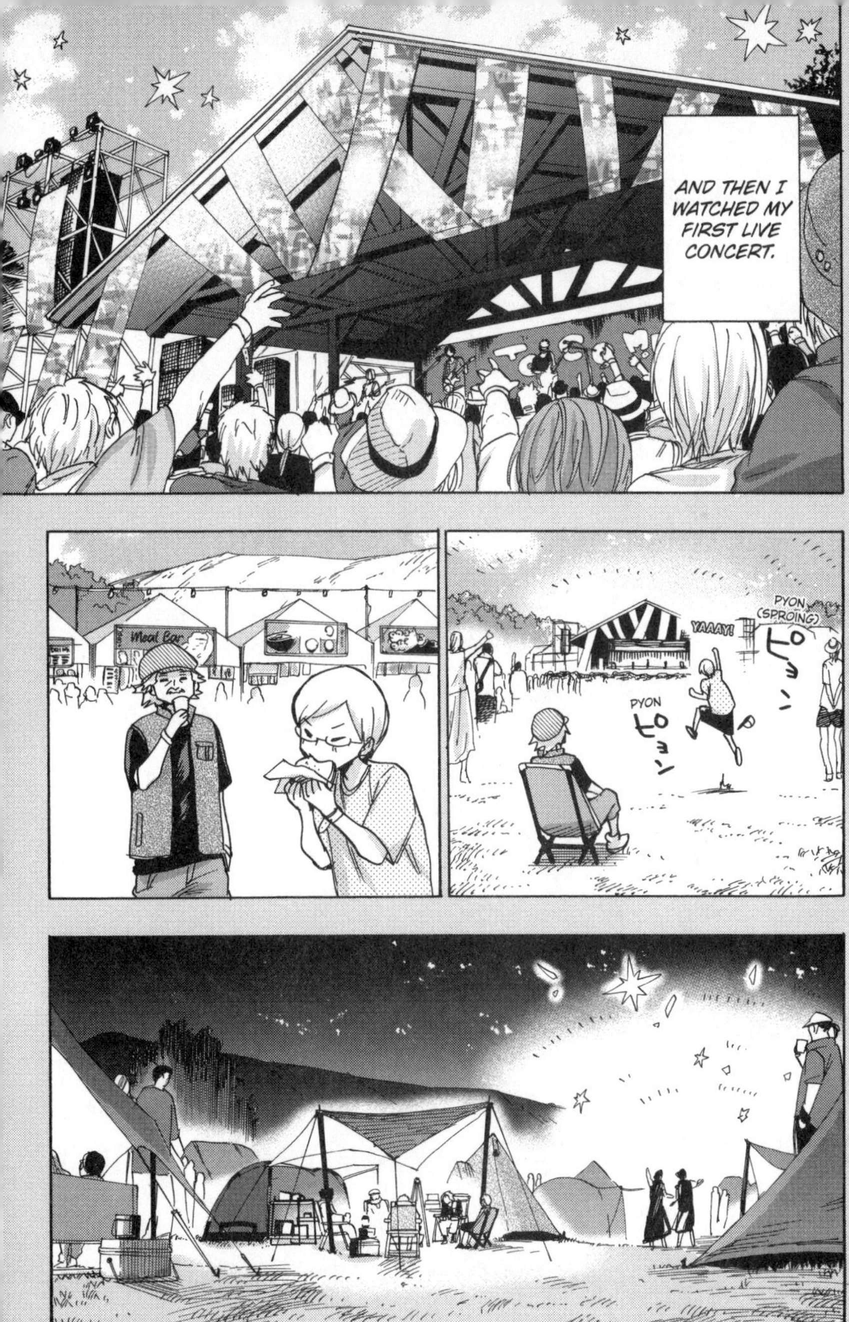
AND THEN I WATCHED MY FIRST LIVE CONCERT.
PYON (SPROING)
ピョン
YAAAY!
PYON
ピョン

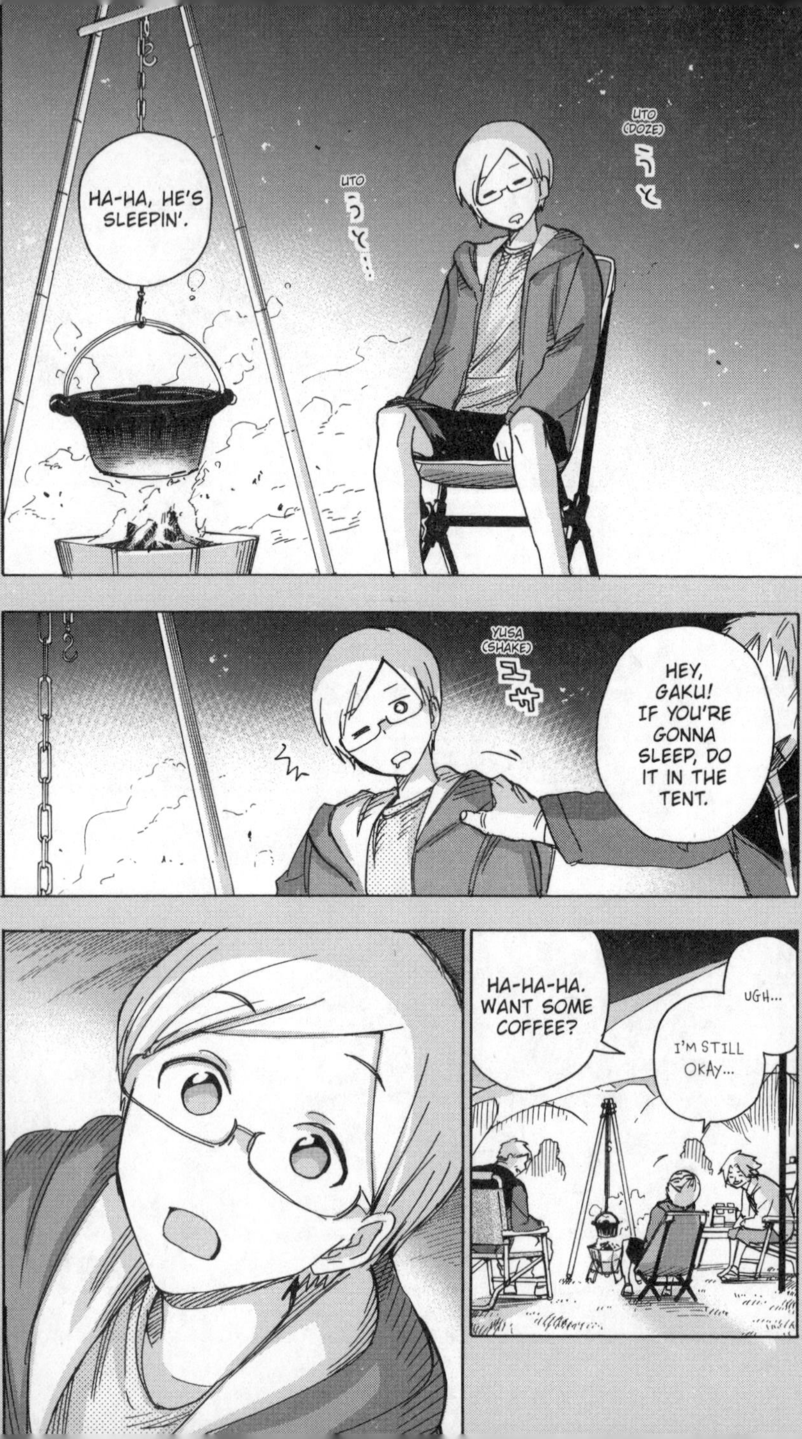
UTO (DOZE)
うと
UTO
うと…
HA-HA, HE'S SLEEPIN'.
HEY, GAKU! IF YOU'RE GONNA SLEEP, DO IT IN THE TENT.
YUSA (SHAKE)
ユサ
UGH...
I'M STILL OKAY...
HA-HA-HA. WANT SOME COFFEE?

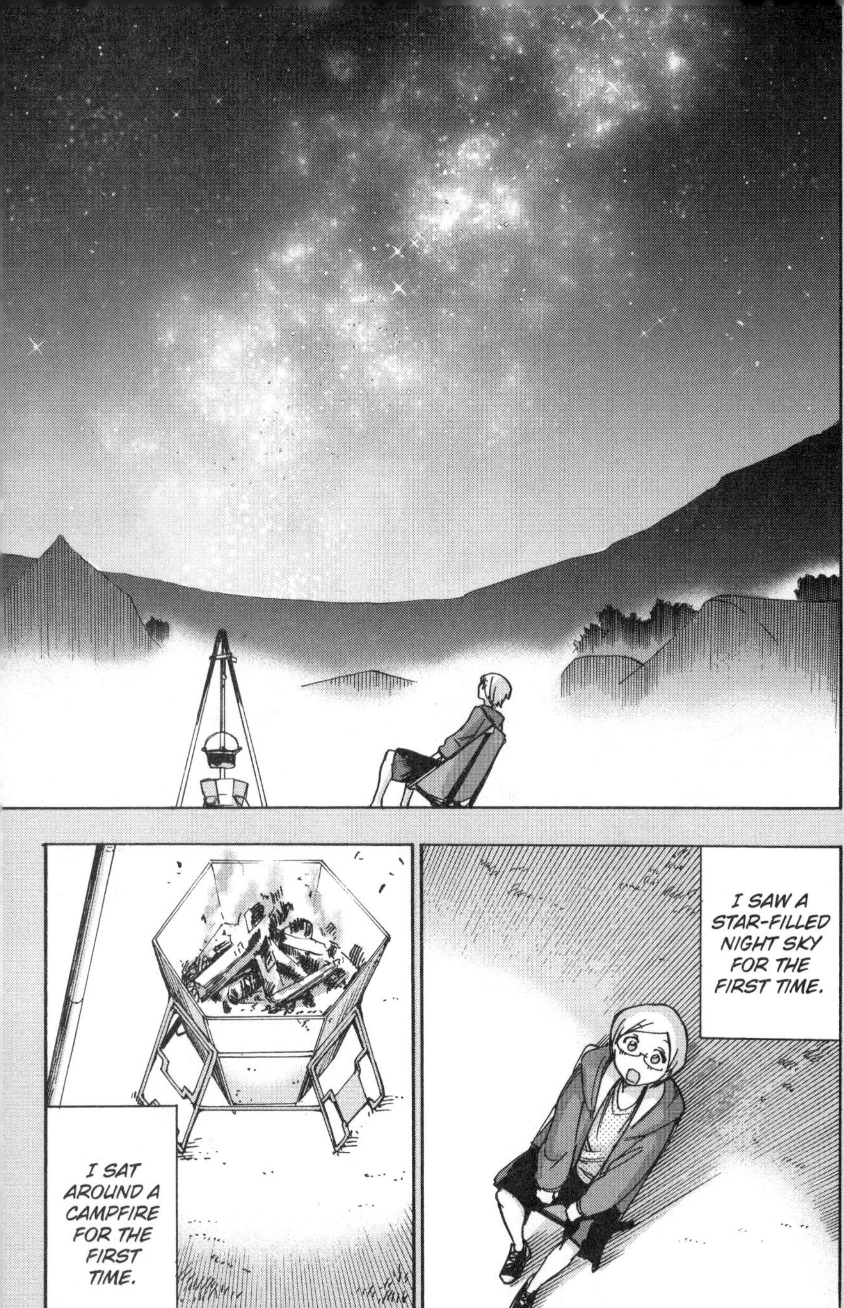
I SAW A STAR-FILLED NIGHT SKY FOR THE FIRST TIME.
I SAT AROUND A CAMPFIRE FOR THE FIRST TIME.

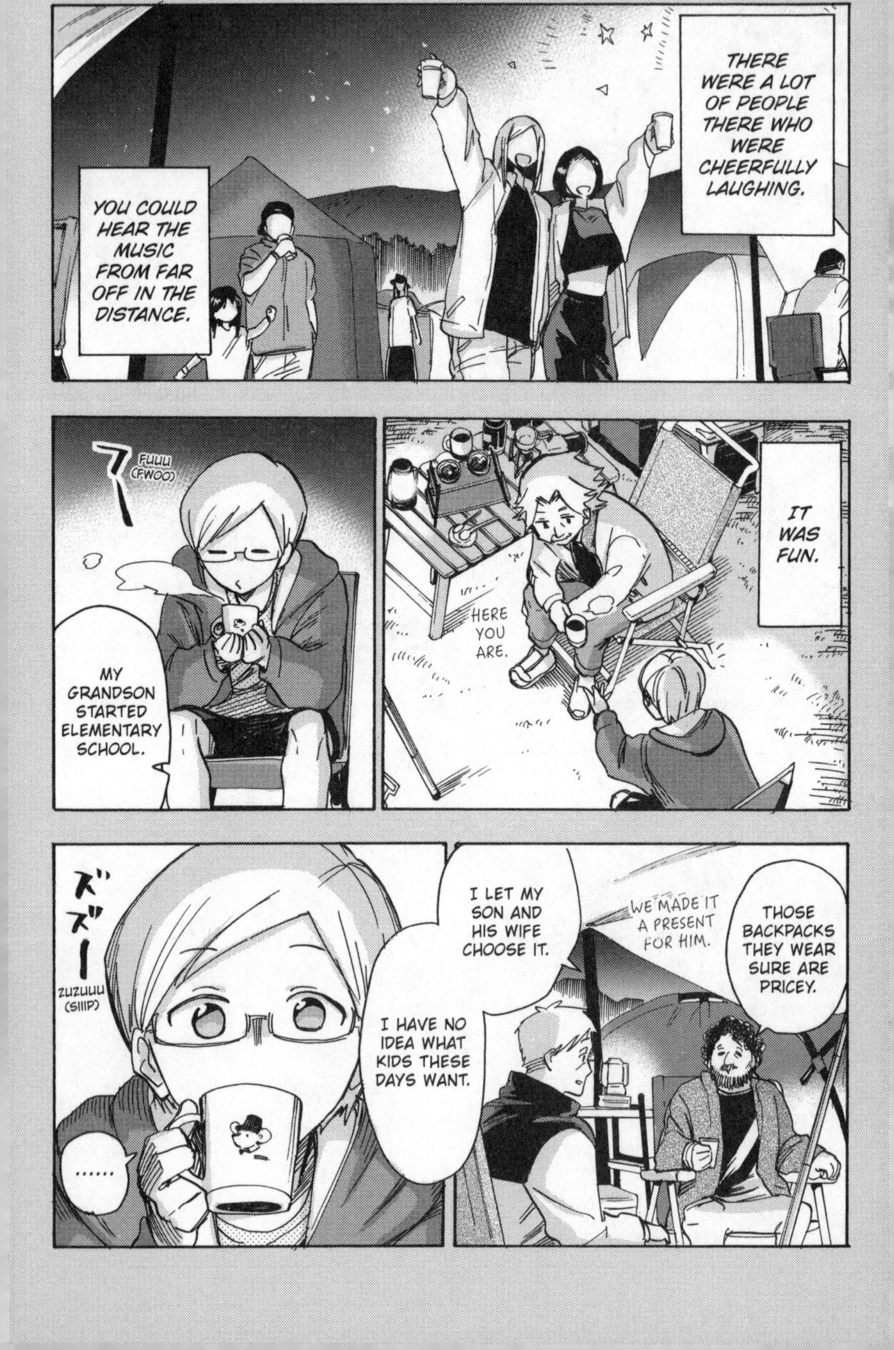
THERE WERE A LOT OF PEOPLE THERE WHO WERE CHEERFULLY LAUGHING.
YOU COULD HEAR THE MUSIC FROM FAR OFF IN THE DISTANCE.
IT WAS FUN.
HERE YOU ARE.
FUUU (FWOO)
MY GRANDSON STARTED ELEMENTARY SCHOOL.
THOSE BACKPACKS THEY WEAR SURE ARE PRICEY.
WE MADE IT A PRESENT FOR HIM.
I LET MY SON AND HIS WIFE CHOOSE IT.
I HAVE NO IDEA WHAT KIDS THESE DAYS WANT.
ズズー
ZUZUUU (SIIIP)
......

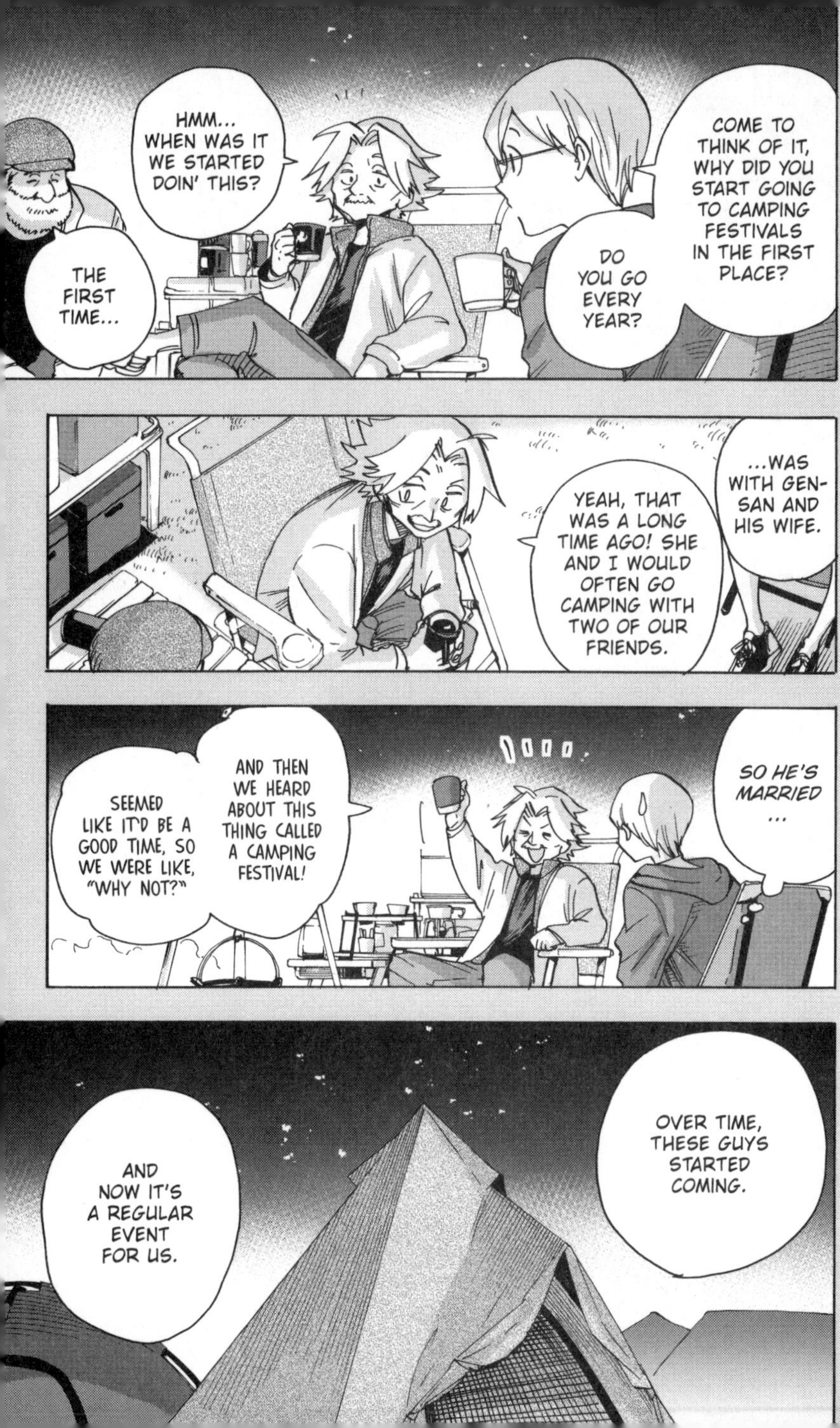
COME TO THINK OF IT, WHY DID YOU START GOING TO CAMPING FESTIVALS IN THE FIRST PLACE?
DO YOU GO EVERY YEAR?
HMM... WHEN WAS IT WE STARTED DOIN' THIS?
THE FIRST TIME...
...WAS WITH GEN-SAN AND HIS WIFE.
YEAH, THAT WAS A LONG TIME AGO! SHE AND I WOULD OFTEN GO CAMPING WITH TWO OF OUR FRIENDS.
SO HE'S MARRIED...
AND THEN WE HEARD ABOUT THIS THING CALLED A CAMPING FESTIVAL!
SEEMED LIKE IT'D BE A GOOD TIME, SO WE WERE LIKE, "WHY NOT?"
OVER TIME, THESE GUYS STARTED COMING.
AND NOW IT'S A REGULAR EVENT FOR US.

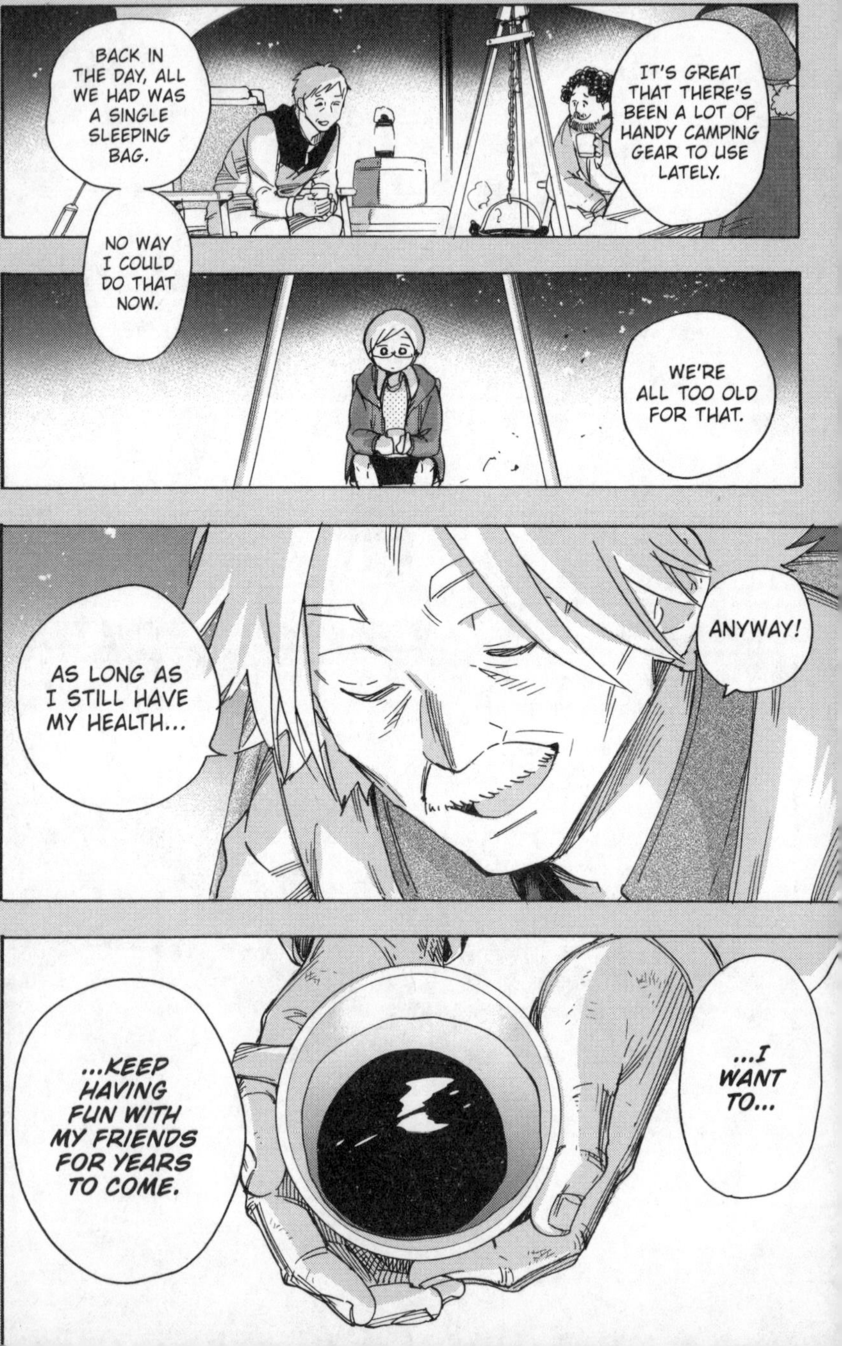
IT'S GREAT THAT THERE'S BEEN A LOT OF HANDY CAMPING GEAR TO USE LATELY.
BACK IN THE DAY, ALL WE HAD WAS A SINGLE SLEEPING BAG.
NO WAY I COULD DO THAT NOW.
WE'RE ALL TOO OLD FOR THAT.
ANYWAY!
AS LONG AS I STILL HAVE MY HEALTH...
...I WANT TO...
...KEEP HAVING FUN WITH MY FRIENDS FOR YEARS TO COME.

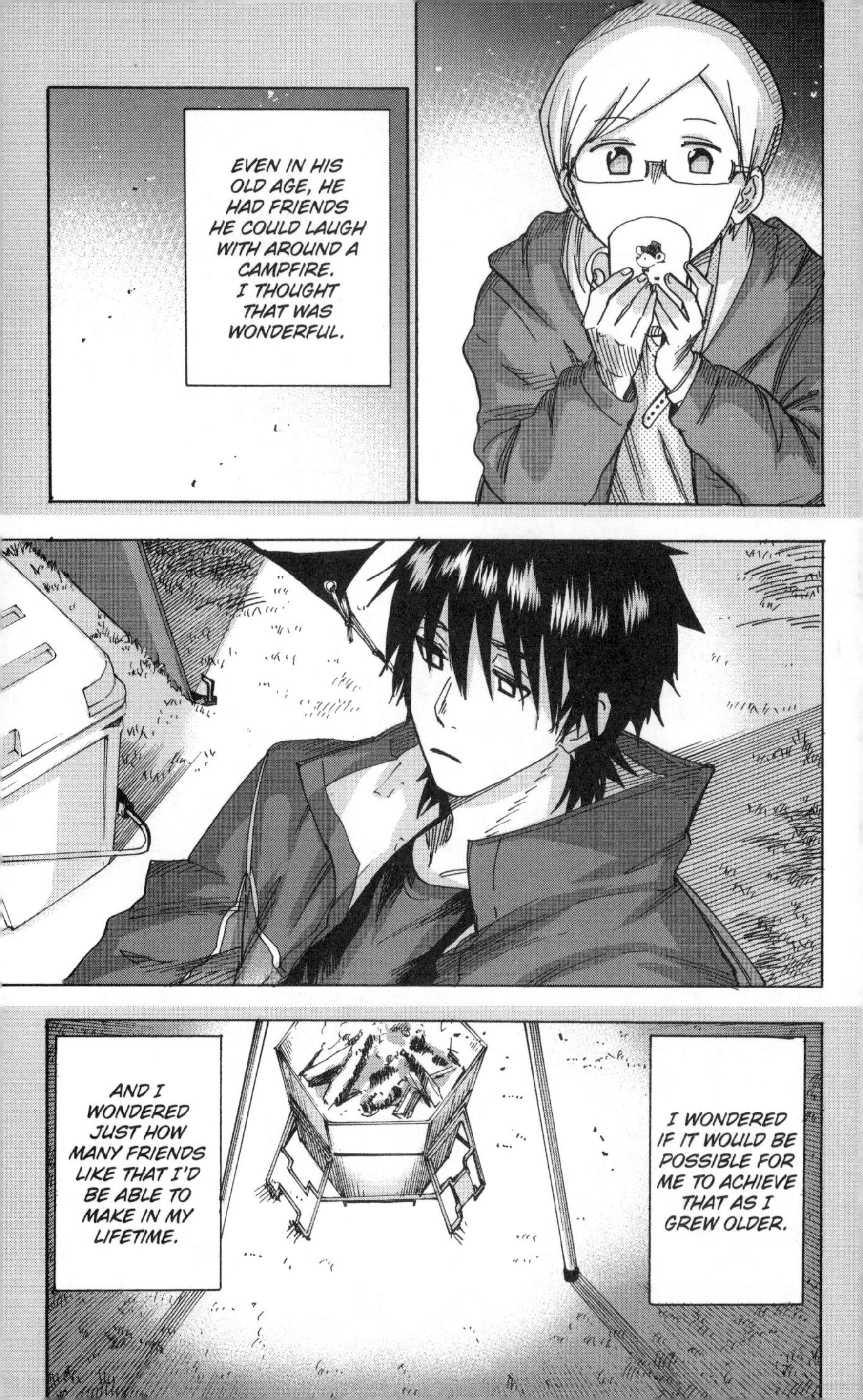
EVEN IN HIS OLD AGE, HE HAD FRIENDS HE COULD LAUGH WITH AROUND A CAMPFIRE. I THOUGHT THAT WAS WONDERFUL.
I WONDERED IF IT WOULD BE POSSIBLE FOR ME TO ACHIEVE THAT AS I GREW OLDER.
AND I WONDERED JUST HOW MANY FRIENDS LIKE THAT I'D BE ABLE TO MAKE IN MY LIFETIME.

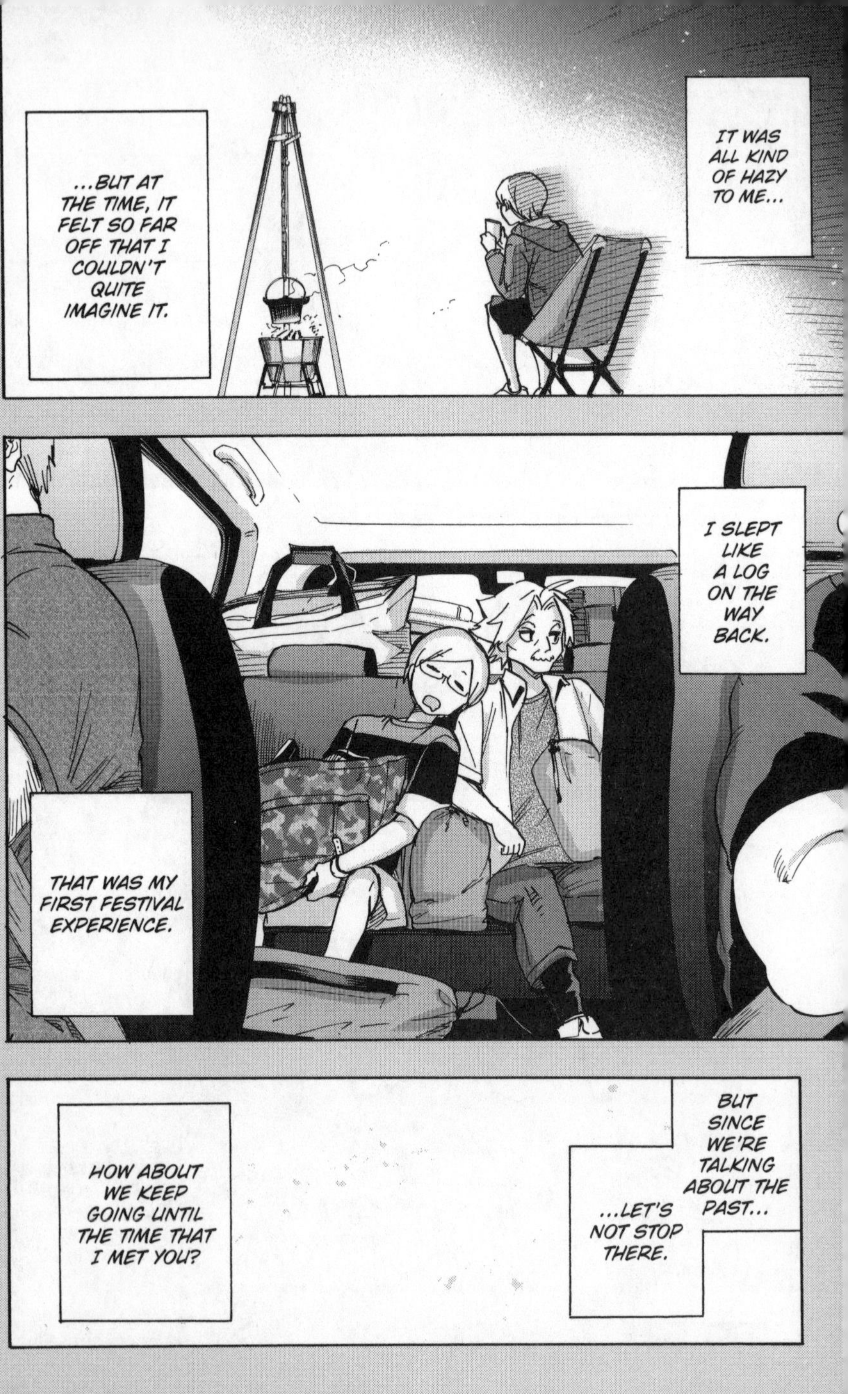
IT WAS ALL KIND OF HAZY TO ME...
...BUT AT THE TIME, IT FELT SO FAR OFF THAT I COULDN'T QUITE IMAGINE IT.
I SLEPT LIKE A LOG ON THE WAY BACK.
THAT WAS MY FIRST FESTIVAL EXPERIENCE.
BUT SINCE WE'RE TALKING ABOUT THE PAST...
...LET'S NOT STOP THERE.
HOW ABOUT WE KEEP GOING UNTIL THE TIME THAT I MET YOU?

Days on Fes

Days on Fes

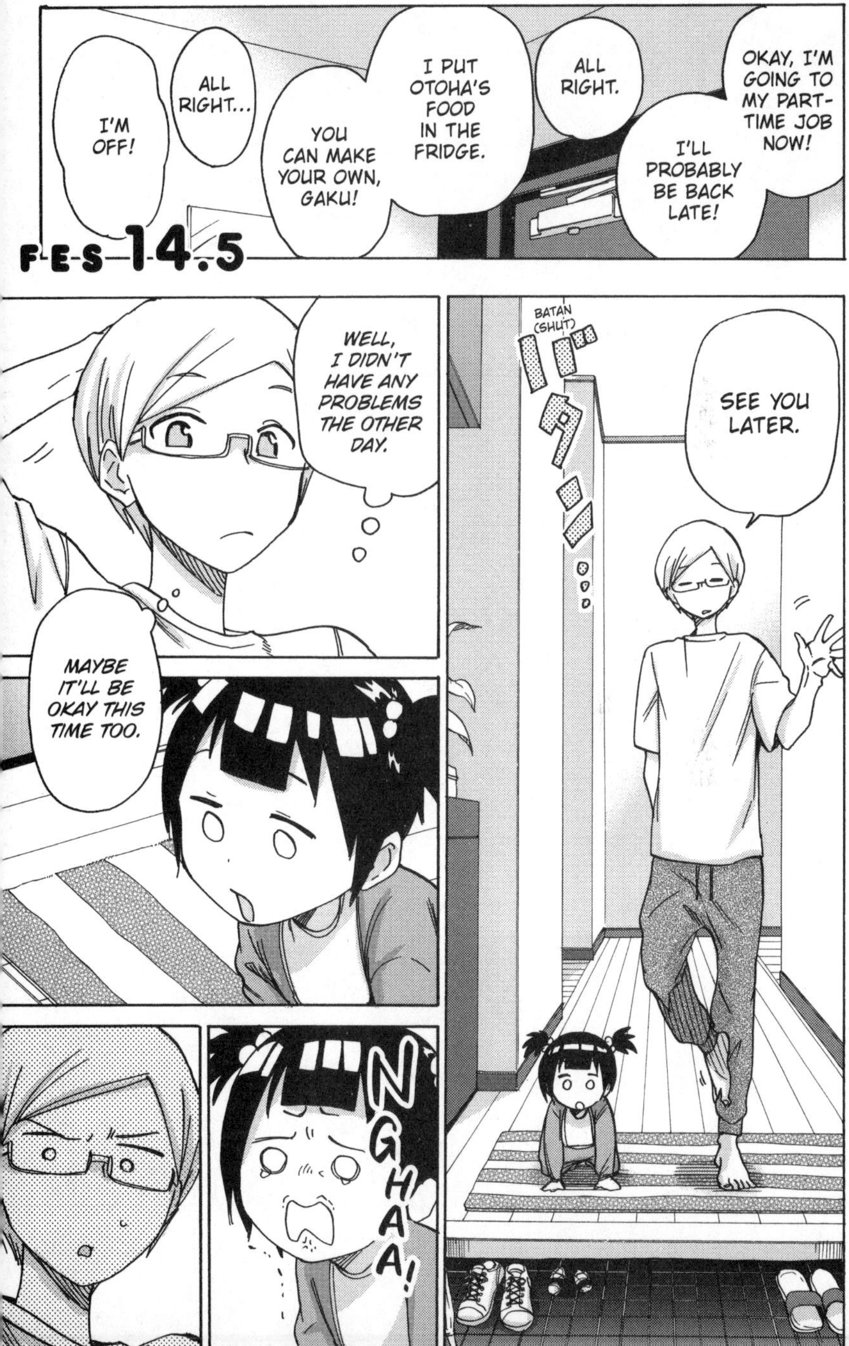
OKAY, I'M GOING TO MY PART-TIME JOB NOW!
I'LL PROBABLY BE BACK LATE!
ALL RIGHT.
I PUT OTOHA'S FOOD IN THE FRIDGE.
YOU CAN MAKE YOUR OWN, GAKU!
ALL RIGHT...
I'M OFF!
F-E-S 14.5
SEE YOU LATER.
BATAN (SHUT)
WELL, I DIDN'T HAVE ANY PROBLEMS THE OTHER DAY.
MAYBE IT'LL BE OKAY THIS TIME TOO.
NGHAA!

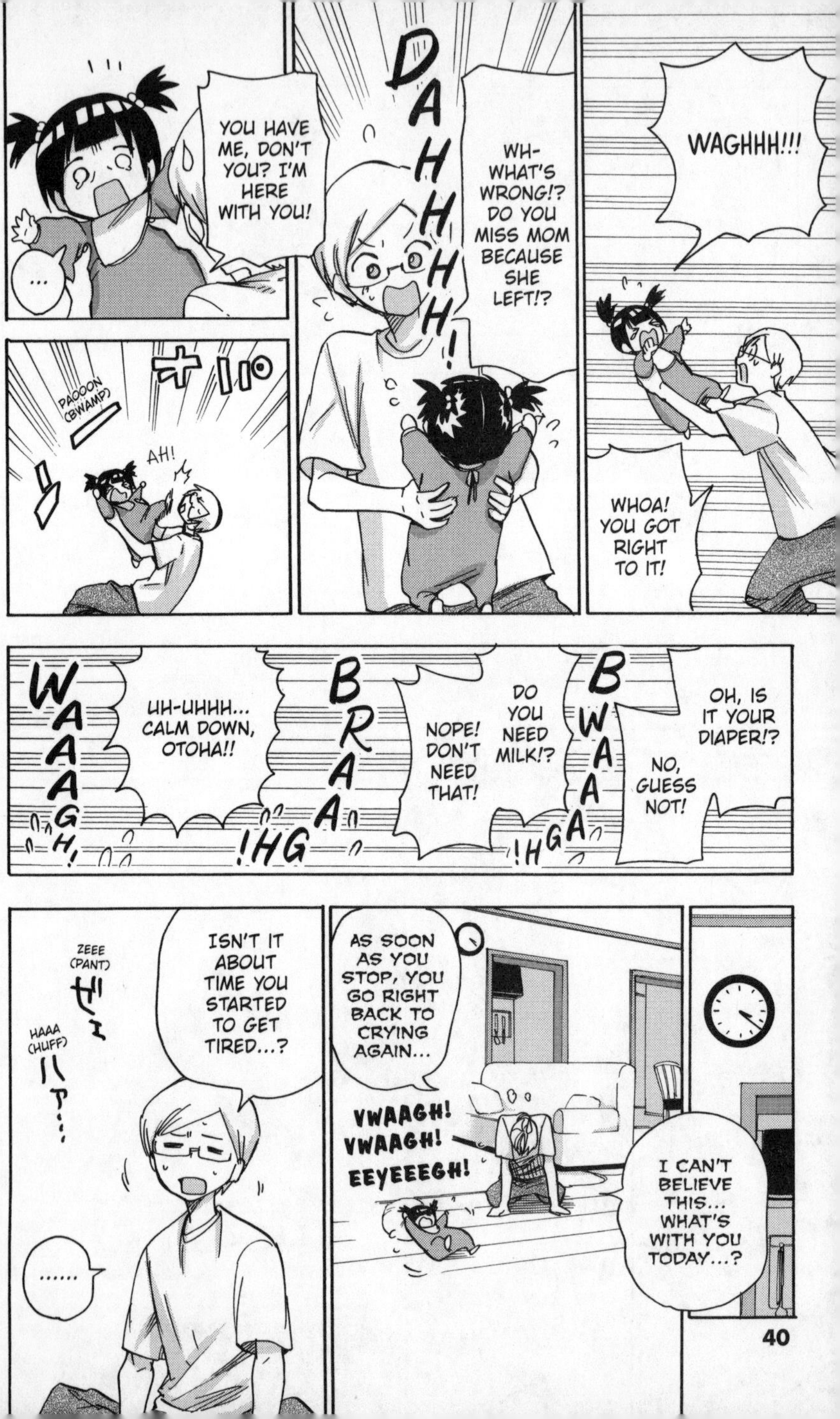
WAGHHH!!!
WHOA! YOU GOT RIGHT TO IT!
DAHHHHH!
WH- WHAT'S WRONG!? DO YOU MISS MOM BECAUSE SHE LEFT!?
YOU HAVE ME, DON'T YOU? I'M HERE WITH YOU!
...
PAOOON (BWAMP)
AH!
OH, IS IT YOUR DIAPER!?
NO, GUESS NOT!
BWAAAGH!
DO YOU NEED MILK!?
NOPE! DON'T NEED THAT!
BRAAAGH!
UH-UHHH... CALM DOWN, OTOHA!!
WAAAAGH!
AS SOON AS YOU STOP, YOU GO RIGHT BACK TO CRYING AGAIN...
VWAAGH! VWAAGH! EEYEEEGH!
I CAN'T BELIEVE THIS... WHAT'S WITH YOU TODAY...?
ISN'T IT ABOUT TIME YOU STARTED TO GET TIRED...?
ZEEE (PANT) ゼェ
HAAA (HUFF) ハァ...
......

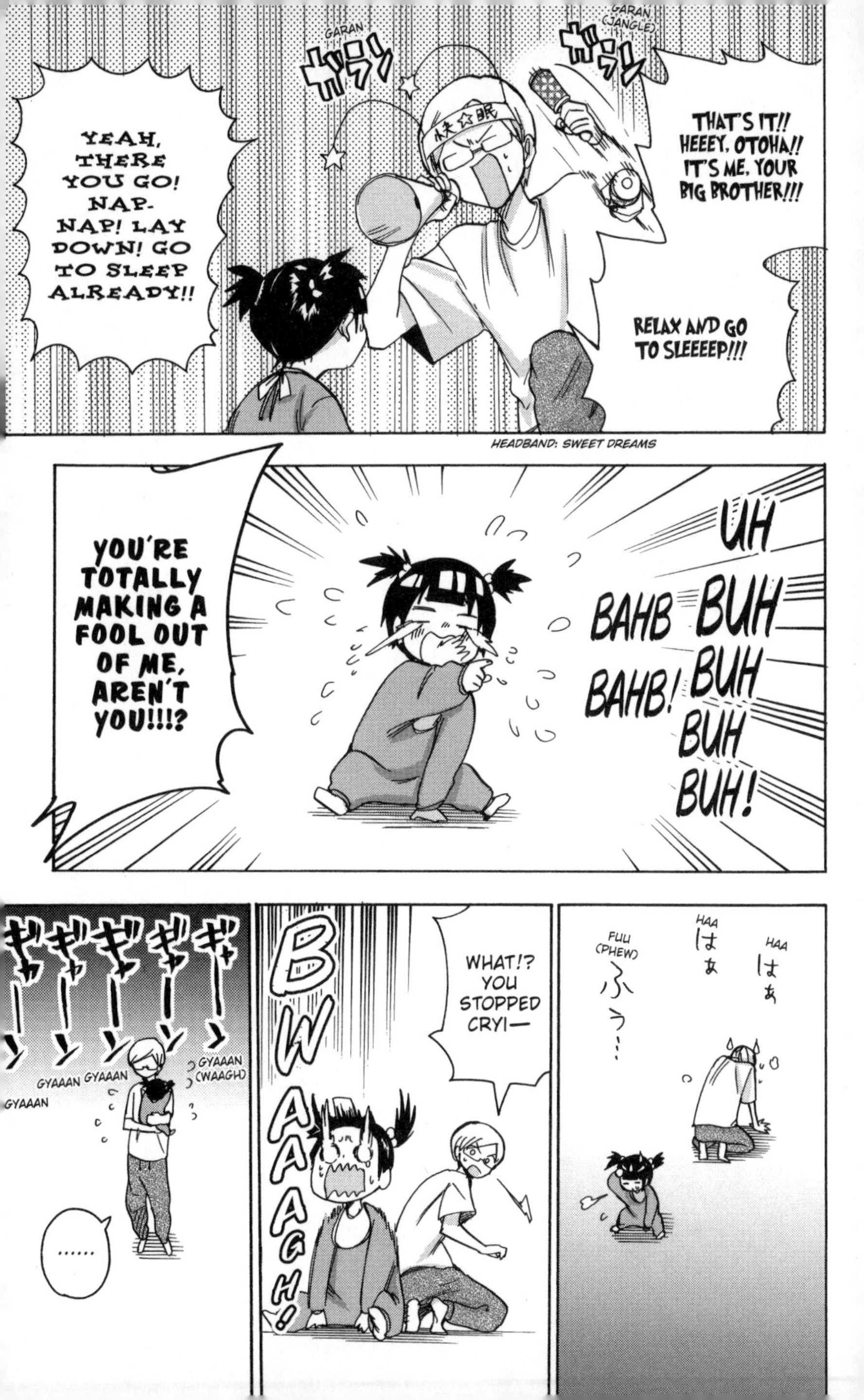
ガラン
GARAN (JANGLE)
THAT'S IT!! HEEEY, OTOHA!! IT'S ME, YOUR BIG BROTHER!!!
ガラン
GARAN
YEAH, THERE YOU GO! NAP-NAP! LAY DOWN! GO TO SLEEP ALREADY!!
RELAX AND GO TO SLEEEEP!!!
HEADBAND: SWEET DREAMS
UH BUH BUH BUH BUH!
BAHB BAHB!
YOU'RE TOTALLY MAKING A FOOL OUT OF ME, AREN'T YOU!!!?
はぁ
HAA
はぁ
HAA
ふぅ…
FUU (PHEW)
WHAT!? YOU STOPPED CRYI—
BWAAAAGH!
ギャーン
GYAAAN (WAAGH)
ギャーン
GYAAAN
ギャーン
GYAAAN
ギャーン
GYAAAN
……

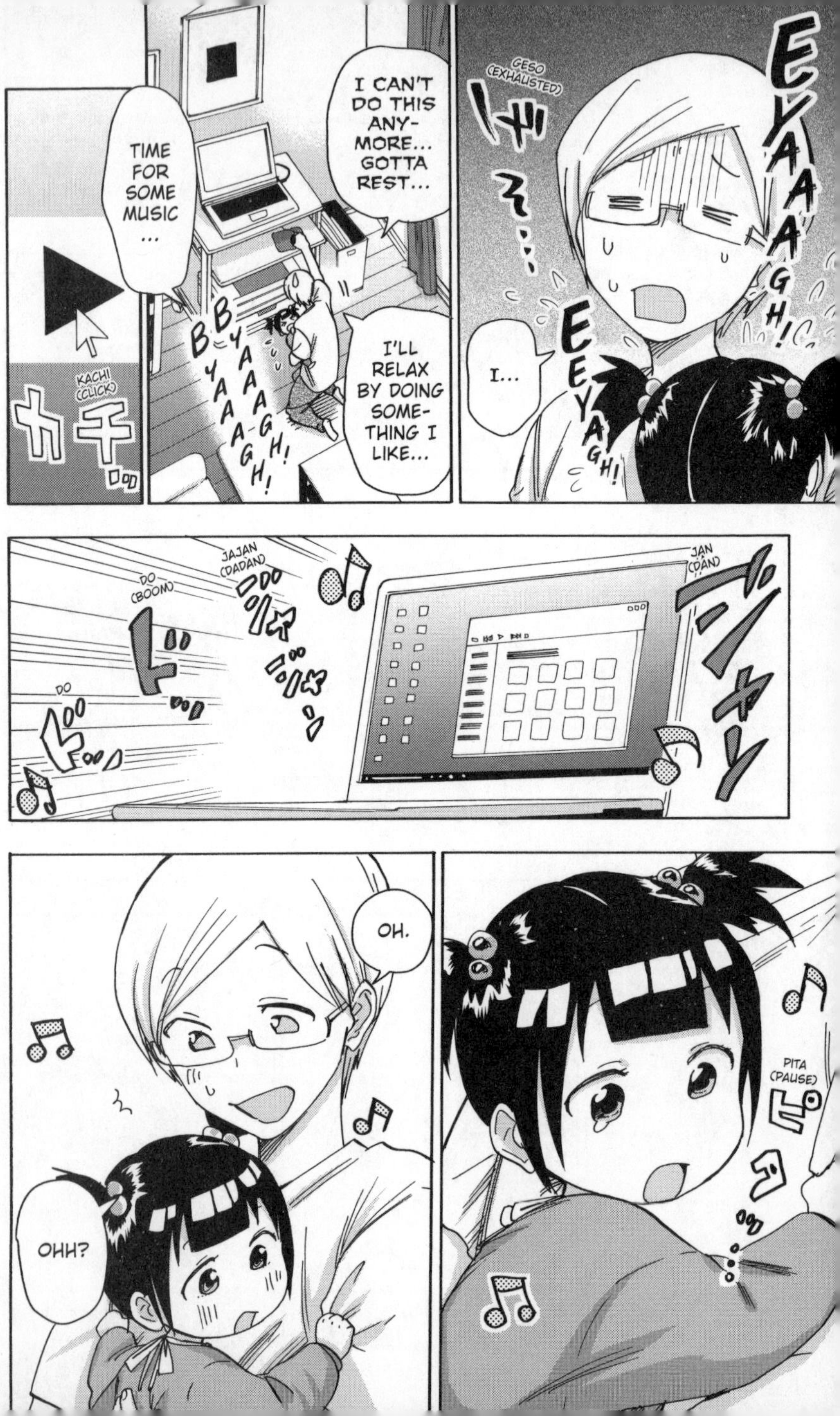
EYAAAAGH!
GESO (EXHAUSTED)
EEYAGH!
I...
I CAN'T DO THIS ANYMORE... GOTTA REST...
I'LL RELAX BY DOING SOMETHING I LIKE...
BYAAAAGH!
BYAAAGH!
TIME FOR SOME MUSIC ...
KACHI (CLICK)
JAN (DADAN)
JAJAN (DADAN)
DO (BOOM)
DO
PITA (PAUSE)
OH.
OHH?

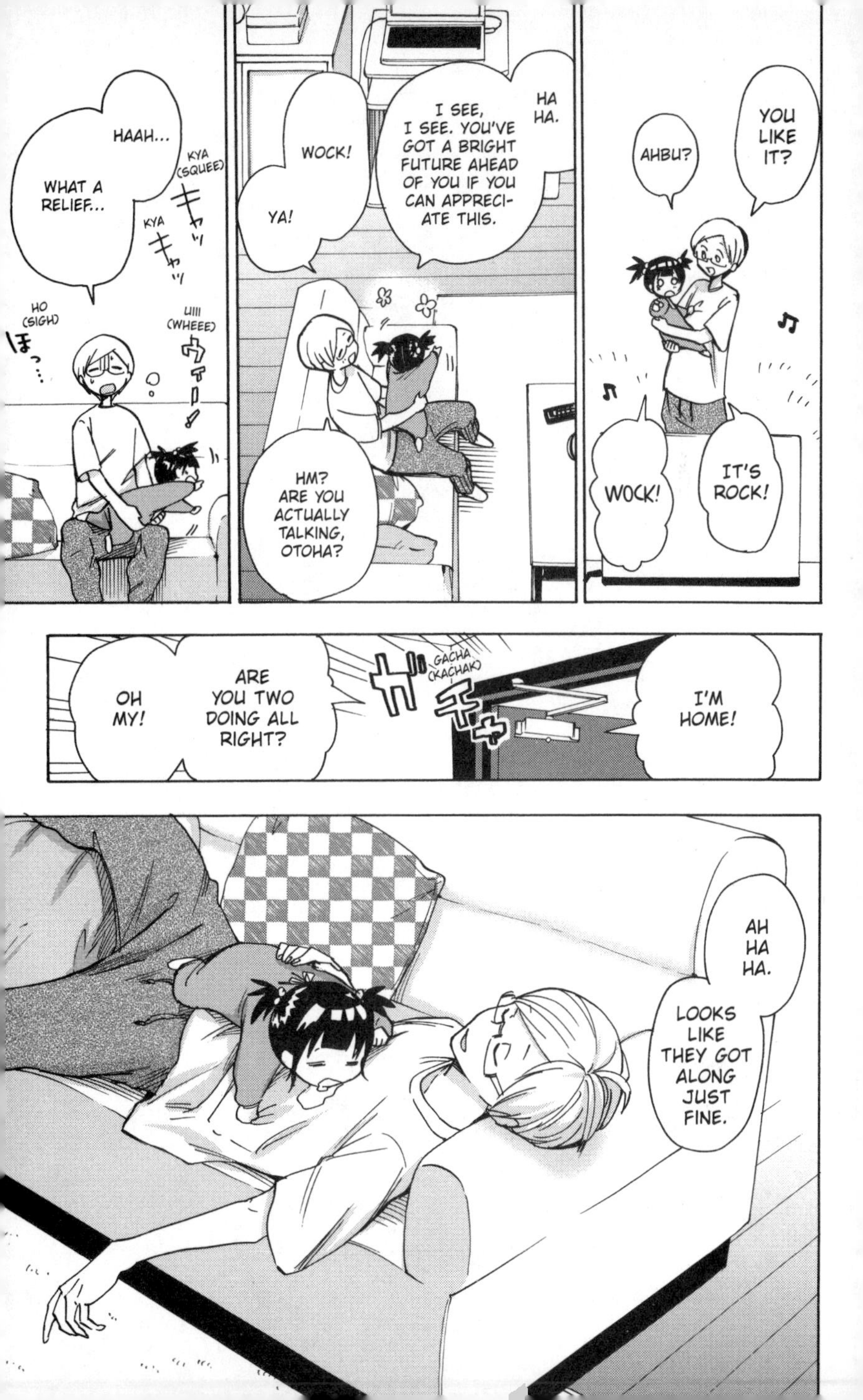
YOU LIKE IT?
AHBU?
IT'S ROCK!
WOCK!
HA HA.
I SEE, I SEE. YOU'VE GOT A BRIGHT FUTURE AHEAD OF YOU IF YOU CAN APPRECIATE THIS.
WOCK!
YA!
HM? ARE YOU ACTUALLY TALKING, OTOHA?
HAAH...
WHAT A RELIEF...
KYA (SQUEE)
KYA
UIII (WHEEE)
HO (SIGH)
I'M HOME!
GACHA (KACHAK)
ARE YOU TWO DOING ALL RIGHT?
OH MY!
AH HA HA.
LOOKS LIKE THEY GOT ALONG JUST FINE.

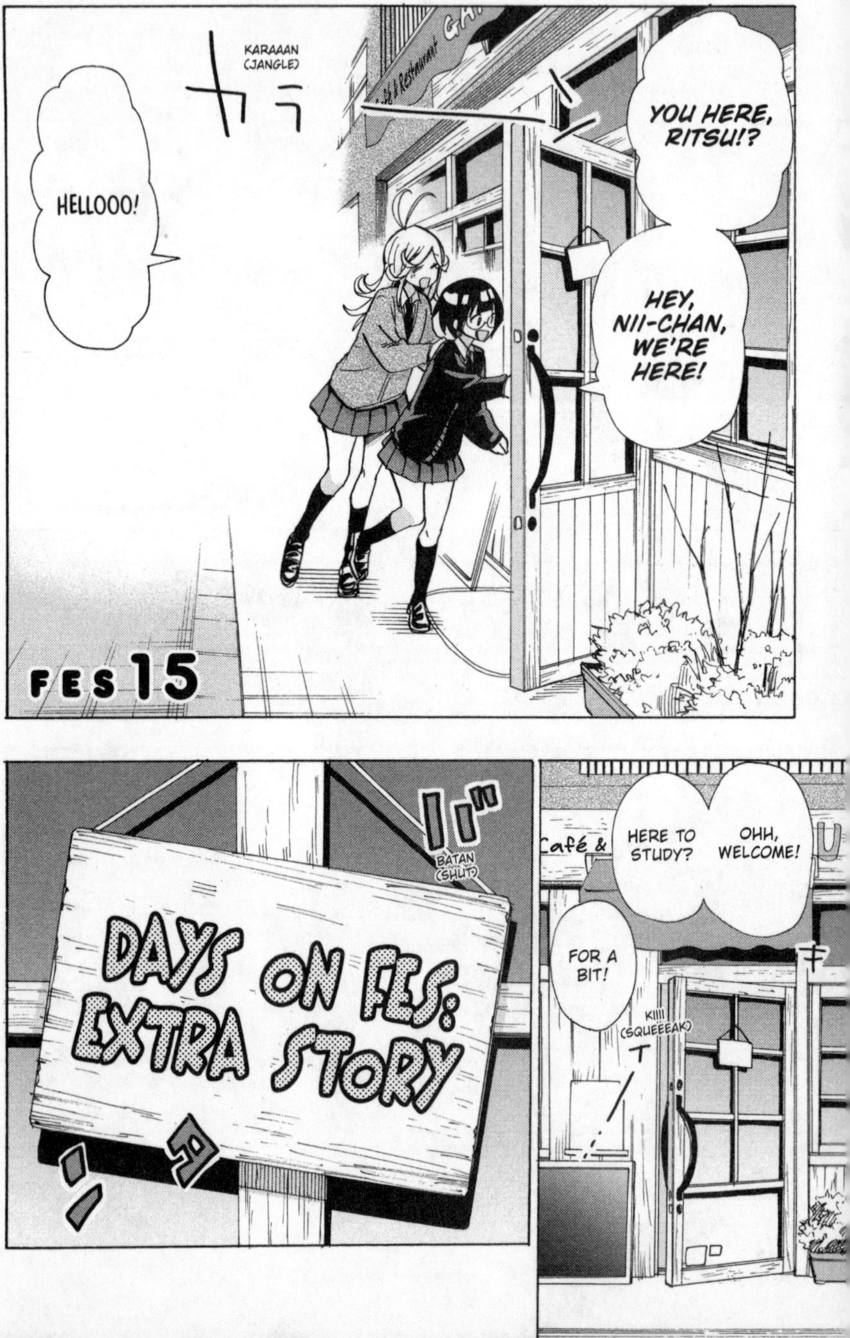
YOU HERE, RITSU!?
HEY, NII-CHAN, WE'RE HERE!
KARAAAN (JANGLE)
HELLOOO!
FES 15
OHH, WELCOME!
HERE TO STUDY?
FOR A BIT!
KIIII (SQUEEEAK)
BATAN (SHUT)
DAYS ON FES: EXTRA STORY

EVERYONE'S STRENGTHS AND WEAKNESSES

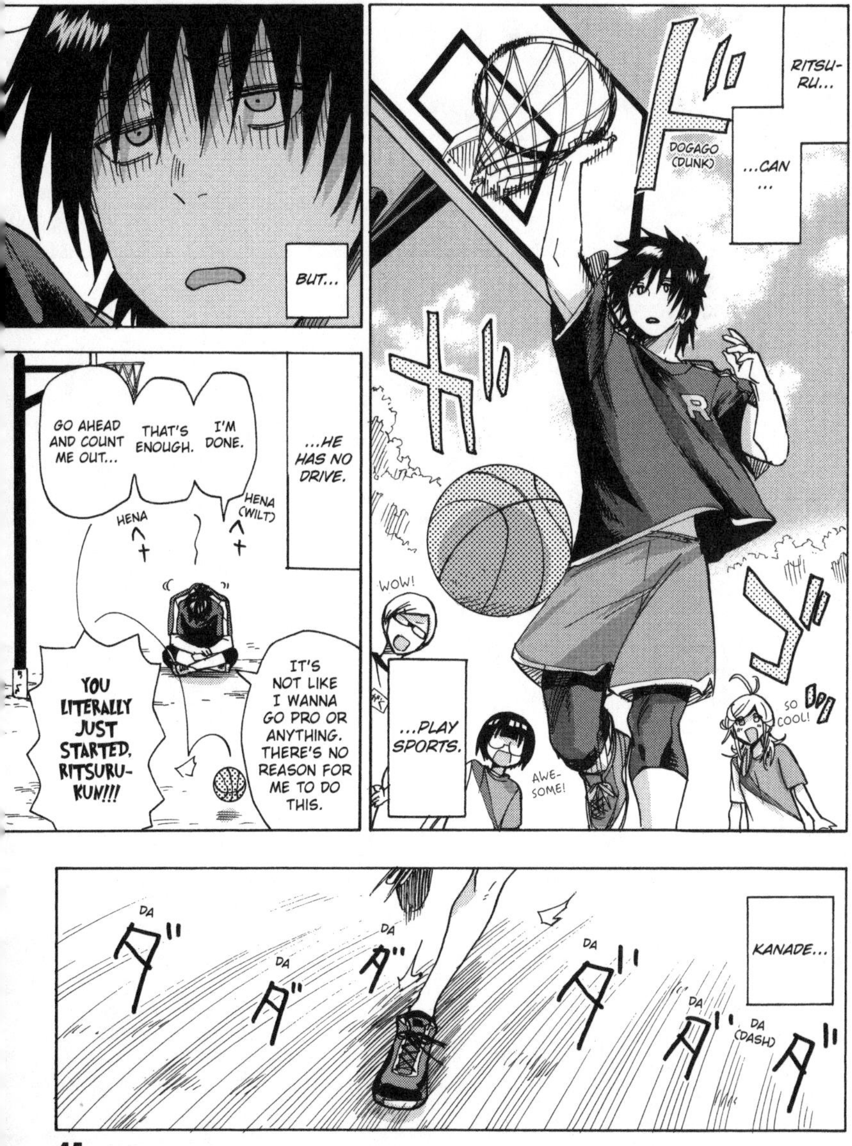

RITSURU...
...CAN ...
DOGAGO (DUNK)
WOW!
SO COOL!
...PLAY SPORTS.
AWESOME!
BUT...
...HE HAS NO DRIVE.
I'M DONE.
THAT'S ENOUGH.
GO AHEAD AND COUNT ME OUT...
HENA (WILT)
HENA
IT'S NOT LIKE I WANNA GO PRO OR ANYTHING. THERE'S NO REASON FOR ME TO DO THIS.
YOU LITERALLY JUST STARTED, RITSURU-KUN!!!
KANADE...
DA (DASH)
DA
DA
DA
DA
DA

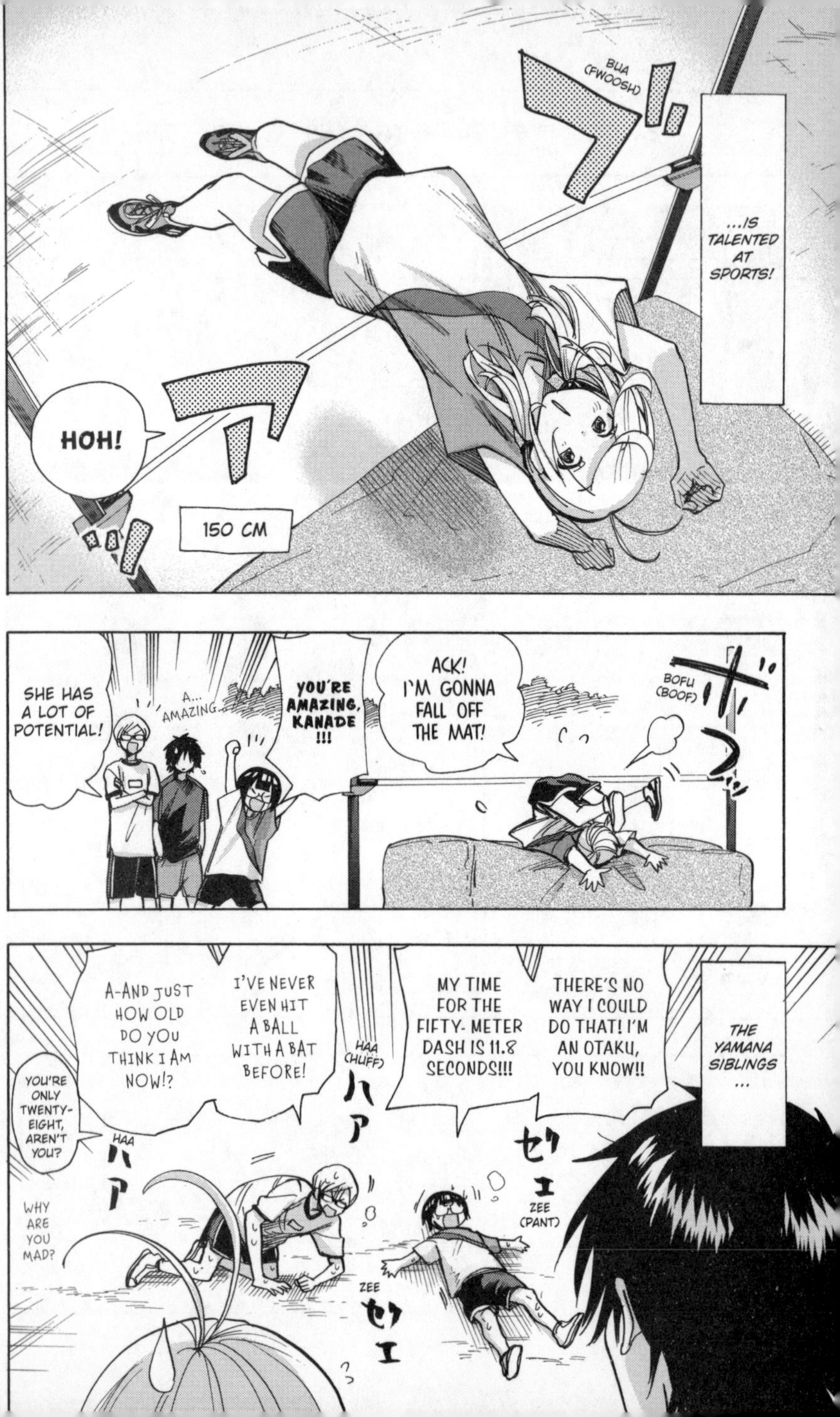
...IS TALENTED AT SPORTS!
BUA (FWOOSH)
HOH!
150 CM
BOFU (BOOF)
ACK! I'M GONNA FALL OFF THE MAT!
YOU'RE AMAZING, KANADE!!!
A... AMAZING...
SHE HAS A LOT OF POTENTIAL!
THE YAMANA SIBLINGS...
THERE'S NO WAY I COULD DO THAT! I'M AN OTAKU, YOU KNOW!!
MY TIME FOR THE FIFTY-METER DASH IS 11.8 SECONDS!!!
HAA (CHUFF)
I'VE NEVER EVEN HIT A BALL WITH A BAT BEFORE!
A-AND JUST HOW OLD DO YOU THINK I AM NOW!?
YOU'RE ONLY TWENTY-EIGHT, AREN'T YOU?
HAA
ZEE (PANT)
WHY ARE YOU MAD?
ZEE

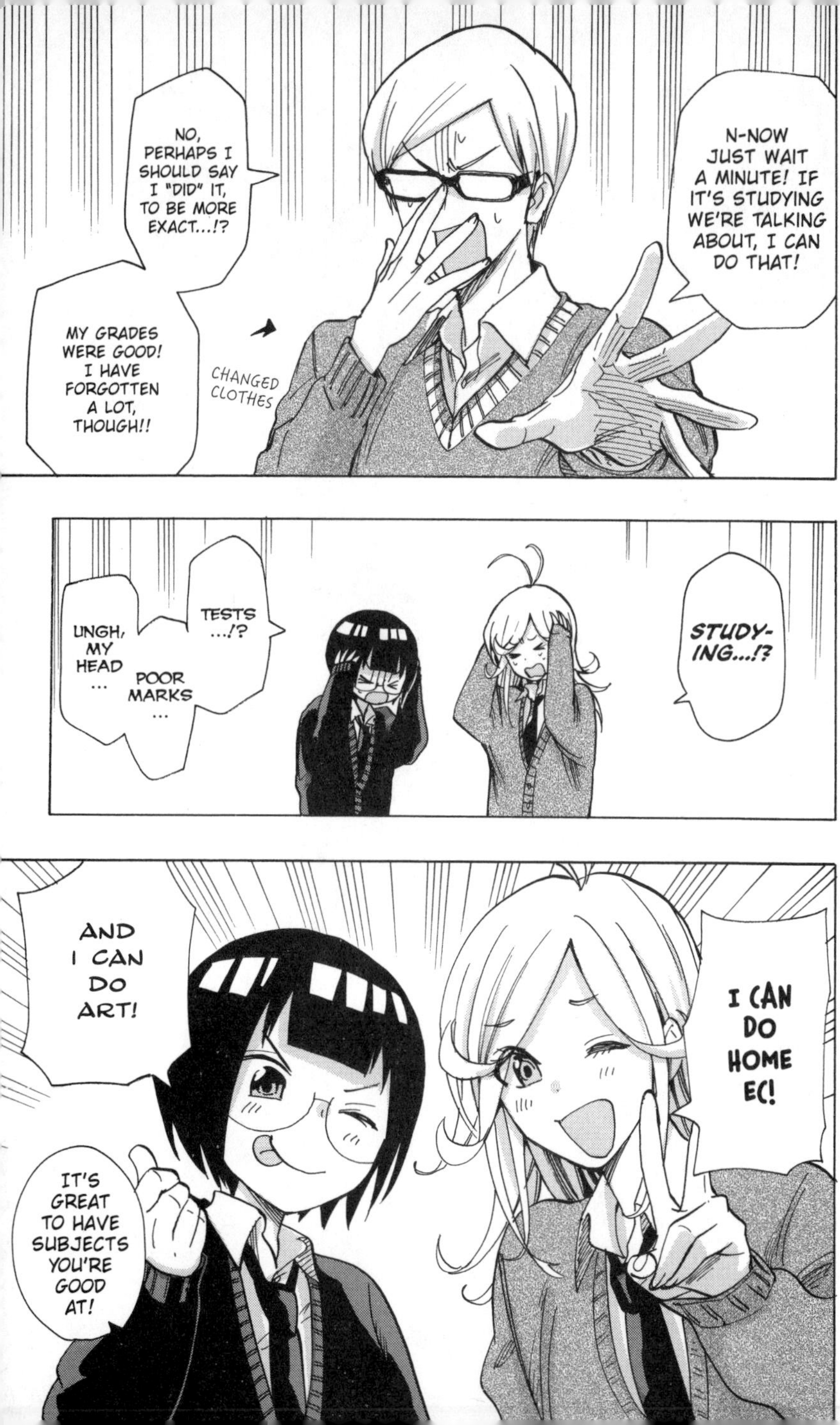
N-NOW JUST WAIT A MINUTE! IF IT'S STUDYING WE'RE TALKING ABOUT, I CAN DO THAT!
NO, PERHAPS I SHOULD SAY I "DID" IT, TO BE MORE EXACT...!?
CHANGED CLOTHES
MY GRADES WERE GOOD! I HAVE FORGOTTEN A LOT, THOUGH!!
STUDYING...!?
TESTS...!?
POOR MARKS...
UNGH, MY HEAD...
I CAN DO HOME EC!
AND I CAN DO ART!
IT'S GREAT TO HAVE SUBJECTS YOU'RE GOOD AT!

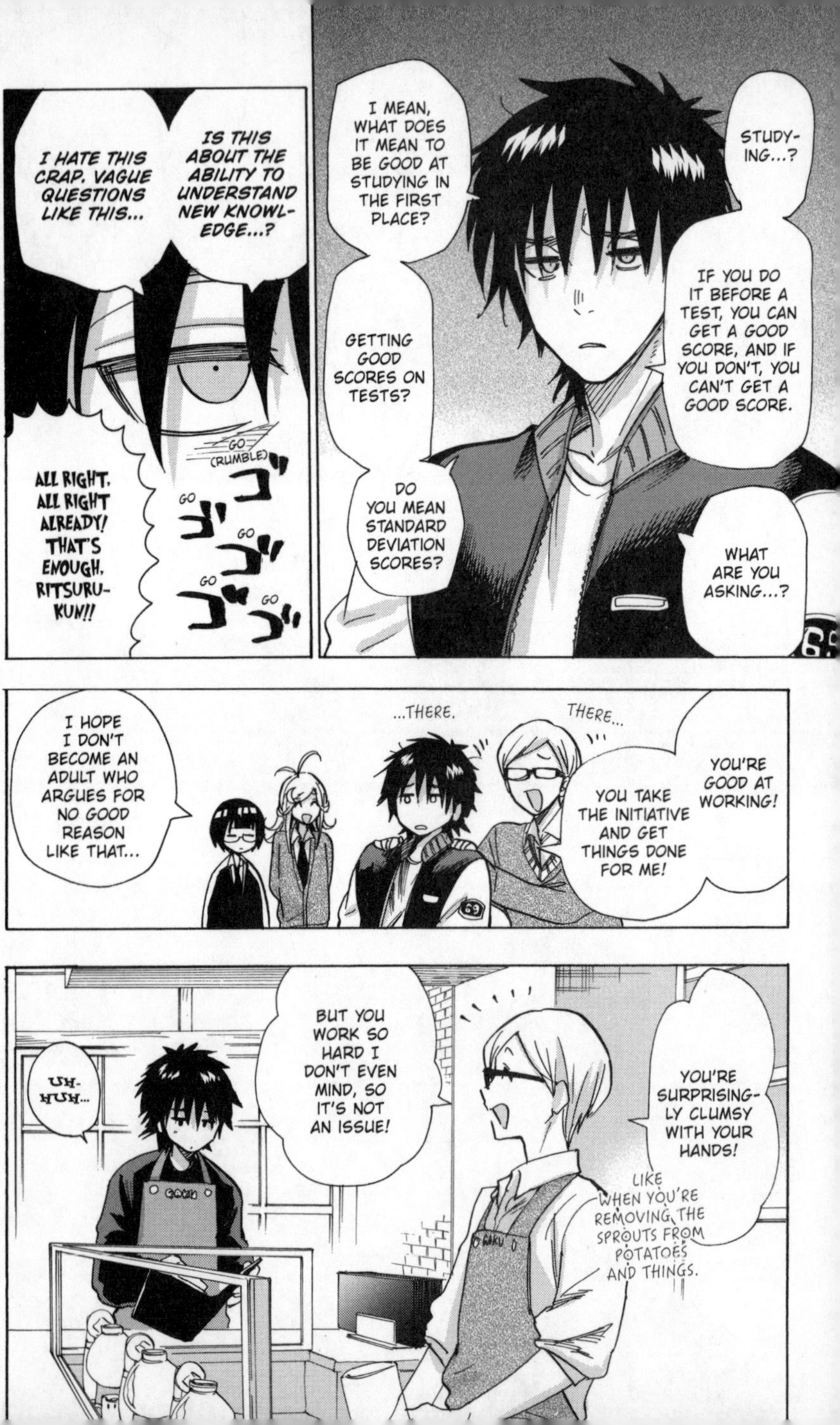

STUDYING...?
IF YOU DO IT BEFORE A TEST, YOU CAN GET A GOOD SCORE, AND IF YOU DON'T, YOU CAN'T GET A GOOD SCORE.
WHAT ARE YOU ASKING...?
I MEAN, WHAT DOES IT MEAN TO BE GOOD AT STUDYING IN THE FIRST PLACE?
GETTING GOOD SCORES ON TESTS?
DO YOU MEAN STANDARD DEVIATION SCORES?
IS THIS ABOUT THE ABILITY TO UNDERSTAND NEW KNOWLEDGE...?
I HATE THIS CRAP. VAGUE QUESTIONS LIKE THIS...
GO (RUMBLE) GO GO GO GO
ALL RIGHT. ALL RIGHT ALREADY! THAT'S ENOUGH, RITSURU-KUN!!
YOU'RE GOOD AT WORKING!
THERE...
YOU TAKE THE INITIATIVE AND GET THINGS DONE FOR ME!
...THERE.
I HOPE I DON'T BECOME AN ADULT WHO ARGUES FOR NO GOOD REASON LIKE THAT...
YOU'RE SURPRISINGLY CLUMSY WITH YOUR HANDS!
LIKE WHEN YOU'RE REMOVING THE SPROUTS FROM POTATOES AND THINGS.
BUT YOU WORK SO HARD I DON'T EVEN MIND, SO IT'S NOT AN ISSUE!
UH-HUH...

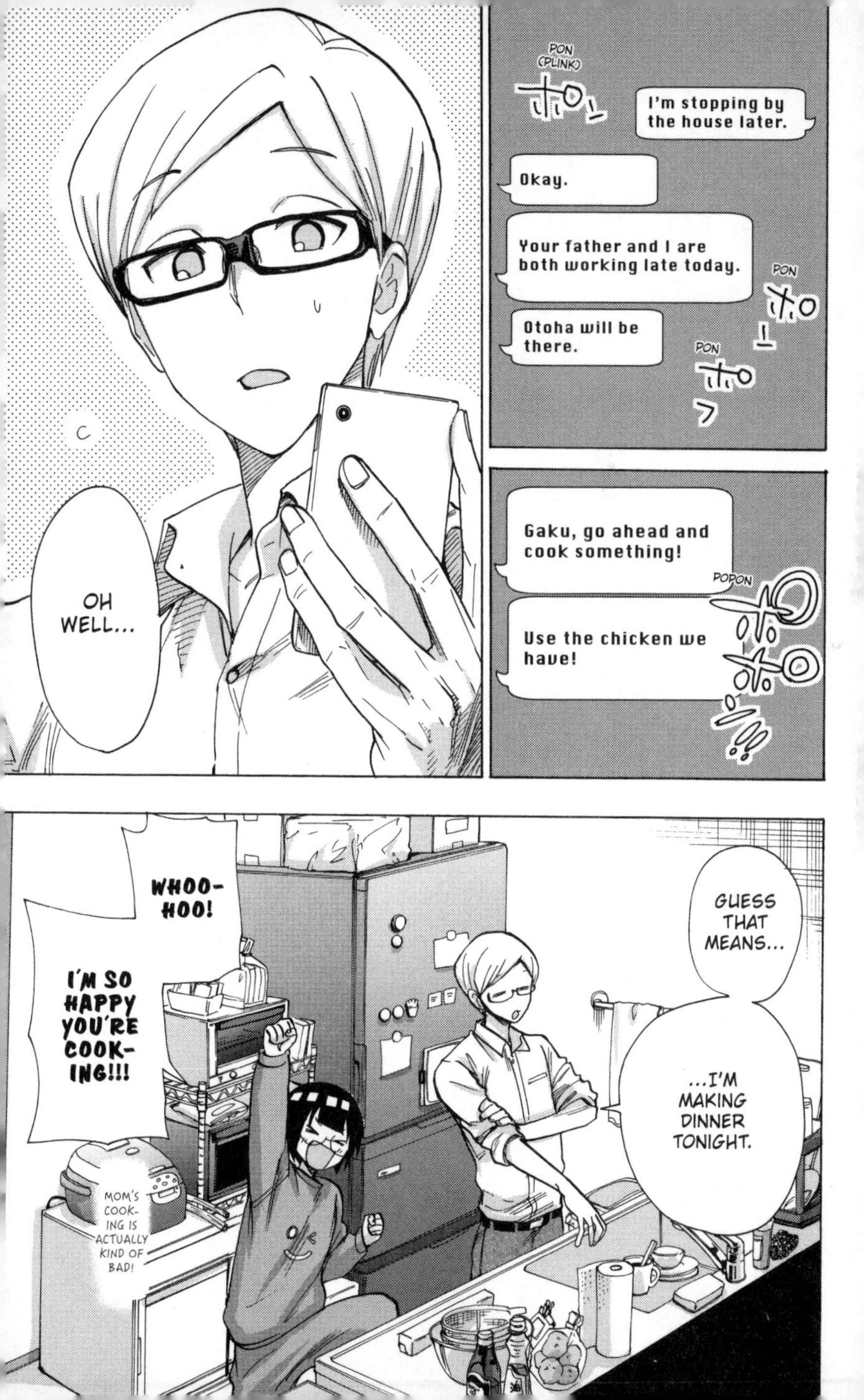
PON (PLINK)
I'm stopping by the house later.
Okay.
Your father and I are both working late today.
PON
Otoha will be there.
PON
Gaku, go ahead and cook something!
POPON
Use the chicken we have!
OH WELL...
GUESS THAT MEANS...
...I'M MAKING DINNER TONIGHT.
WHOO-HOO!
I'M SO HAPPY YOU'RE COOKING!!!
MOM'S COOKING IS ACTUALLY KIND OF BAD!

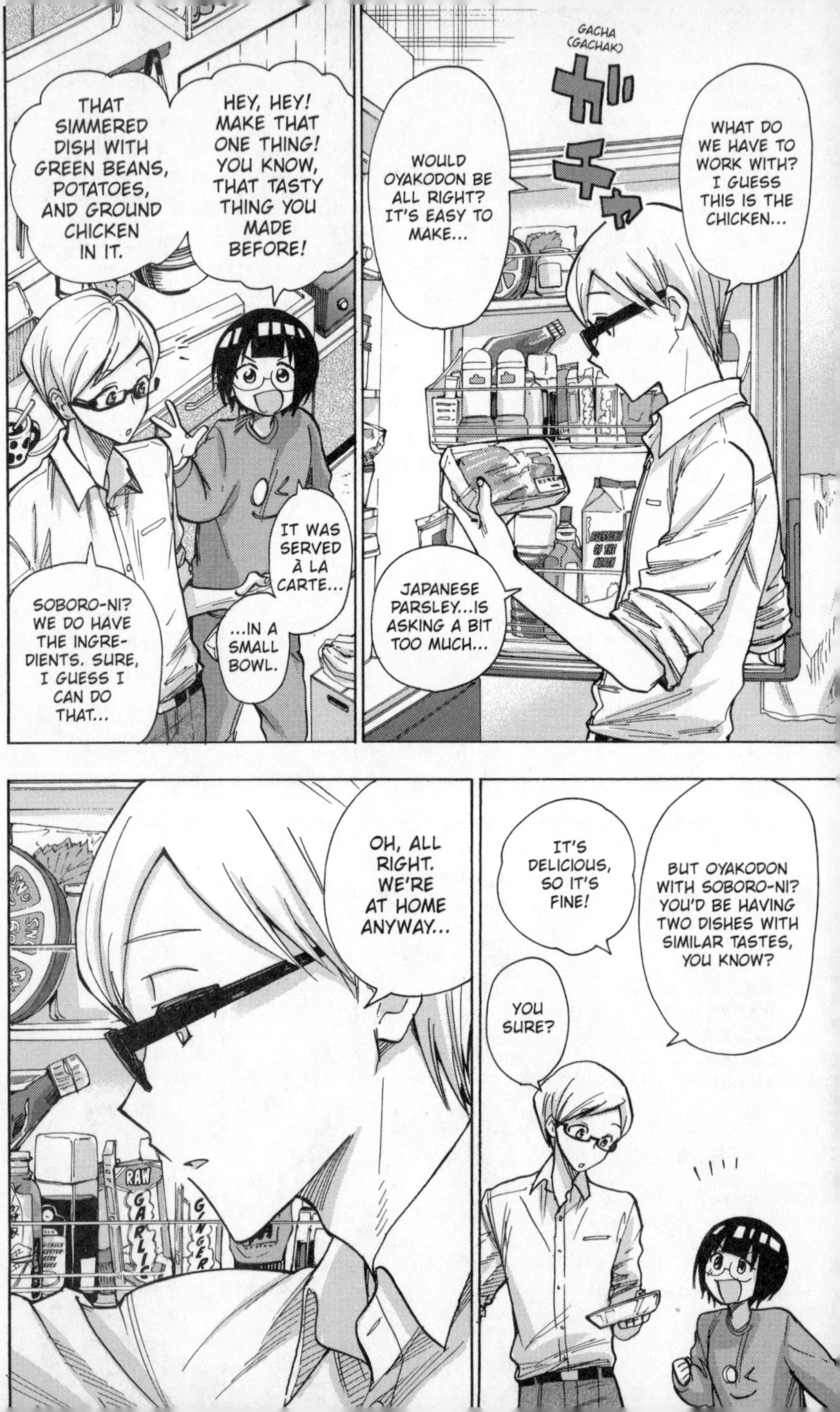
GACHA (GACHAK)
WHAT DO WE HAVE TO WORK WITH? I GUESS THIS IS THE CHICKEN...
WOULD OYAKODON BE ALL RIGHT? IT'S EASY TO MAKE...
JAPANESE PARSLEY...IS ASKING A BIT TOO MUCH...
HEY, HEY! MAKE THAT ONE THING! YOU KNOW, THAT TASTY THING YOU MADE BEFORE!
THAT SIMMERED DISH WITH GREEN BEANS, POTATOES, AND GROUND CHICKEN IN IT.
IT WAS SERVED À LA CARTE...
...IN A SMALL BOWL.
SOBORO-NI? WE DO HAVE THE INGREDIENTS. SURE, I GUESS I CAN DO THAT...
BUT OYAKODON WITH SOBORO-NI? YOU'D BE HAVING TWO DISHES WITH SIMILAR TASTES, YOU KNOW?
IT'S DELICIOUS, SO IT'S FINE!
YOU SURE?
OH, ALL RIGHT. WE'RE AT HOME ANYWAY...
RAW GARLIC
GINGER

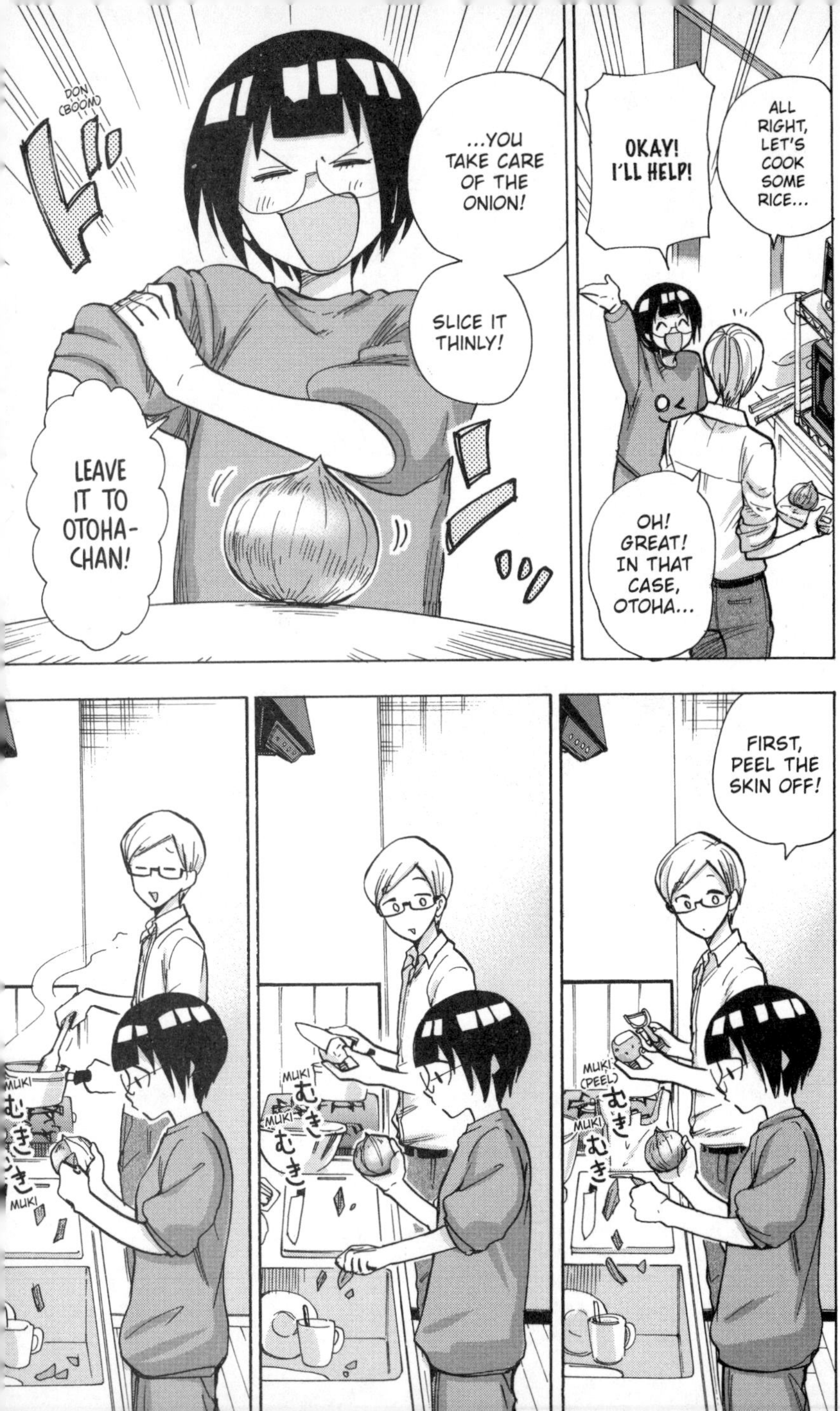
ALL RIGHT, LET'S COOK SOME RICE...
OKAY! I'LL HELP!
OH! GREAT! IN THAT CASE, OTOHA...
...YOU TAKE CARE OF THE ONION!
SLICE IT THINLY!
DON (BOOM)
LEAVE IT TO OTOHA-CHAN!
FIRST, PEEL THE SKIN OFF!
MUKI (PEEL) むき
MUKI むき
MUKI むき
MUKI むき
MUKI むき
むき MUKI

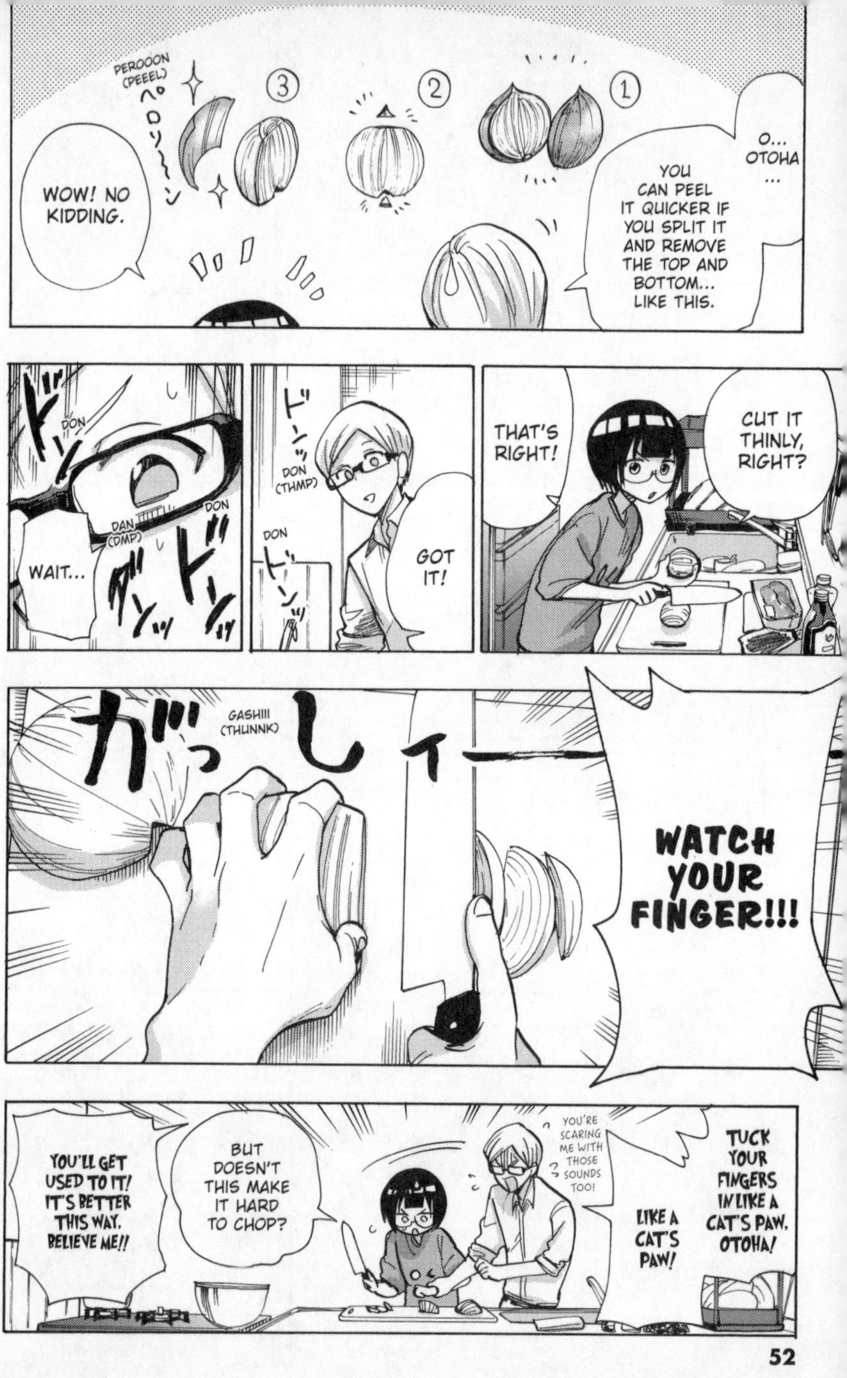
O... OTOHA ...
YOU CAN PEEL IT QUICKER IF YOU SPLIT IT AND REMOVE THE TOP AND BOTTOM... LIKE THIS.
1
2
3
PEROOON (PEEEL)
ペロリ～ン
WOW! NO KIDDING.
CUT IT THINLY, RIGHT?
THAT'S RIGHT!
ドーンッ
DON (THMP)
GOT IT!
DON
ドーンッ
DON
ドッ
DON
ドッ
DAN (DMP)
ダンッ
WAIT...
WATCH YOUR FINGER!!!
GASHIII (THUNNK)
がっしイー
TUCK YOUR FINGERS IN LIKE A CAT'S PAW, OTOHA!
LIKE A CAT'S PAW!
YOU'RE SCARING ME WITH THOSE SOUNDS TOO!
BUT DOESN'T THIS MAKE IT HARD TO CHOP?
YOU'LL GET USED TO IT! IT'S BETTER THIS WAY. BELIEVE ME!!

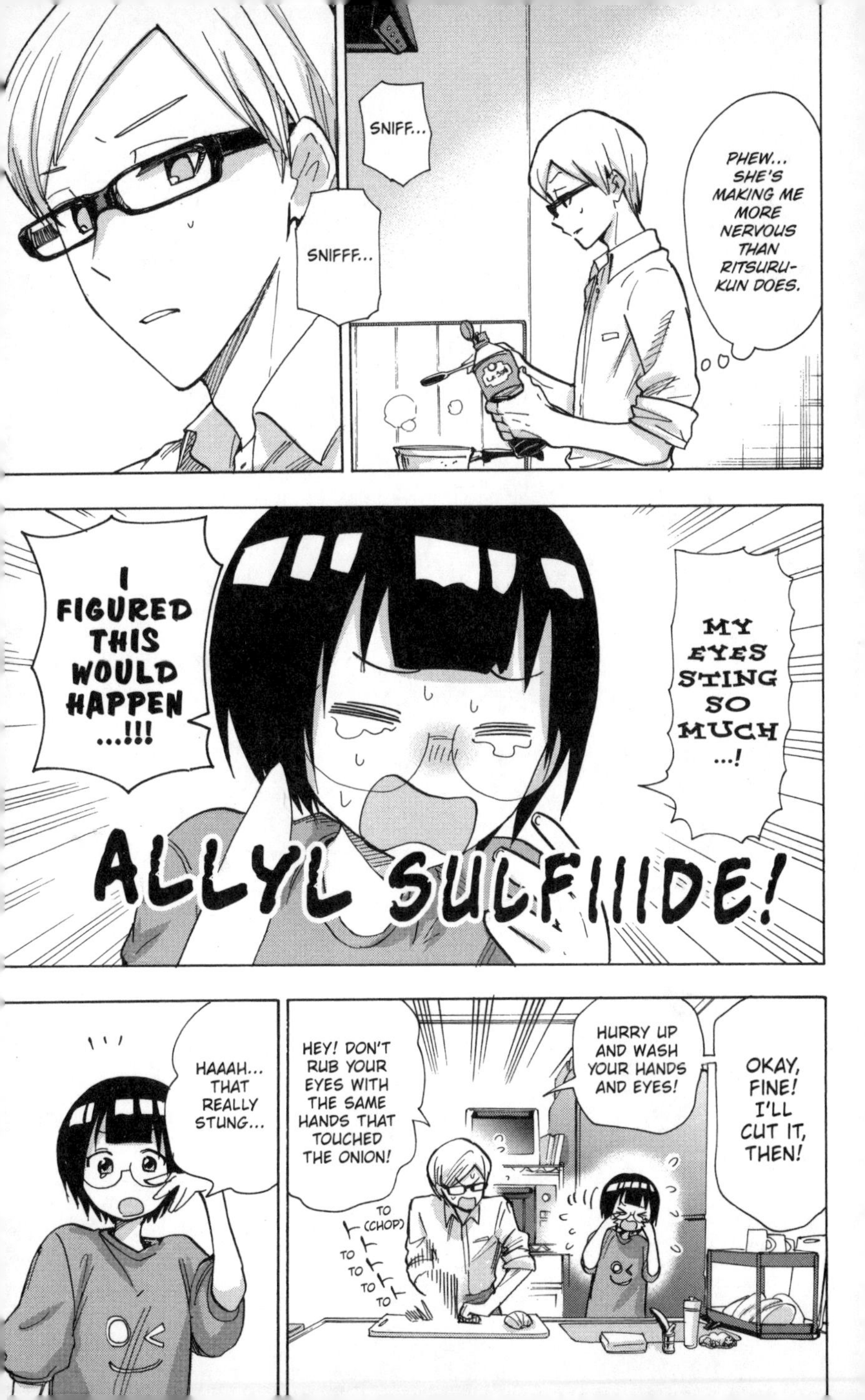
PHEW... SHE'S MAKING ME MORE NERVOUS THAN RITSURU-KUN DOES.
SNIFF...
SNIFFF...
MY EYES STING SO MUCH...!
I FIGURED THIS WOULD HAPPEN...!!!
ALLYL SULFIIDE!
OKAY, FINE! I'LL CUT IT, THEN!
HURRY UP AND WASH YOUR HANDS AND EYES!
HEY! DON'T RUB YOUR EYES WITH THE SAME HANDS THAT TOUCHED THE ONION!
TO (CHOP)
TO TO TO TO
HAAAH... THAT REALLY STUNG...

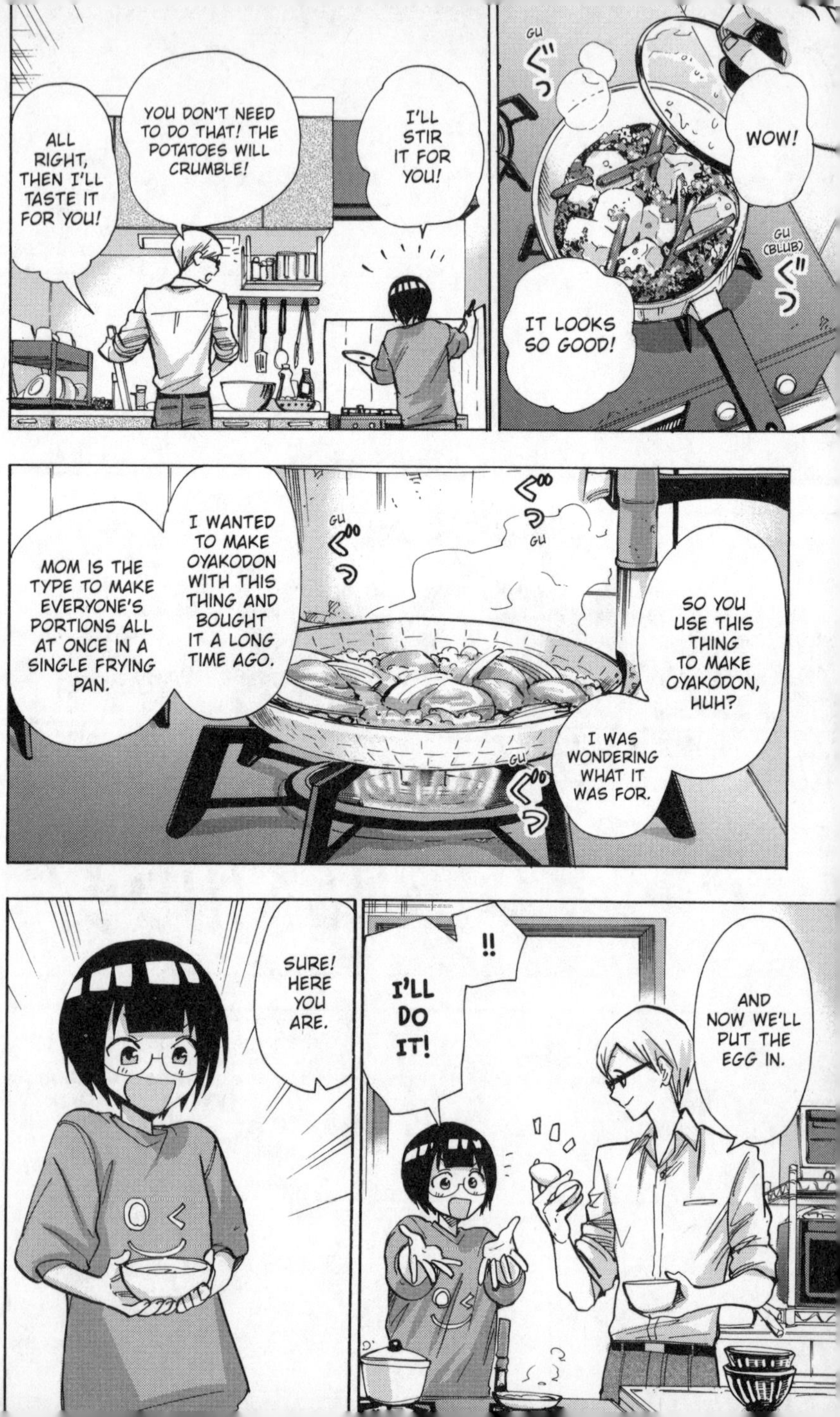
GU
WOW!
GU (BLUB)
IT LOOKS SO GOOD!
I'LL STIR IT FOR YOU!
YOU DON'T NEED TO DO THAT! THE POTATOES WILL CRUMBLE!
ALL RIGHT, THEN I'LL TASTE IT FOR YOU!
SO YOU USE THIS THING TO MAKE OYAKODON, HUH?
I WAS WONDERING WHAT IT WAS FOR.
GU
GU
GU
I WANTED TO MAKE OYAKODON WITH THIS THING AND BOUGHT IT A LONG TIME AGO.
MOM IS THE TYPE TO MAKE EVERYONE'S PORTIONS ALL AT ONCE IN A SINGLE FRYING PAN.
AND NOW WE'LL PUT THE EGG IN.
!!
I'LL DO IT!
SURE! HERE YOU ARE.

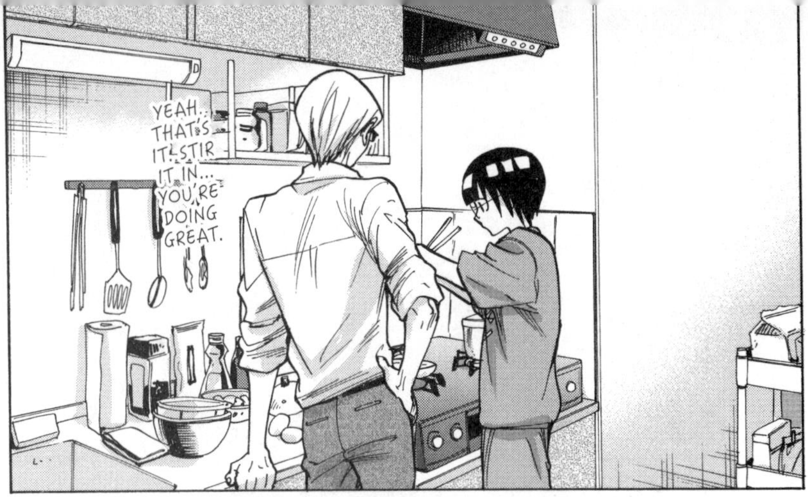
YEAH. THAT'S IT. STIR IT IN... YOU'RE DOING GREAT.

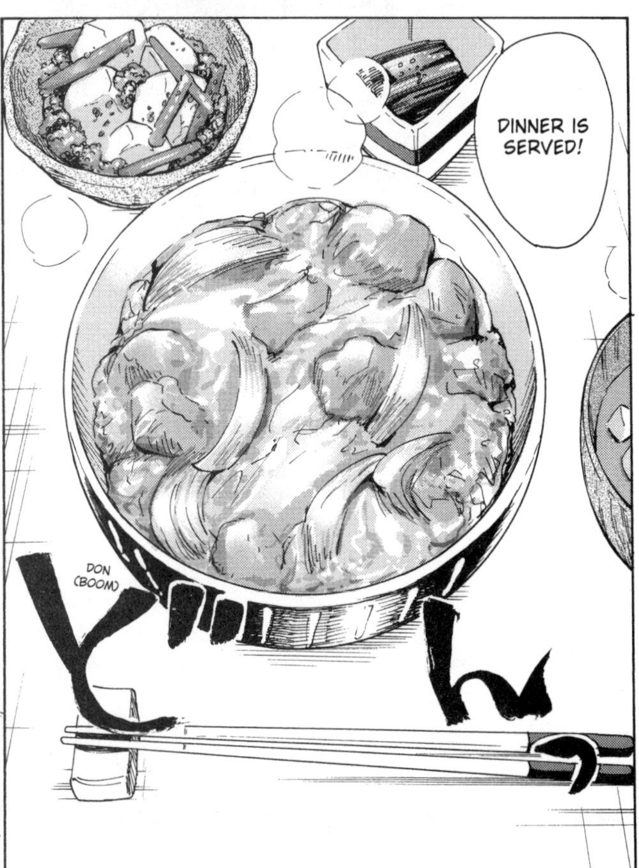
DINNER IS SERVED!
DON (BOOM)

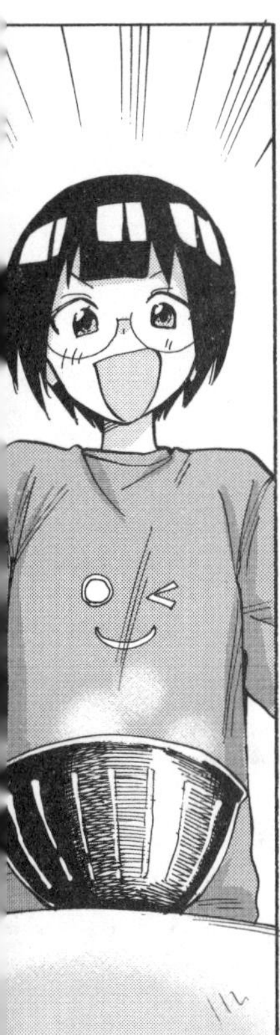

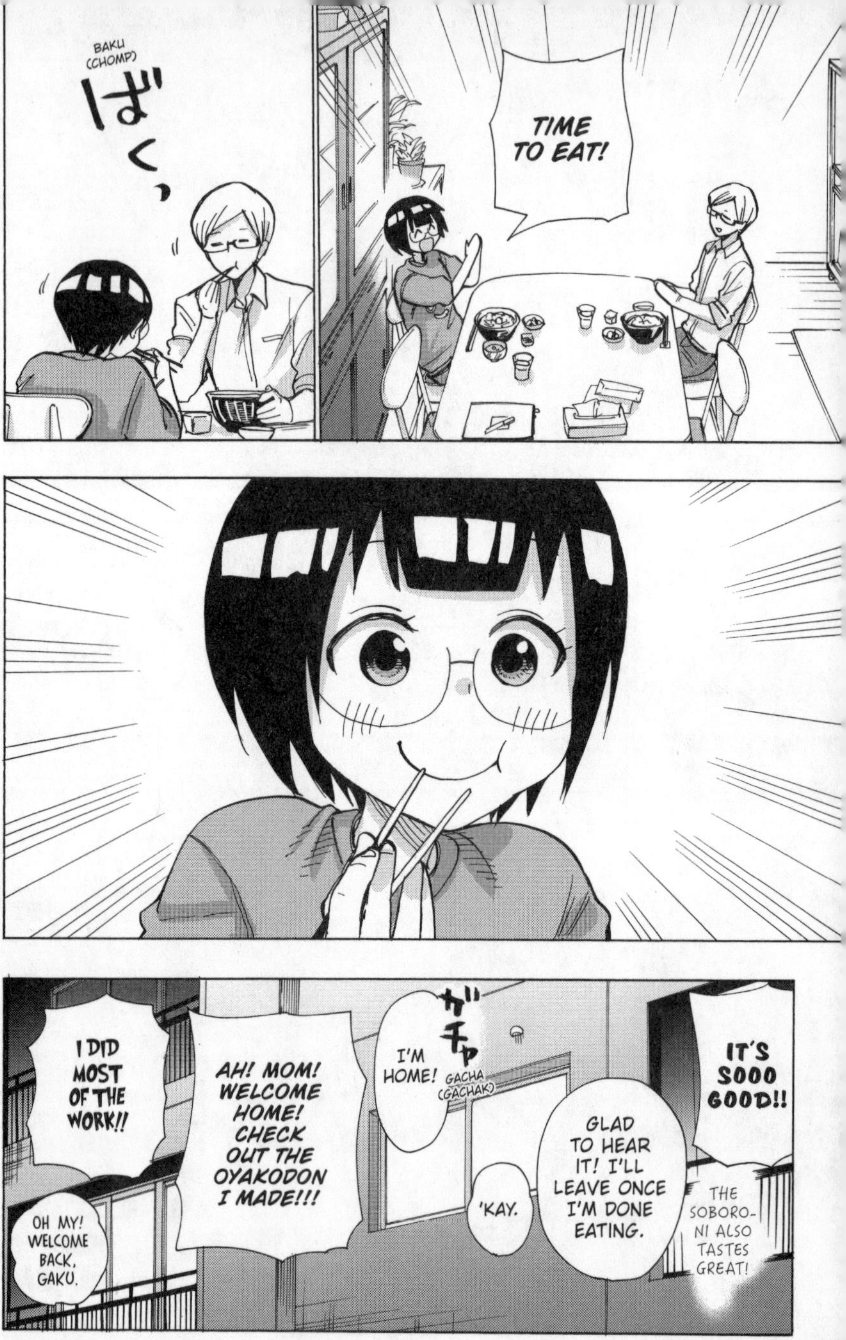
TIME TO EAT!
BAKU (CHOMP)
ばく
IT'S SOOO GOOD!!
THE SOBORO-NI ALSO TASTES GREAT!
GLAD TO HEAR IT! I'LL LEAVE ONCE I'M DONE EATING.
ガチャ
GACHA (GACHAK)
I'M HOME!
'KAY.
AH! MOM! WELCOME HOME! CHECK OUT THE OYAKODON I MADE!!!
I DID MOST OF THE WORK!!
OH MY! WELCOME BACK, GAKU.

FES 15.5

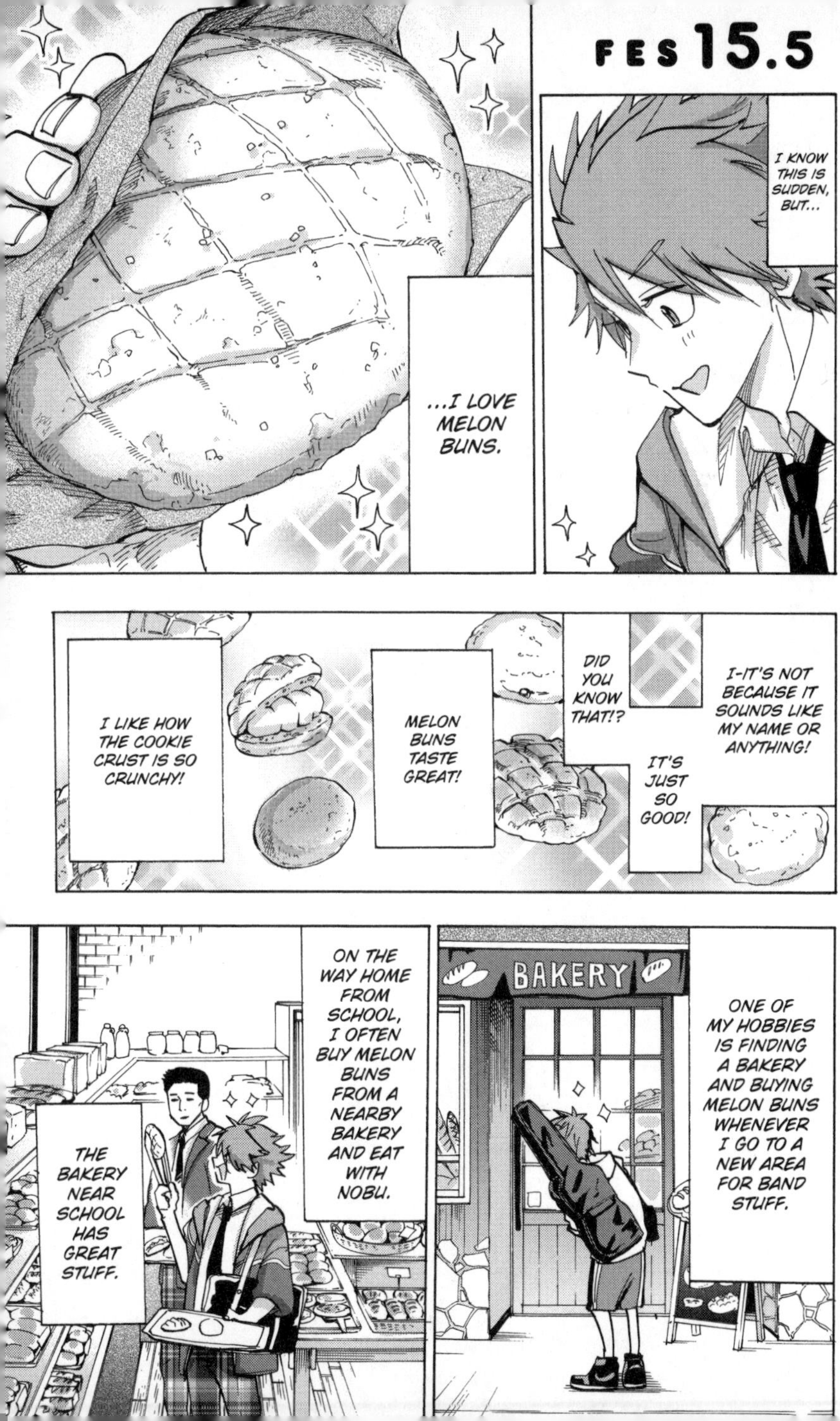
I KNOW THIS IS SUDDEN, BUT...
...I LOVE MELON BUNS.
I-IT'S NOT BECAUSE IT SOUNDS LIKE MY NAME OR ANYTHING!
IT'S JUST SO GOOD!
DID YOU KNOW THAT!?
MELON BUNS TASTE GREAT!
I LIKE HOW THE COOKIE CRUST IS SO CRUNCHY!
ONE OF MY HOBBIES IS FINDING A BAKERY AND BUYING MELON BUNS WHENEVER I GO TO A NEW AREA FOR BAND STUFF.
BAKERY
ON THE WAY HOME FROM SCHOOL, I OFTEN BUY MELON BUNS FROM A NEARBY BAKERY AND EAT WITH NOBU.
THE BAKERY NEAR SCHOOL HAS GREAT STUFF.

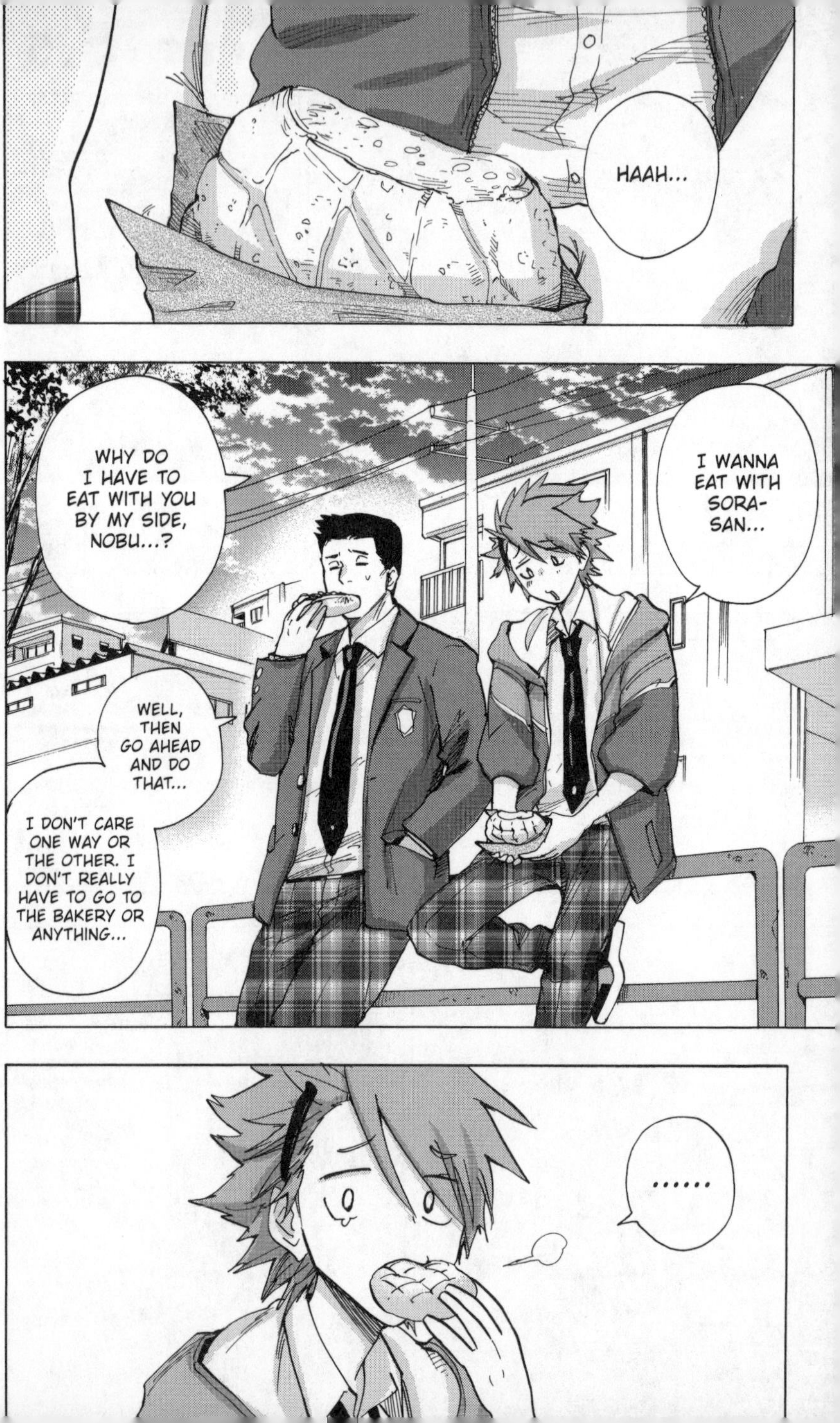
HAAH...
I WANNA EAT WITH SORA-SAN...
WHY DO I HAVE TO EAT WITH YOU BY MY SIDE, NOBU...?
WELL, THEN GO AHEAD AND DO THAT...
I DON'T CARE ONE WAY OR THE OTHER. I DON'T REALLY HAVE TO GO TO THE BAKERY OR ANYTHING...
......

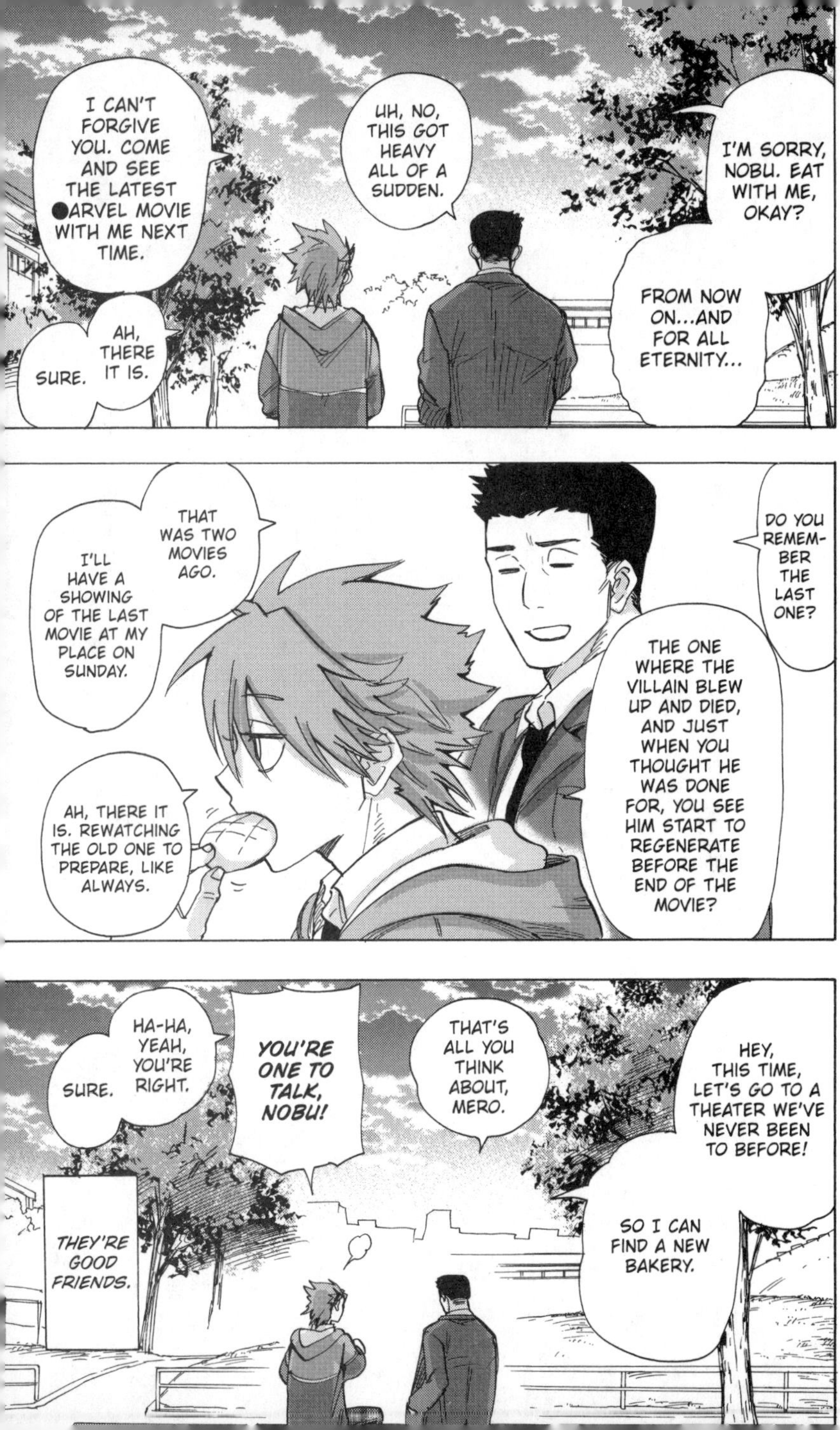
I'M SORRY, NOBU. EAT WITH ME, OKAY?
FROM NOW ON...AND FOR ALL ETERNITY...
UH, NO, THIS GOT HEAVY ALL OF A SUDDEN.
I CAN'T FORGIVE YOU. COME AND SEE THE LATEST ●ARVEL MOVIE WITH ME NEXT TIME.
AH, THERE IT IS.
SURE.
DO YOU REMEMBER THE LAST ONE?
THE ONE WHERE THE VILLAIN BLEW UP AND DIED, AND JUST WHEN YOU THOUGHT HE WAS DONE FOR, YOU SEE HIM START TO REGENERATE BEFORE THE END OF THE MOVIE?
THAT WAS TWO MOVIES AGO.
I'LL HAVE A SHOWING OF THE LAST MOVIE AT MY PLACE ON SUNDAY.
AH, THERE IT IS. REWATCHING THE OLD ONE TO PREPARE, LIKE ALWAYS.
HEY, THIS TIME, LET'S GO TO A THEATER WE'VE NEVER BEEN TO BEFORE!
SO I CAN FIND A NEW BAKERY.
THAT'S ALL YOU THINK ABOUT, MERO.
YOU'RE ONE TO TALK, NOBU!
HA-HA, YEAH, YOU'RE RIGHT.
SURE.
THEY'RE GOOD FRIENDS.

Days on Fes

FES 16

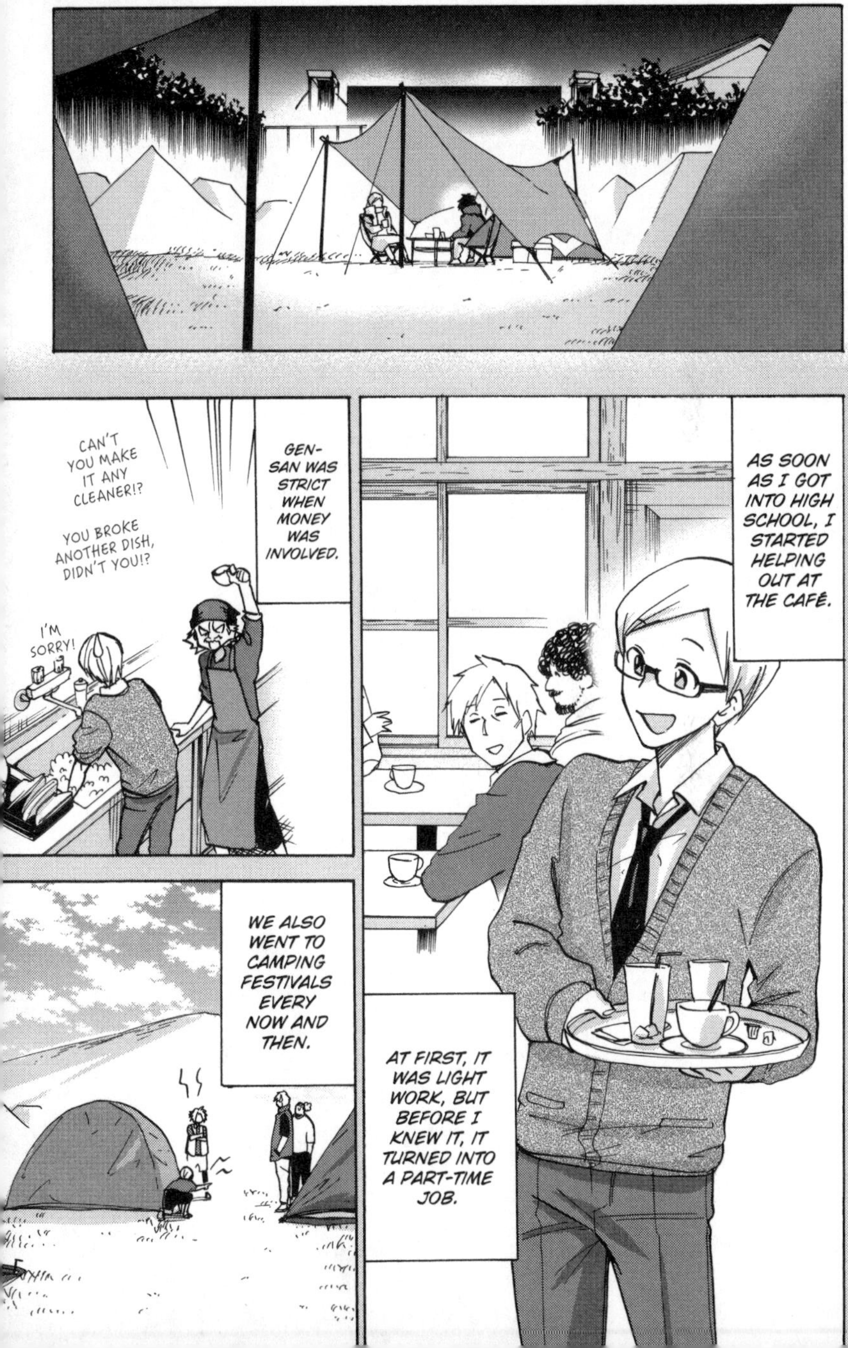
AS SOON AS I GOT INTO HIGH SCHOOL, I STARTED HELPING OUT AT THE CAFÉ.
AT FIRST, IT WAS LIGHT WORK, BUT BEFORE I KNEW IT, IT TURNED INTO A PART-TIME JOB.
GEN-SAN WAS STRICT WHEN MONEY WAS INVOLVED.
CAN'T YOU MAKE IT ANY CLEANER!?
YOU BROKE ANOTHER DISH, DIDN'T YOU!?
I'M SORRY!
WE ALSO WENT TO CAMPING FESTIVALS EVERY NOW AND THEN.

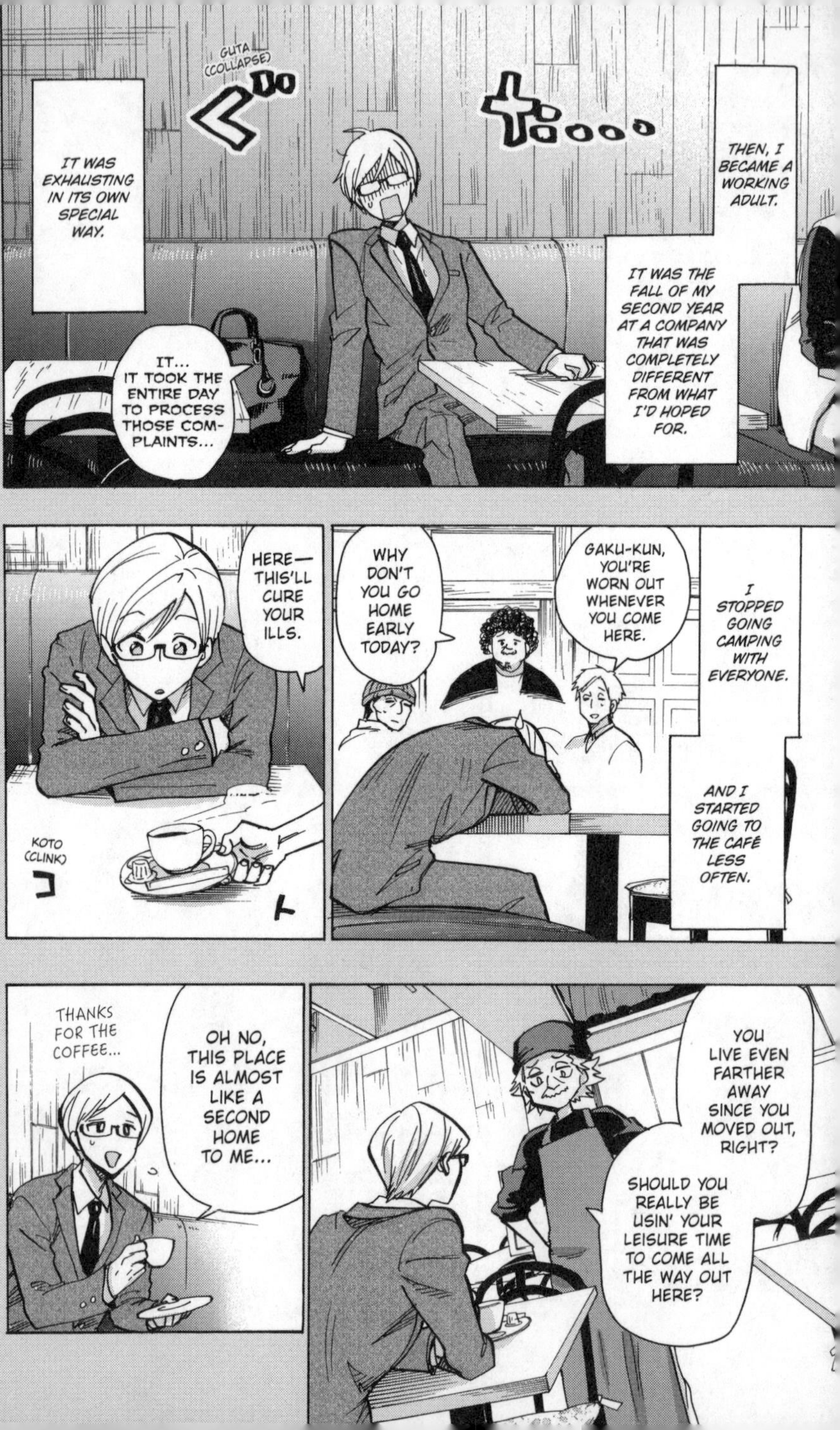
THEN, I BECAME A WORKING ADULT.
IT WAS THE FALL OF MY SECOND YEAR AT A COMPANY THAT WAS COMPLETELY DIFFERENT FROM WHAT I'D HOPED FOR.
GUTA (COLLAPSE)
IT WAS EXHAUSTING IN ITS OWN SPECIAL WAY.
IT... IT TOOK THE ENTIRE DAY TO PROCESS THOSE COM-PLAINTS...
I STOPPED GOING CAMPING WITH EVERYONE.
AND I STARTED GOING TO THE CAFÉ LESS OFTEN.
GAKU-KUN, YOU'RE WORN OUT WHENEVER YOU COME HERE.
WHY DON'T YOU GO HOME EARLY TODAY?
HERE—THIS'LL CURE YOUR ILLS.
KOTO (CLINK)
YOU LIVE EVEN FARTHER AWAY SINCE YOU MOVED OUT, RIGHT?
SHOULD YOU REALLY BE USIN' YOUR LEISURE TIME TO COME ALL THE WAY OUT HERE?
OH NO, THIS PLACE IS ALMOST LIKE A SECOND HOME TO ME...
THANKS FOR THE COFFEE...

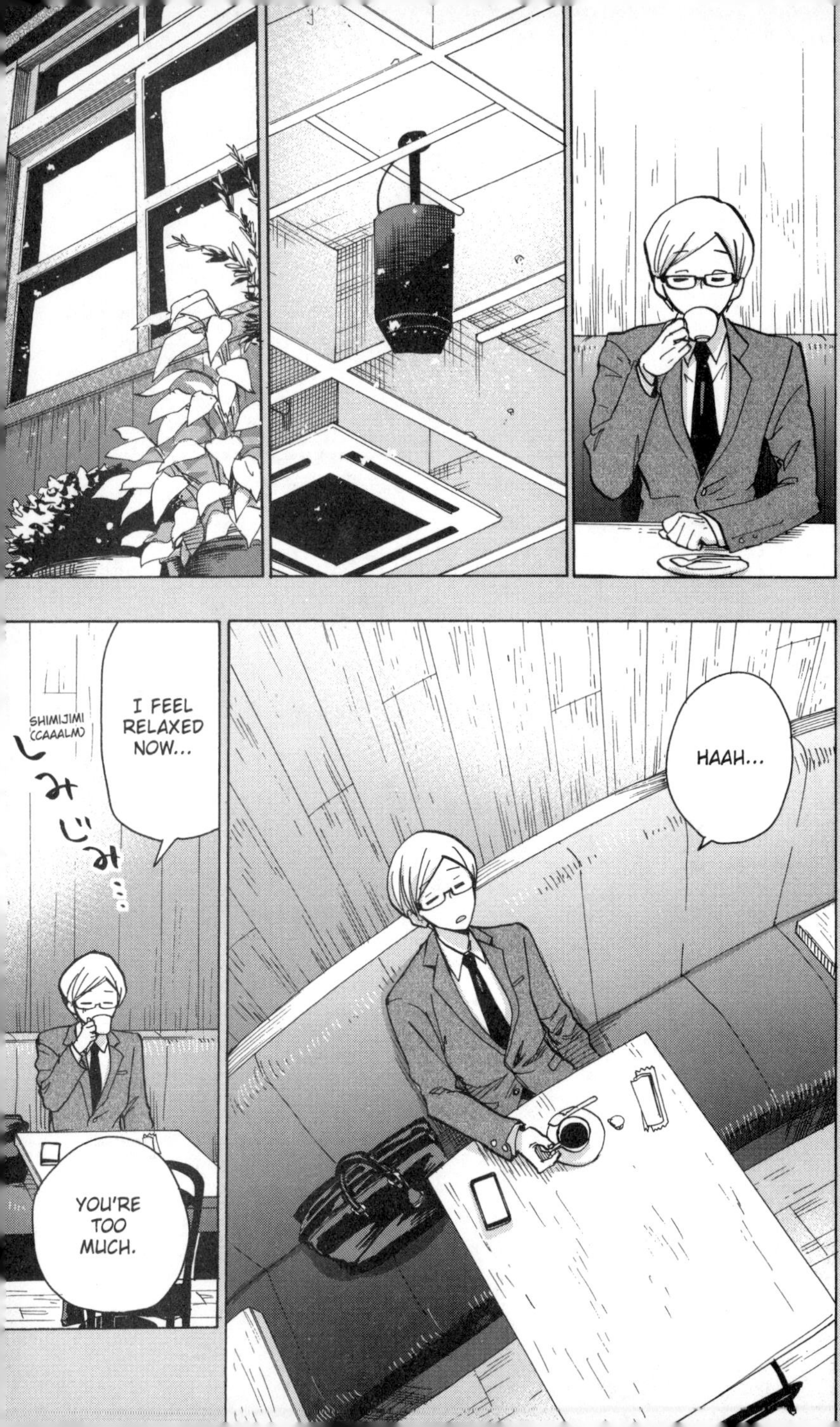
HAAH...
I FEEL RELAXED NOW...
SHIMIJIMI (CAAALM)
しみじみ…
YOU'RE TOO MUCH.

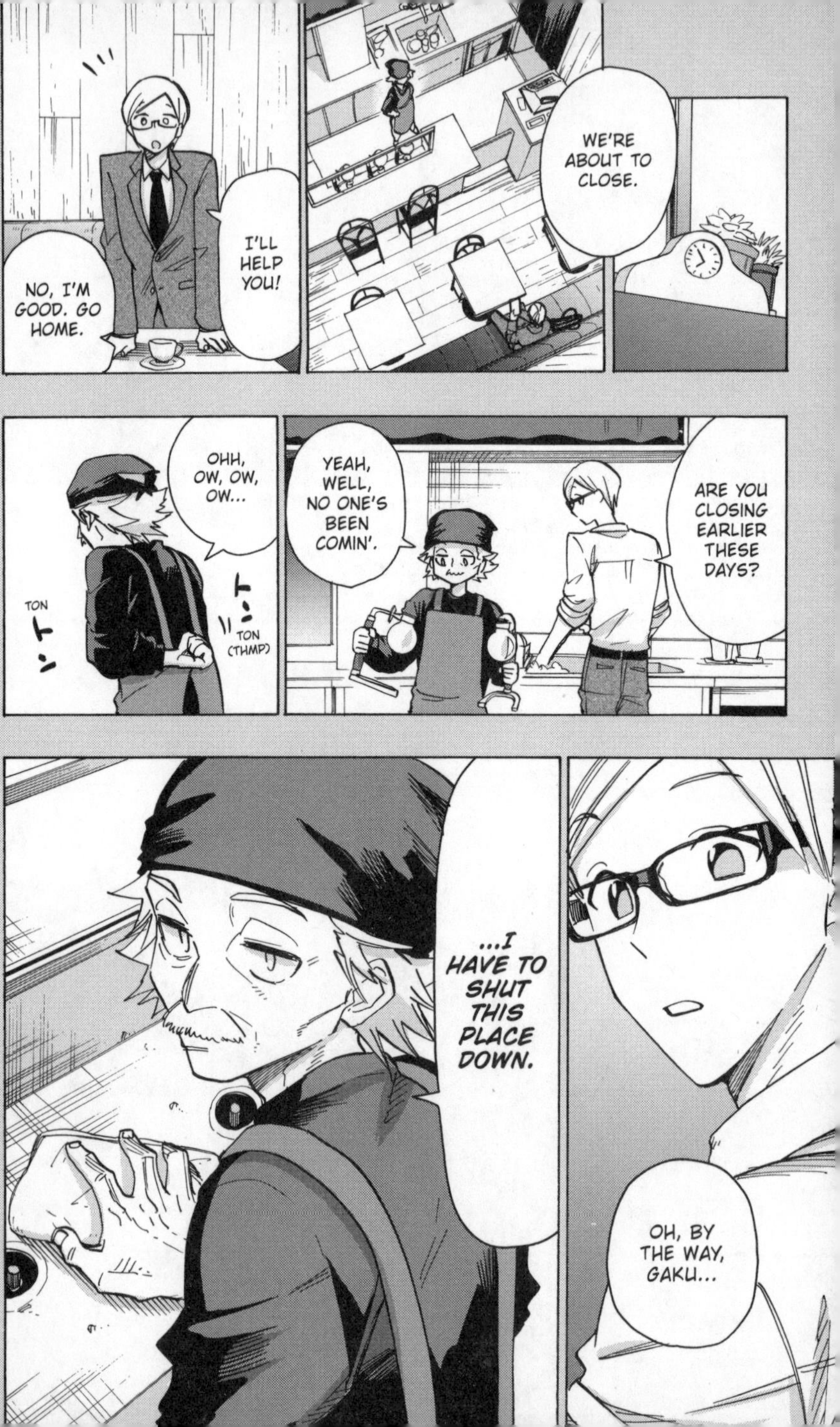
WE'RE ABOUT TO CLOSE.
I'LL HELP YOU!
NO, I'M GOOD. GO HOME.
ARE YOU CLOSING EARLIER THESE DAYS?
YEAH, WELL, NO ONE'S BEEN COMIN'.
OHH, OW, OW, OW...
トン
TON (THMP)
トン
TON
OH, BY THE WAY, GAKU...
...I HAVE TO SHUT THIS PLACE DOWN.

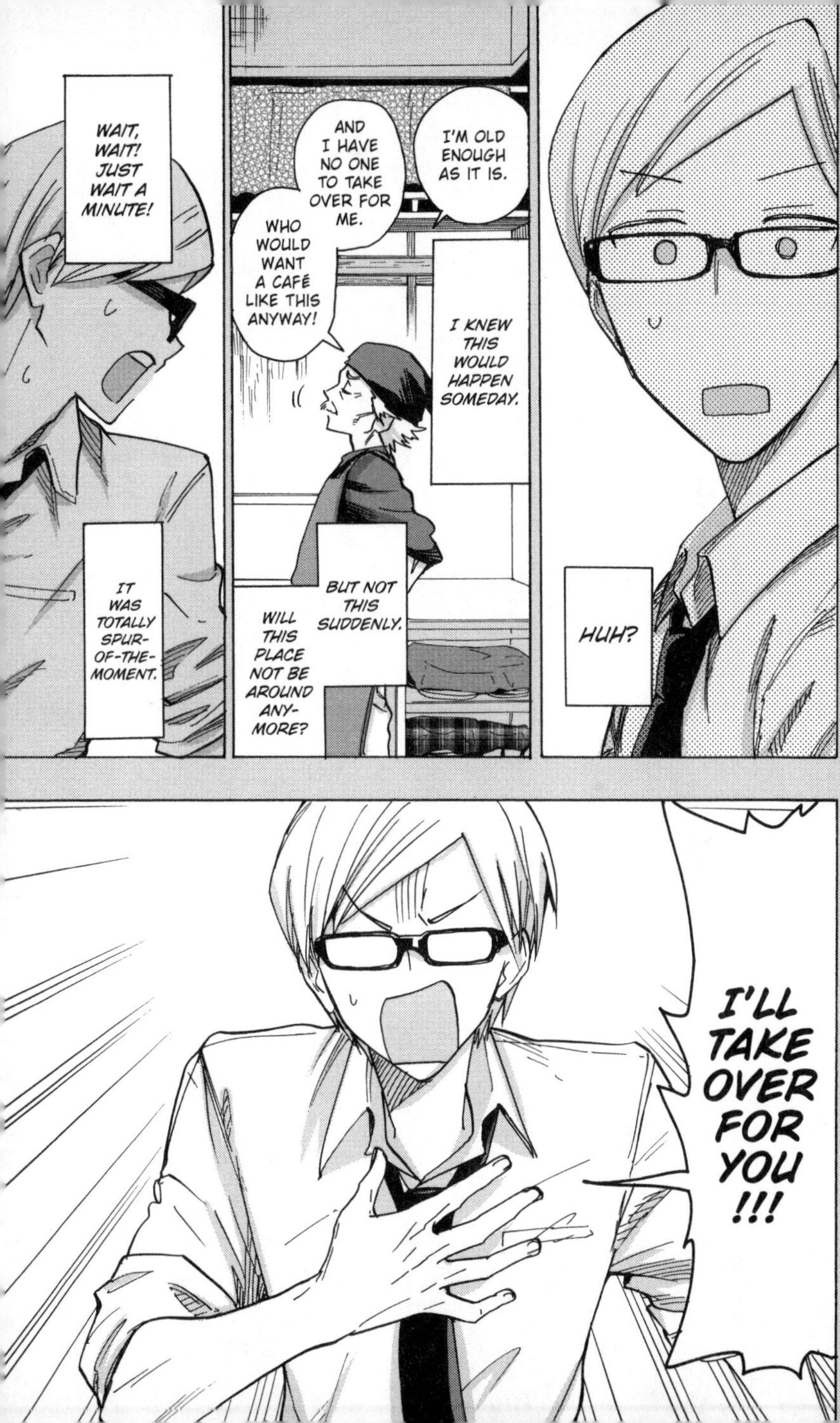
HUH?
I'M OLD ENOUGH AS IT IS.
AND I HAVE NO ONE TO TAKE OVER FOR ME.
WHO WOULD WANT A CAFÉ LIKE THIS ANYWAY!
I KNEW THIS WOULD HAPPEN SOMEDAY.
BUT NOT THIS SUDDENLY.
WILL THIS PLACE NOT BE AROUND ANYMORE?
WAIT, WAIT! JUST WAIT A MINUTE!
IT WAS TOTALLY SPUR-OF-THE-MOMENT.
I'LL TAKE OVER FOR YOU!!!

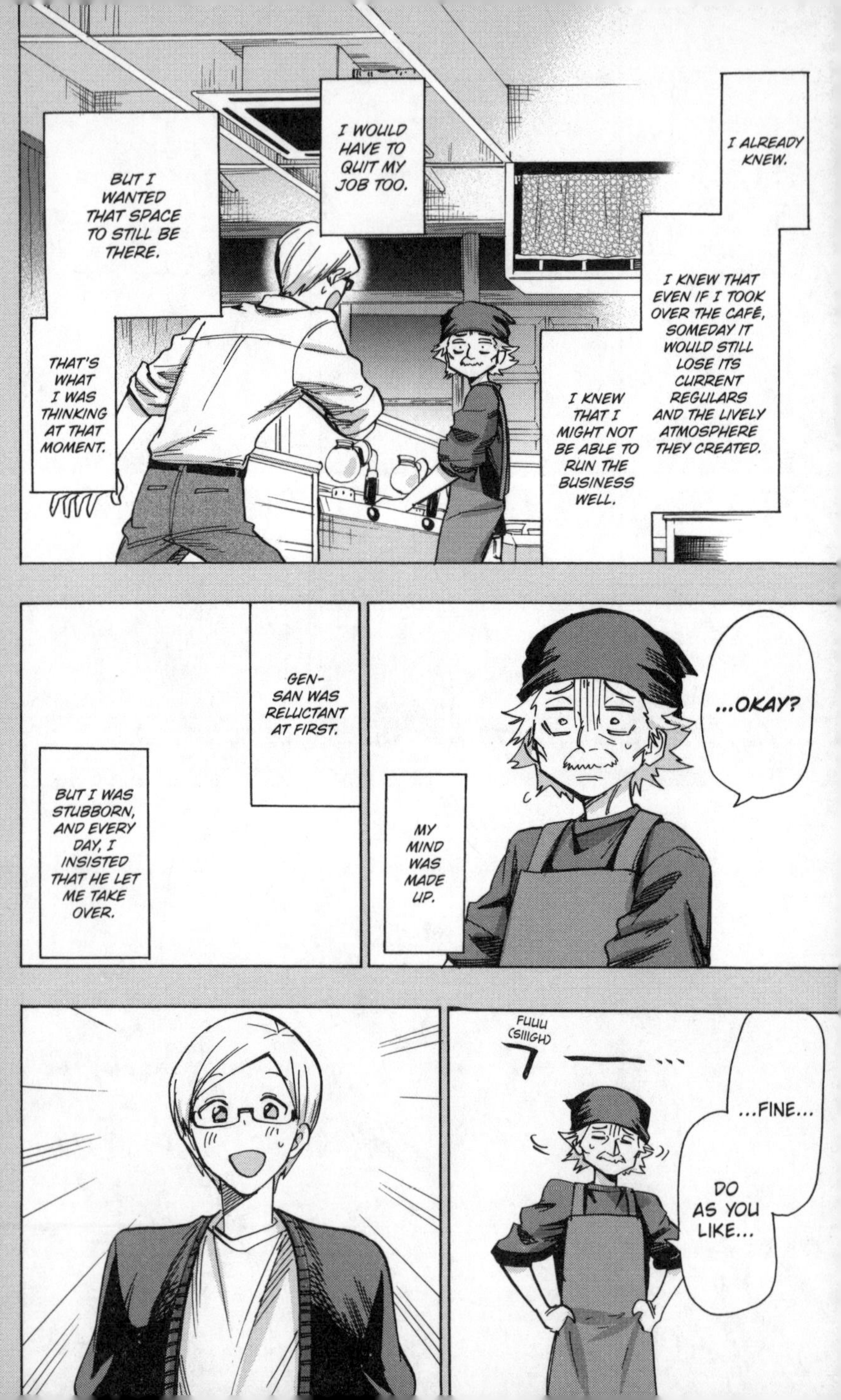
I ALREADY KNEW.
I KNEW THAT EVEN IF I TOOK OVER THE CAFÉ, SOMEDAY IT WOULD STILL LOSE ITS CURRENT REGULARS AND THE LIVELY ATMOSPHERE THEY CREATED.
I KNEW THAT I MIGHT NOT BE ABLE TO RUN THE BUSINESS WELL.
I WOULD HAVE TO QUIT MY JOB TOO.
BUT I WANTED THAT SPACE TO STILL BE THERE.
THAT'S WHAT I WAS THINKING AT THAT MOMENT.
...OKAY?
MY MIND WAS MADE UP.
GEN-SAN WAS RELUCTANT AT FIRST.
BUT I WAS STUBBORN, AND EVERY DAY, I INSISTED THAT HE LET ME TAKE OVER.
FUUU (SIIIGH)
...FINE...
DO AS YOU LIKE...

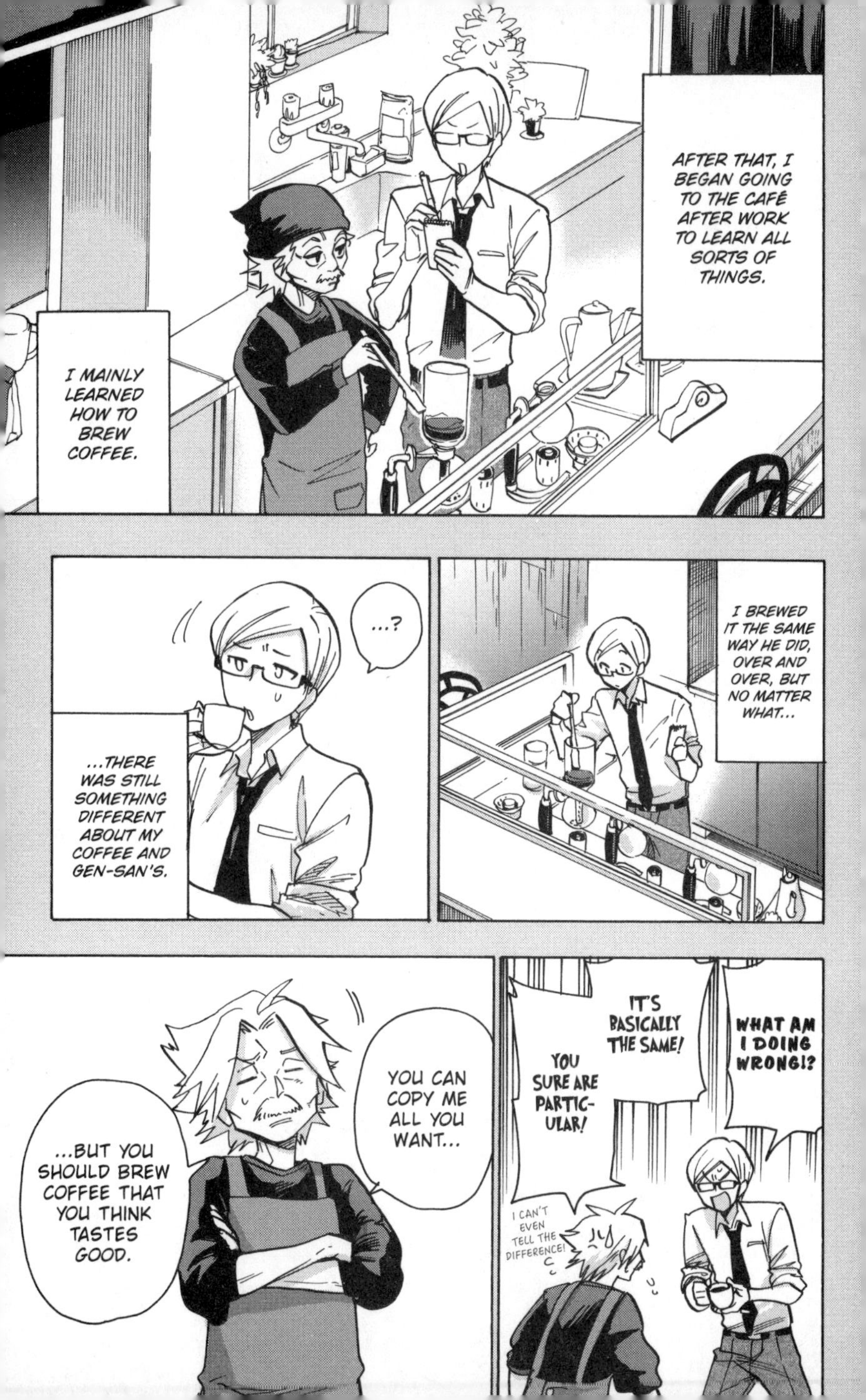
AFTER THAT, I BEGAN GOING TO THE CAFÉ AFTER WORK TO LEARN ALL SORTS OF THINGS.
I MAINLY LEARNED HOW TO BREW COFFEE.
I BREWED IT THE SAME WAY HE DID, OVER AND OVER, BUT NO MATTER WHAT...
...?
...THERE WAS STILL SOMETHING DIFFERENT ABOUT MY COFFEE AND GEN-SAN'S.
WHAT AM I DOING WRONG!?
IT'S BASICALLY THE SAME!
YOU SURE ARE PARTICULAR!
I CAN'T EVEN TELL THE DIFFERENCE!
YOU CAN COPY ME ALL YOU WANT...
...BUT YOU SHOULD BREW COFFEE THAT YOU THINK TASTES GOOD.

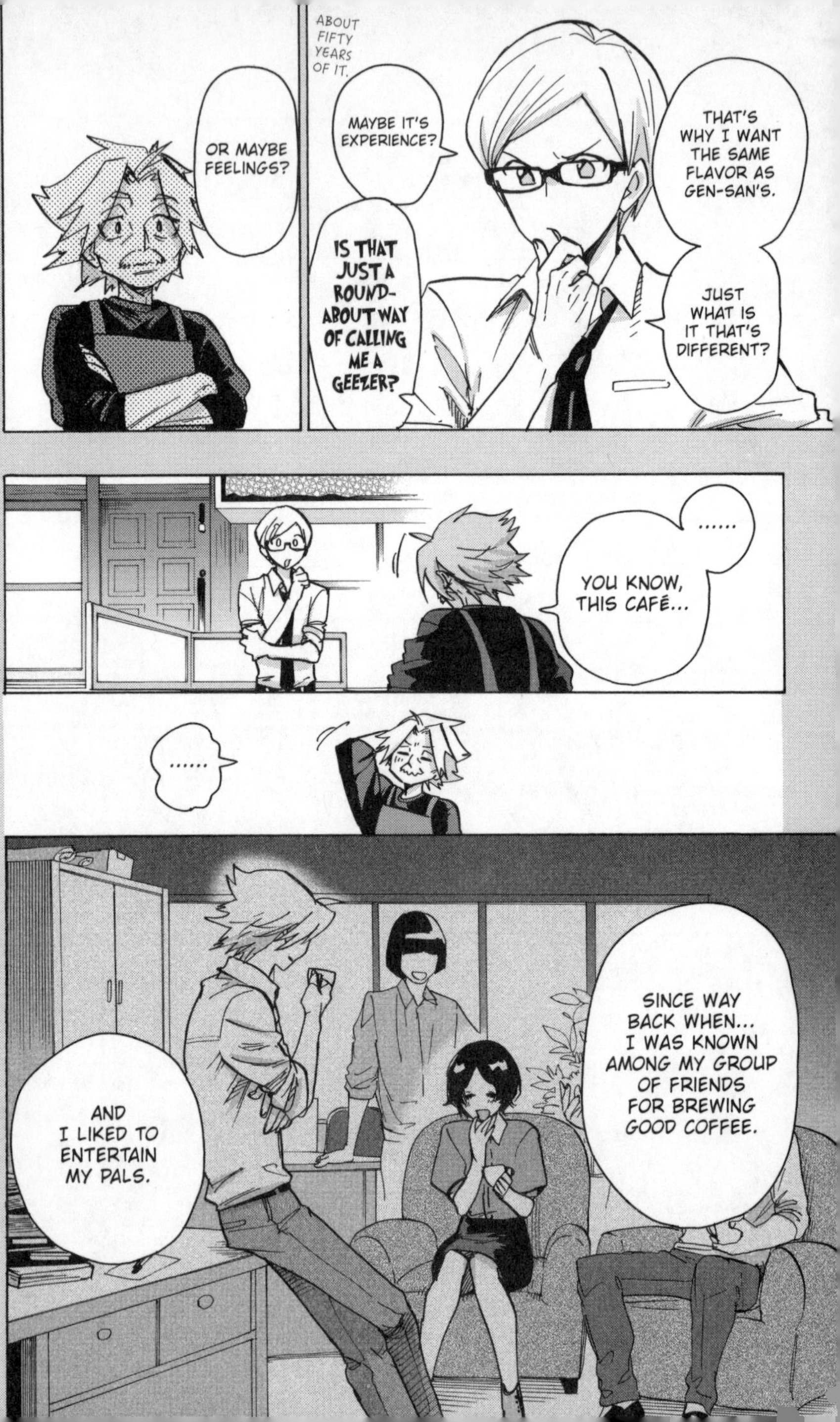
THAT'S WHY I WANT THE SAME FLAVOR AS GEN-SAN'S.
JUST WHAT IS IT THAT'S DIFFERENT?
MAYBE IT'S EXPERIENCE?
ABOUT FIFTY YEARS OF IT.
IS THAT JUST A ROUNDABOUT WAY OF CALLING ME A GEEZER?
OR MAYBE FEELINGS?
......
YOU KNOW, THIS CAFÉ...
......
SINCE WAY BACK WHEN... I WAS KNOWN AMONG MY GROUP OF FRIENDS FOR BREWING GOOD COFFEE.
AND I LIKED TO ENTERTAIN MY PALS.

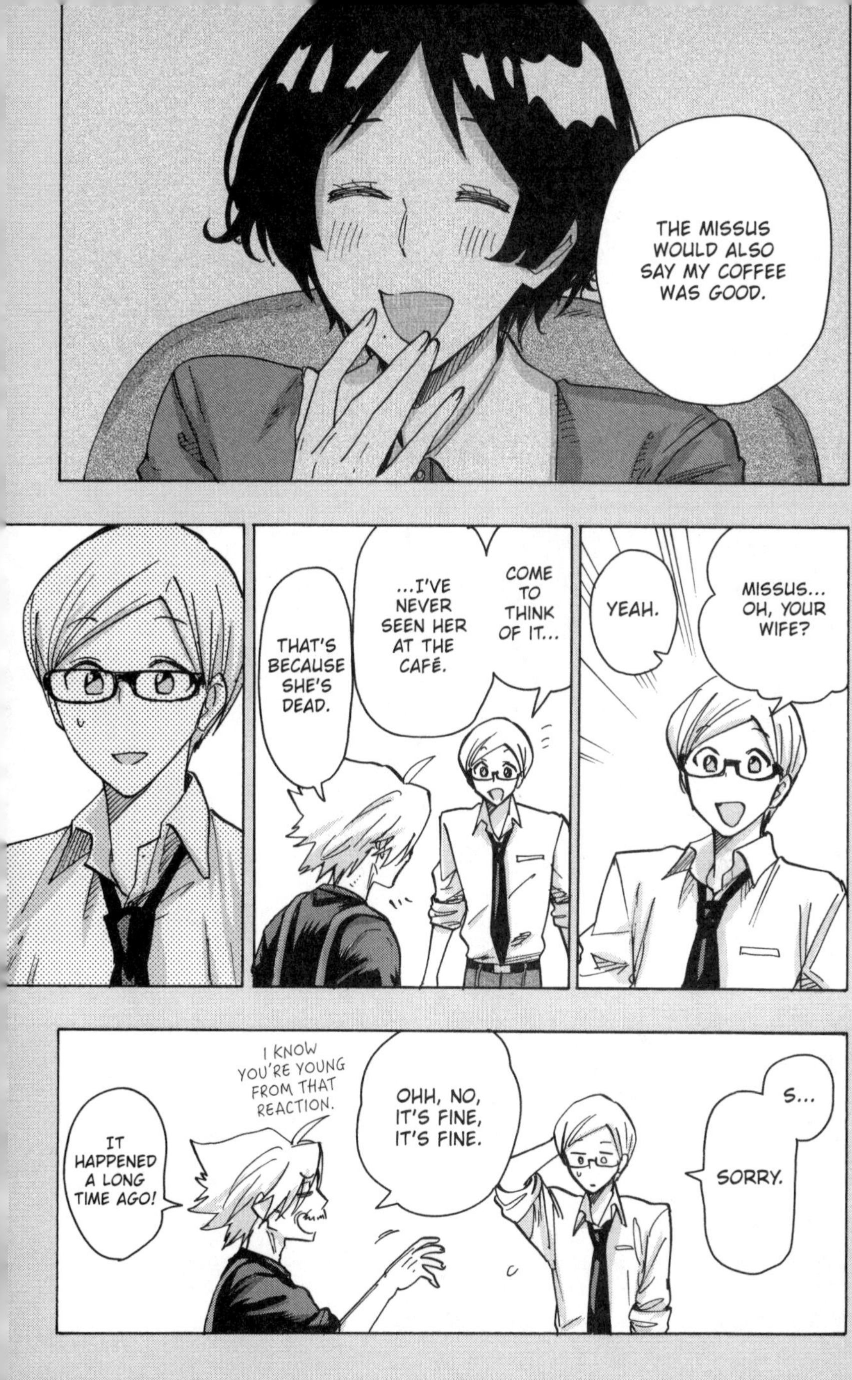
THE MISSUS WOULD ALSO SAY MY COFFEE WAS GOOD.
MISSUS... OH, YOUR WIFE?
YEAH.
COME TO THINK OF IT...
...I'VE NEVER SEEN HER AT THE CAFÉ.
THAT'S BECAUSE SHE'S DEAD.
S...
SORRY.
OHH, NO, IT'S FINE, IT'S FINE.
I KNOW YOU'RE YOUNG FROM THAT REACTION.
IT HAPPENED A LONG TIME AGO!

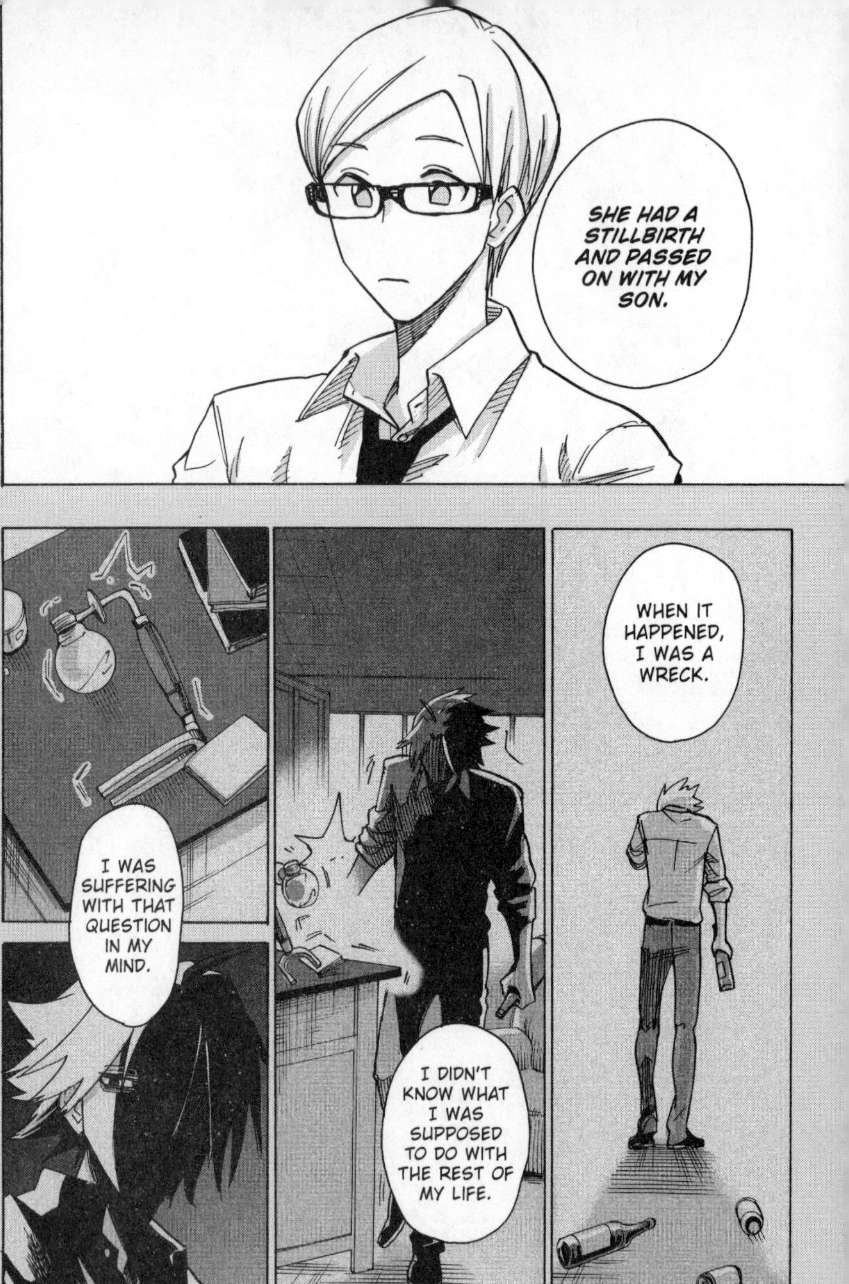
SHE HAD A STILLBIRTH AND PASSED ON WITH MY SON.
WHEN IT HAPPENED, I WAS A WRECK.
I DIDN'T KNOW WHAT I WAS SUPPOSED TO DO WITH THE REST OF MY LIFE.
I WAS SUFFERING WITH THAT QUESTION IN MY MIND.

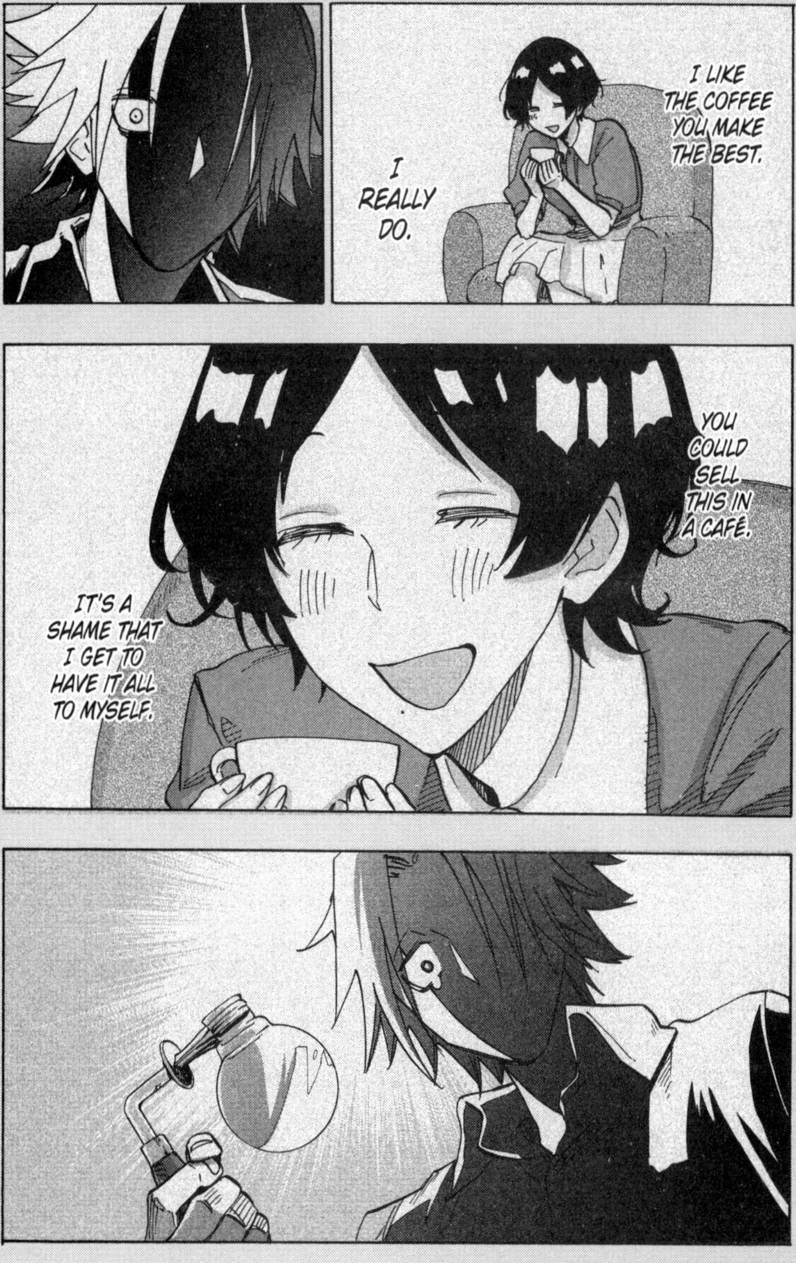
I LIKE THE COFFEE YOU MAKE THE BEST.
I REALLY DO.
YOU COULD SELL THIS IN A CAFÉ.
IT'S A SHAME THAT I GET TO HAVE IT ALL TO MYSELF.

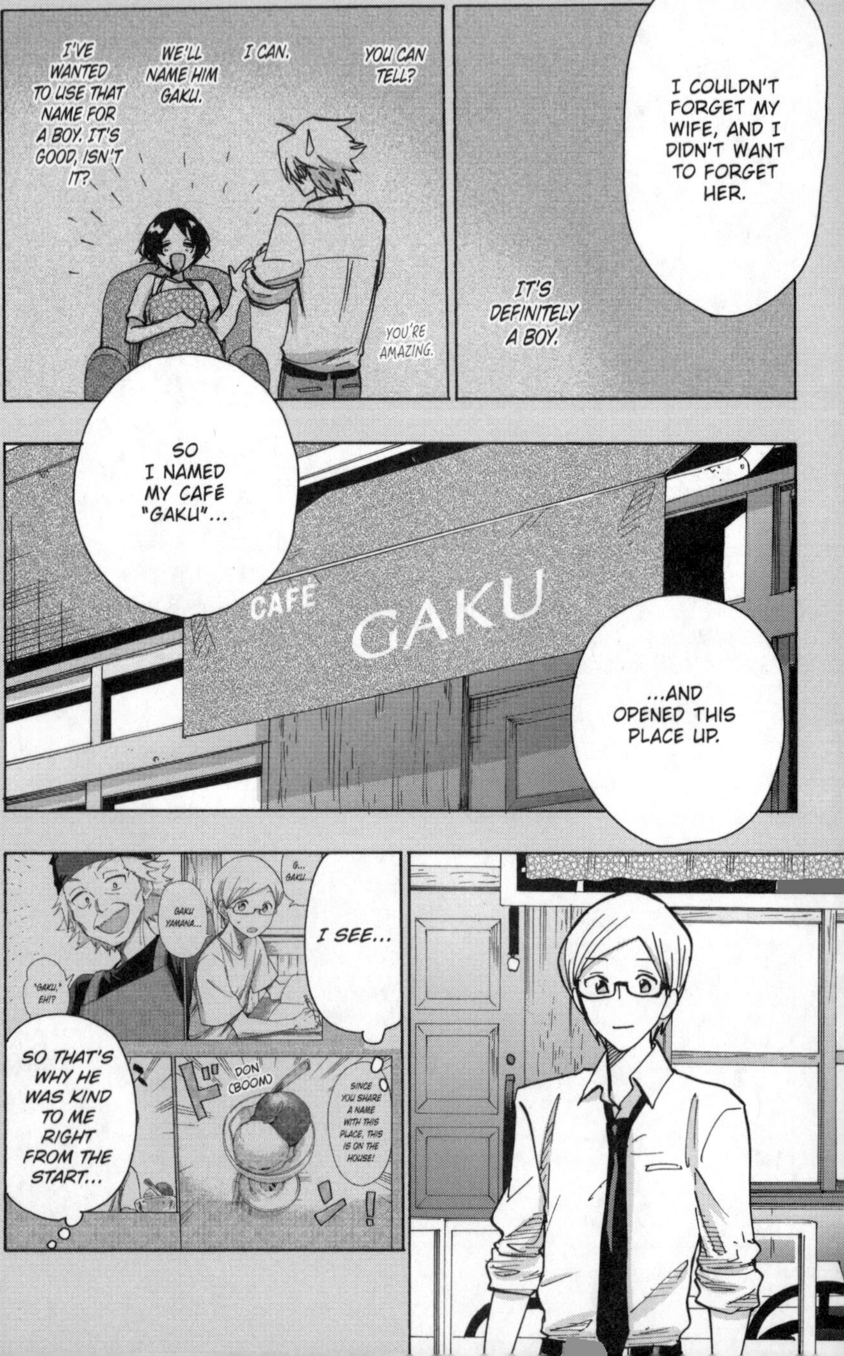
I COULDN'T FORGET MY WIFE, AND I DIDN'T WANT TO FORGET HER.
IT'S DEFINITELY A BOY.
YOU CAN TELL?
I CAN.
WE'LL NAME HIM GAKU.
I'VE WANTED TO USE THAT NAME FOR A BOY. IT'S GOOD, ISN'T IT?
YOU'RE AMAZING.
SO I NAMED MY CAFÉ "GAKU"...
CAFÉ GAKU
...AND OPENED THIS PLACE UP.
G... GAKU...
I SEE...
GAKU YAMANA...
"GAKU," EH?
DON (BOOM)
SINCE YOU SHARE A NAME WITH THIS PLACE, THIS IS ON THE HOUSE!
SO THAT'S WHY HE WAS KIND TO ME RIGHT FROM THE START...

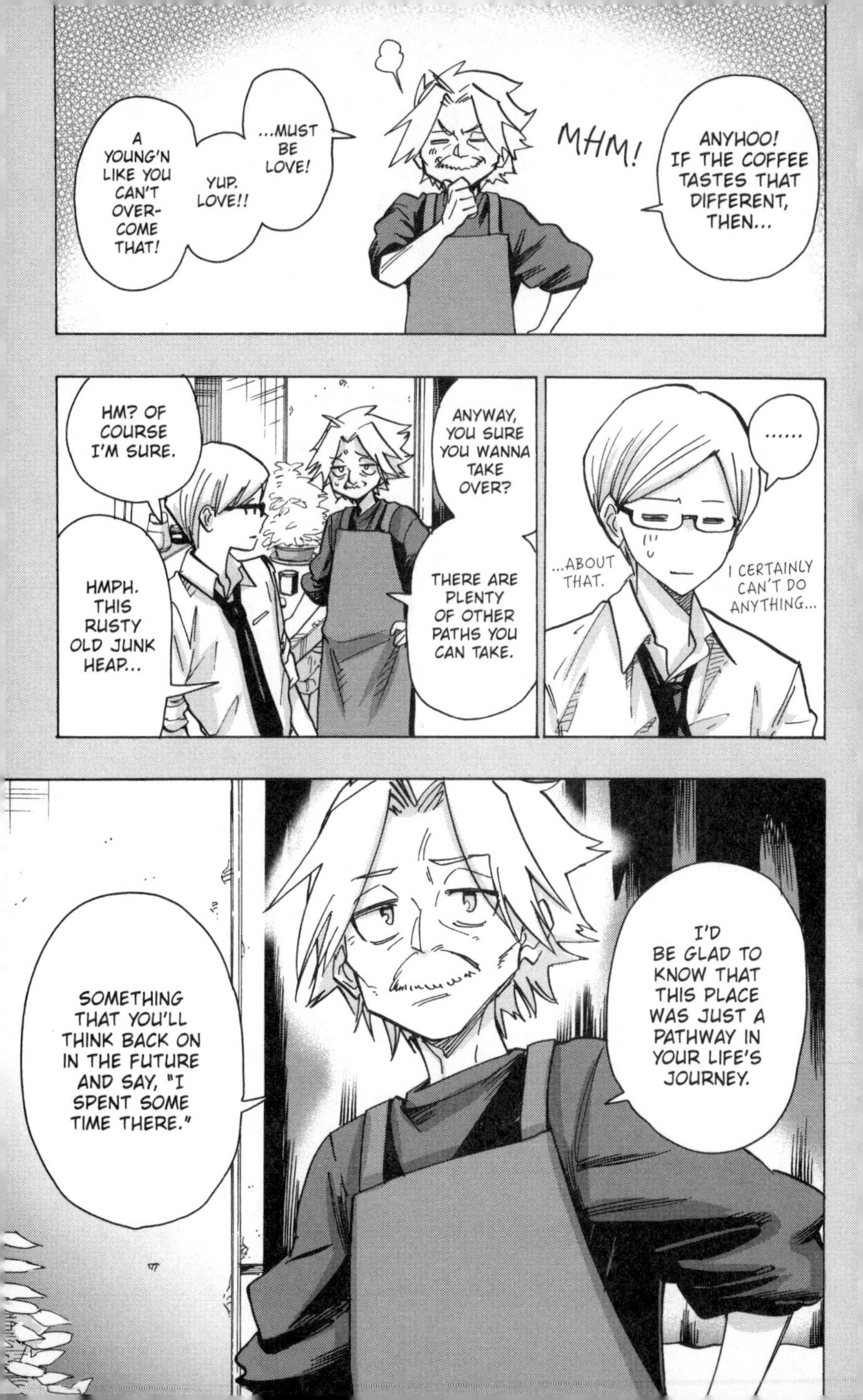
ANYHOO! IF THE COFFEE TASTES THAT DIFFERENT, THEN...
MHM!
...MUST BE LOVE!
YUP. LOVE!!
A YOUNG'N LIKE YOU CAN'T OVER-COME THAT!
......
I CERTAINLY CAN'T DO ANYTHING...
...ABOUT THAT.
ANYWAY, YOU SURE YOU WANNA TAKE OVER?
HM? OF COURSE I'M SURE.
THERE ARE PLENTY OF OTHER PATHS YOU CAN TAKE.
HMPH. THIS RUSTY OLD JUNK HEAP...
I'D BE GLAD TO KNOW THAT THIS PLACE WAS JUST A PATHWAY IN YOUR LIFE'S JOURNEY.
SOMETHING THAT YOU'LL THINK BACK ON IN THE FUTURE AND SAY, "I SPENT SOME TIME THERE."

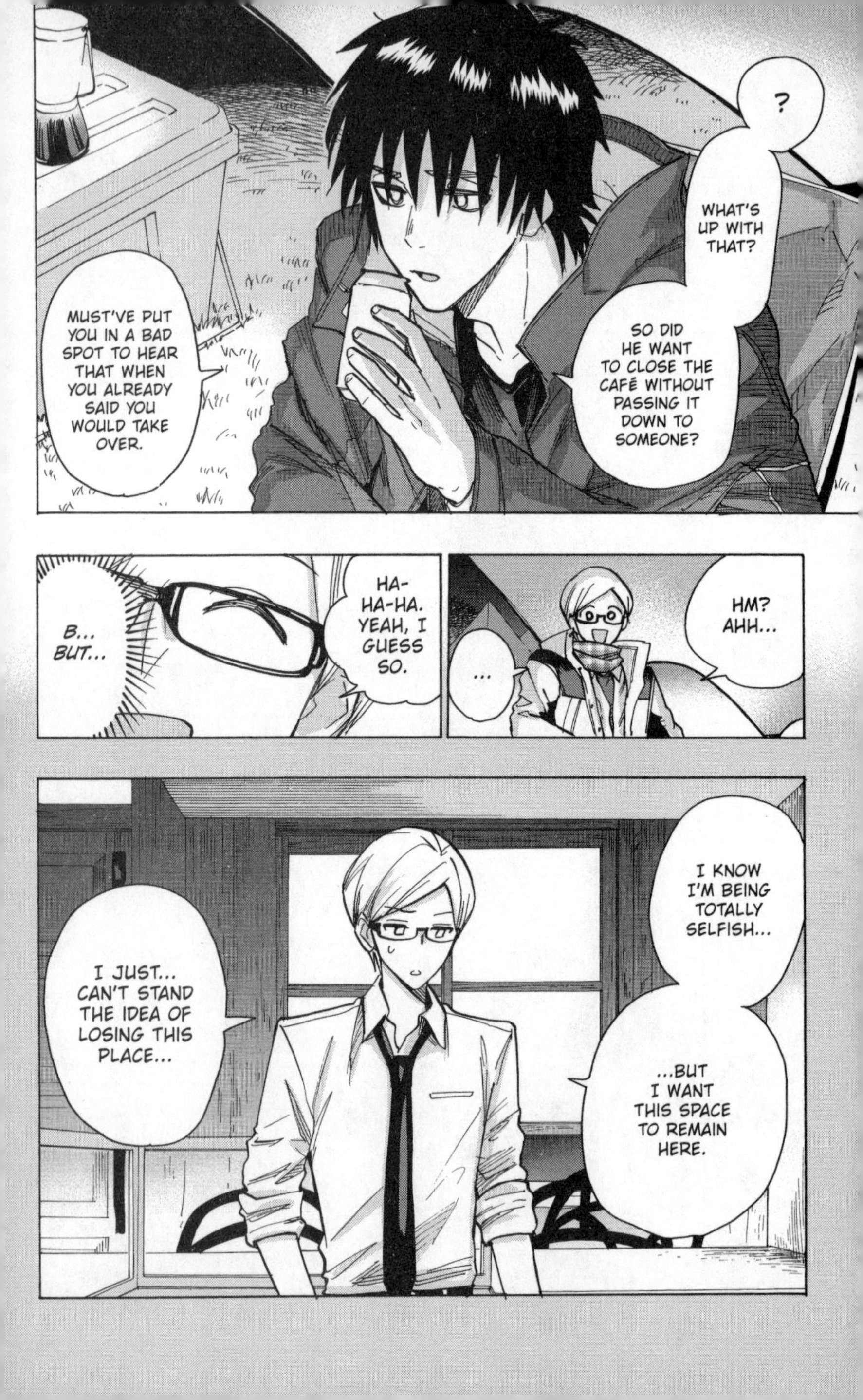
?
WHAT'S UP WITH THAT?
SO DID HE WANT TO CLOSE THE CAFÉ WITHOUT PASSING IT DOWN TO SOMEONE?
MUST'VE PUT YOU IN A BAD SPOT TO HEAR THAT WHEN YOU ALREADY SAID YOU WOULD TAKE OVER.
HM? AHH...
...
HA-HA-HA. YEAH, I GUESS SO.
B... BUT...
I KNOW I'M BEING TOTALLY SELFISH...
...BUT I WANT THIS SPACE TO REMAIN HERE.
I JUST... CAN'T STAND THE IDEA OF LOSING THIS PLACE...

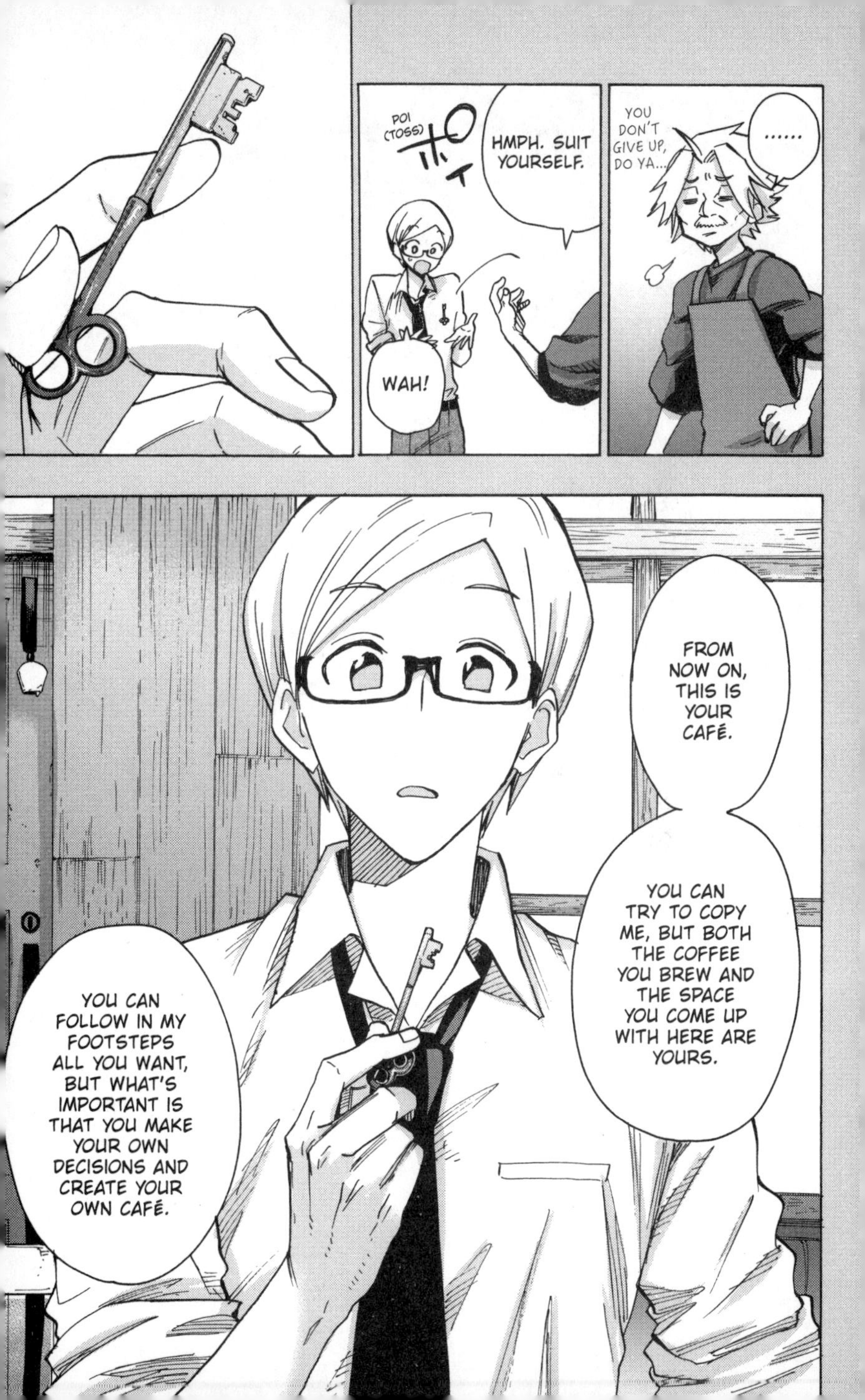
......
YOU DON'T GIVE UP, DO YA...
HMPH. SUIT YOURSELF.
POI (TOSS)
WAH!
FROM NOW ON, THIS IS YOUR CAFÉ.
YOU CAN TRY TO COPY ME, BUT BOTH THE COFFEE YOU BREW AND THE SPACE YOU COME UP WITH HERE ARE YOURS.
YOU CAN FOLLOW IN MY FOOTSTEPS ALL YOU WANT, BUT WHAT'S IMPORTANT IS THAT YOU MAKE YOUR OWN DECISIONS AND CREATE YOUR OWN CAFÉ.

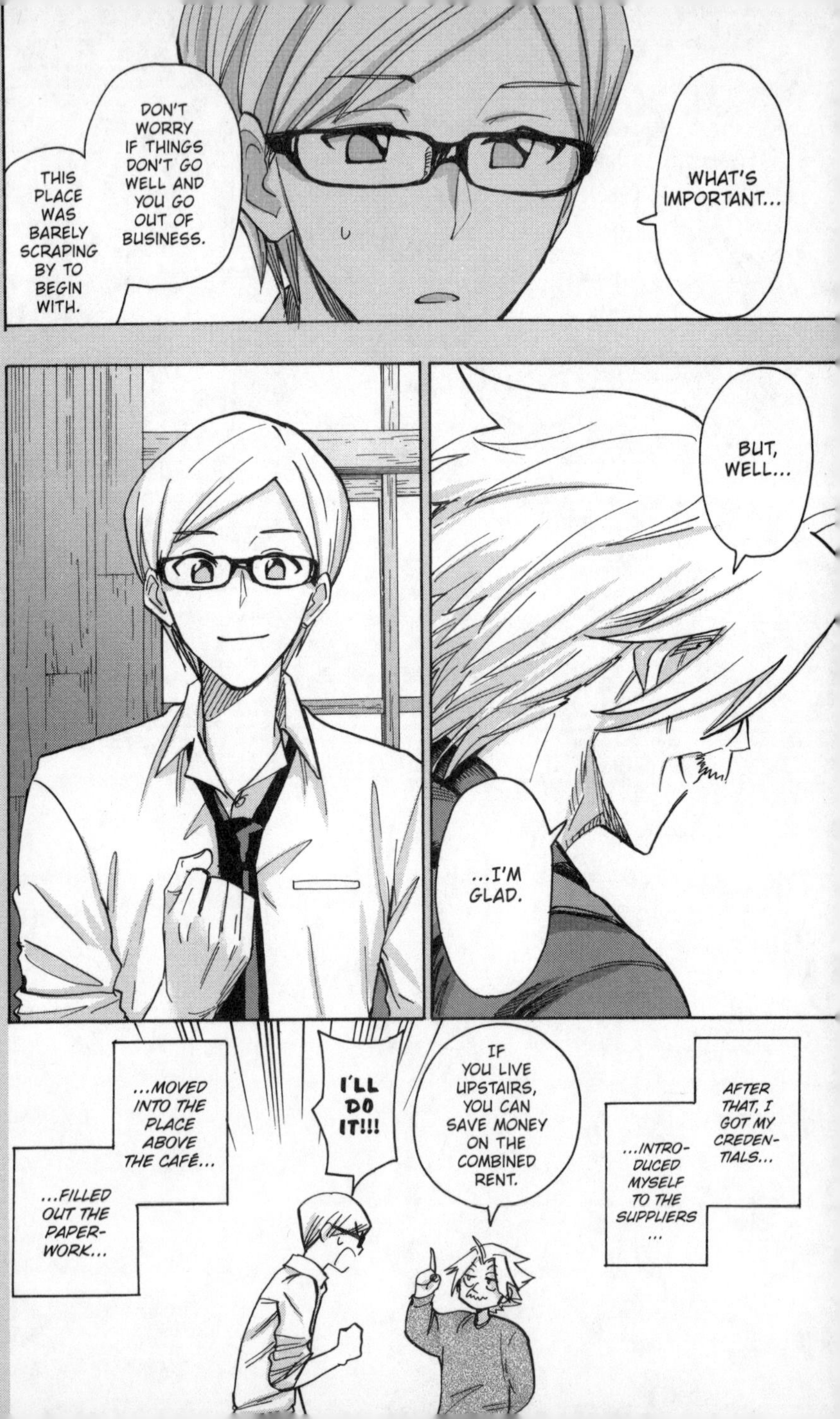
WHAT'S IMPORTANT...
DON'T WORRY IF THINGS DON'T GO WELL AND YOU GO OUT OF BUSINESS.
THIS PLACE WAS BARELY SCRAPING BY TO BEGIN WITH.
BUT, WELL...
...I'M GLAD.
AFTER THAT, I GOT MY CREDEN-TIALS...
...INTRO-DUCED MYSELF TO THE SUPPLIERS ...
IF YOU LIVE UPSTAIRS, YOU CAN SAVE MONEY ON THE COMBINED RENT.
I'LL DO IT!!!
...MOVED INTO THE PLACE ABOVE THE CAFÉ...
...FILLED OUT THE PAPER-WORK...

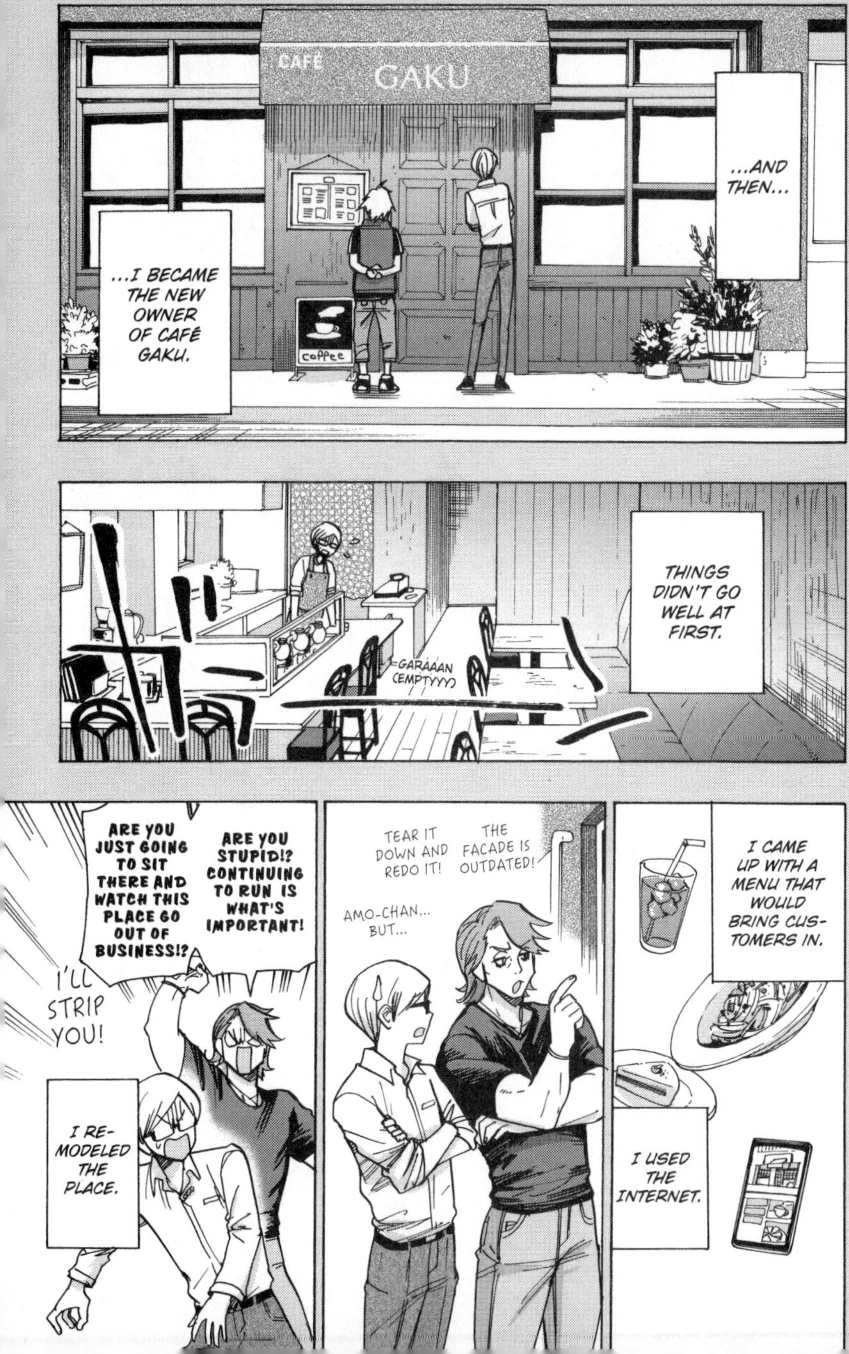
CAFÉ GAKU
coffee
...AND THEN...
...I BECAME THE NEW OWNER OF CAFÉ GAKU.
THINGS DIDN'T GO WELL AT FIRST.
GARAAAN (EMPTYYY)
I CAME UP WITH A MENU THAT WOULD BRING CUS-TOMERS IN.
I USED THE INTERNET.
THE FACADE IS OUTDATED!
TEAR IT DOWN AND REDO IT!
AMO-CHAN... BUT...
ARE YOU STUPID!? CONTINUING TO RUN IS WHAT'S IMPORTANT!
ARE YOU JUST GOING TO SIT THERE AND WATCH THIS PLACE GO OUT OF BUSINESS!?
I'LL STRIP YOU!
I RE-MODELED THE PLACE.

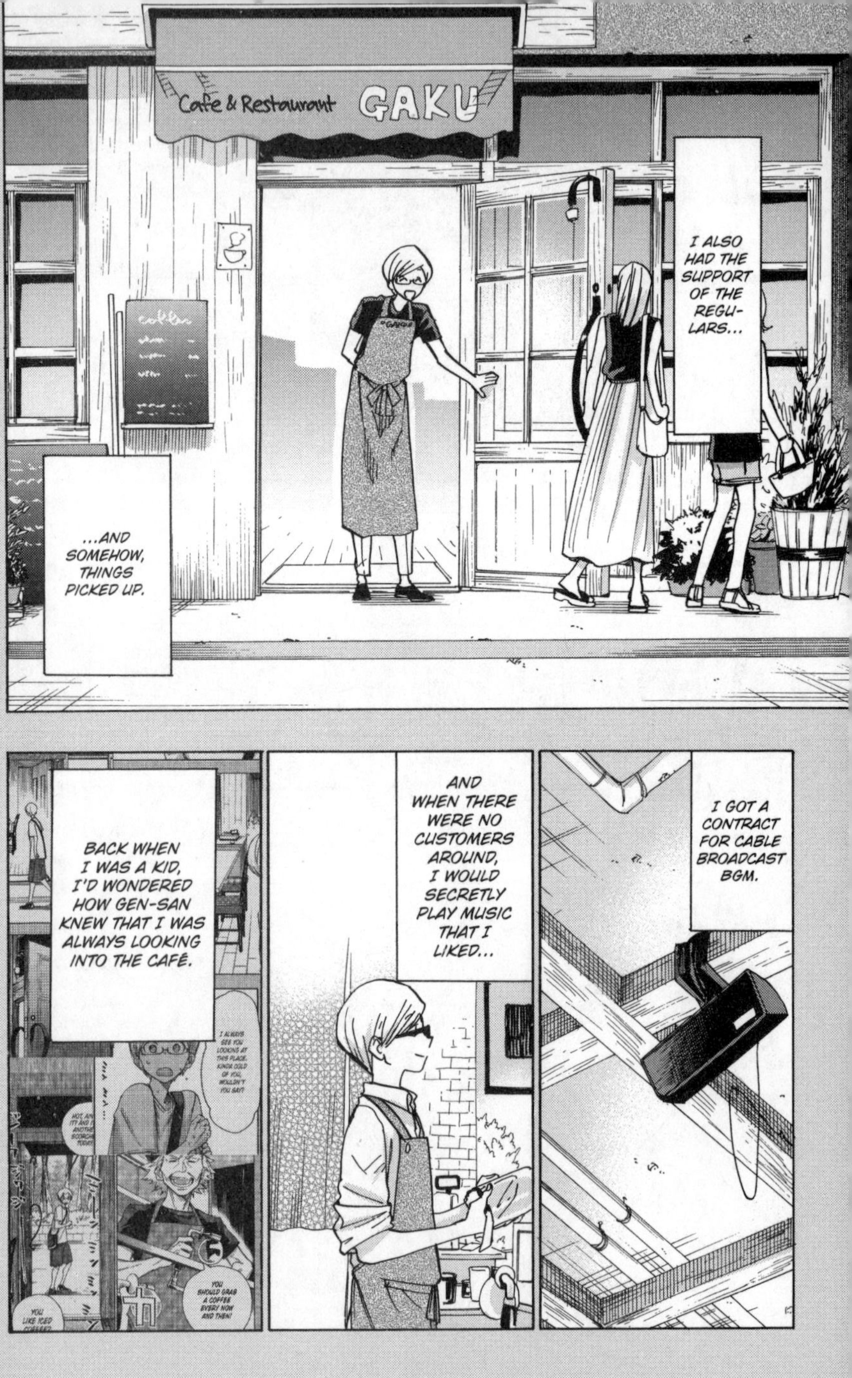
Cafe & Restaurant GAKU
I ALSO HAD THE SUPPORT OF THE REGU-LARS...
...AND SOMEHOW, THINGS PICKED UP.
I GOT A CONTRACT FOR CABLE BROADCAST BGM.
AND WHEN THERE WERE NO CUSTOMERS AROUND, I WOULD SECRETLY PLAY MUSIC THAT I LIKED...
BACK WHEN I WAS A KID, I'D WONDERED HOW GEN-SAN KNEW THAT I WAS ALWAYS LOOKING INTO THE CAFÉ.
I ALWAYS SEE YOU LOOKING AT THIS PLACE. KINDA COLD OF YOU, WOULDN'T YOU SAY?
YOU SHOULD GRAB A COFFEE EVERY NOW AND THEN!

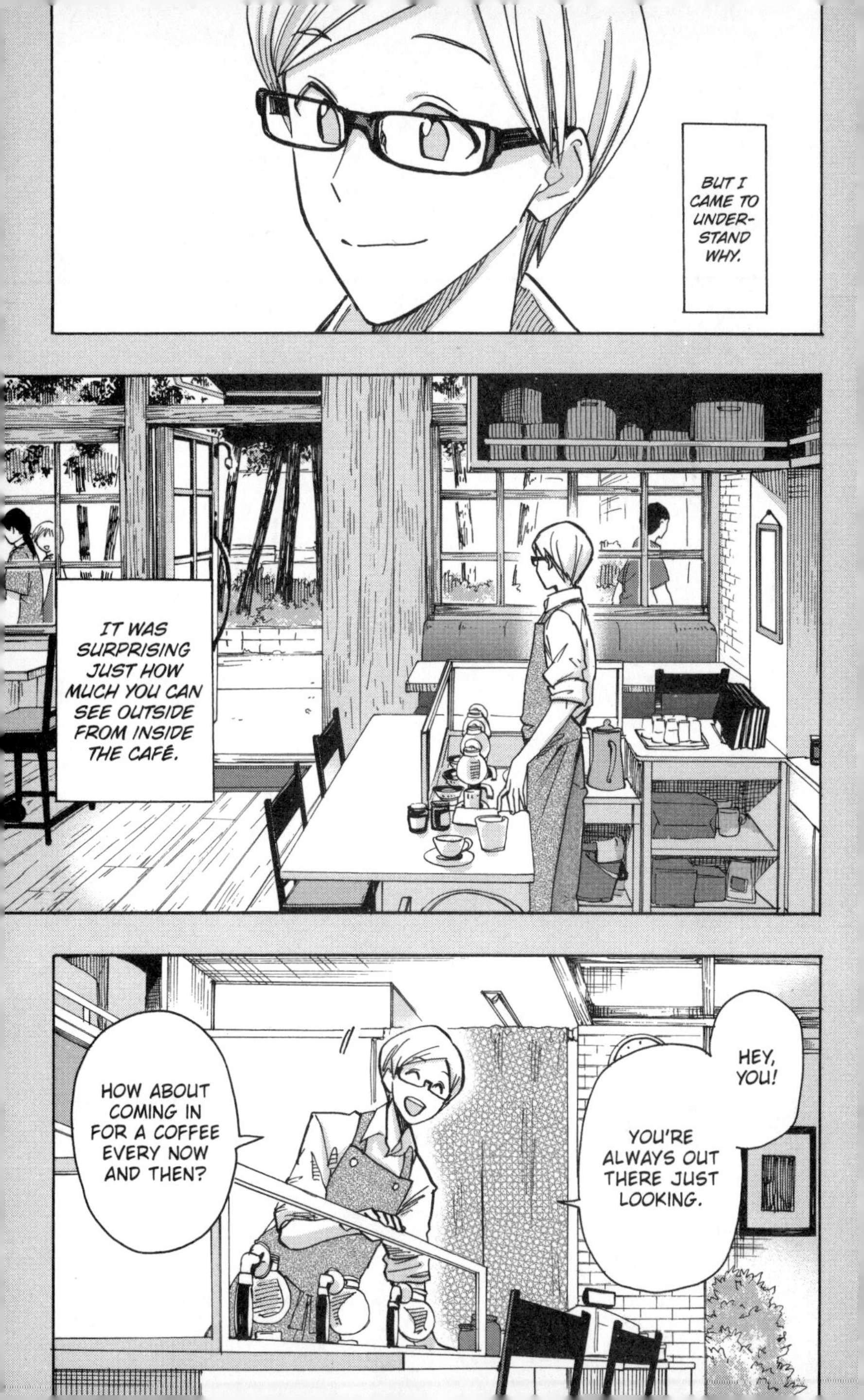
BUT I CAME TO UNDER-STAND WHY.
IT WAS SURPRISING JUST HOW MUCH YOU CAN SEE OUTSIDE FROM INSIDE THE CAFÉ.
HEY, YOU!
YOU'RE ALWAYS OUT THERE JUST LOOKING.
HOW ABOUT COMING IN FOR A COFFEE EVERY NOW AND THEN?

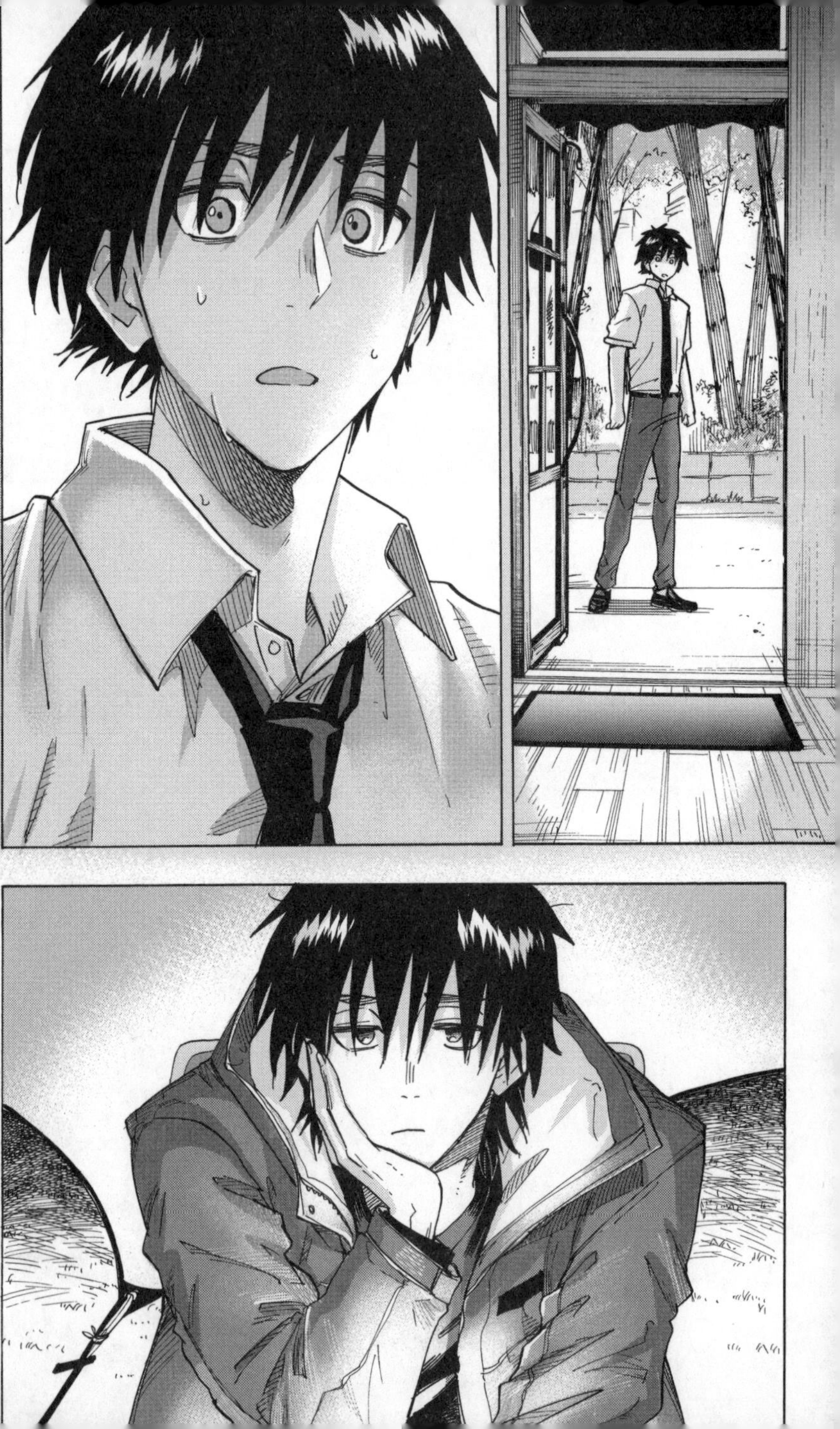

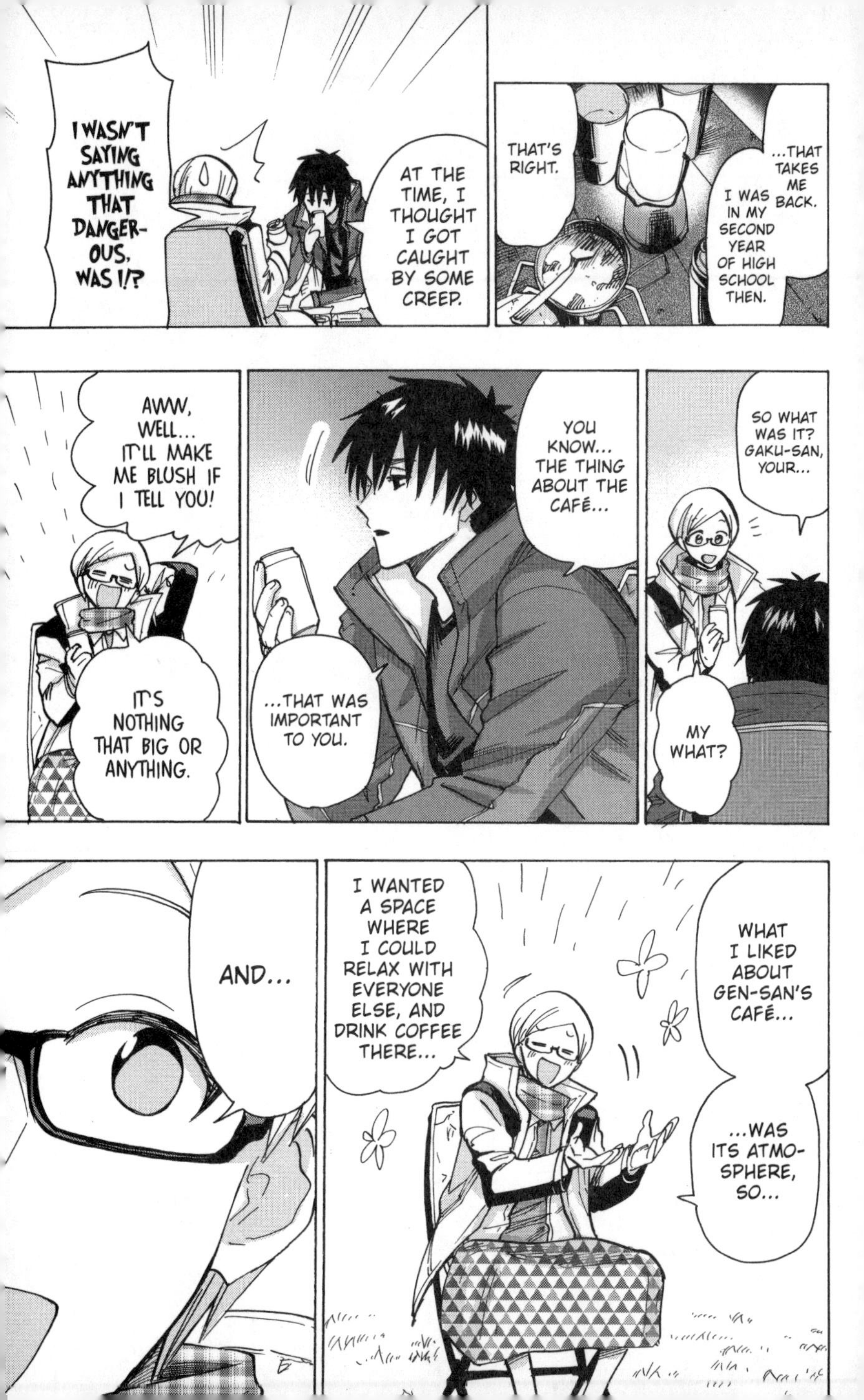
...THAT TAKES ME BACK.
I WAS IN MY SECOND YEAR OF HIGH SCHOOL THEN.
THAT'S RIGHT.
AT THE TIME, I THOUGHT I GOT CAUGHT BY SOME CREEP.
I WASN'T SAYING ANYTHING THAT DANGER-OUS, WAS I!?
SO WHAT WAS IT? GAKU-SAN, YOUR...
MY WHAT?
YOU KNOW... THE THING ABOUT THE CAFÉ...
...THAT WAS IMPORTANT TO YOU.
AWW, WELL... IT'LL MAKE ME BLUSH IF I TELL YOU!
IT'S NOTHING THAT BIG OR ANYTHING.
WHAT I LIKED ABOUT GEN-SAN'S CAFÉ...
...WAS ITS ATMO-SPHERE, SO...
I WANTED A SPACE WHERE I COULD RELAX WITH EVERYONE ELSE, AND DRINK COFFEE THERE...
AND...

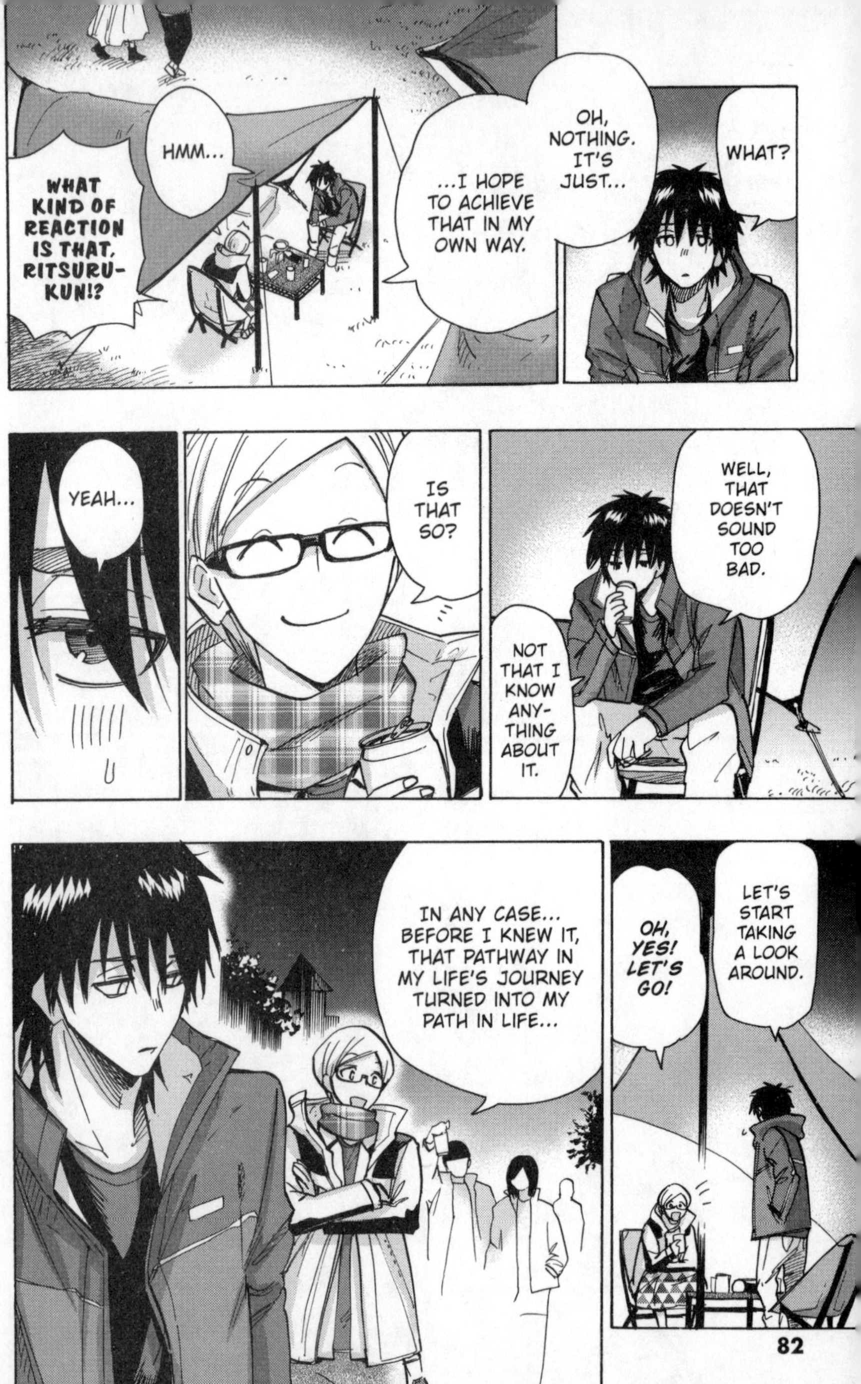
WHAT?
OH, NOTHING. IT'S JUST...
...I HOPE TO ACHIEVE THAT IN MY OWN WAY.
HMM...
WHAT KIND OF REACTION IS THAT, RITSURU-KUN!?
WELL, THAT DOESN'T SOUND TOO BAD.
NOT THAT I KNOW ANY-THING ABOUT IT.
IS THAT SO?
YEAH...
LET'S START TAKING A LOOK AROUND.
OH, YES! LET'S GO!
IN ANY CASE... BEFORE I KNEW IT, THAT PATHWAY IN MY LIFE'S JOURNEY TURNED INTO MY PATH IN LIFE...

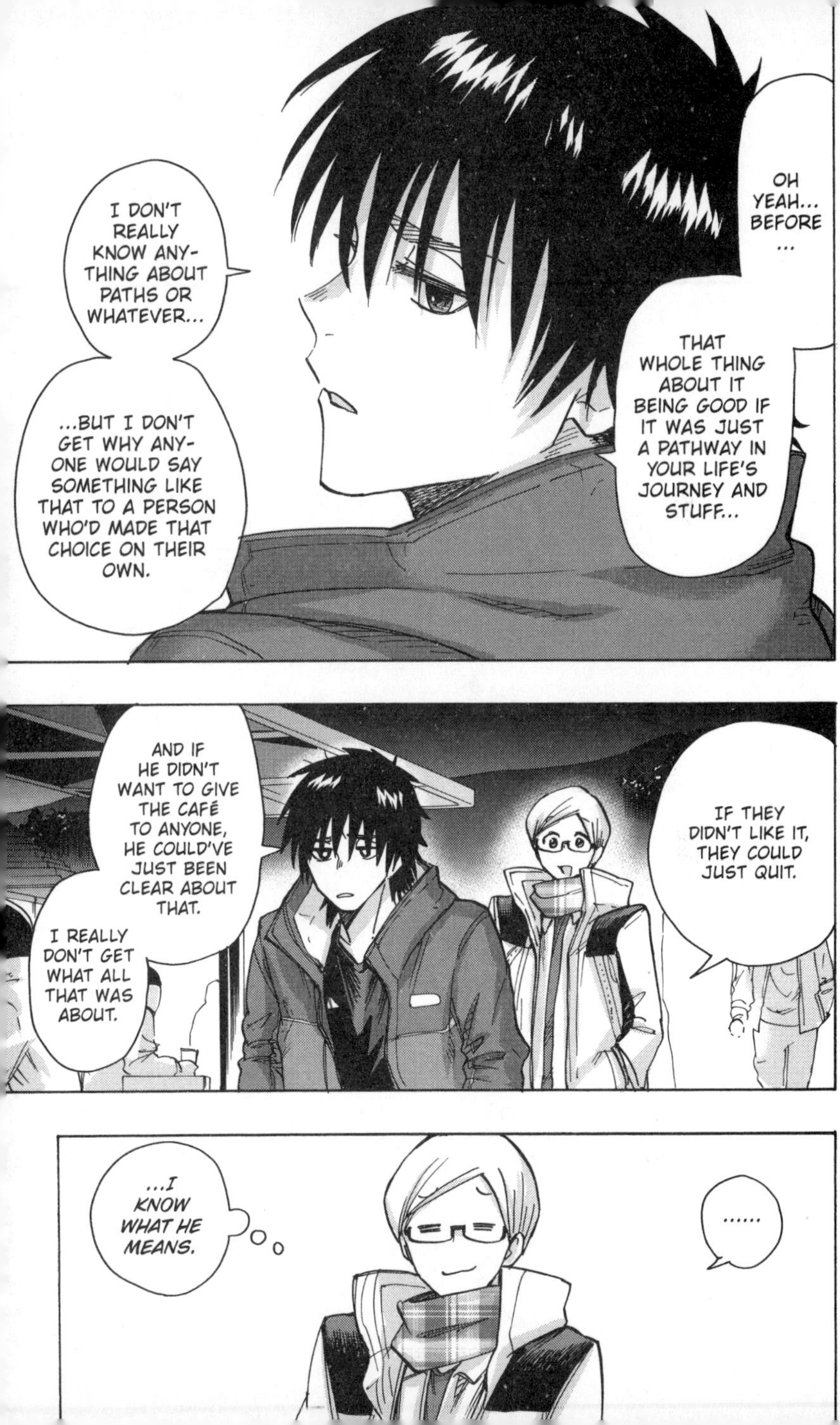
OH YEAH... BEFORE...
THAT WHOLE THING ABOUT IT BEING GOOD IF IT WAS JUST A PATHWAY IN YOUR LIFE'S JOURNEY AND STUFF...
I DON'T REALLY KNOW ANYTHING ABOUT PATHS OR WHATEVER...
...BUT I DON'T GET WHY ANYONE WOULD SAY SOMETHING LIKE THAT TO A PERSON WHO'D MADE THAT CHOICE ON THEIR OWN.
IF THEY DIDN'T LIKE IT, THEY COULD JUST QUIT.
AND IF HE DIDN'T WANT TO GIVE THE CAFÉ TO ANYONE, HE COULD'VE JUST BEEN CLEAR ABOUT THAT.
I REALLY DON'T GET WHAT ALL THAT WAS ABOUT.
......
...I KNOW WHAT HE MEANS.

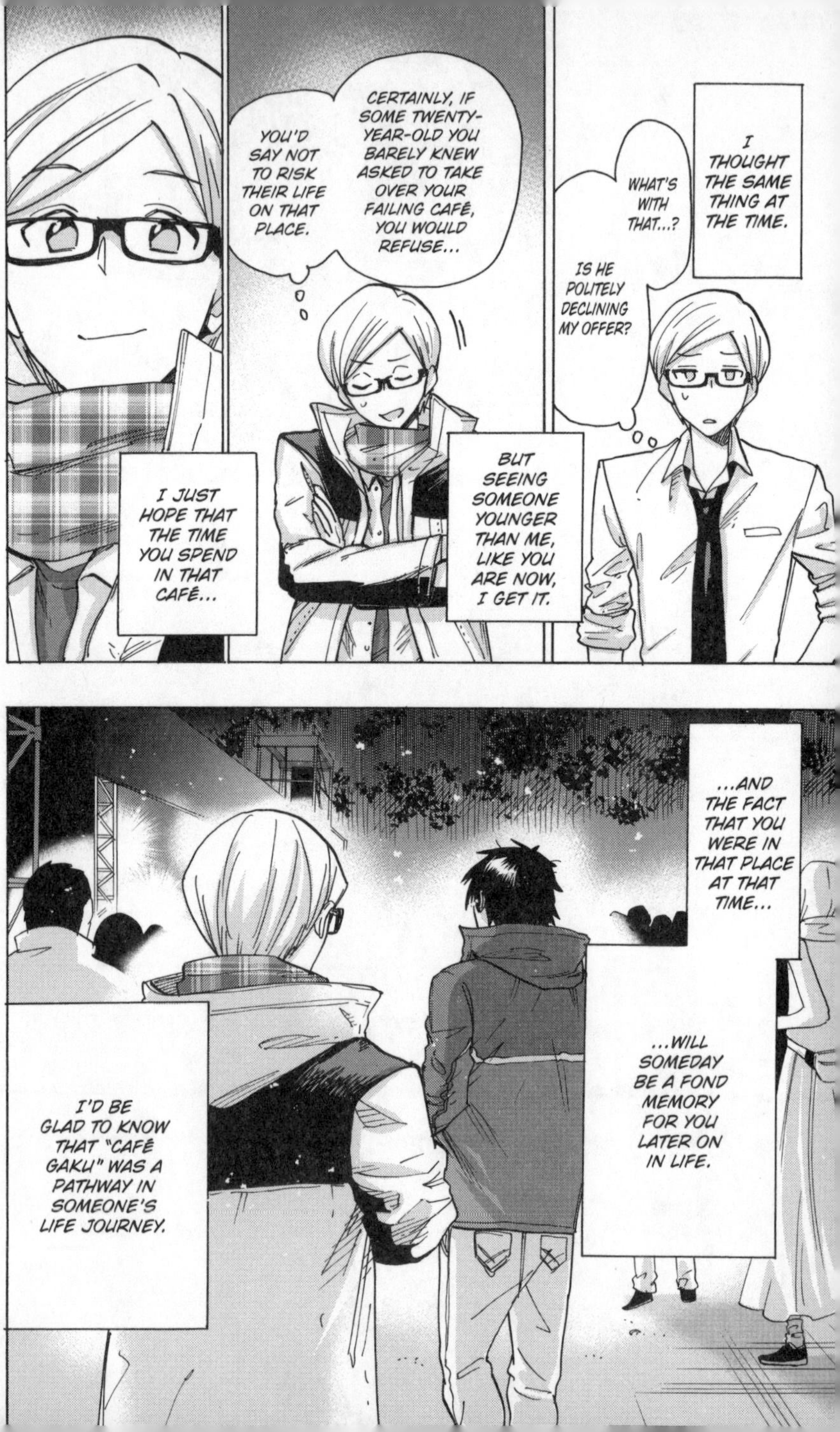
I THOUGHT THE SAME THING AT THE TIME.
WHAT'S WITH THAT...?
IS HE POLITELY DECLINING MY OFFER?
CERTAINLY, IF SOME TWENTY-YEAR-OLD YOU BARELY KNEW ASKED TO TAKE OVER YOUR FAILING CAFÉ, YOU WOULD REFUSE...
YOU'D SAY NOT TO RISK THEIR LIFE ON THAT PLACE.
BUT SEEING SOMEONE YOUNGER THAN ME, LIKE YOU ARE NOW, I GET IT.
I JUST HOPE THAT THE TIME YOU SPEND IN THAT CAFÉ...
...AND THE FACT THAT YOU WERE IN THAT PLACE AT THAT TIME...
...WILL SOMEDAY BE A FOND MEMORY FOR YOU LATER ON IN LIFE.
I'D BE GLAD TO KNOW THAT "CAFÉ GAKU" WAS A PATHWAY IN SOMEONE'S LIFE JOURNEY.

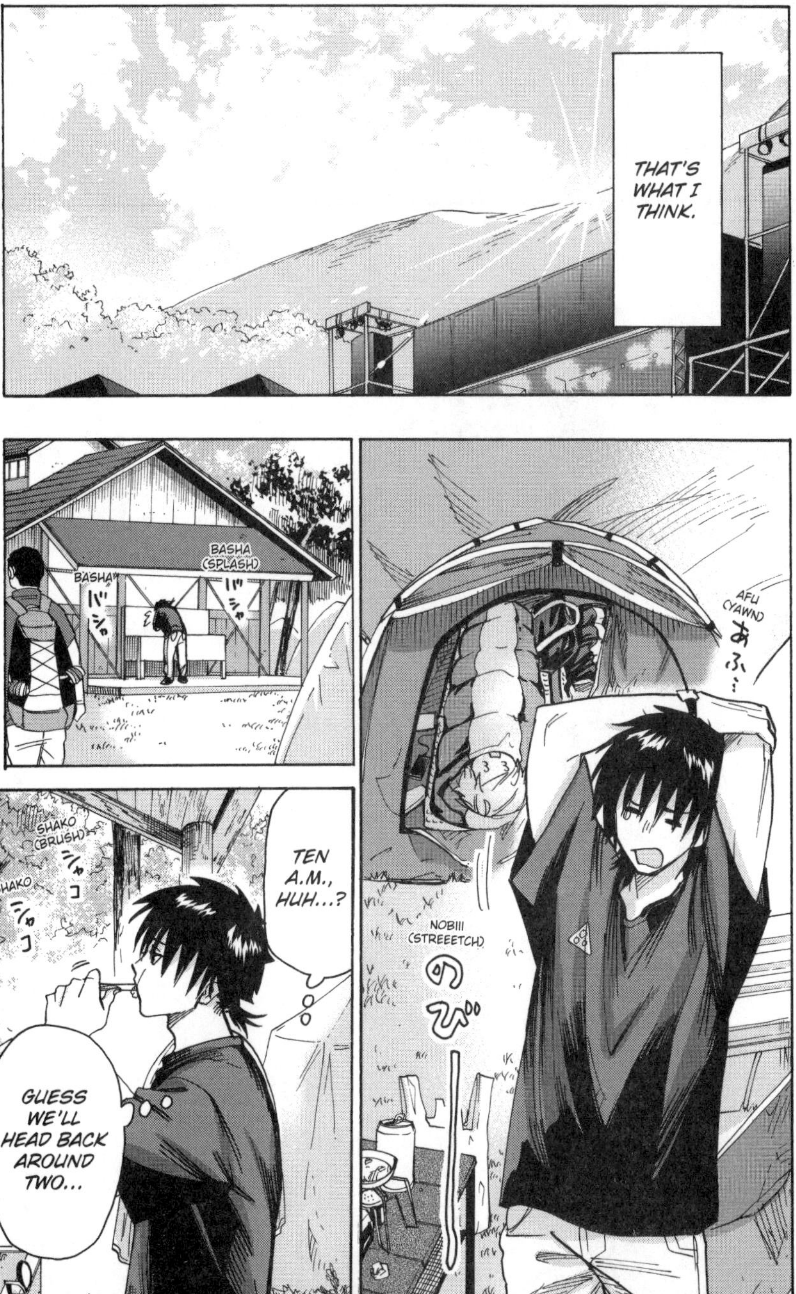
THAT'S WHAT I THINK.
AFU (YAWN)
あふ…
NOBIII (STREEETCH)
のび
BASHA (SPLASH)
バシャ
BASHA
バシャ
SHAKO (BRUSH)
シャコ
SHAKO
シャコ
TEN A.M., HUH...?
GUESS WE'LL HEAD BACK AROUND TWO...

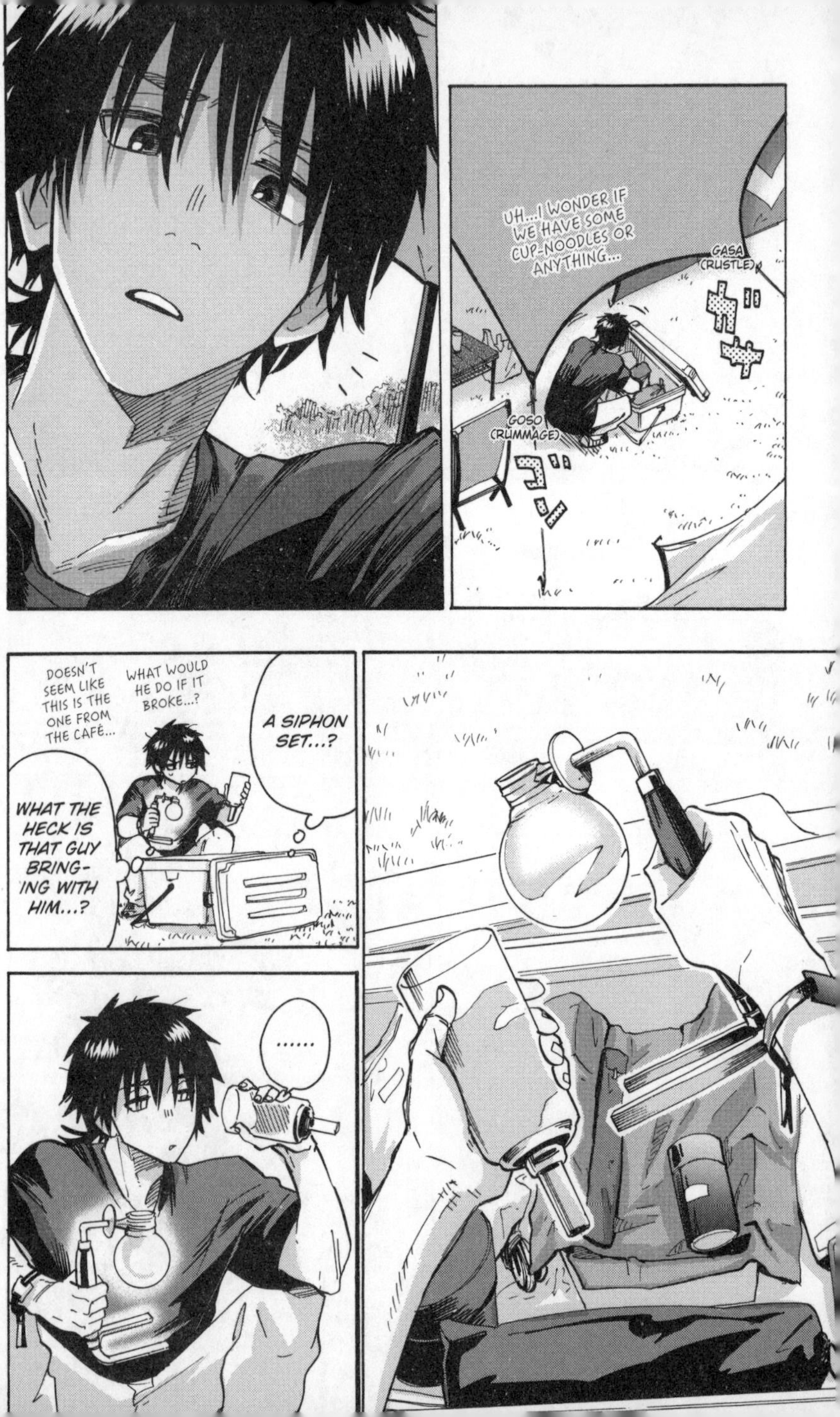
UH...I WONDER IF WE HAVE SOME CUP-NOODLES OR ANYTHING...
GASA (RUSTLE)
GOSO (RUMMAGE)
A SIPHON SET...?
WHAT WOULD HE DO IF IT BROKE...?
DOESN'T SEEM LIKE THIS IS THE ONE FROM THE CAFÉ...
WHAT THE HECK IS THAT GUY BRING-ING WITH HIM...?
......

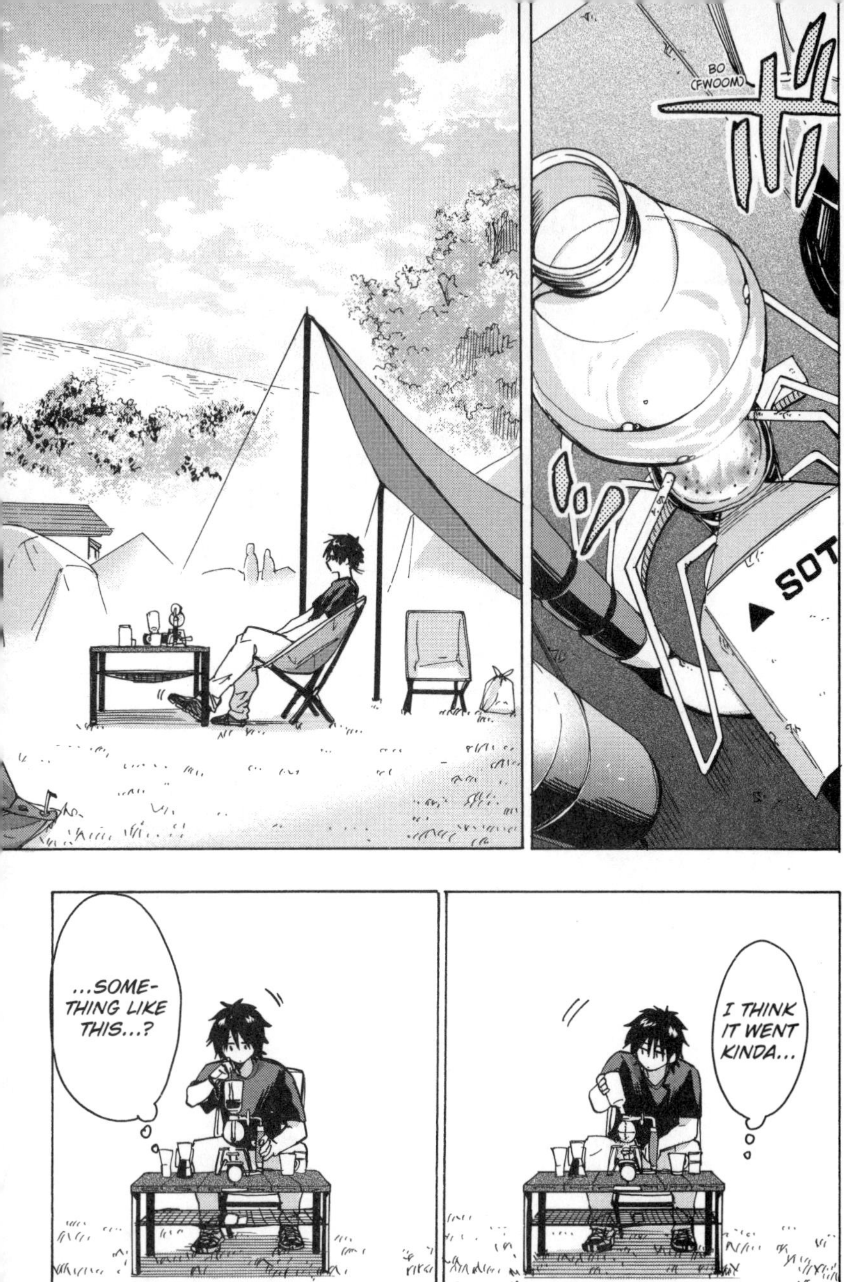
BO
(FWOOM)
SOT
I THINK IT WENT KINDA...
...SOME-THING LIKE THIS...?

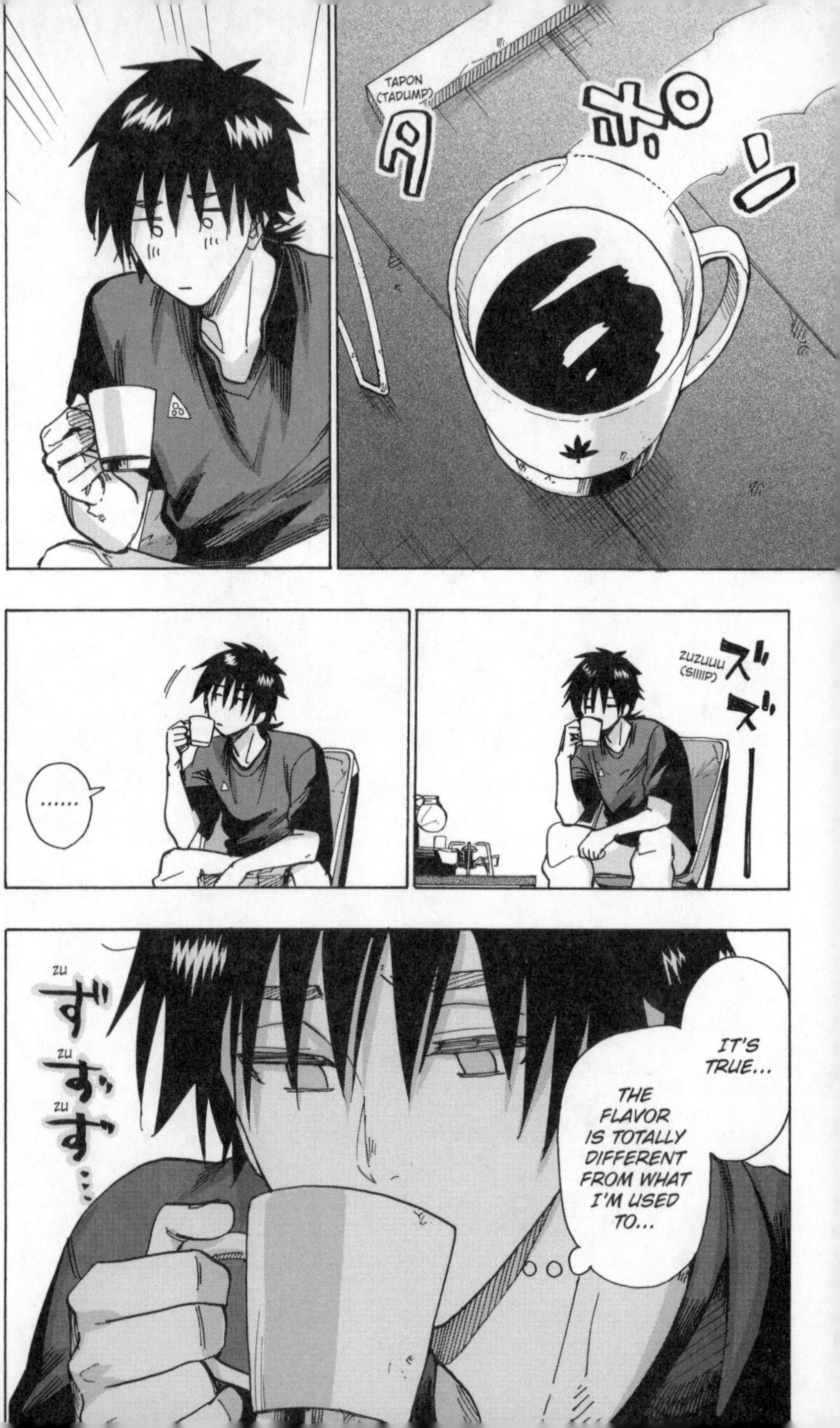
TAPON (TADUMP)
タポン
ZUZUUU (SIIIP)
ズズー
......
zu zu zu
ずずず
IT'S TRUE...
THE FLAVOR IS TOTALLY DIFFERENT FROM WHAT I'M USED TO...

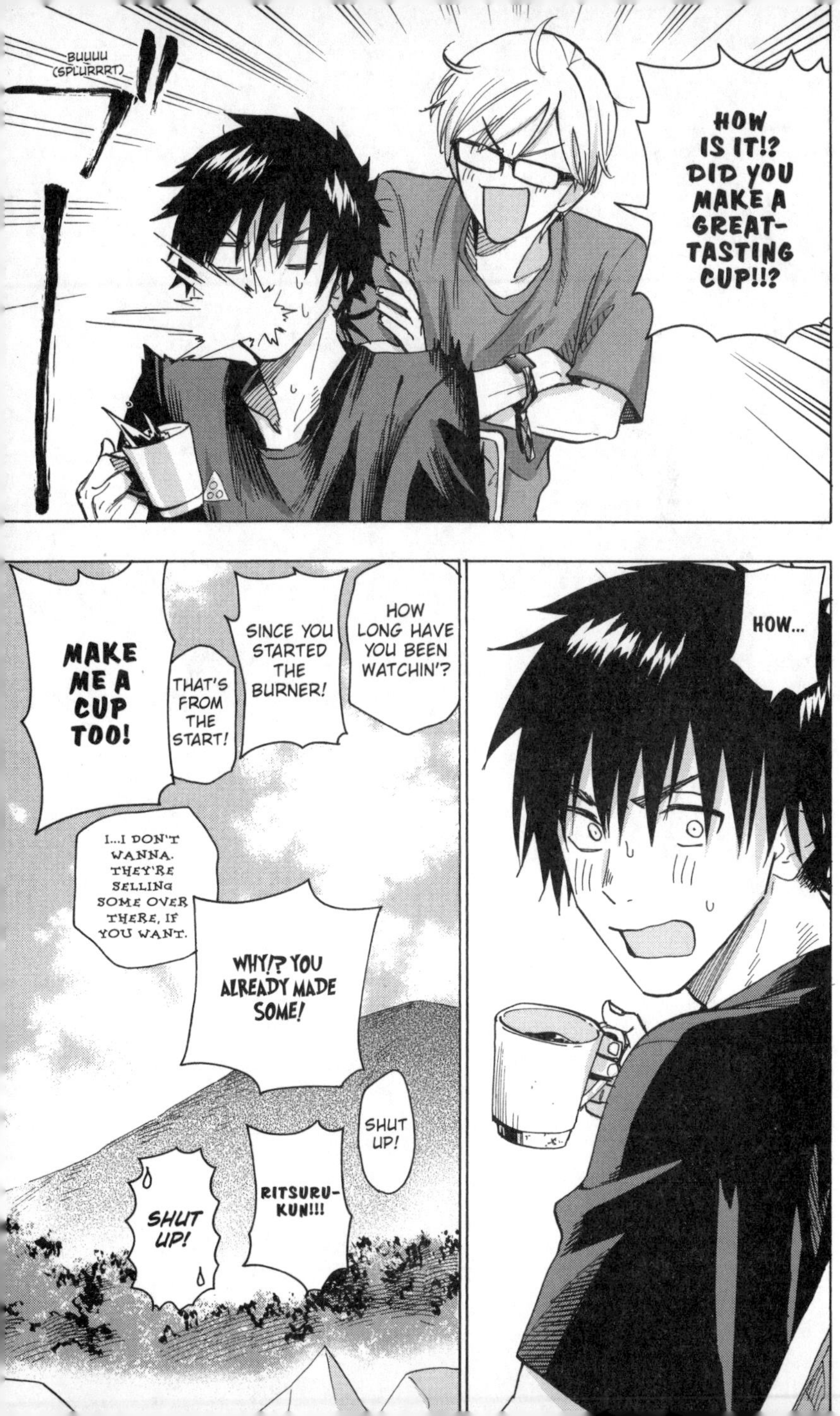
HOW IS IT!? DID YOU MAKE A GREAT-TASTING CUP!!?
BUUUU (SPLURRRT)
HOW...
HOW LONG HAVE YOU BEEN WATCHIN'?
SINCE YOU STARTED THE BURNER!
THAT'S FROM THE START!
MAKE ME A CUP TOO!
I...I DON'T WANNA. THEY'RE SELLING SOME OVER THERE, IF YOU WANT.
WHY!? YOU ALREADY MADE SOME!
SHUT UP!
RITSURU-KUN!!!
SHUT UP!

Days on Fes

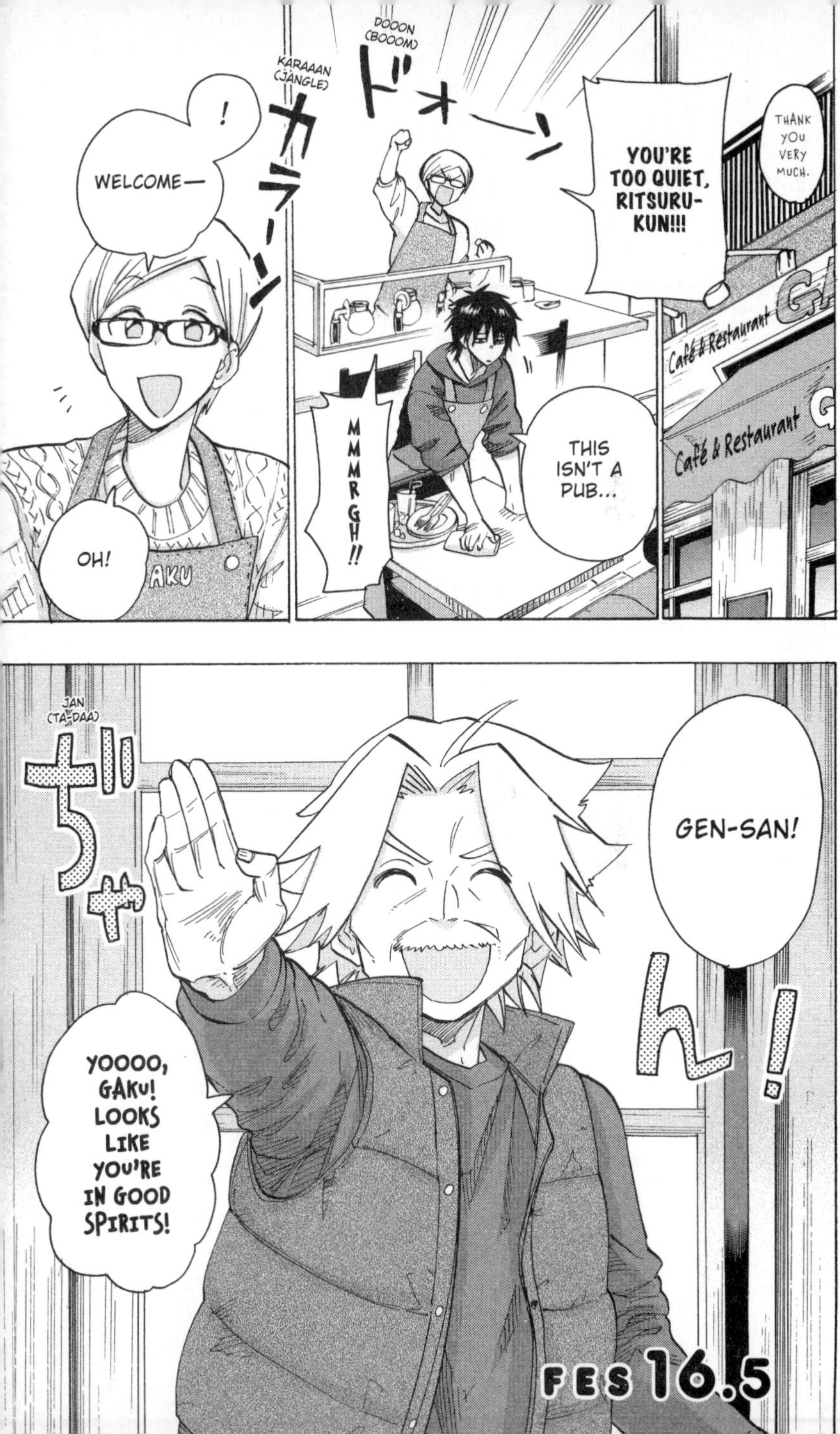
THANK YOU VERY MUCH.
Café & Restaurant
Café & Restaurant
DOOON (BOOOM)
ドオーン
YOU'RE TOO QUIET, RITSURU-KUN!!!
THIS ISN'T A PUB...
MMMRGH!!
KARAAAN (JANGLE)
カラーン
!
WELCOME—
OH!
GEN-SAN!
JAN (TA-DAA)
ぢゃん!
YOOOO, GAKU! LOOKS LIKE YOU'RE IN GOOD SPIRITS!
FES 16.5

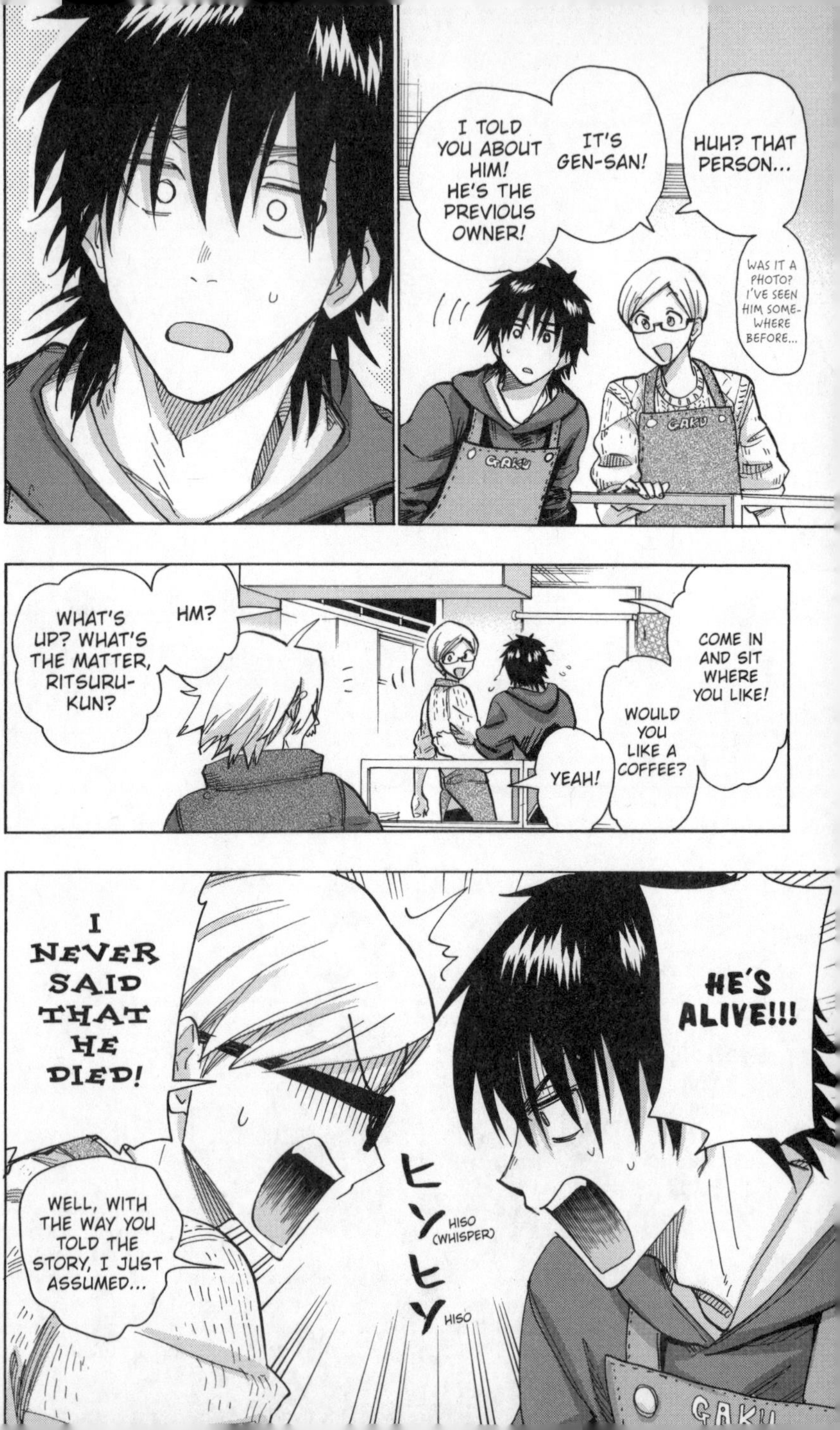
HUH? THAT PERSON...
WAS IT A PHOTO? I'VE SEEN HIM SOME-WHERE BEFORE...
IT'S GEN-SAN!
I TOLD YOU ABOUT HIM! HE'S THE PREVIOUS OWNER!
GAKU
GAKU
COME IN AND SIT WHERE YOU LIKE!
WOULD YOU LIKE A COFFEE?
YEAH!
HM?
WHAT'S UP? WHAT'S THE MATTER, RITSURU-KUN?
HE'S ALIVE!!!
I NEVER SAID THAT HE DIED!
ヒソ HISO (WHISPER)
ヒソ HISO
WELL, WITH THE WAY YOU TOLD THE STORY, I JUST ASSUMED...
GAKU

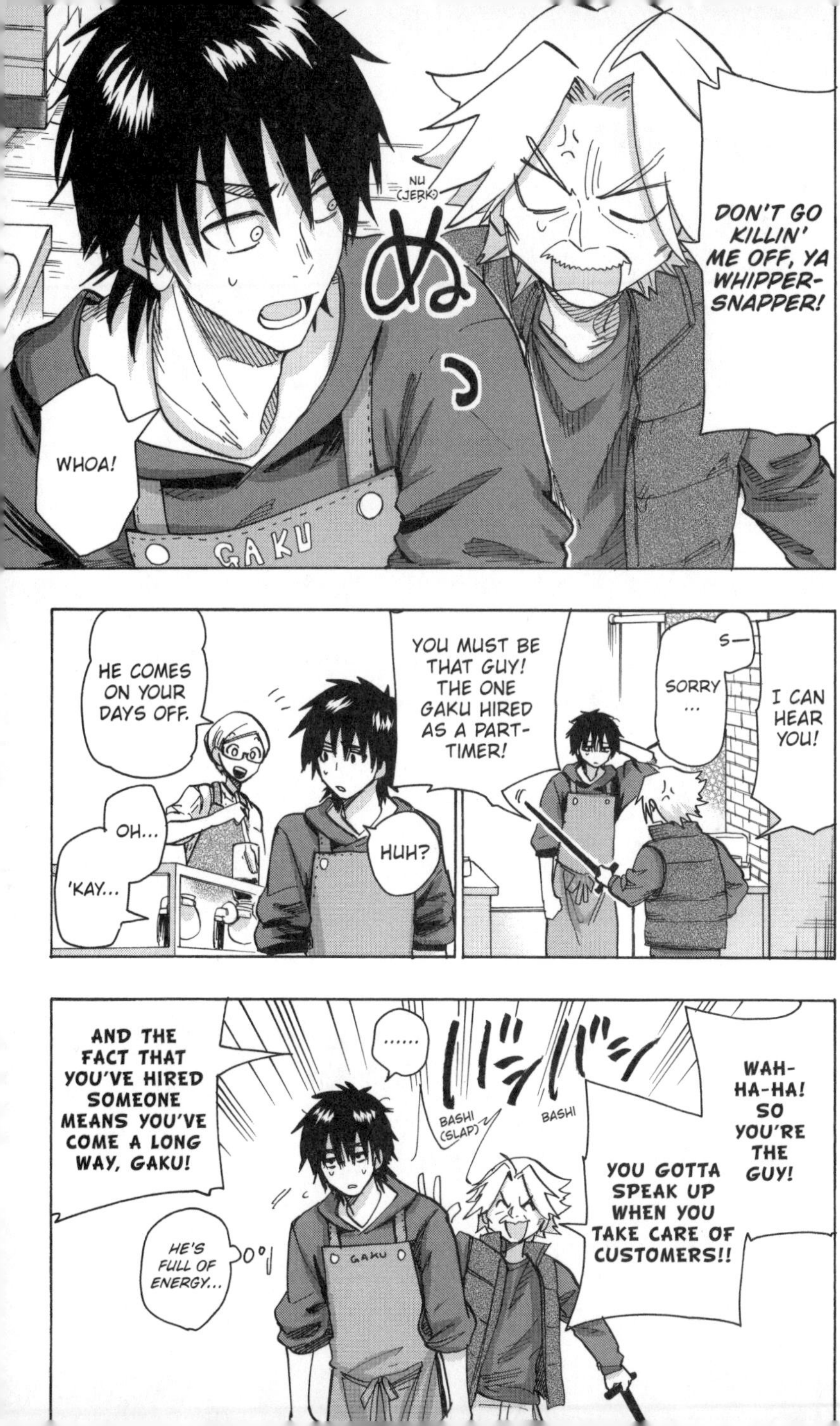
DON'T GO KILLIN' ME OFF, YA WHIPPER-SNAPPER!
NU (JERK)
WHOA!
I CAN HEAR YOU!
S— SORRY …
YOU MUST BE THAT GUY! THE ONE GAKU HIRED AS A PART-TIMER!
HE COMES ON YOUR DAYS OFF.
HUH?
OH… 'KAY…
WAH-HA-HA! SO YOU'RE THE GUY!
BASHI
BASHI (SLAP)
YOU GOTTA SPEAK UP WHEN YOU TAKE CARE OF CUSTOMERS!!
……
AND THE FACT THAT YOU'VE HIRED SOMEONE MEANS YOU'VE COME A LONG WAY, GAKU!
HE'S FULL OF ENERGY…

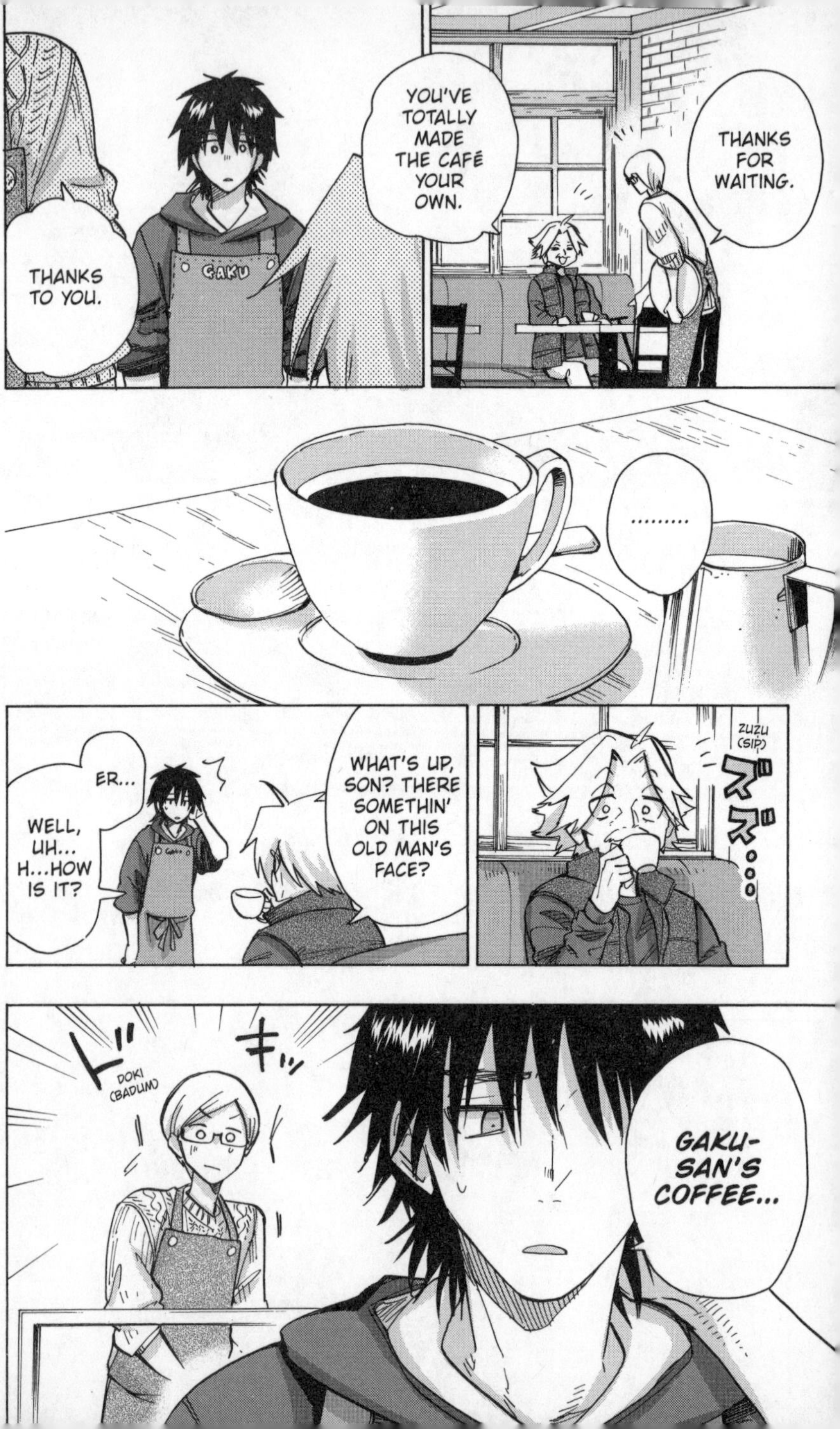
THANKS FOR WAITING.
YOU'VE TOTALLY MADE THE CAFÉ YOUR OWN.
GAKU
THANKS TO YOU.
....
ZUZU (SIP)
WHAT'S UP, SON? THERE SOMETHIN' ON THIS OLD MAN'S FACE?
ER...
WELL, UH... H...HOW IS IT?
GAKU-SAN'S COFFEE...
DOKI (BADUM)

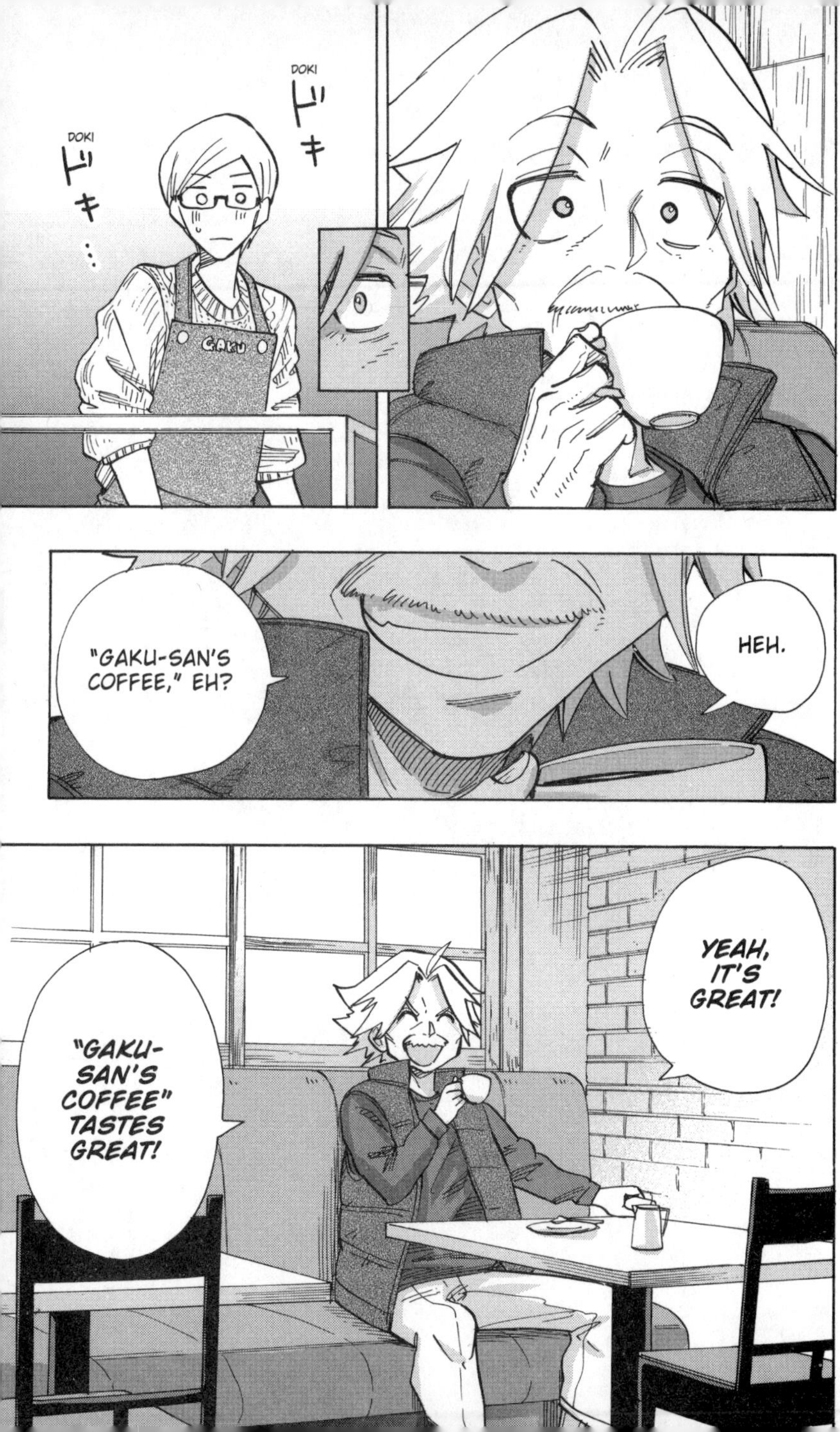
DOKI
ドキ
DOKI
ドキ…
HEH.
"GAKU-SAN'S COFFEE," EH?
YEAH, IT'S GREAT!
"GAKU-SAN'S COFFEE" TASTES GREAT!

Days on Fes

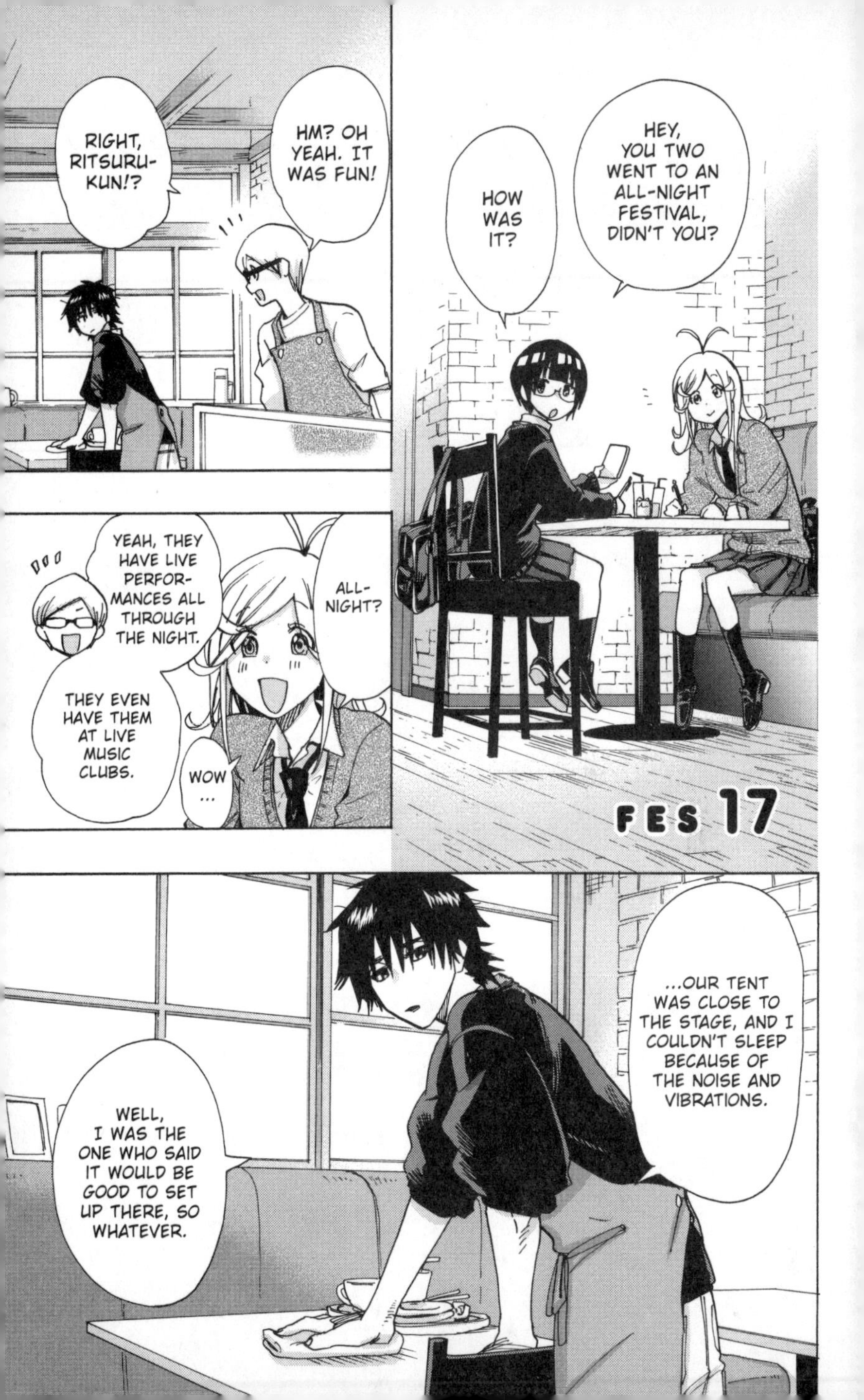
HEY, YOU TWO WENT TO AN ALL-NIGHT FESTIVAL, DIDN'T YOU?
HOW WAS IT?
FES 17
HM? OH YEAH. IT WAS FUN!
RIGHT, RITSURU-KUN!?
ALL-NIGHT?
YEAH, THEY HAVE LIVE PERFORMANCES ALL THROUGH THE NIGHT.
THEY EVEN HAVE THEM AT LIVE MUSIC CLUBS.
WOW ...
...OUR TENT WAS CLOSE TO THE STAGE, AND I COULDN'T SLEEP BECAUSE OF THE NOISE AND VIBRATIONS.
WELL, I WAS THE ONE WHO SAID IT WOULD BE GOOD TO SET UP THERE, SO WHATEVER.

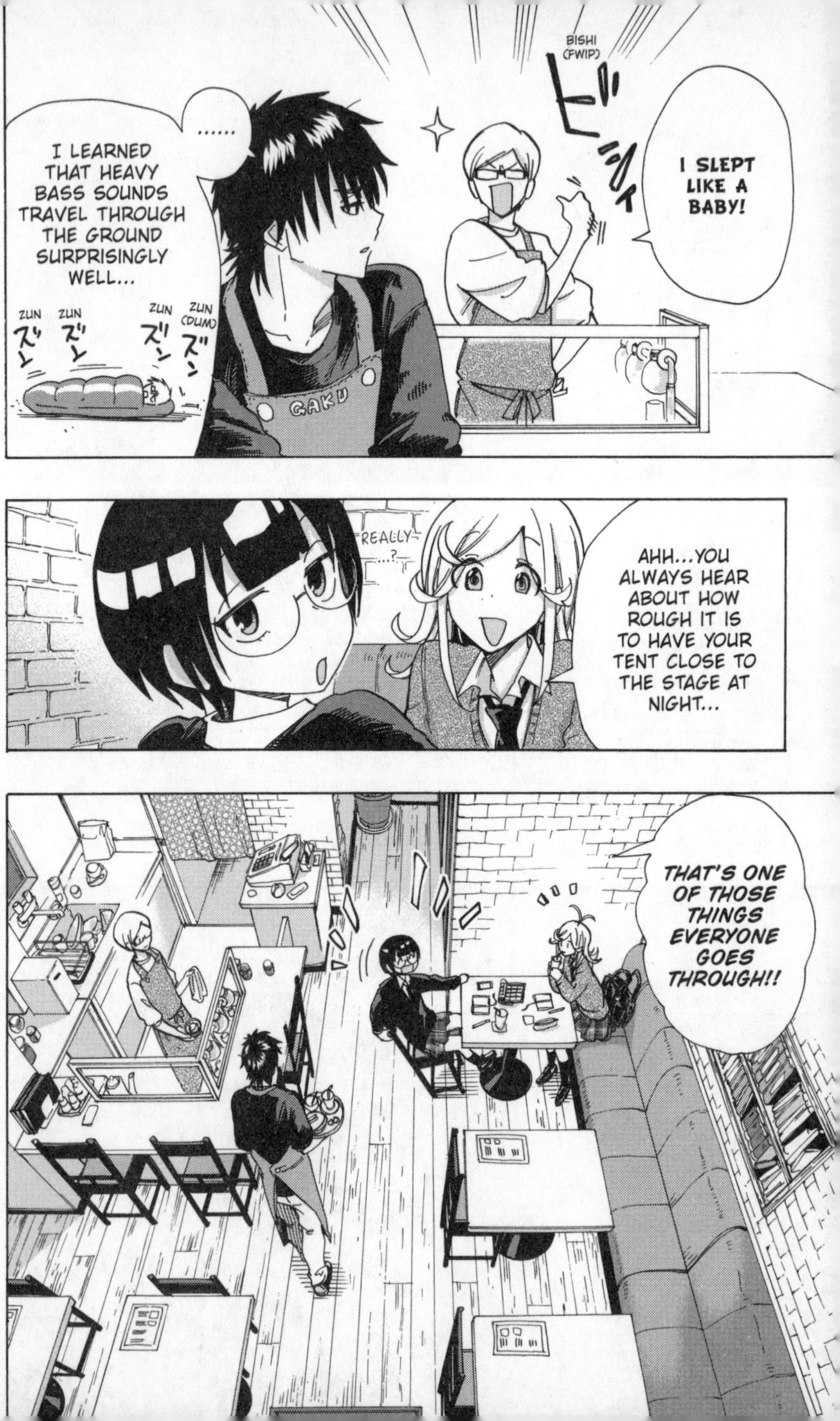
I SLEPT LIKE A BABY!
BISHI (FWIP)
......
I LEARNED THAT HEAVY BASS SOUNDS TRAVEL THROUGH THE GROUND SURPRISINGLY WELL...
ZUN (DUM)
ZUN
ZUN
ZUN
GAKU
AHH...YOU ALWAYS HEAR ABOUT HOW ROUGH IT IS TO HAVE YOUR TENT CLOSE TO THE STAGE AT NIGHT...
REALLY ...?
THAT'S ONE OF THOSE THINGS EVERYONE GOES THROUGH!!

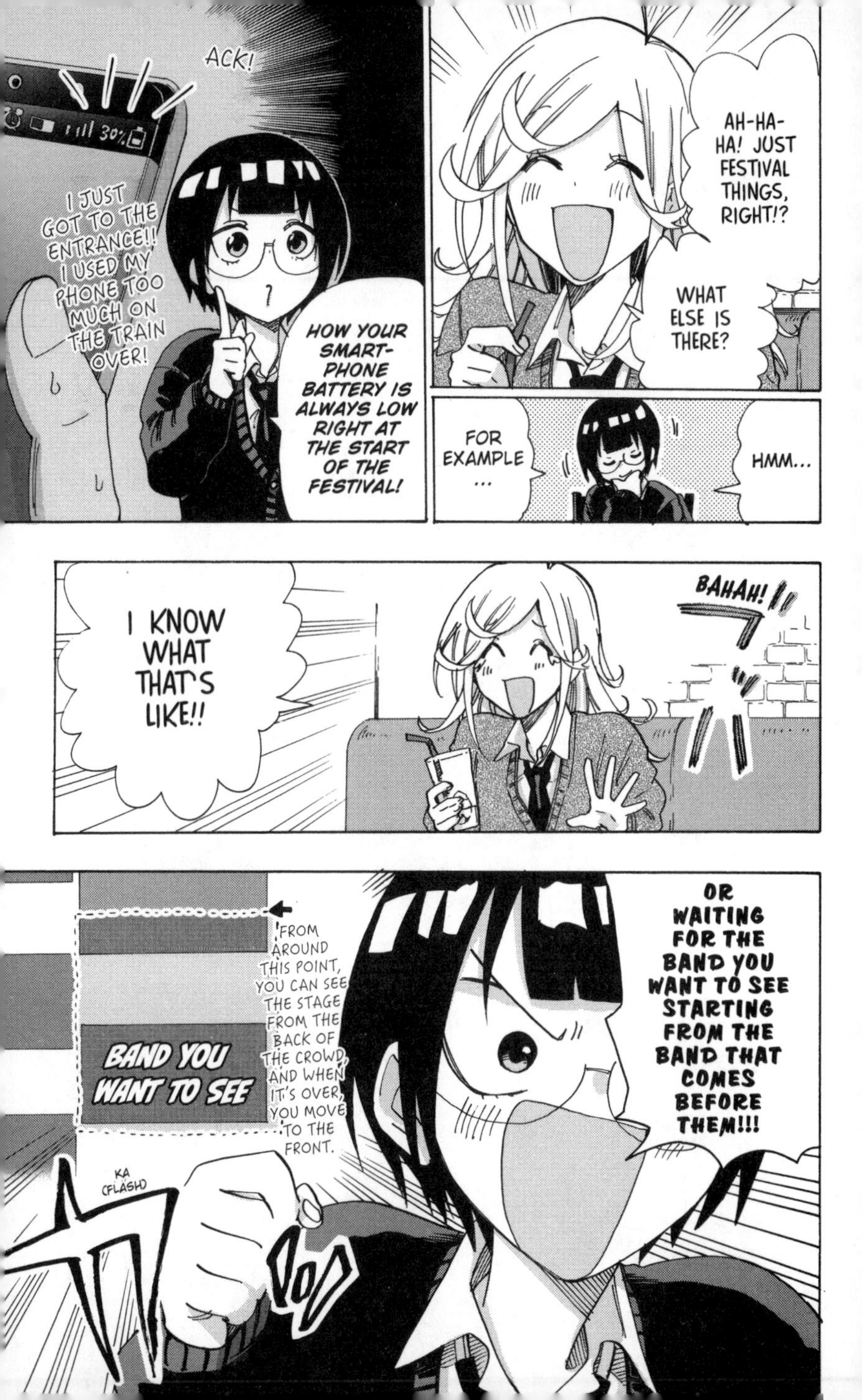
AH-HA-HA! JUST FESTIVAL THINGS, RIGHT!?
WHAT ELSE IS THERE?
HMM...
FOR EXAMPLE ...
ACK!
HOW YOUR SMART-PHONE BATTERY IS ALWAYS LOW RIGHT AT THE START OF THE FESTIVAL!
I JUST GOT TO THE ENTRANCE!! I USED MY PHONE TOO MUCH ON THE TRAIN OVER!
30%
BAHAH!
I KNOW WHAT THAT'S LIKE!!
OR WAITING FOR THE BAND YOU WANT TO SEE STARTING FROM THE BAND THAT COMES BEFORE THEM!!!
FROM AROUND THIS POINT, YOU CAN SEE THE STAGE FROM THE BACK OF THE CROWD, AND WHEN IT'S OVER, YOU MOVE TO THE FRONT.
BAND YOU WANT TO SEE
KA (FLASH)

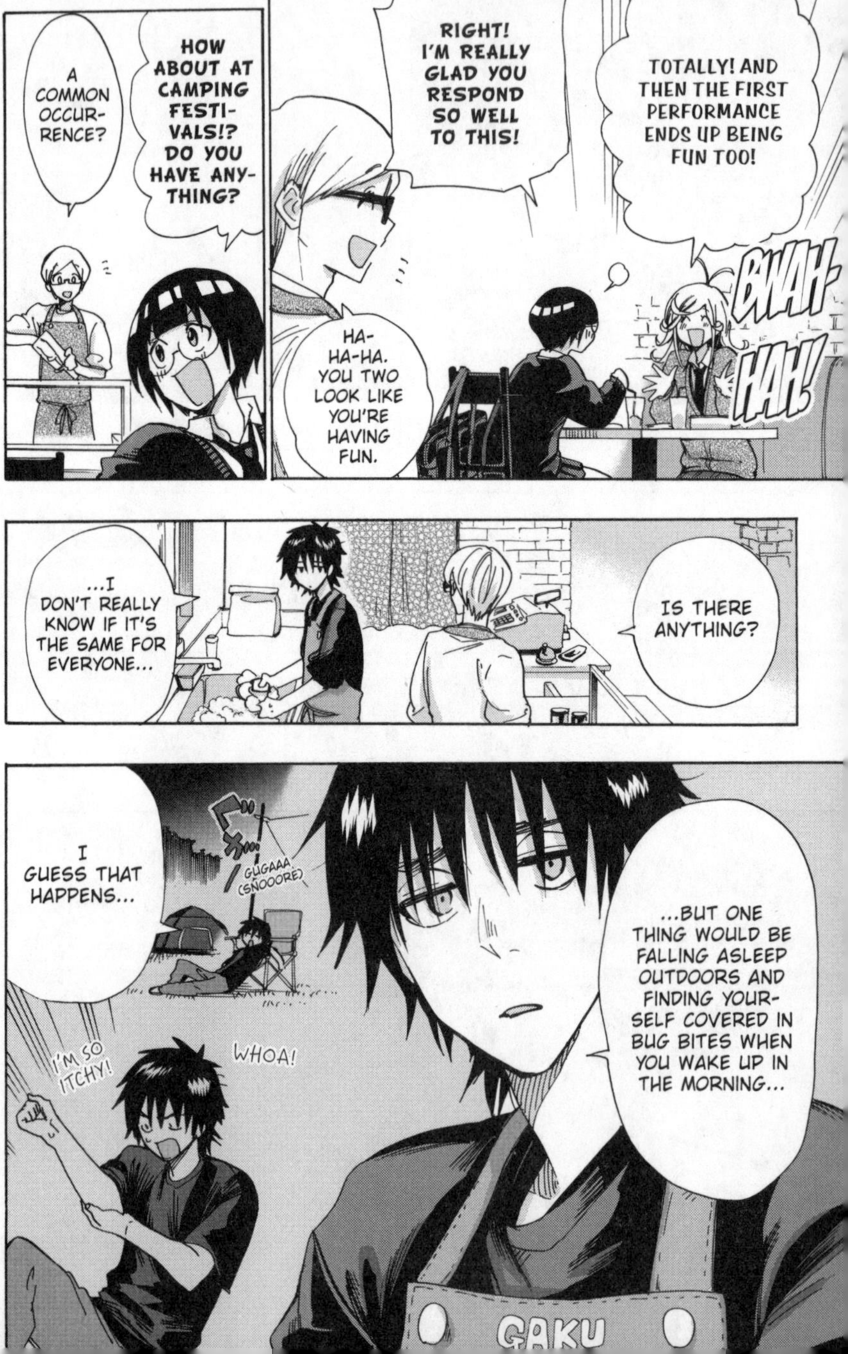
TOTALLY! AND THEN THE FIRST PERFORMANCE ENDS UP BEING FUN TOO!
BWAH-HAH!
RIGHT! I'M REALLY GLAD YOU RESPOND SO WELL TO THIS!
HA-HA-HA. YOU TWO LOOK LIKE YOU'RE HAVING FUN.
HOW ABOUT AT CAMPING FESTIVALS!? DO YOU HAVE ANYTHING?
A COMMON OCCURRENCE?
IS THERE ANYTHING?
...I DON'T REALLY KNOW IF IT'S THE SAME FOR EVERYONE...
...BUT ONE THING WOULD BE FALLING ASLEEP OUTDOORS AND FINDING YOURSELF COVERED IN BUG BITES WHEN YOU WAKE UP IN THE MORNING...
GUGAAA (SÑOOORE)
WHOA!
I'M SO ITCHY!
I GUESS THAT HAPPENS...
GAKU

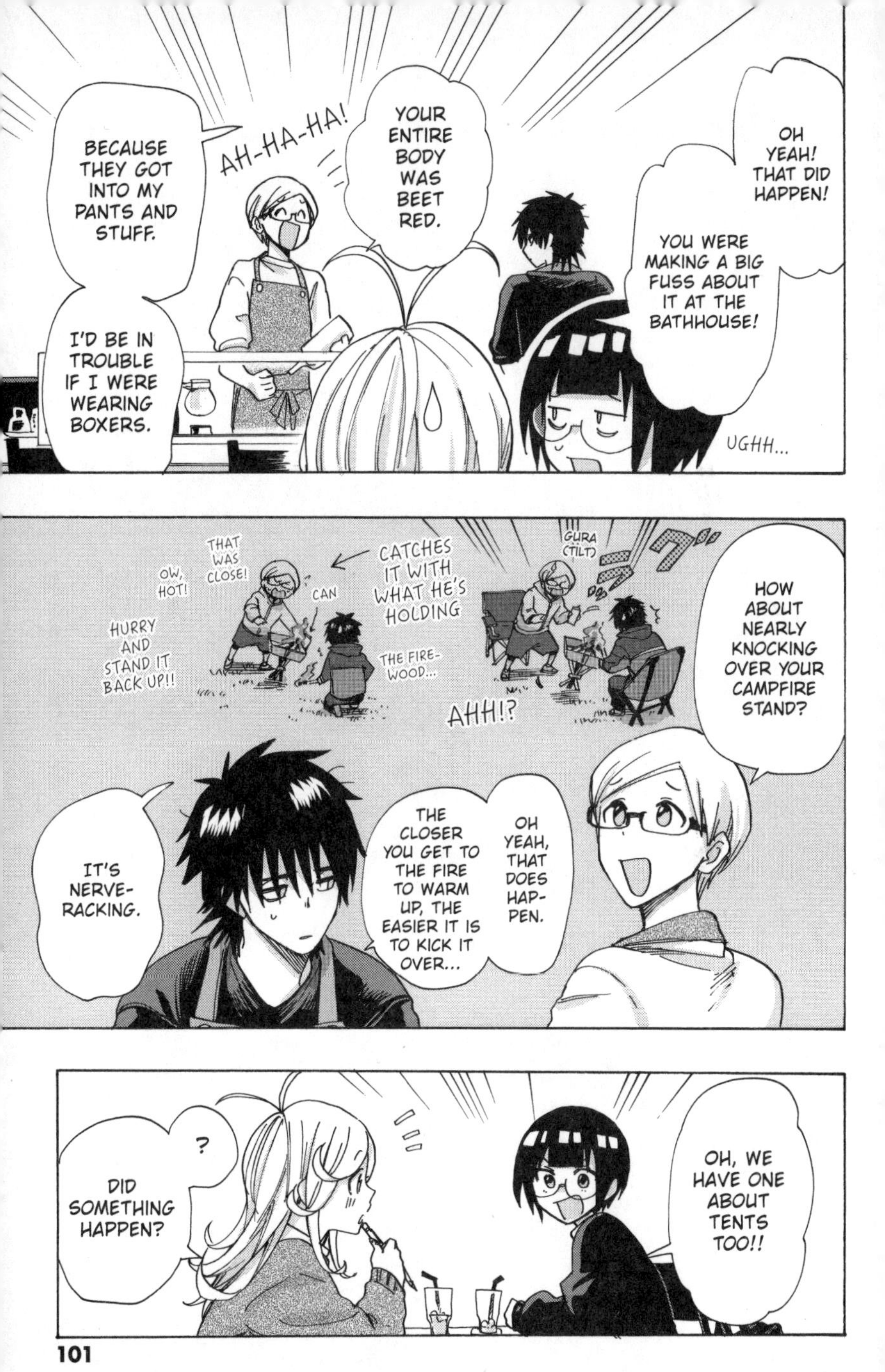
OH YEAH! THAT DID HAPPEN!
YOU WERE MAKING A BIG FUSS ABOUT IT AT THE BATHHOUSE!
UGHH...
YOUR ENTIRE BODY WAS BEET RED.
AH-HA-HA!
BECAUSE THEY GOT INTO MY PANTS AND STUFF.
I'D BE IN TROUBLE IF I WERE WEARING BOXERS.
HOW ABOUT NEARLY KNOCKING OVER YOUR CAMPFIRE STAND?
GURA (TILT)
AHH!?
CATCHES IT WITH WHAT HE'S HOLDING
THE FIRE-WOOD...
CAN
THAT WAS CLOSE!
OW, HOT!
HURRY AND STAND IT BACK UP!!
OH YEAH, THAT DOES HAP-PEN.
THE CLOSER YOU GET TO THE FIRE TO WARM UP, THE EASIER IT IS TO KICK IT OVER...
IT'S NERVE-RACKING.
OH, WE HAVE ONE ABOUT TENTS TOO!!
?
DID SOMETHING HAPPEN?

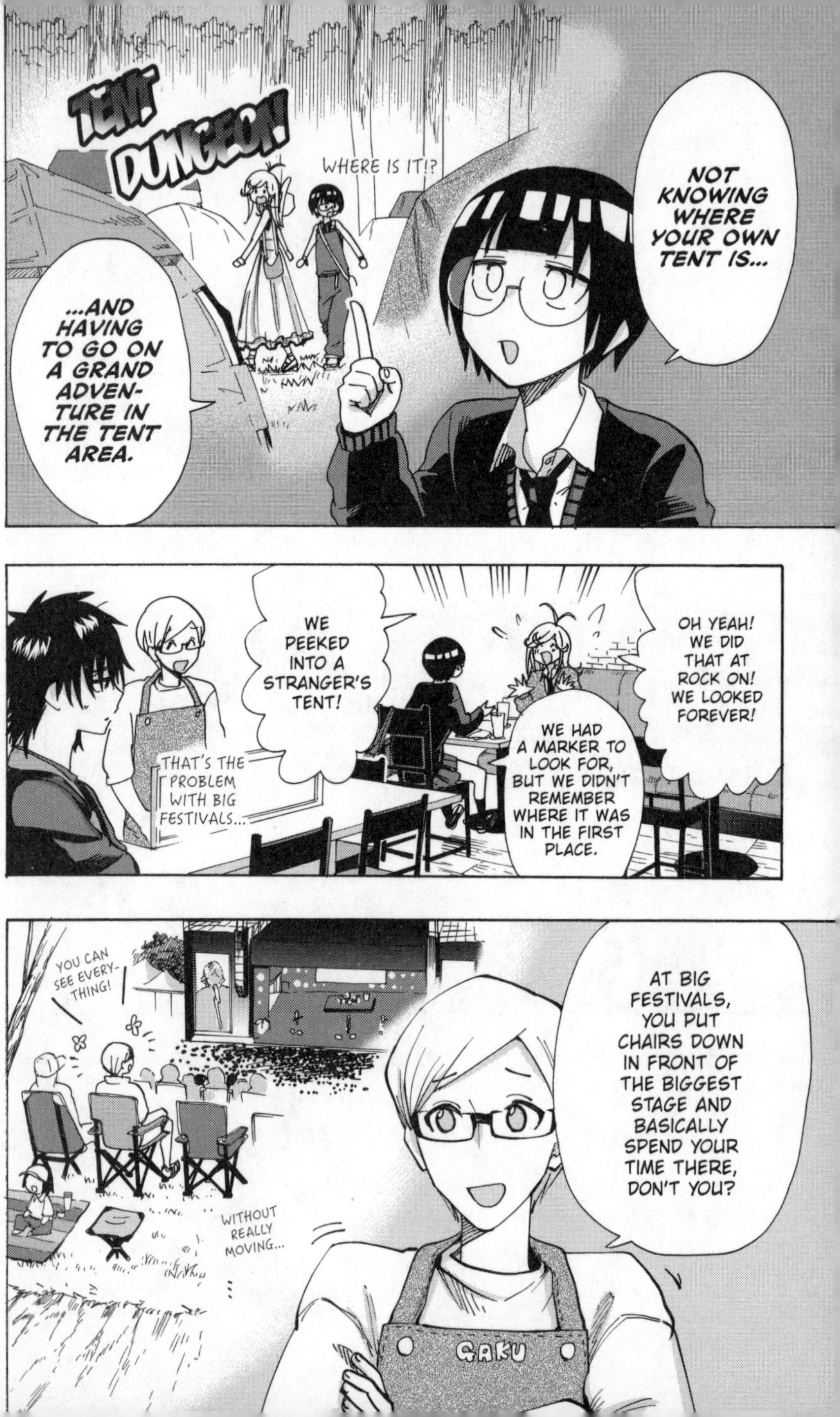
NOT KNOWING WHERE YOUR OWN TENT IS...
WHERE IS IT!?
TENT DUNGEON!
...AND HAVING TO GO ON A GRAND ADVENTURE IN THE TENT AREA.
OH YEAH! WE DID THAT AT ROCK ON! WE LOOKED FOREVER!
WE HAD A MARKER TO LOOK FOR, BUT WE DIDN'T REMEMBER WHERE IT WAS IN THE FIRST PLACE.
WE PEEKED INTO A STRANGER'S TENT!
THAT'S THE PROBLEM WITH BIG FESTIVALS...
AT BIG FESTIVALS, YOU PUT CHAIRS DOWN IN FRONT OF THE BIGGEST STAGE AND BASICALLY SPEND YOUR TIME THERE, DON'T YOU?
WITHOUT REALLY MOVING...
YOU CAN SEE EVERYTHING!
GAKU

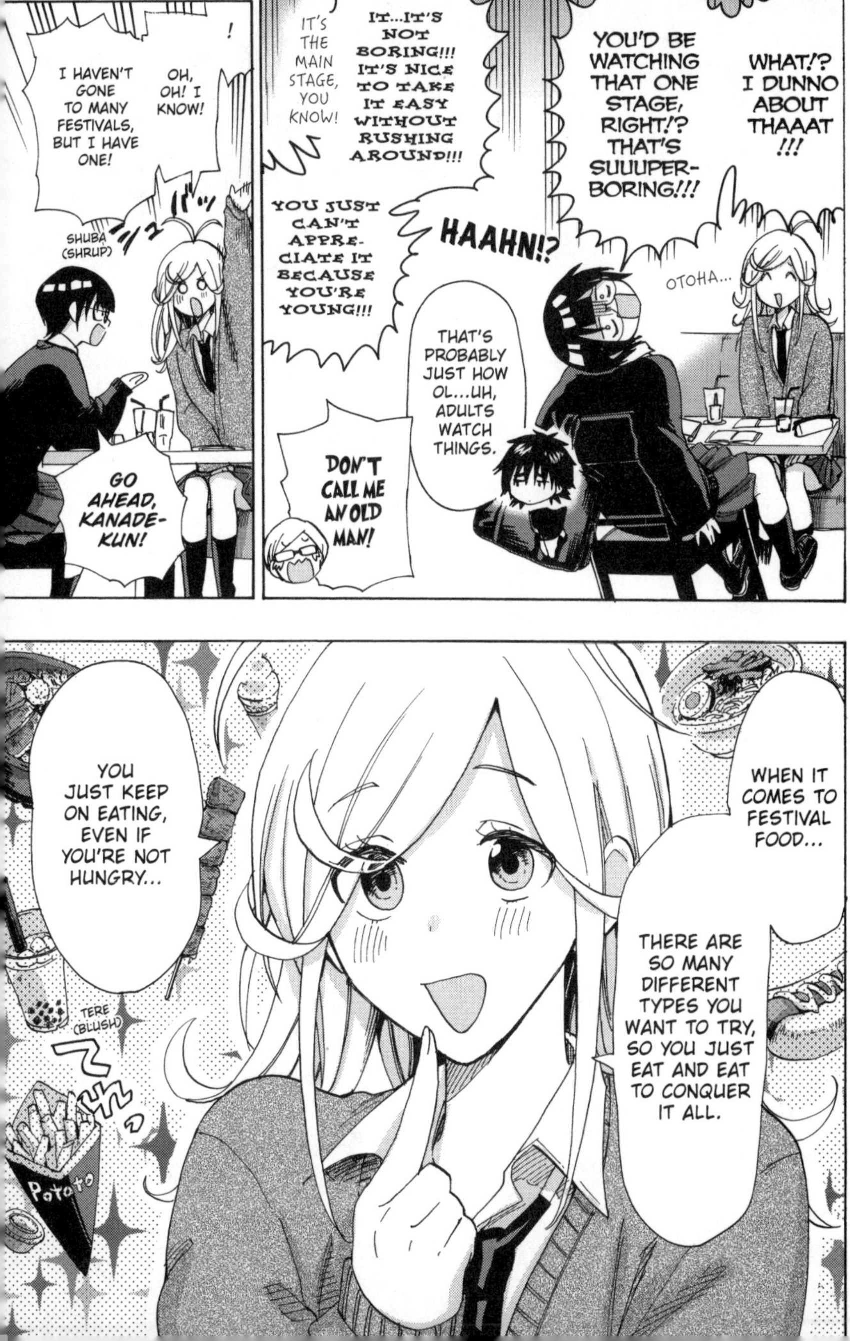
WHAT!? I DUNNO ABOUT THAAAT!!!
YOU'D BE WATCHING THAT ONE STAGE, RIGHT!? THAT'S SUUUPER-BORING!!!
OTOHA...
HAAHN!?
IT...IT'S NOT BORING!!! IT'S NICE TO TAKE IT EASY WITHOUT RUSHING AROUND!!!
IT'S THE MAIN STAGE, YOU KNOW!
YOU JUST CAN'T APPRECIATE IT BECAUSE YOU'RE YOUNG!!!
THAT'S PROBABLY JUST HOW OL...UH, ADULTS WATCH THINGS.
DON'T CALL ME AN OLD MAN!
!
OH, OH! I KNOW!
I HAVEN'T GONE TO MANY FESTIVALS, BUT I HAVE ONE!
SHUBA (SHRUP)
GO AHEAD, KANADE-KUN!
WHEN IT COMES TO FESTIVAL FOOD...
THERE ARE SO MANY DIFFERENT TYPES YOU WANT TO TRY, SO YOU JUST EAT AND EAT TO CONQUER IT ALL.
YOU JUST KEEP ON EATING, EVEN IF YOU'RE NOT HUNGRY...
TERE (BLUSH)
Potato

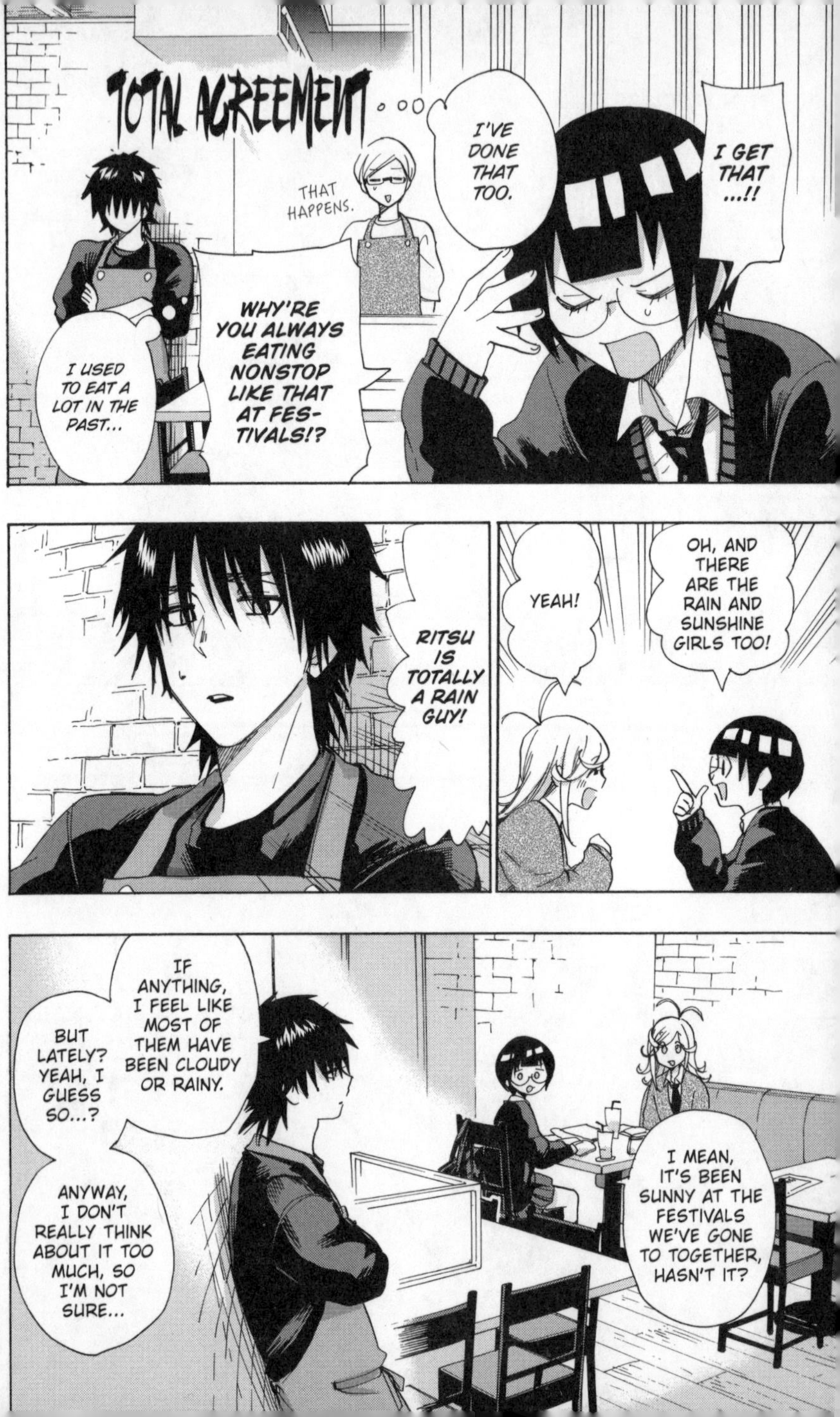
I GET THAT ...!!
I'VE DONE THAT TOO.
TOTAL AGREEMENT! . . .
THAT HAPPENS.
WHY'RE YOU ALWAYS EATING NONSTOP LIKE THAT AT FES-TIVALS!?
I USED TO EAT A LOT IN THE PAST...
OH, AND THERE ARE THE RAIN AND SUNSHINE GIRLS TOO!
YEAH!
RITSU IS TOTALLY A RAIN GUY!
I MEAN, IT'S BEEN SUNNY AT THE FESTIVALS WE'VE GONE TO TOGETHER, HASN'T IT?
IF ANYTHING, I FEEL LIKE MOST OF THEM HAVE BEEN CLOUDY OR RAINY.
BUT LATELY? YEAH, I GUESS SO...?
ANYWAY, I DON'T REALLY THINK ABOUT IT TOO MUCH, SO I'M NOT SURE...

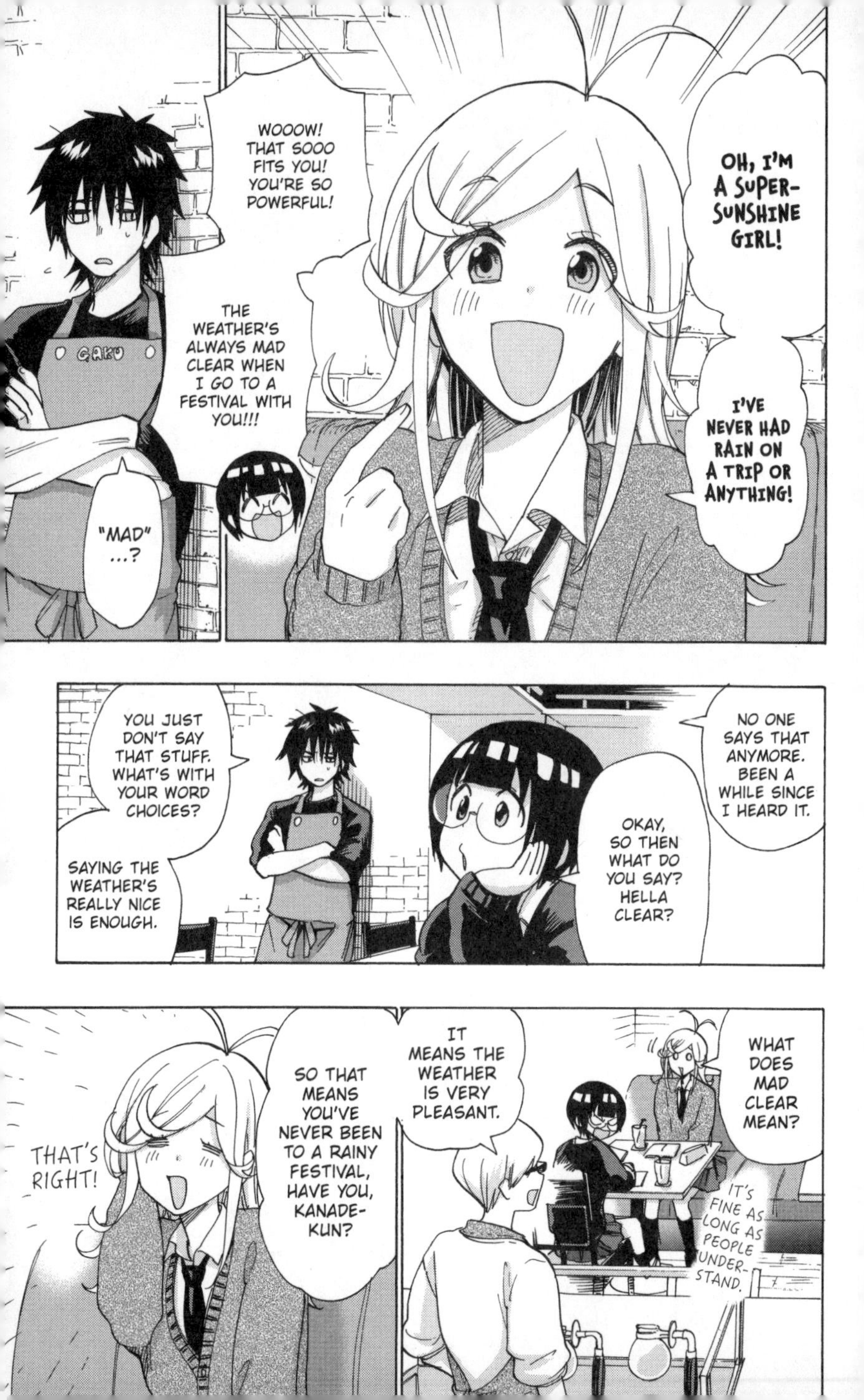
OH, I'M A SUPER-SUNSHINE GIRL!
I'VE NEVER HAD RAIN ON A TRIP OR ANYTHING!
WOOOW! THAT SOOO FITS YOU! YOU'RE SO POWERFUL!
THE WEATHER'S ALWAYS MAD CLEAR WHEN I GO TO A FESTIVAL WITH YOU!!!
GAKU
"MAD" ...?
NO ONE SAYS THAT ANYMORE. BEEN A WHILE SINCE I HEARD IT.
OKAY, SO THEN WHAT DO YOU SAY? HELLA CLEAR?
YOU JUST DON'T SAY THAT STUFF. WHAT'S WITH YOUR WORD CHOICES?
SAYING THE WEATHER'S REALLY NICE IS ENOUGH.
WHAT DOES MAD CLEAR MEAN?
IT'S FINE AS LONG AS PEOPLE UNDERSTAND.
IT MEANS THE WEATHER IS VERY PLEASANT.
SO THAT MEANS YOU'VE NEVER BEEN TO A RAINY FESTIVAL, HAVE YOU, KANADE-KUN?
THAT'S RIGHT!

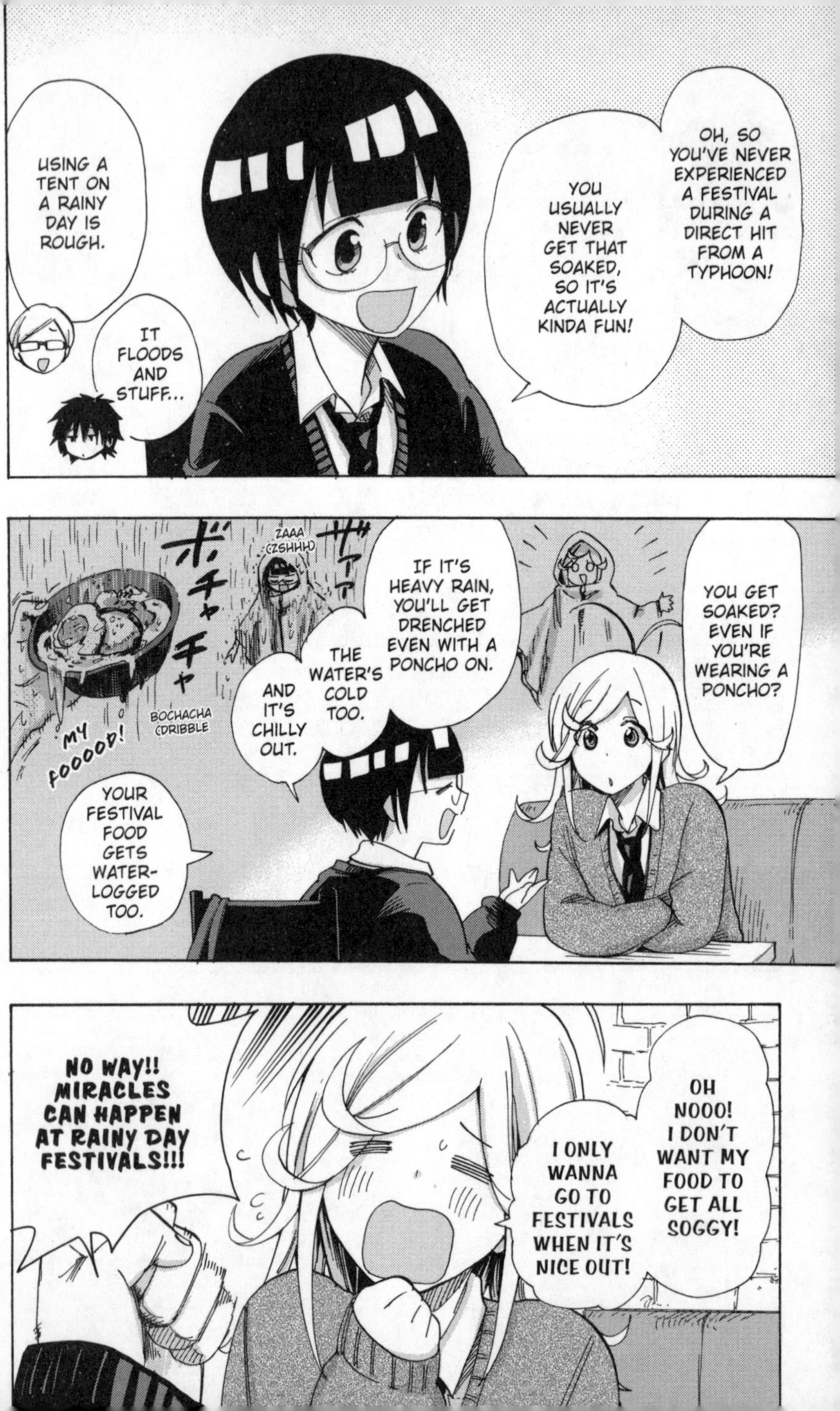
OH, SO YOU'VE NEVER EXPERIENCED A FESTIVAL DURING A DIRECT HIT FROM A TYPHOON!
YOU USUALLY NEVER GET THAT SOAKED, SO IT'S ACTUALLY KINDA FUN!
USING A TENT ON A RAINY DAY IS ROUGH.
IT FLOODS AND STUFF...
YOU GET SOAKED? EVEN IF YOU'RE WEARING A PONCHO?
IF IT'S HEAVY RAIN, YOU'LL GET DRENCHED EVEN WITH A PONCHO ON.
THE WATER'S COLD TOO.
AND IT'S CHILLY OUT.
ZAAA (ZSHHH)
BOCHACHA (DRIBBLE)
MY FOOOOD!
YOUR FESTIVAL FOOD GETS WATER-LOGGED TOO.
OH NOOO! I DON'T WANT MY FOOD TO GET ALL SOGGY!
I ONLY WANNA GO TO FESTIVALS WHEN IT'S NICE OUT!
NO WAY!! MIRACLES CAN HAPPEN AT RAINY DAY FESTIVALS!!!

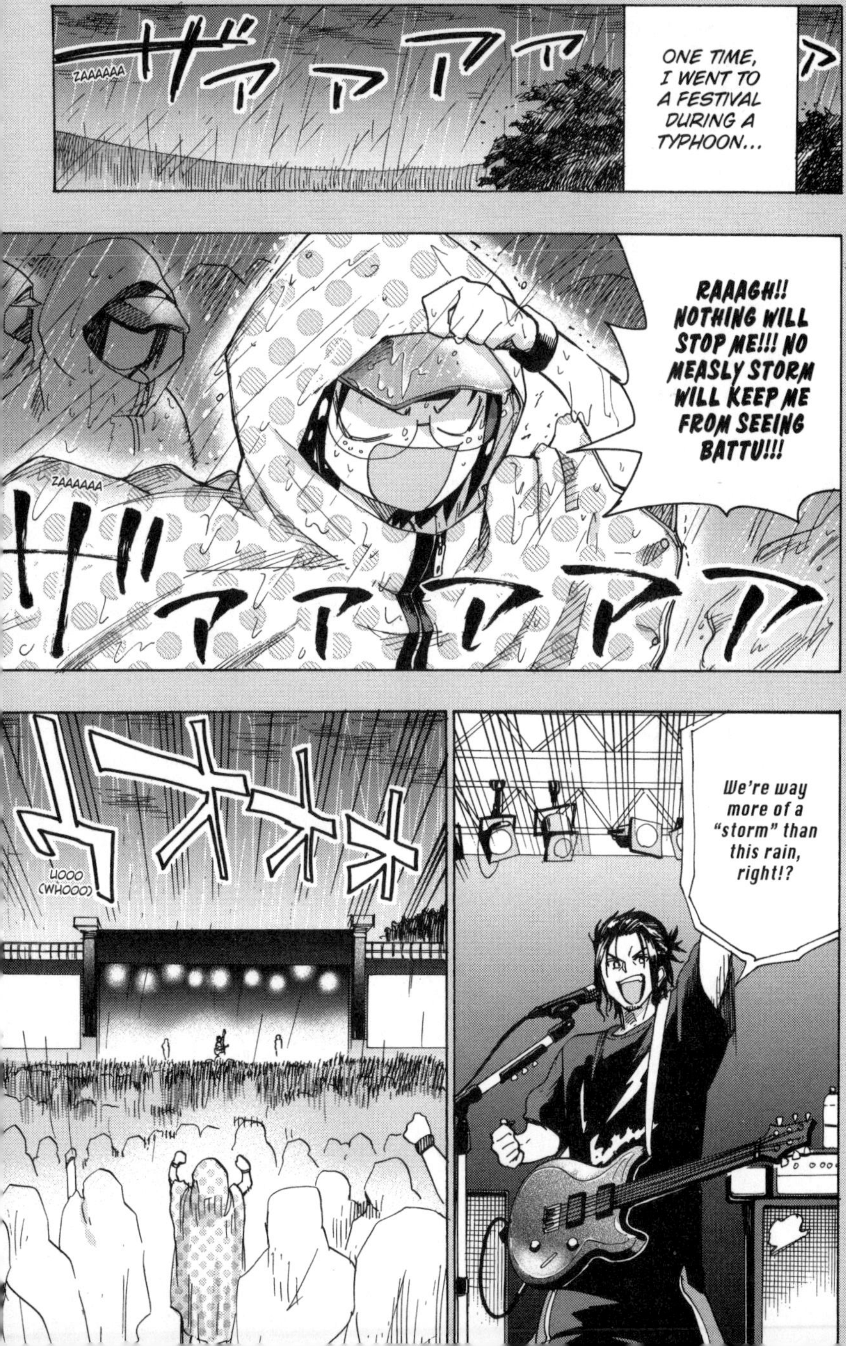
ONE TIME, I WENT TO A FESTIVAL DURING A TYPHOON…
ZAAAAAA
RAAAGH!! NOTHING WILL STOP ME!!! NO MEASLY STORM WILL KEEP ME FROM SEEING BATTU!!!
ZAAAAAA
We're way more of a "storm" than this rain, right!?
UOOO (WHOOO)

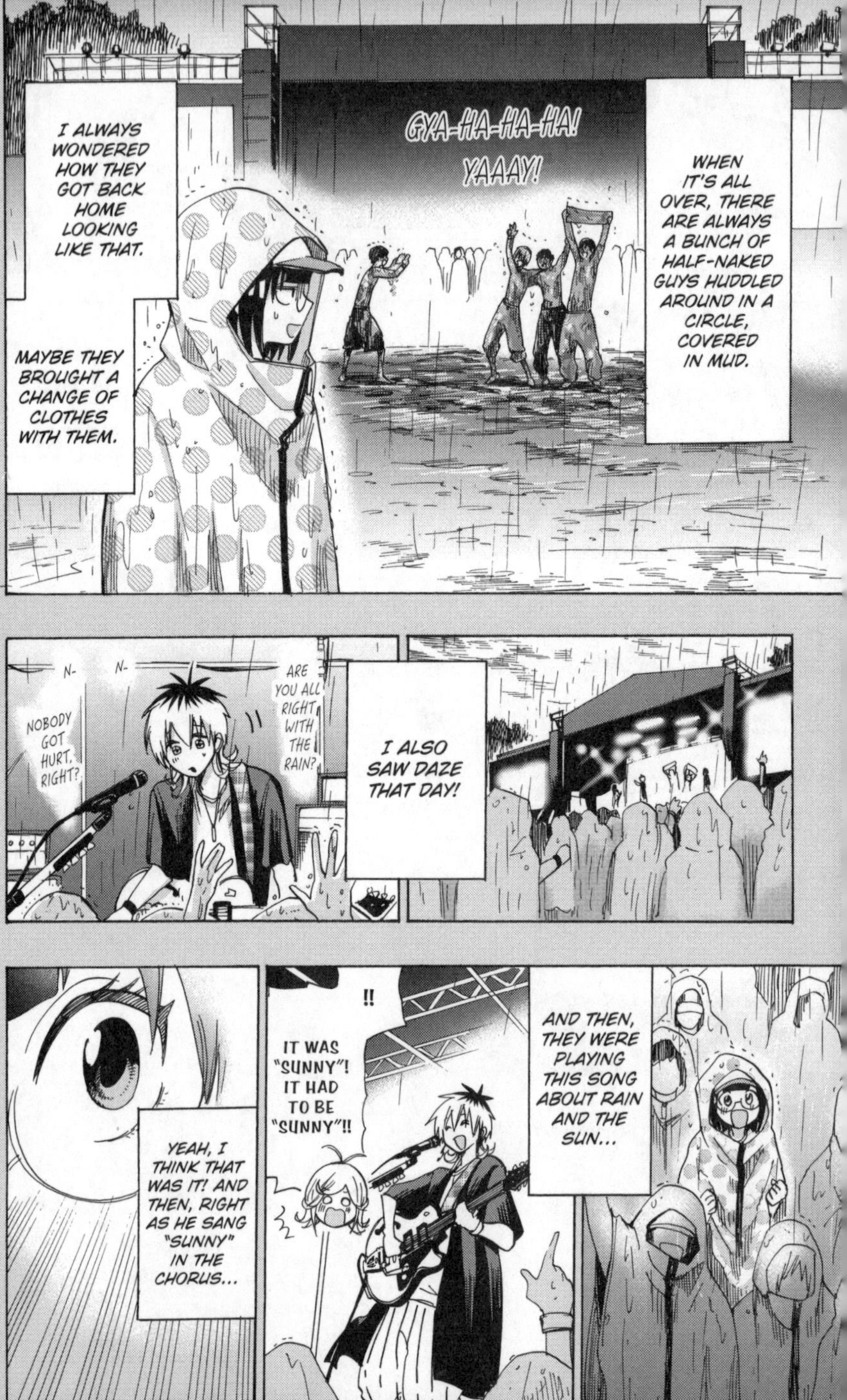
WHEN IT'S ALL OVER, THERE ARE ALWAYS A BUNCH OF HALF-NAKED GUYS HUDDLED AROUND IN A CIRCLE, COVERED IN MUD.
GYA-HA-HA-HA!
YAAAY!
I ALWAYS WONDERED HOW THEY GOT BACK HOME LOOKING LIKE THAT.
MAYBE THEY BROUGHT A CHANGE OF CLOTHES WITH THEM.
I ALSO SAW DAZE THAT DAY!
ARE YOU ALL RIGHT WITH THE RAIN?
N-
N-
NOBODY GOT HURT, RIGHT?
AND THEN, THEY WERE PLAYING THIS SONG ABOUT RAIN AND THE SUN...
!!
IT WAS "SUNNY"! IT HAD TO BE "SUNNY"!!
YEAH, I THINK THAT WAS IT! AND THEN, RIGHT AS HE SANG "SUNNY" IN THE CHORUS...

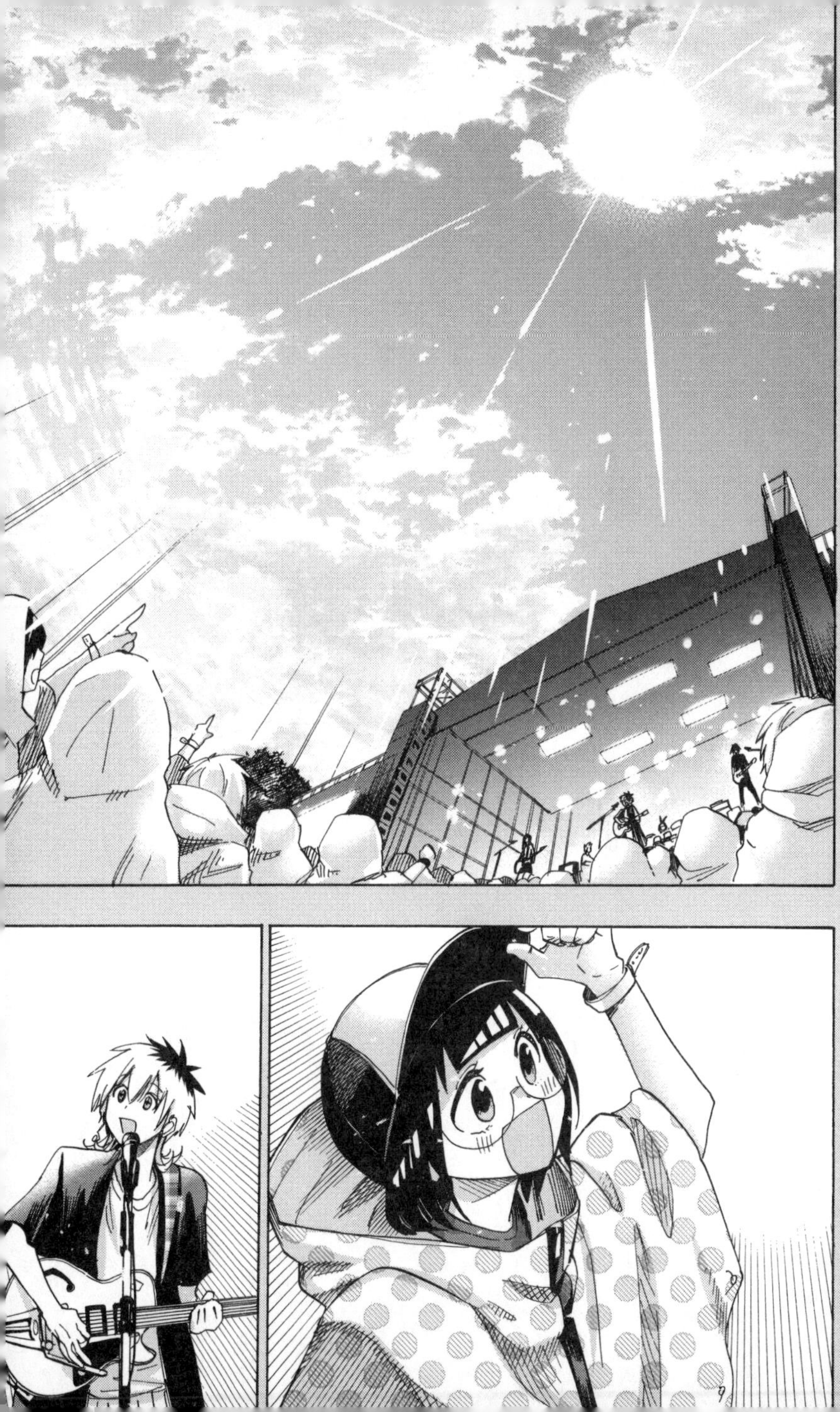

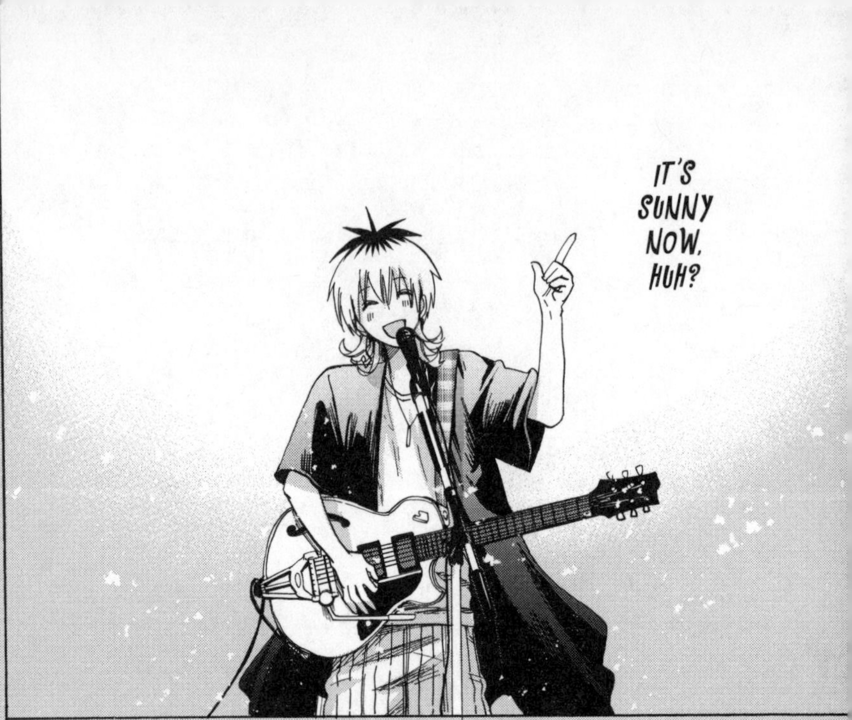
IT'S SUNNY NOW, HUH?
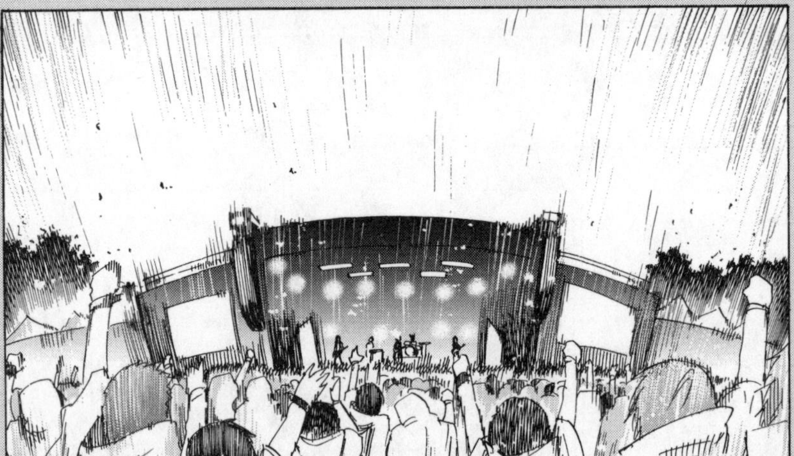

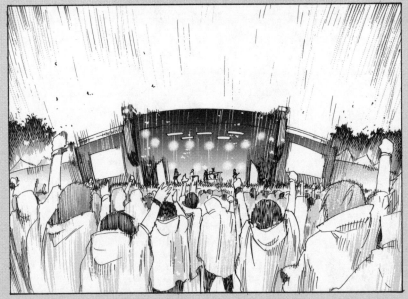

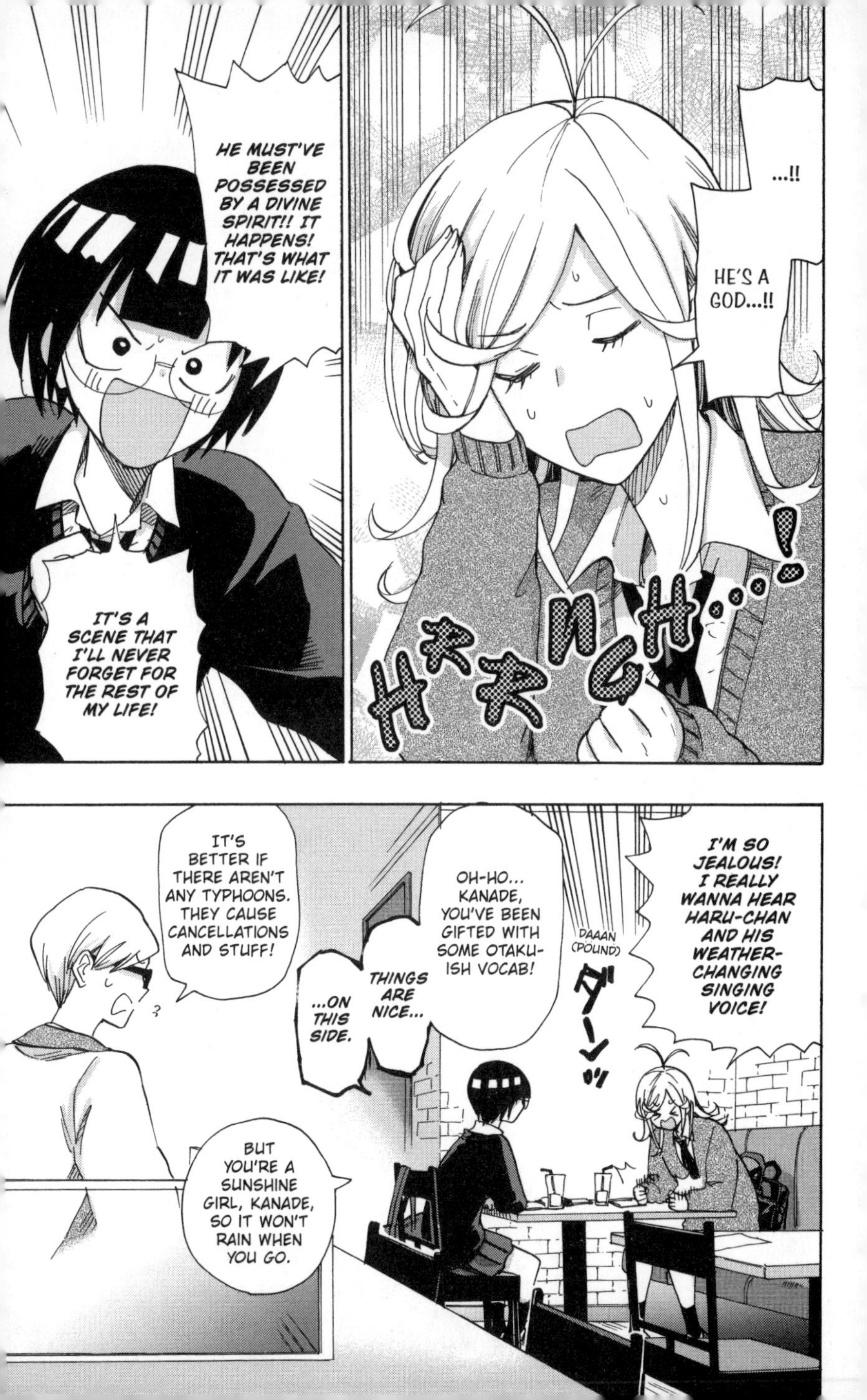
...!!
HE'S A GOD...!!
HNNGH..!
HE MUST'VE BEEN POSSESSED BY A DIVINE SPIRIT!! IT HAPPENS! THAT'S WHAT IT WAS LIKE!
IT'S A SCENE THAT I'LL NEVER FORGET FOR THE REST OF MY LIFE!
I'M SO JEALOUS! I REALLY WANNA HEAR HARU-CHAN AND HIS WEATHER-CHANGING SINGING VOICE!
DAAAN (POUND)
OH-HO... KANADE, YOU'VE BEEN GIFTED WITH SOME OTAKU-ISH VOCAB!
THINGS ARE NICE...
...ON THIS SIDE.
IT'S BETTER IF THERE AREN'T ANY TYPHOONS. THEY CAUSE CANCELLATIONS AND STUFF!
?
BUT YOU'RE A SUNSHINE GIRL, KANADE, SO IT WON'T RAIN WHEN YOU GO.

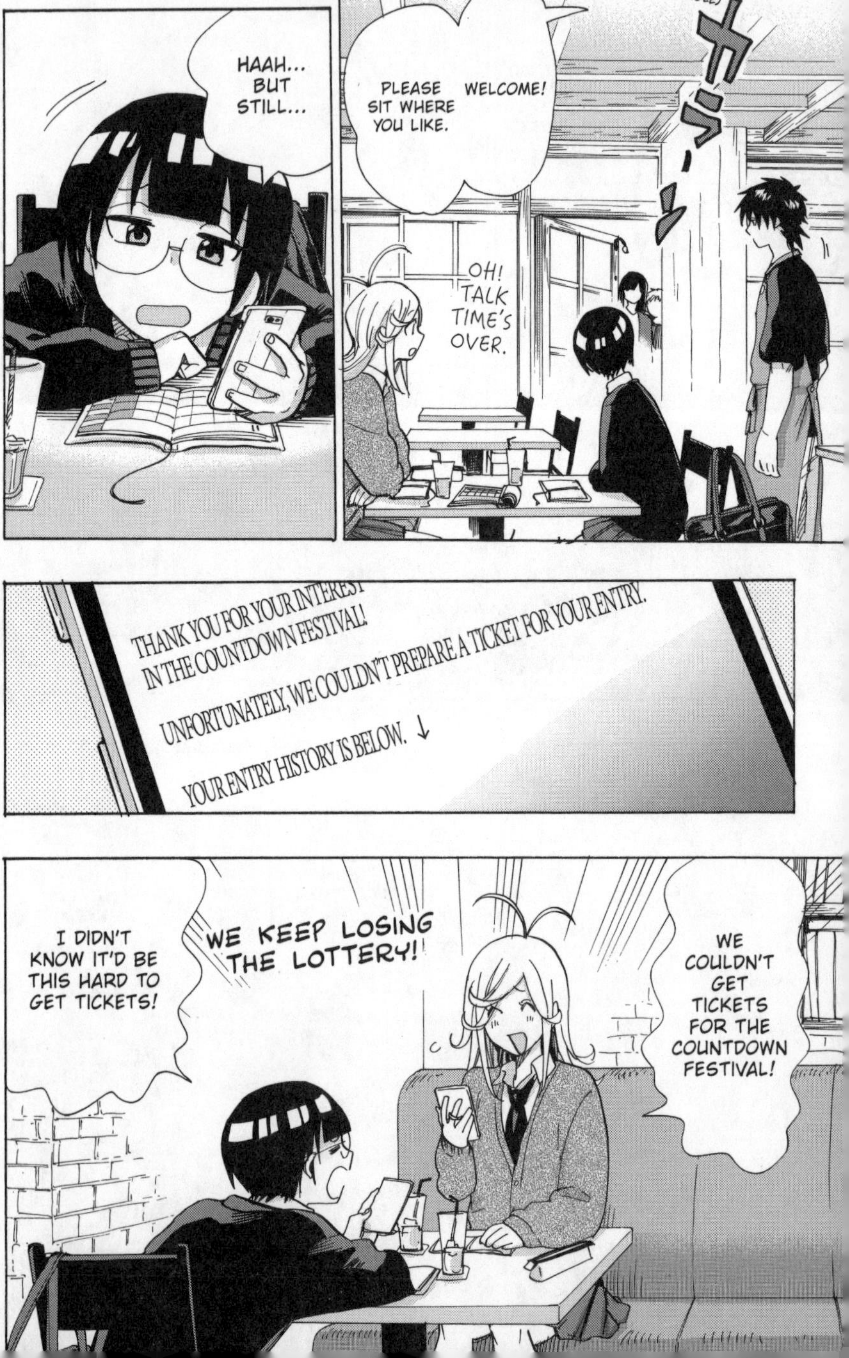
KARAAN (JANGLE)
WELCOME!
PLEASE SIT WHERE YOU LIKE.
OH! TALK TIME'S OVER.
HAAH... BUT STILL...
THANK YOU FOR YOUR INTEREST IN THE COUNTDOWN FESTIVAL!
UNFORTUNATELY, WE COULDN'T PREPARE A TICKET FOR YOUR ENTRY.
YOUR ENTRY HISTORY IS BELOW. ↓
WE COULDN'T GET TICKETS FOR THE COUNTDOWN FESTIVAL!
WE KEEP LOSING THE LOTTERY!
I DIDN'T KNOW IT'D BE THIS HARD TO GET TICKETS!

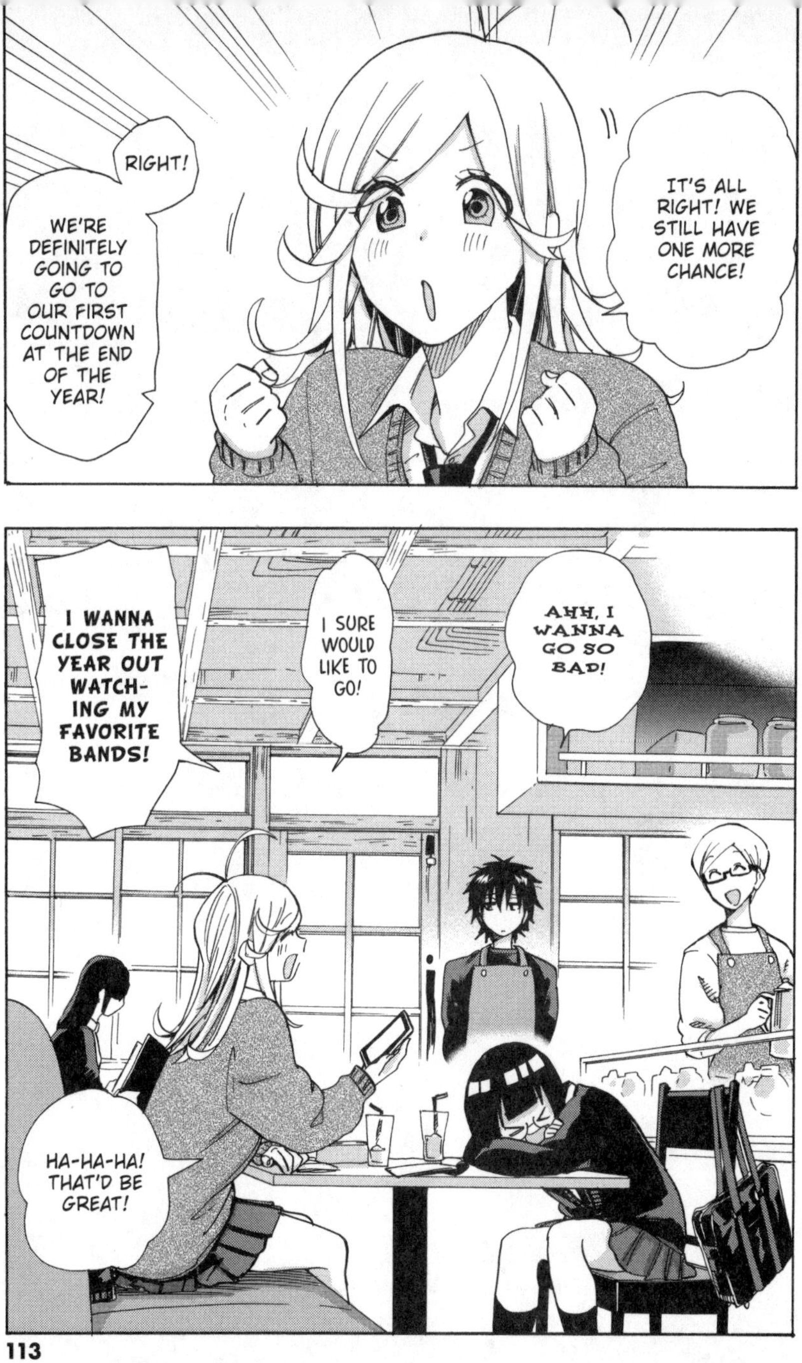
IT'S ALL RIGHT! WE STILL HAVE ONE MORE CHANCE!
RIGHT!
WE'RE DEFINITELY GOING TO GO TO OUR FIRST COUNTDOWN AT THE END OF THE YEAR!
AHH, I WANNA GO SO BAD!
I SURE WOULD LIKE TO GO!
I WANNA CLOSE THE YEAR OUT WATCHING MY FAVORITE BANDS!
HA-HA-HA! THAT'D BE GREAT!

Days on Fes

FES 17.5

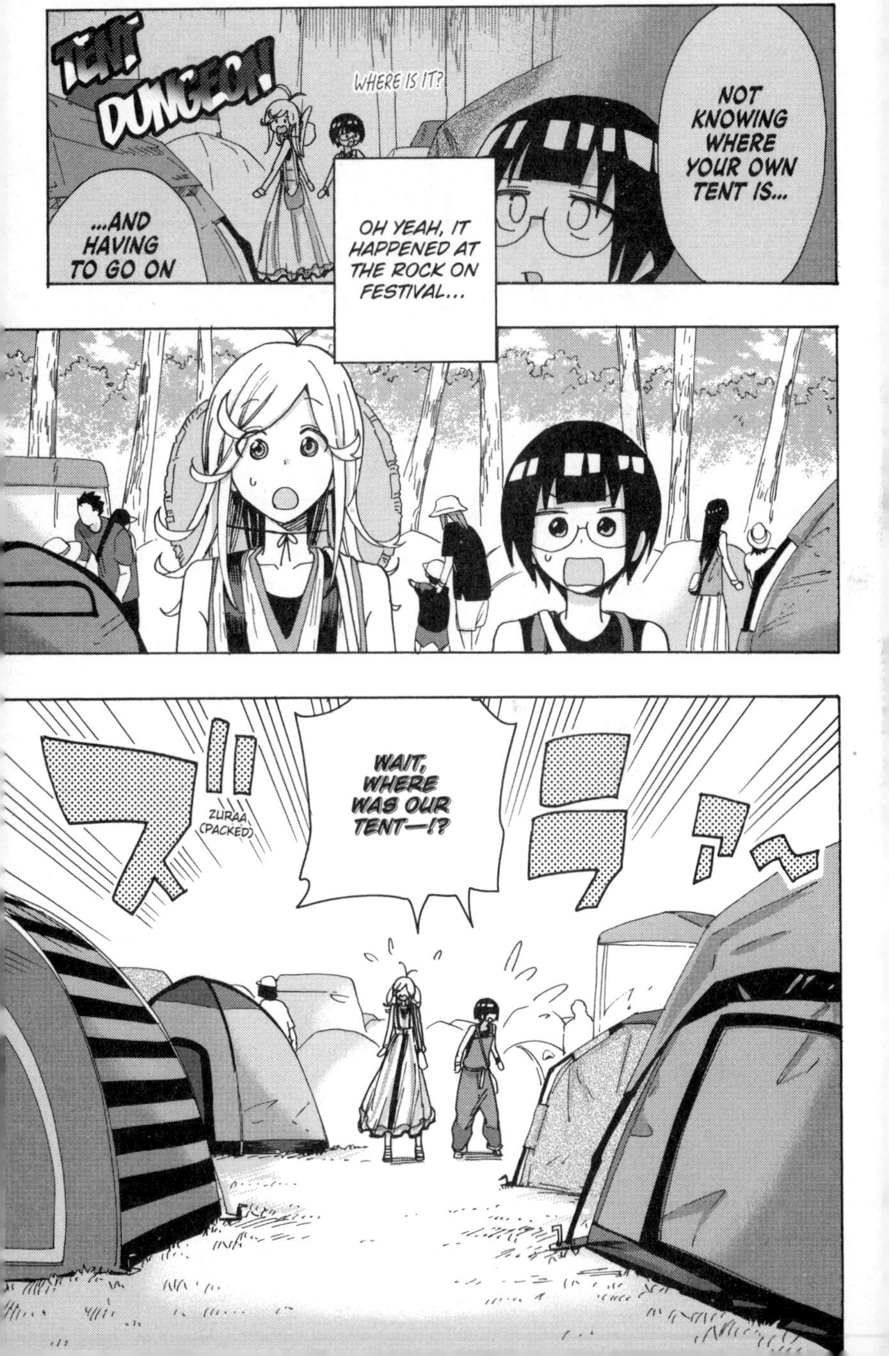
NOT KNOWING WHERE YOUR OWN TENT IS...
WHERE IS IT?
TENT DUNGEON!
...AND HAVING TO GO ON
OH YEAH, IT HAPPENED AT THE ROCK ON FESTIVAL...
WAIT, WHERE WAS OUR TENT—!?
ZURAA (PACKED)

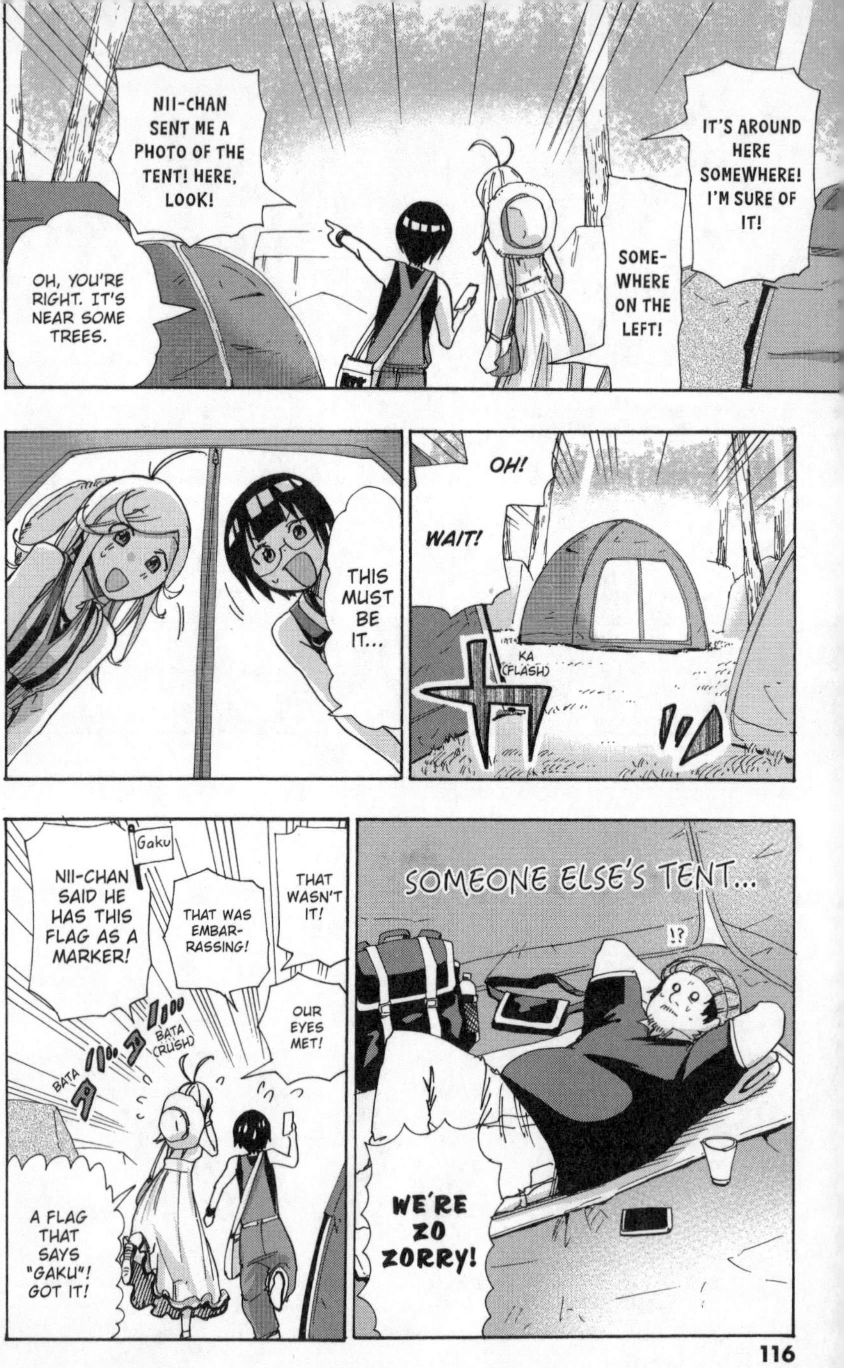
IT'S AROUND HERE SOMEWHERE! I'M SURE OF IT!
SOME-WHERE ON THE LEFT!
NII-CHAN SENT ME A PHOTO OF THE TENT! HERE, LOOK!
OH, YOU'RE RIGHT. IT'S NEAR SOME TREES.
OH!
WAIT!
KA (FLASH)
THIS MUST BE IT...
SOMEONE ELSE'S TENT...
!?
WE'RE ZO ZORRY!
THAT WASN'T IT!
THAT WAS EMBARRASSING!
Gaku
NII-CHAN SAID HE HAS THIS FLAG AS A MARKER!
OUR EYES MET!
BATA (RUSH)
BATA
A FLAG THAT SAYS "GAKU"! GOT IT!

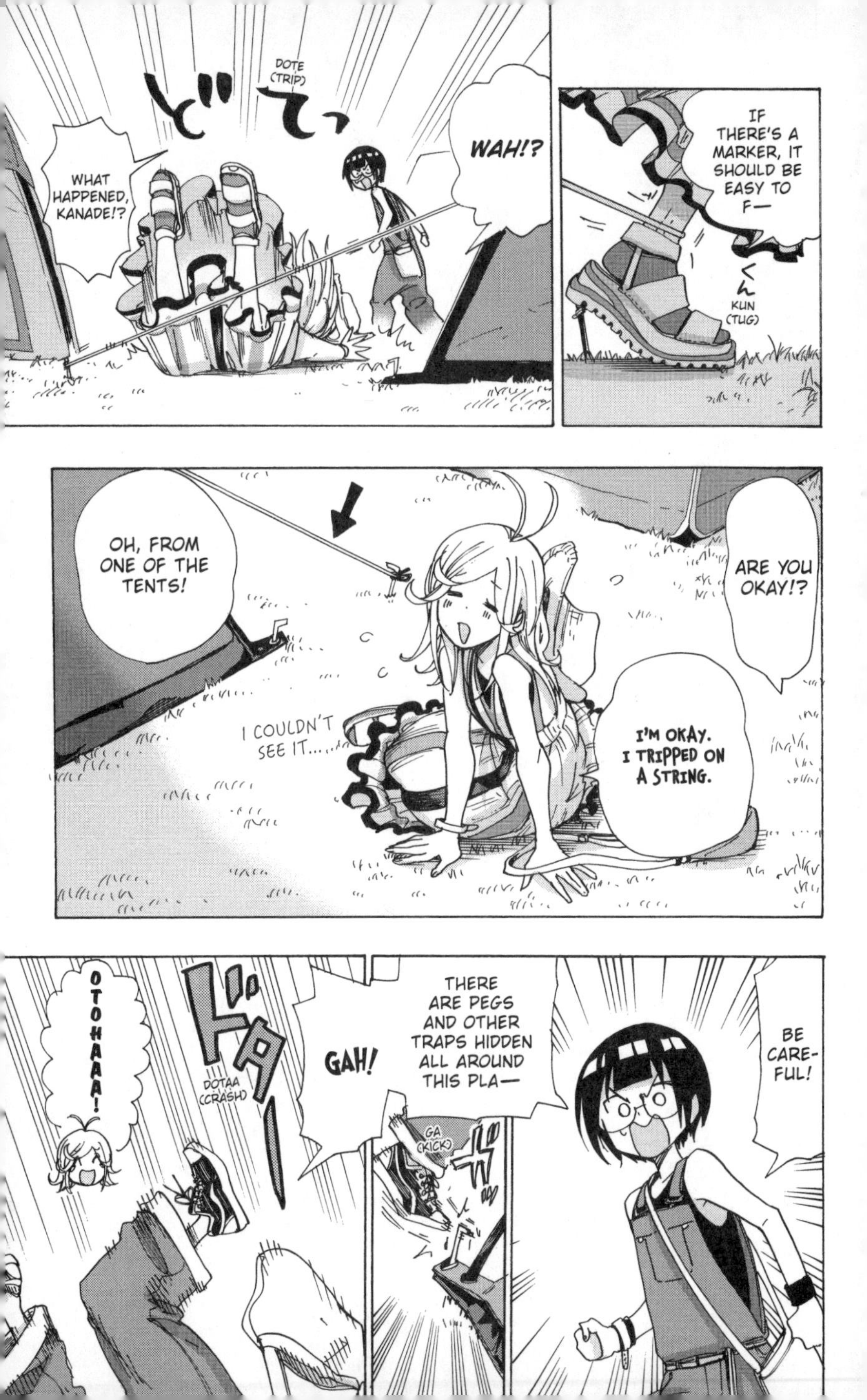
IF THERE'S A MARKER, IT SHOULD BE EASY TO F—
くん
KUN (TUG)
WAH!?
どてっ
DOTE (TRIP)
WHAT HAPPENED, KANADE!?
ARE YOU OKAY!?
I'M OKAY. I TRIPPED ON A STRING.
OH, FROM ONE OF THE TENTS!
I COULDN'T SEE IT......
BE CARE-FUL!
THERE ARE PEGS AND OTHER TRAPS HIDDEN ALL AROUND THIS PLA—
GA (KICK)
GAH!
ドター
DOTAA (CRASH)
OTOHAAA!

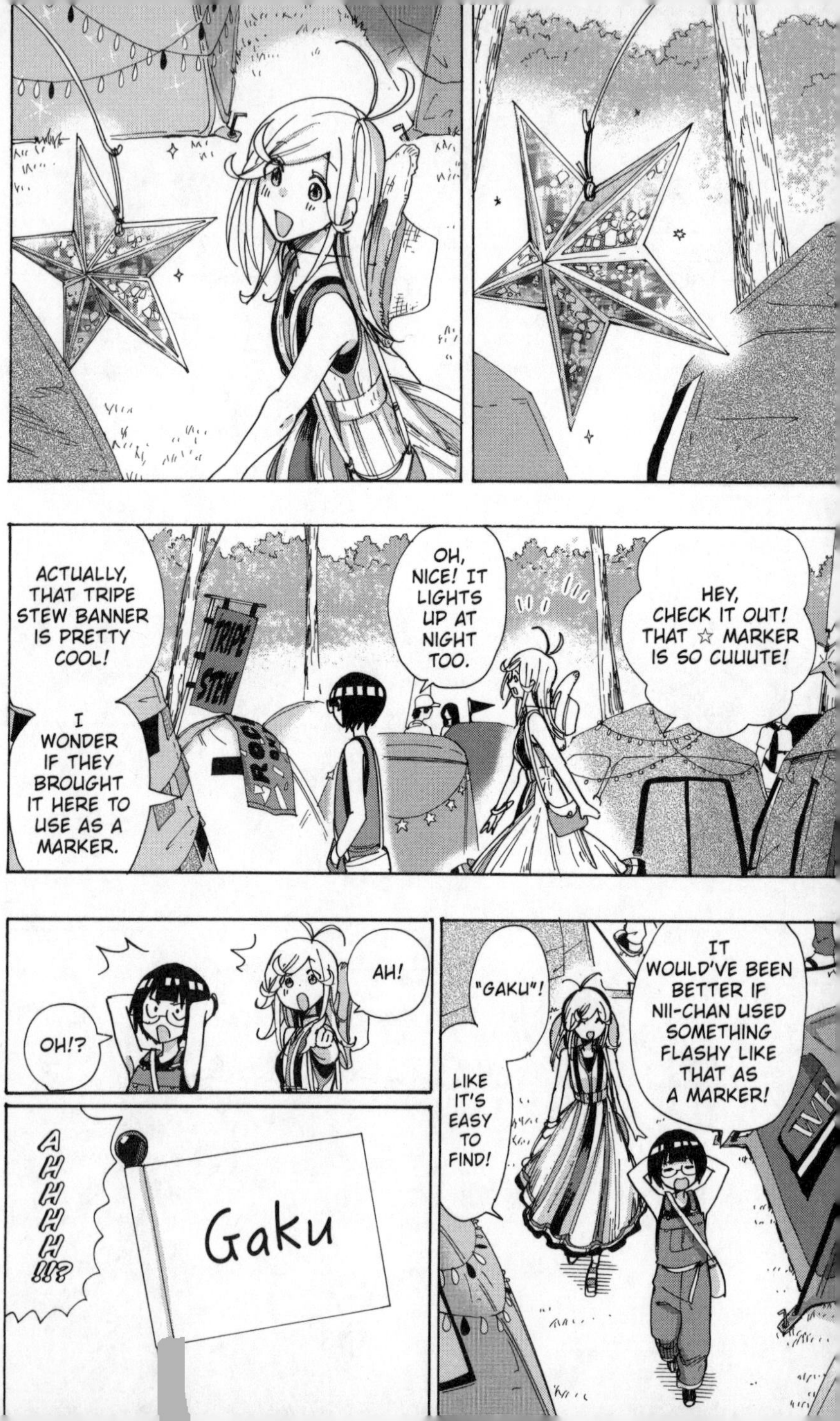
HEY, CHECK IT OUT! THAT ☆ MARKER IS SO CUUUTE!
OH, NICE! IT LIGHTS UP AT NIGHT TOO.
TRIPE STEW
ACTUALLY, THAT TRIPE STEW BANNER IS PRETTY COOL!
I WONDER IF THEY BROUGHT IT HERE TO USE AS A MARKER.
IT WOULD'VE BEEN BETTER IF NII-CHAN USED SOMETHING FLASHY LIKE THAT AS A MARKER!
"GAKU"!
LIKE IT'S EASY TO FIND!
AH!
OH!?
Gaku
AHHHHH!!?

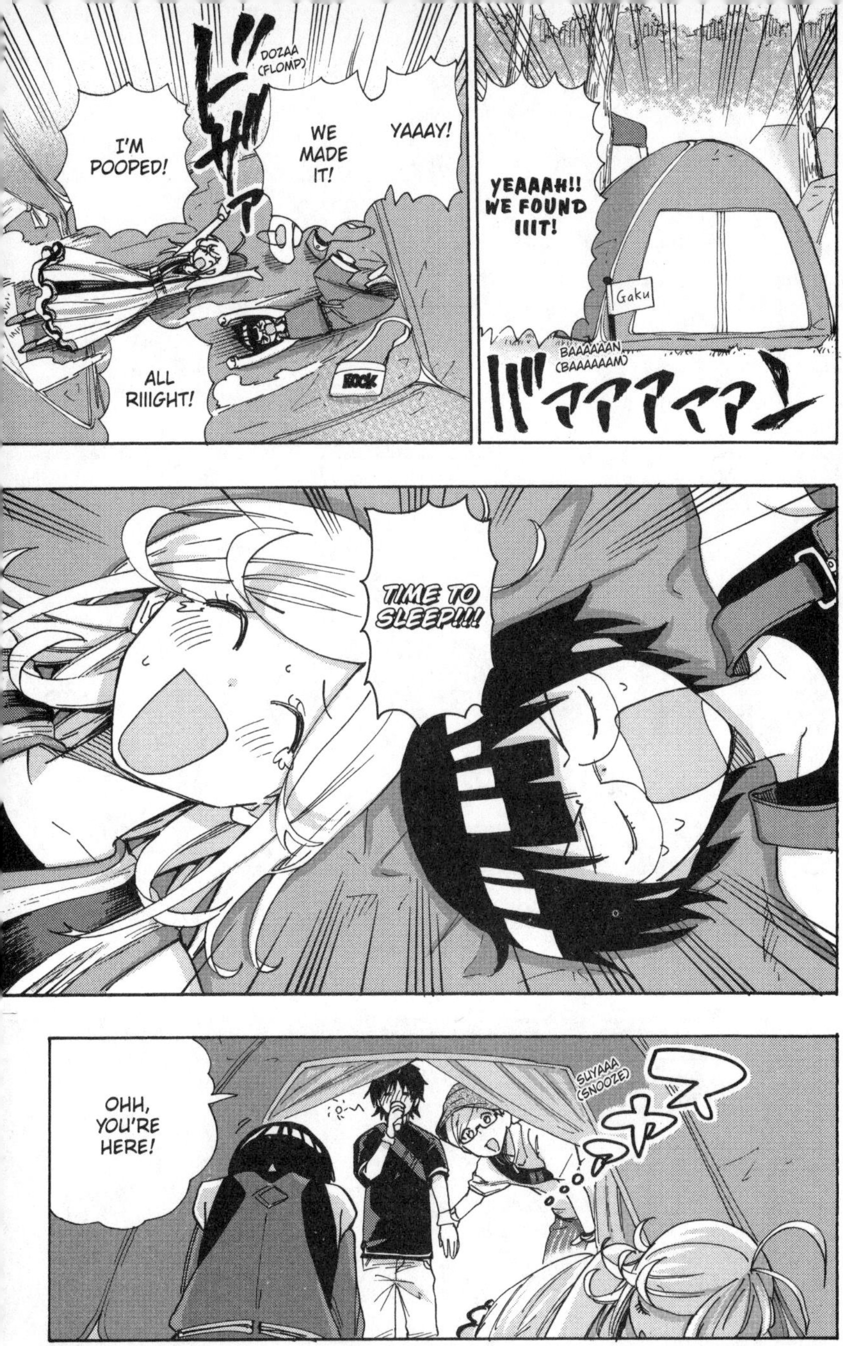
YEAAAH!! WE FOUND IIIT!
Gaku
BAAAAAAN (BAAAAAAM)
YAAAY!
WE MADE IT!
DOZAA (FLOMP)
I'M POOPED!
ROCK
ALL RIIIGHT!
TIME TO SLEEP!!!
SUYAAA (SNOOZE)
OHH, YOU'RE HERE!

Days on Fes

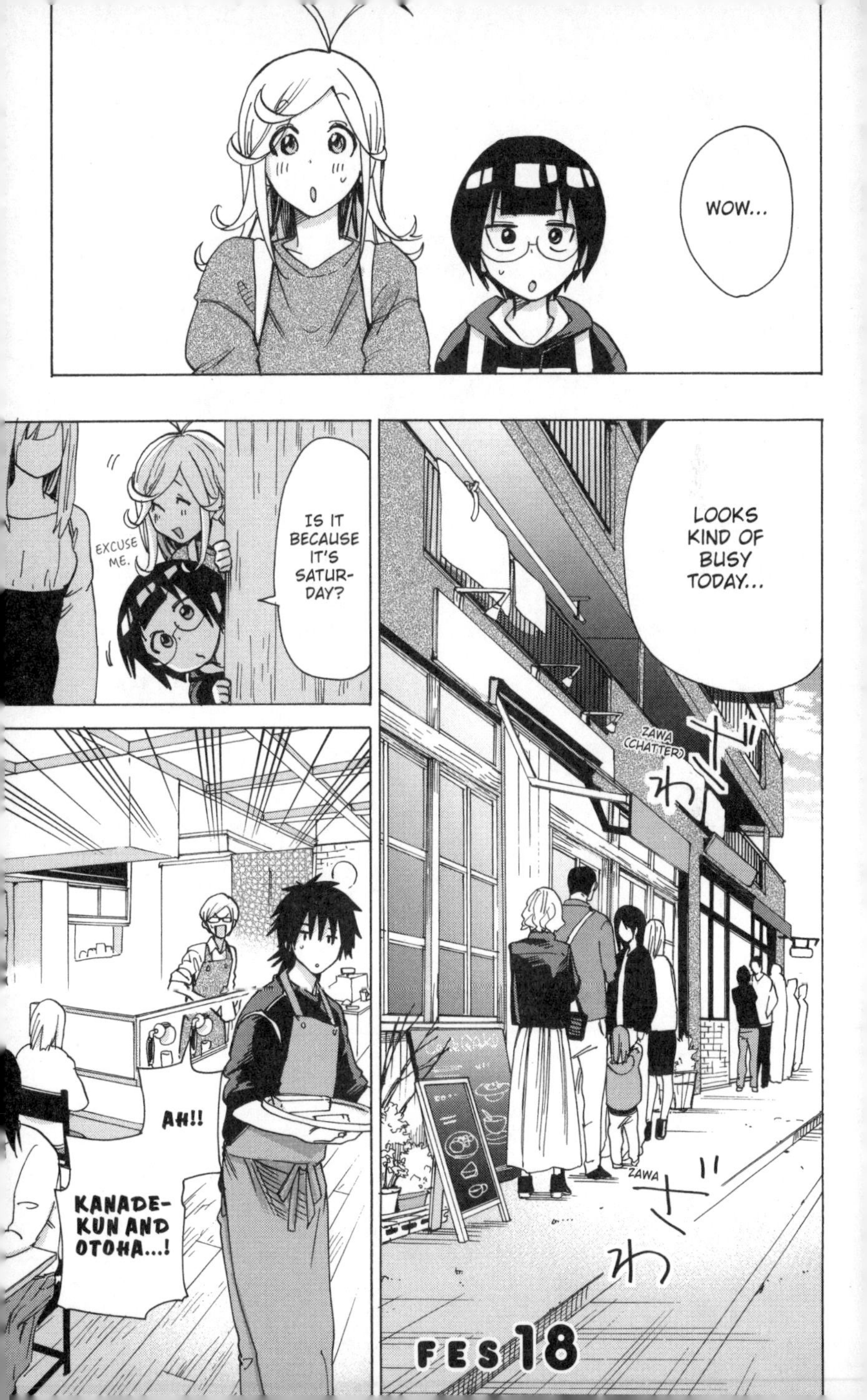
WOW...
LOOKS KIND OF BUSY TODAY...
ZAWA (CHATTER)
ZAWA
FES 18
IS IT BECAUSE IT'S SATUR-DAY?
EXCUSE ME.
AH!!
KANADE-KUN AND OTOHA...!

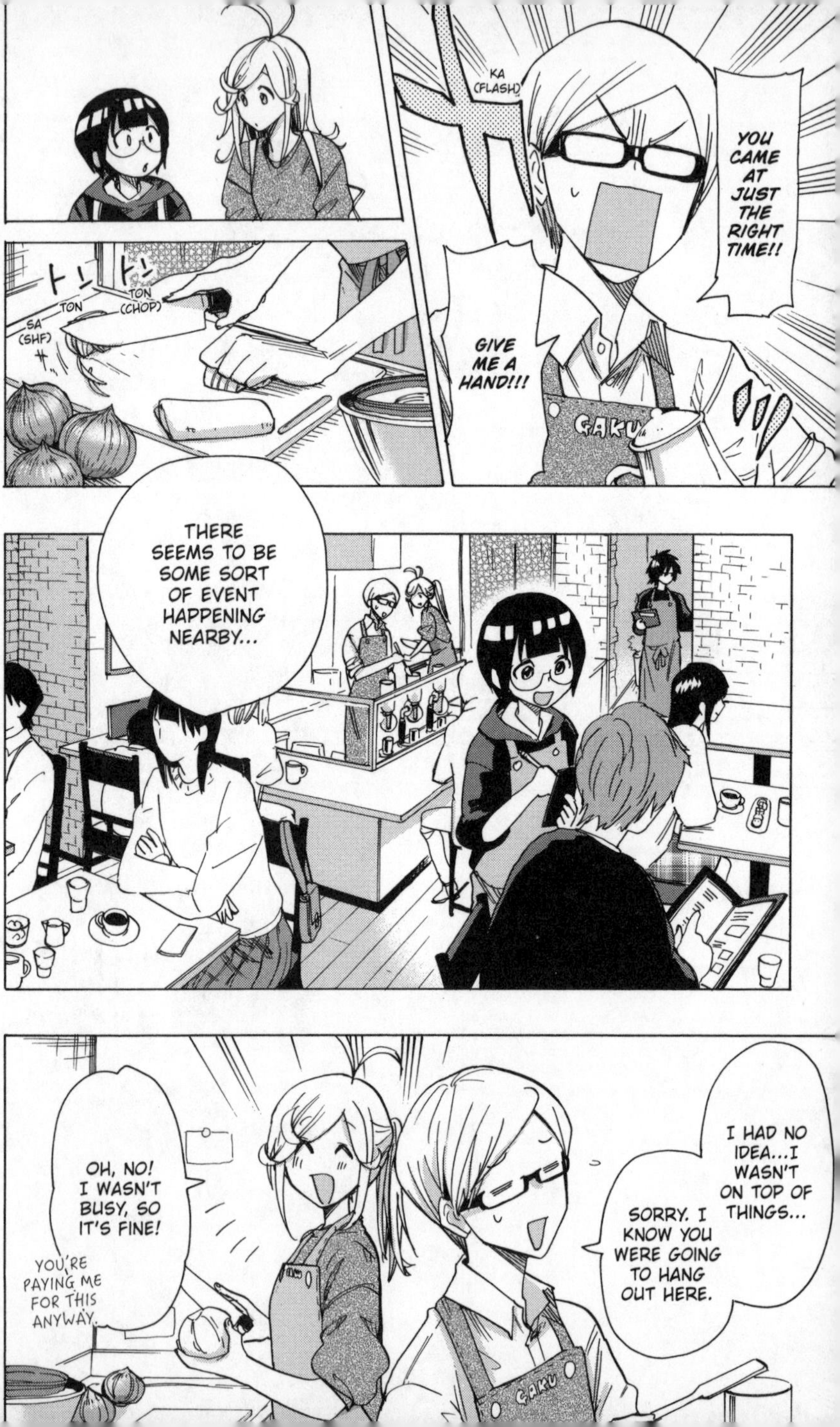
KA (FLASH)
YOU CAME AT JUST THE RIGHT TIME!!
GIVE ME A HAND!!!
TON
TON (CHOP)
SA (SHF)
THERE SEEMS TO BE SOME SORT OF EVENT HAPPENING NEARBY...
I HAD NO IDEA...I WASN'T ON TOP OF THINGS...
SORRY. I KNOW YOU WERE GOING TO HANG OUT HERE.
OH, NO! I WASN'T BUSY, SO IT'S FINE!
YOU'RE PAYING ME FOR THIS ANYWAY.

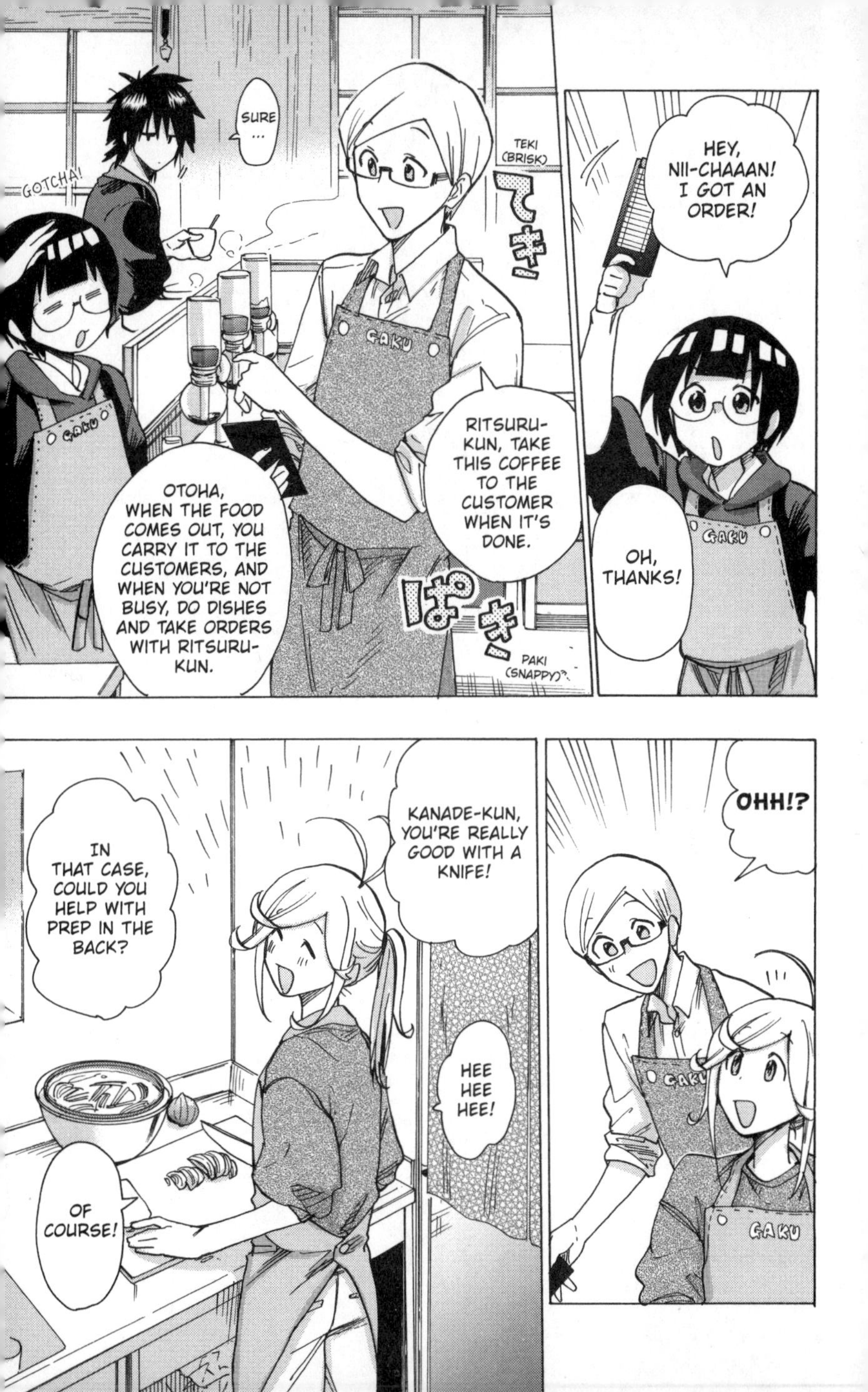
HEY, NII-CHAAAN! I GOT AN ORDER!
OH, THANKS!
TEKI (BRISK)
てき
RITSURU-KUN, TAKE THIS COFFEE TO THE CUSTOMER WHEN IT'S DONE.
SURE ...
GOTCHA!
OTOHA, WHEN THE FOOD COMES OUT, YOU CARRY IT TO THE CUSTOMERS, AND WHEN YOU'RE NOT BUSY, DO DISHES AND TAKE ORDERS WITH RITSURU-KUN.
ぱき
PAKI (SNAPPY)?
OHH!?
KANADE-KUN, YOU'RE REALLY GOOD WITH A KNIFE!
HEE HEE HEE!
IN THAT CASE, COULD YOU HELP WITH PREP IN THE BACK?
OF COURSE!

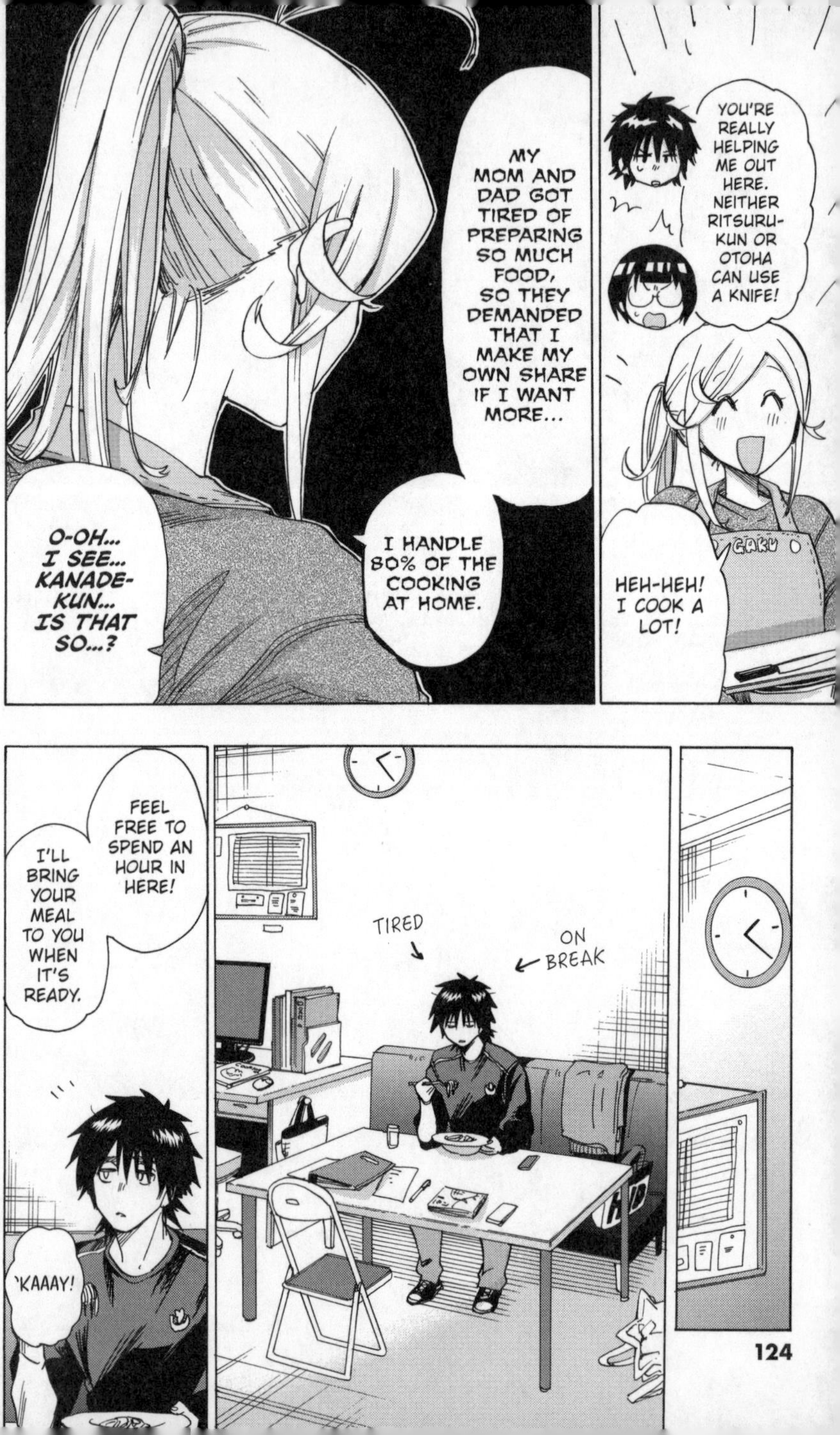
YOU'RE REALLY HELPING ME OUT HERE. NEITHER RITSURU-KUN OR OTOHA CAN USE A KNIFE!
HEH-HEH! I COOK A LOT!
GAKU
MY MOM AND DAD GOT TIRED OF PREPARING SO MUCH FOOD, SO THEY DEMANDED THAT I MAKE MY OWN SHARE IF I WANT MORE...
I HANDLE 80% OF THE COOKING AT HOME.
O-OH... I SEE... KANADE-KUN... IS THAT SO...?
TIRED
ON BREAK
FEEL FREE TO SPEND AN HOUR IN HERE!
I'LL BRING YOUR MEAL TO YOU WHEN IT'S READY.
'KAAAY!

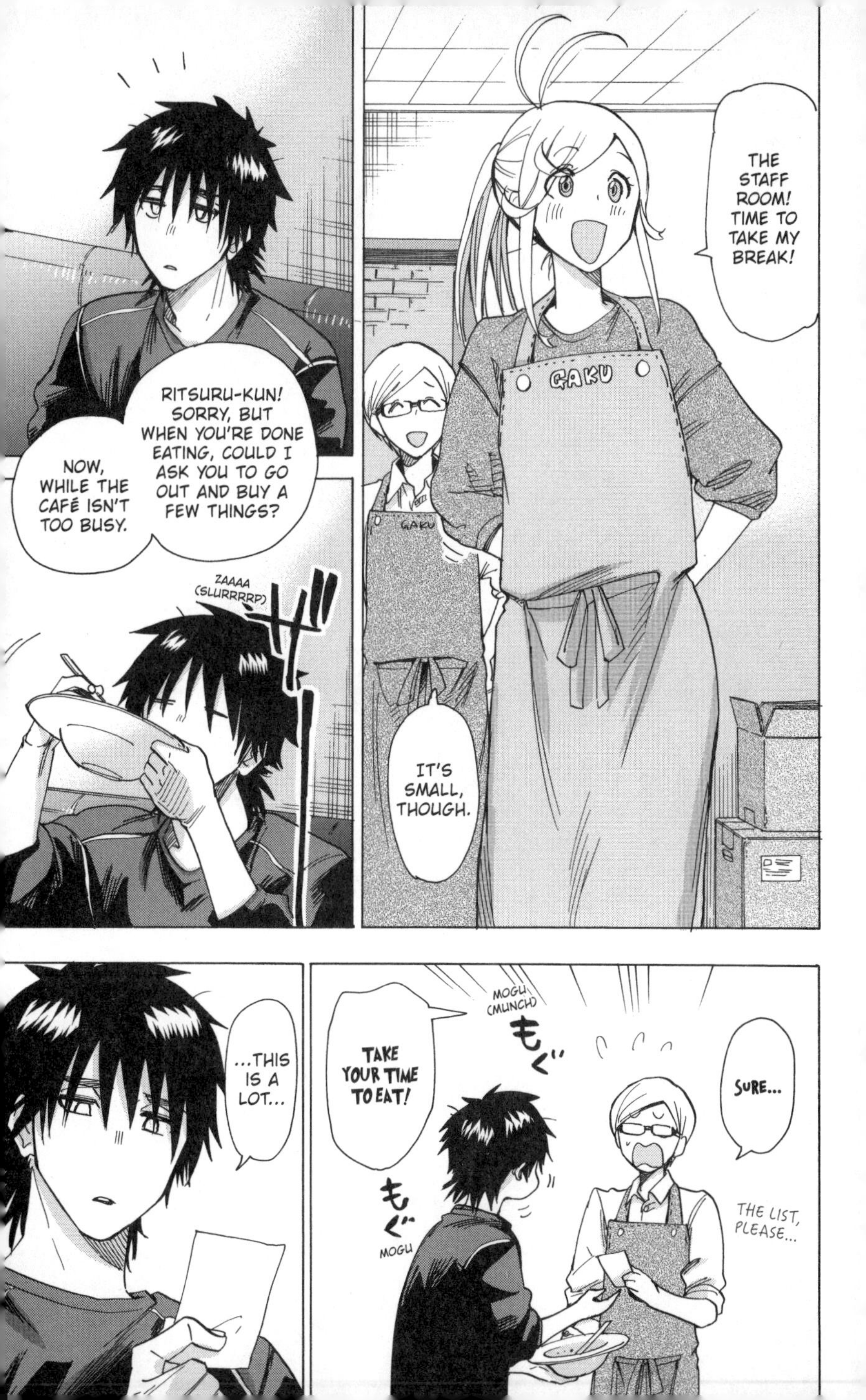
THE STAFF ROOM! TIME TO TAKE MY BREAK!
GAKU
GAKU
IT'S SMALL, THOUGH.
RITSURU-KUN! SORRY, BUT WHEN YOU'RE DONE EATING, COULD I ASK YOU TO GO OUT AND BUY A FEW THINGS?
NOW, WHILE THE CAFÉ ISN'T TOO BUSY.
ZAAAA (SLURRRRP)
SURE...
THE LIST, PLEASE...
MOGU (MUNCH)
TAKE YOUR TIME TO EAT!
MOGU
...THIS IS A LOT...

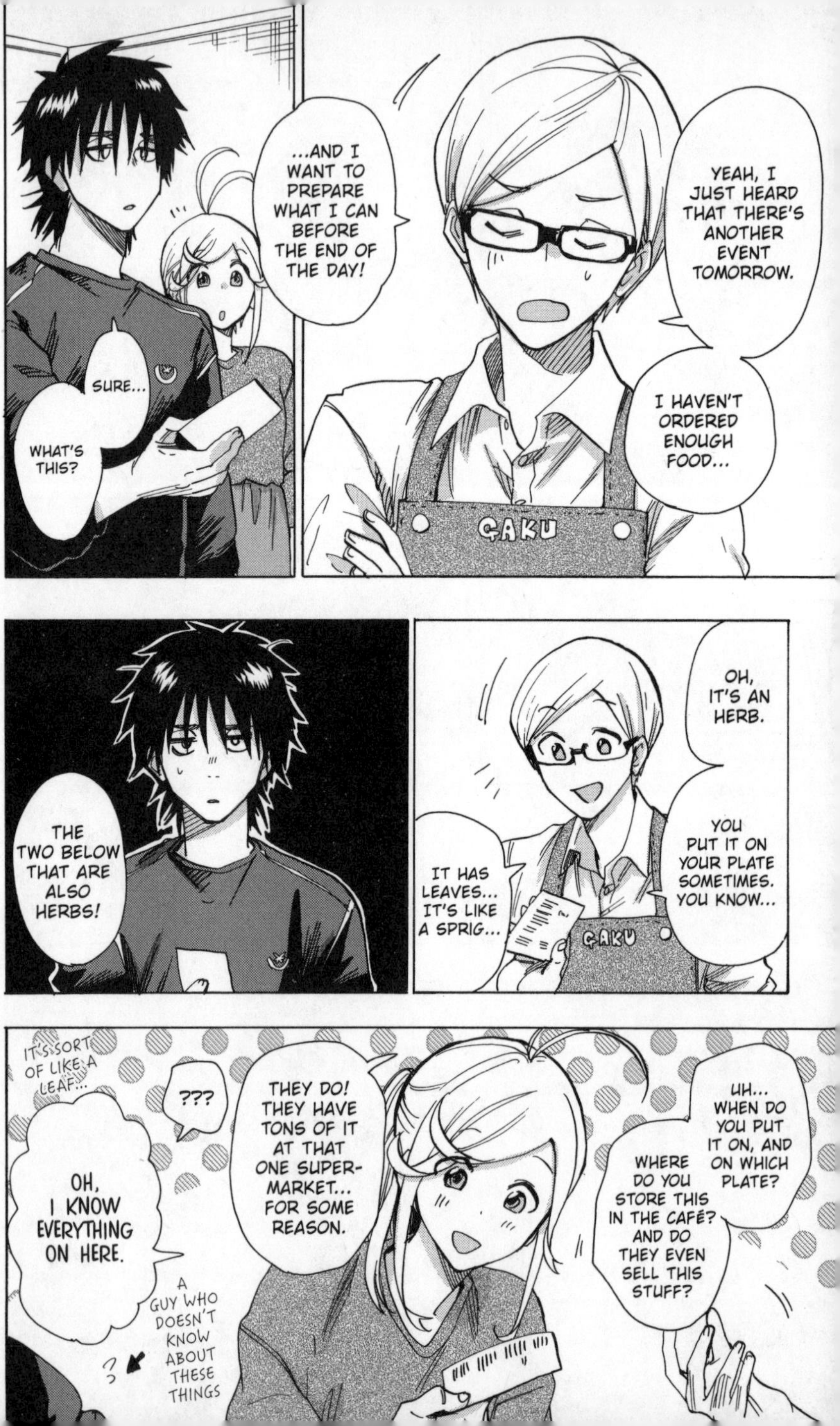
YEAH, I JUST HEARD THAT THERE'S ANOTHER EVENT TOMORROW.
I HAVEN'T ORDERED ENOUGH FOOD...
...AND I WANT TO PREPARE WHAT I CAN BEFORE THE END OF THE DAY!
SURE...
WHAT'S THIS?
GAKU
OH, IT'S AN HERB.
YOU PUT IT ON YOUR PLATE SOMETIMES. YOU KNOW...
IT HAS LEAVES... IT'S LIKE A SPRIG...
GAKU
THE TWO BELOW THAT ARE ALSO HERBS!
UH... WHEN DO YOU PUT IT ON, AND ON WHICH PLATE?
WHERE DO YOU STORE THIS IN THE CAFÉ? AND DO THEY EVEN SELL THIS STUFF?
THEY DO! THEY HAVE TONS OF IT AT THAT ONE SUPER-MARKET... FOR SOME REASON.
???
IT'S SORT OF LIKE A LEAF...
OH, I KNOW EVERYTHING ON HERE.
A GUY WHO DOESN'T KNOW ABOUT THESE THINGS
?

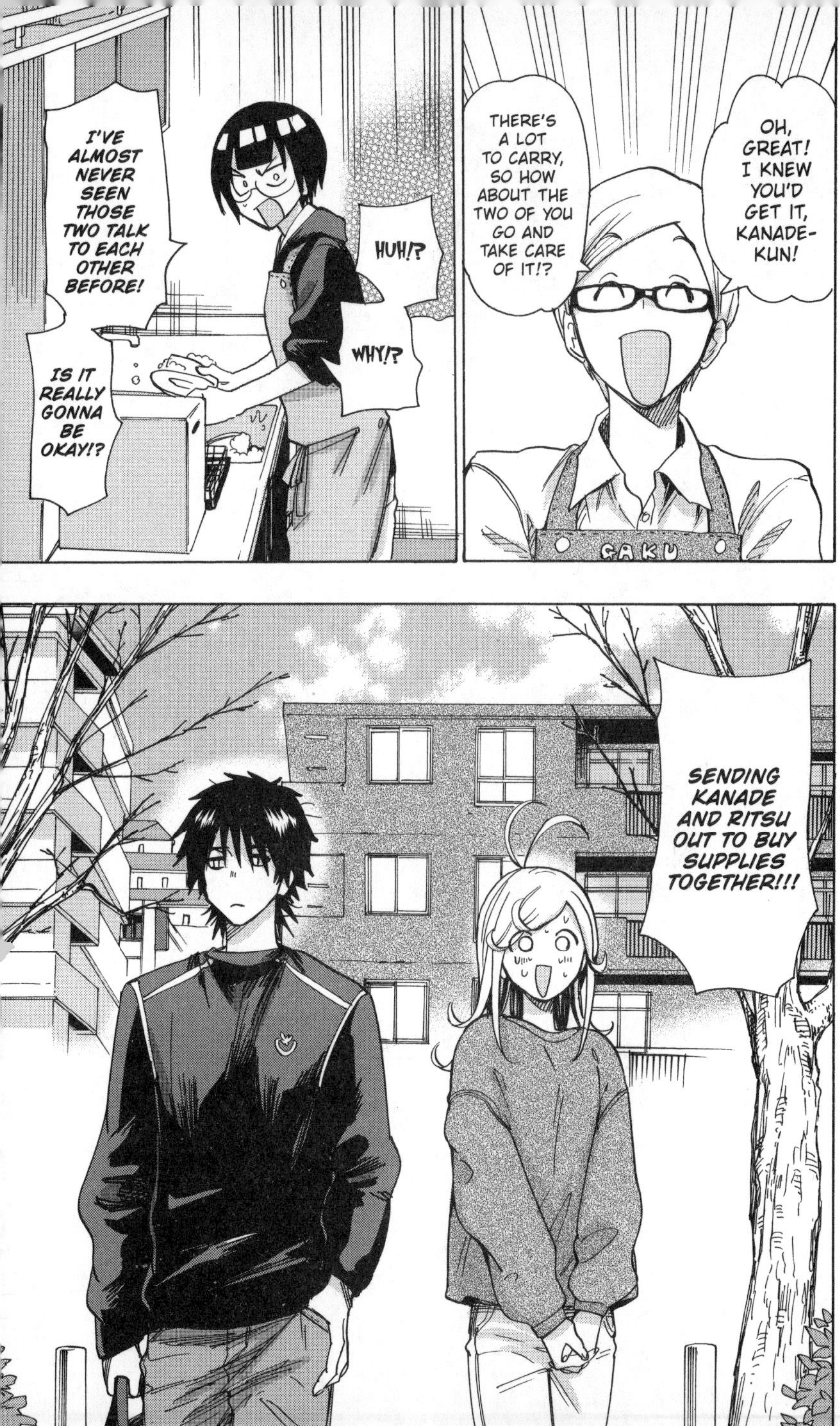
OH, GREAT! I KNEW YOU'D GET IT, KANADE-KUN!
THERE'S A LOT TO CARRY, SO HOW ABOUT THE TWO OF YOU GO AND TAKE CARE OF IT!?
GAKU
HUH!?
WHY!?
I'VE ALMOST NEVER SEEN THOSE TWO TALK TO EACH OTHER BEFORE!
IS IT REALLY GONNA BE OKAY!?
SENDING KANADE AND RITSU OUT TO BUY SUPPLIES TOGETHER!!!

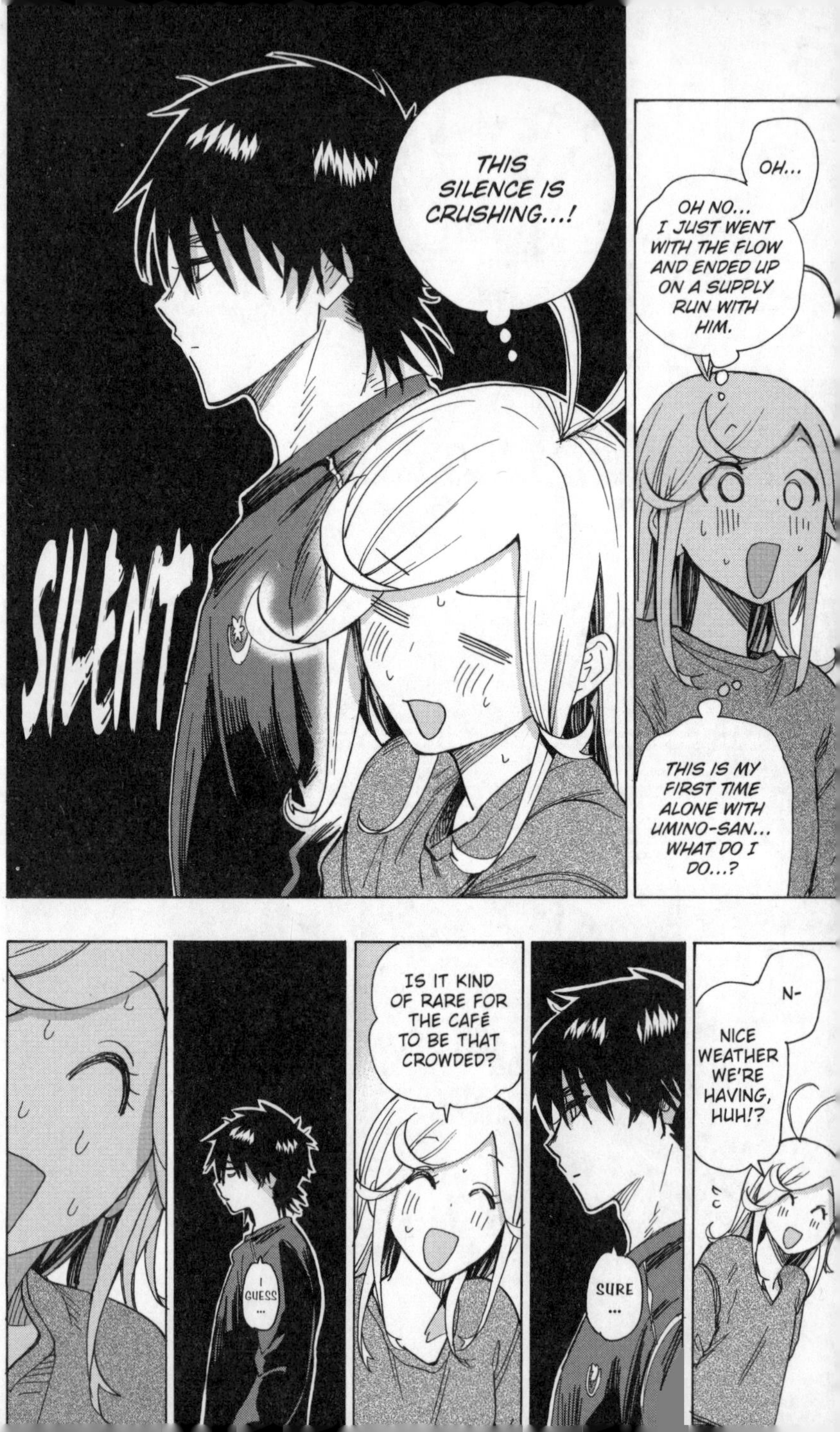
OH...
OH NO... I JUST WENT WITH THE FLOW AND ENDED UP ON A SUPPLY RUN WITH HIM.
THIS IS MY FIRST TIME ALONE WITH UMINO-SAN... WHAT DO I DO...?
THIS SILENCE IS CRUSHING...!
SILENT
N-
NICE WEATHER WE'RE HAVING, HUH!?
SURE ...
IS IT KIND OF RARE FOR THE CAFÉ TO BE THAT CROWDED?
I GUESS ...

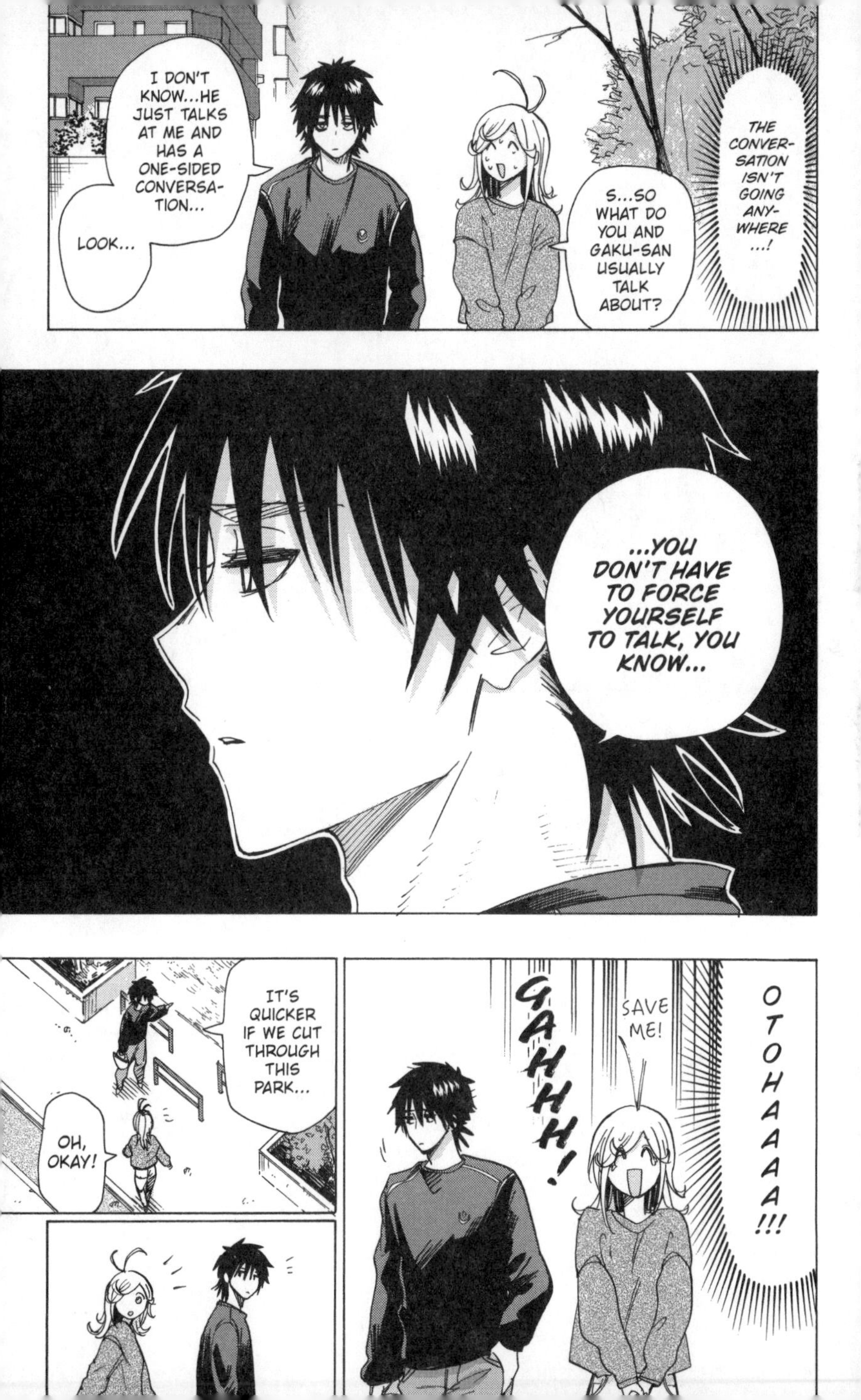
THE CONVER-SATION ISN'T GOING ANY-WHERE ...!
S...SO WHAT DO YOU AND GAKU-SAN USUALLY TALK ABOUT?
I DON'T KNOW...HE JUST TALKS AT ME AND HAS A ONE-SIDED CONVERSA-TION...
LOOK...
...YOU DON'T HAVE TO FORCE YOURSELF TO TALK, YOU KNOW...
OTOHAAAAAA!!!
SAVE ME!
GAHHH!
IT'S QUICKER IF WE CUT THROUGH THIS PARK...
OH, OKAY!

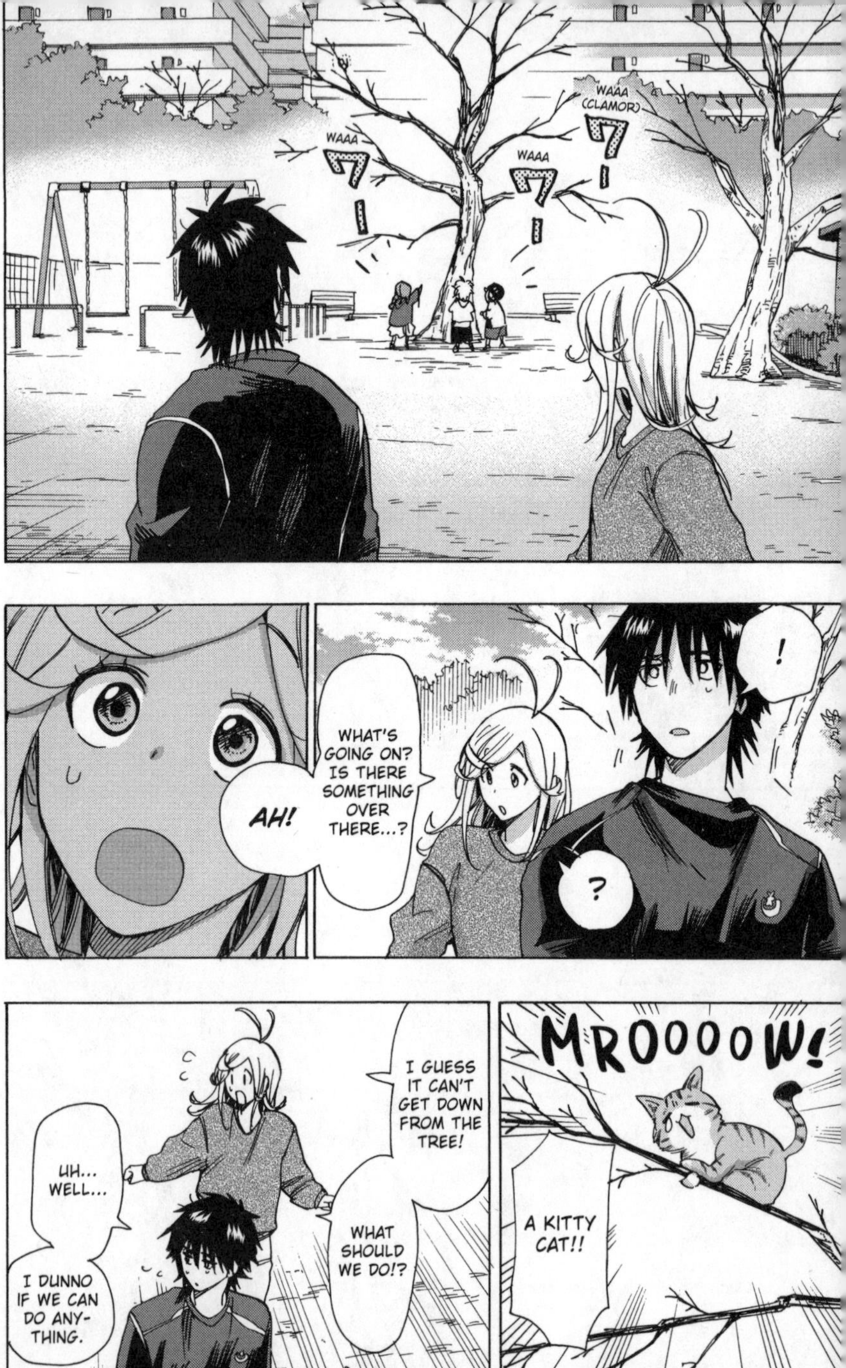
WAAA (CLAMOR)
WAAA
WAAA
!
?
WHAT'S GOING ON? IS THERE SOMETHING OVER THERE...?
AH!
MROOOOW!
A KITTY CAT!!
I GUESS IT CAN'T GET DOWN FROM THE TREE!
WHAT SHOULD WE DO!?
UH... WELL...
I DUNNO IF WE CAN DO ANYTHING.

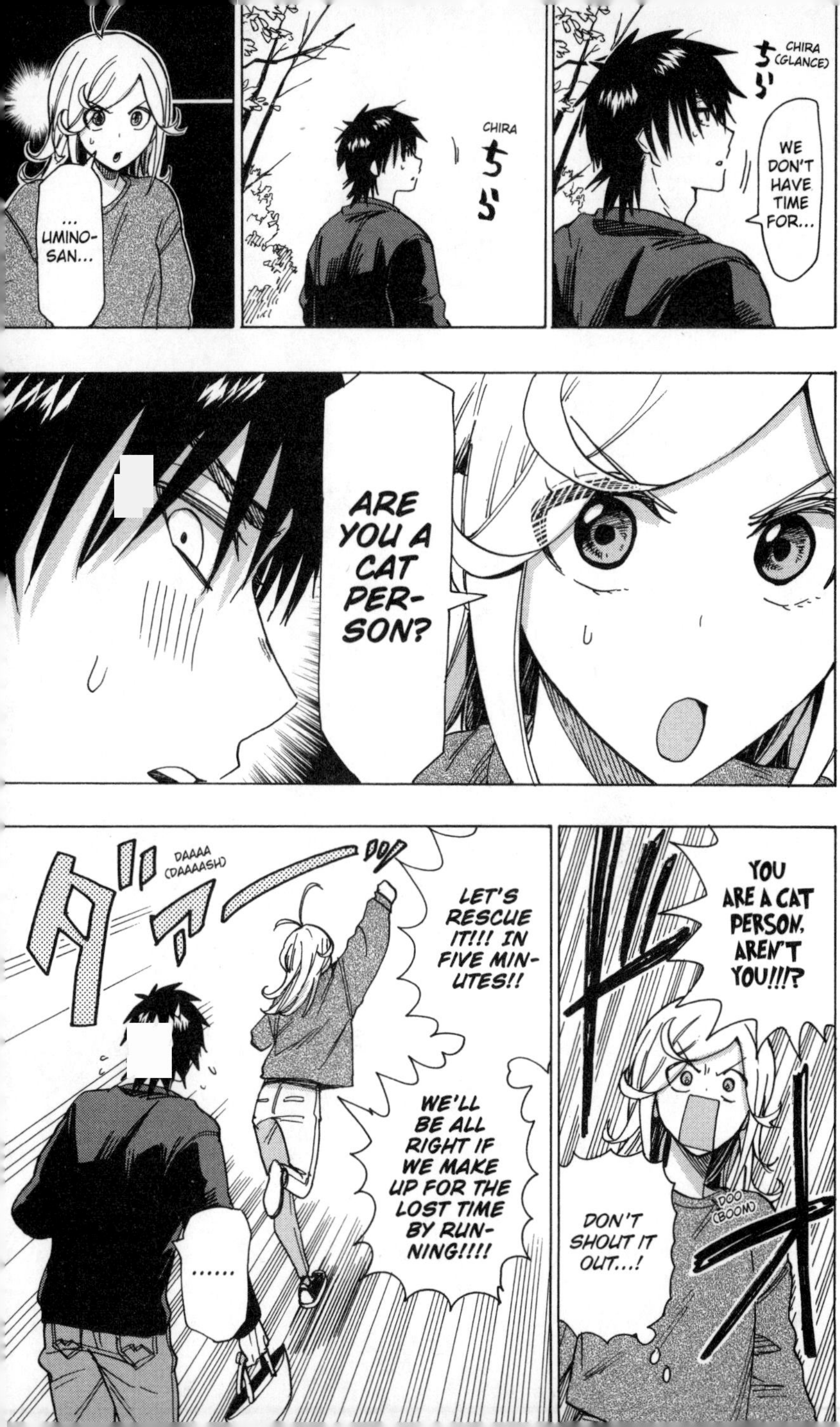
ちら
CHIRA (GLANCE)
WE DON'T HAVE TIME FOR...
ちら
CHIRA
... UMINO-SAN...
ARE YOU A CAT PER-SON?
YOU ARE A CAT PERSON, AREN'T YOU!!!?
DOO (BOOM)
DON'T SHOUT IT OUT...!
DO
LET'S RESCUE IT!!! IN FIVE MIN-UTES!!
WE'LL BE ALL RIGHT IF WE MAKE UP FOR THE LOST TIME BY RUN-NING!!!!
DAAAA (DAAAASH)
......

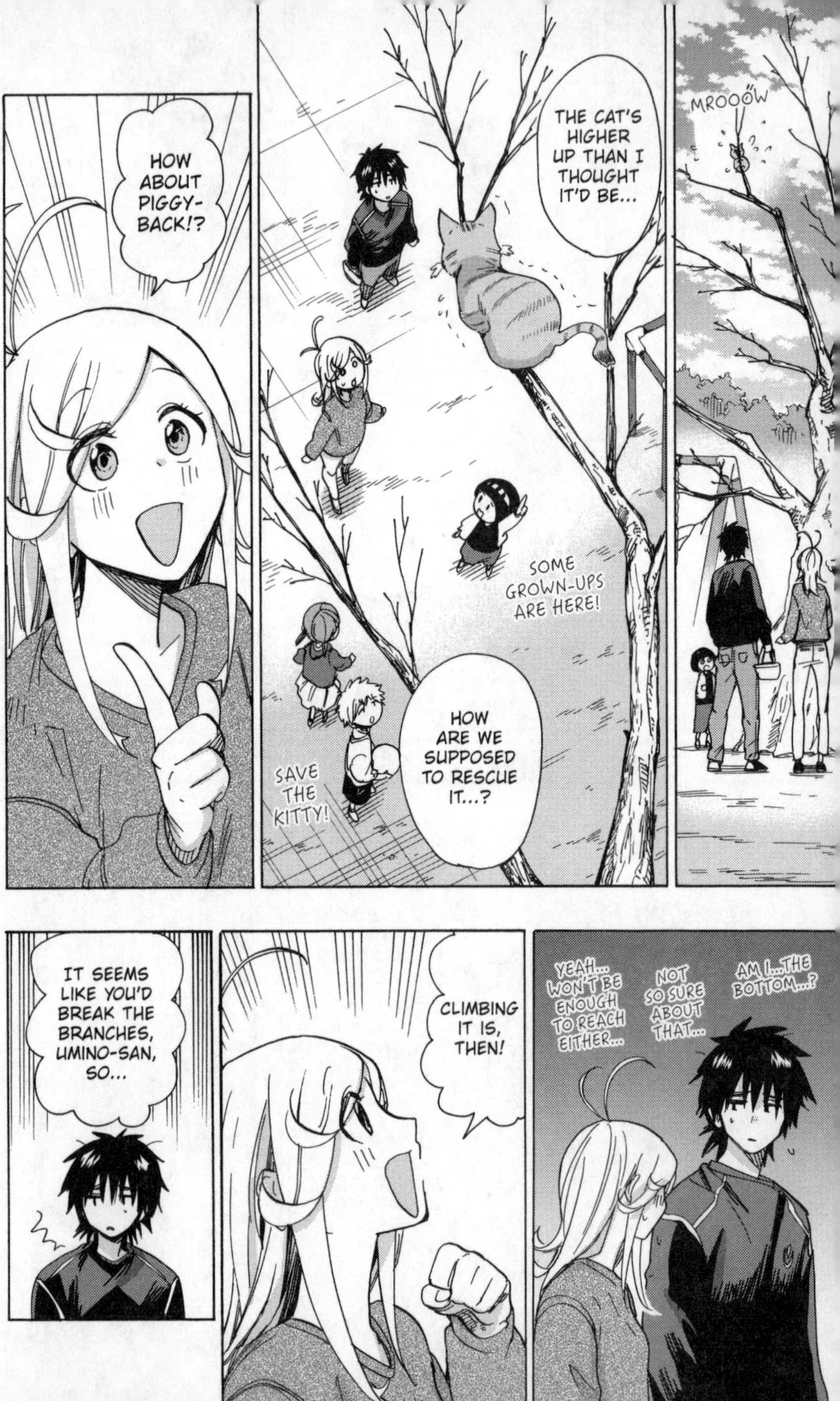
MROOOW
THE CAT'S HIGHER UP THAN I THOUGHT IT'D BE...
SOME GROWN-UPS ARE HERE!
HOW ARE WE SUPPOSED TO RESCUE IT...?
SAVE THE KITTY!
HOW ABOUT PIGGY-BACK!?
AM I...THE BOTTOM...?
NOT SO SURE ABOUT THAT...
YEAH... WON'T BE ENOUGH TO REACH EITHER...
CLIMBING IT IS, THEN!
IT SEEMS LIKE YOU'D BREAK THE BRANCHES, UMINO-SAN, SO...

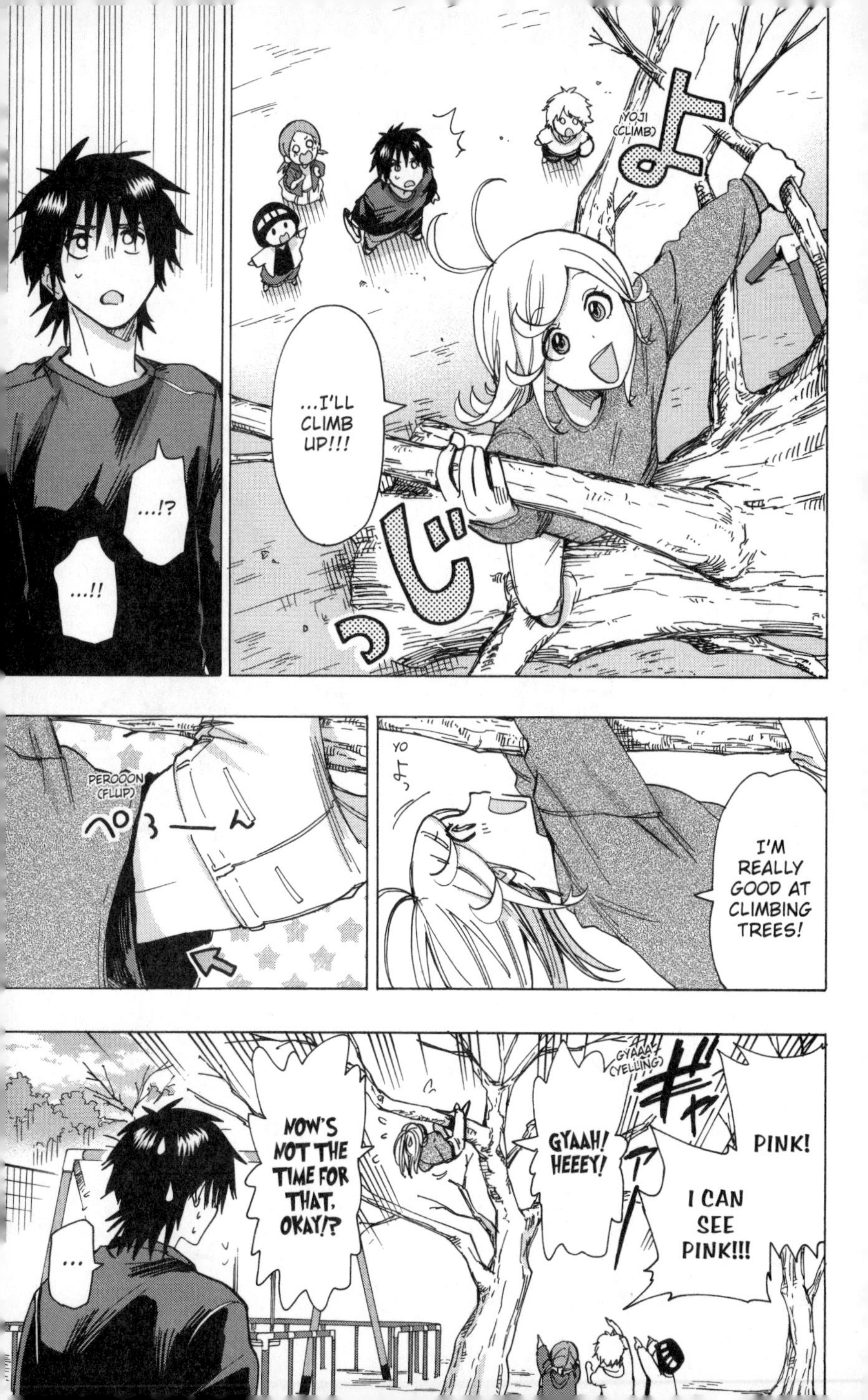

YOJI (CLIMB)
よ
...I'LL CLIMB UP!!!
じっ
...!?
...!!
YO
よ
I'M REALLY GOOD AT CLIMBING TREES!
PEROOON (FLUP)
へろーん
GYAAA! (YELLING)
ギャア
PINK!
I CAN SEE PINK!!!
GYAAH! HEEEY!
NOW'S NOT THE TIME FOR THAT, OKAY!?
...

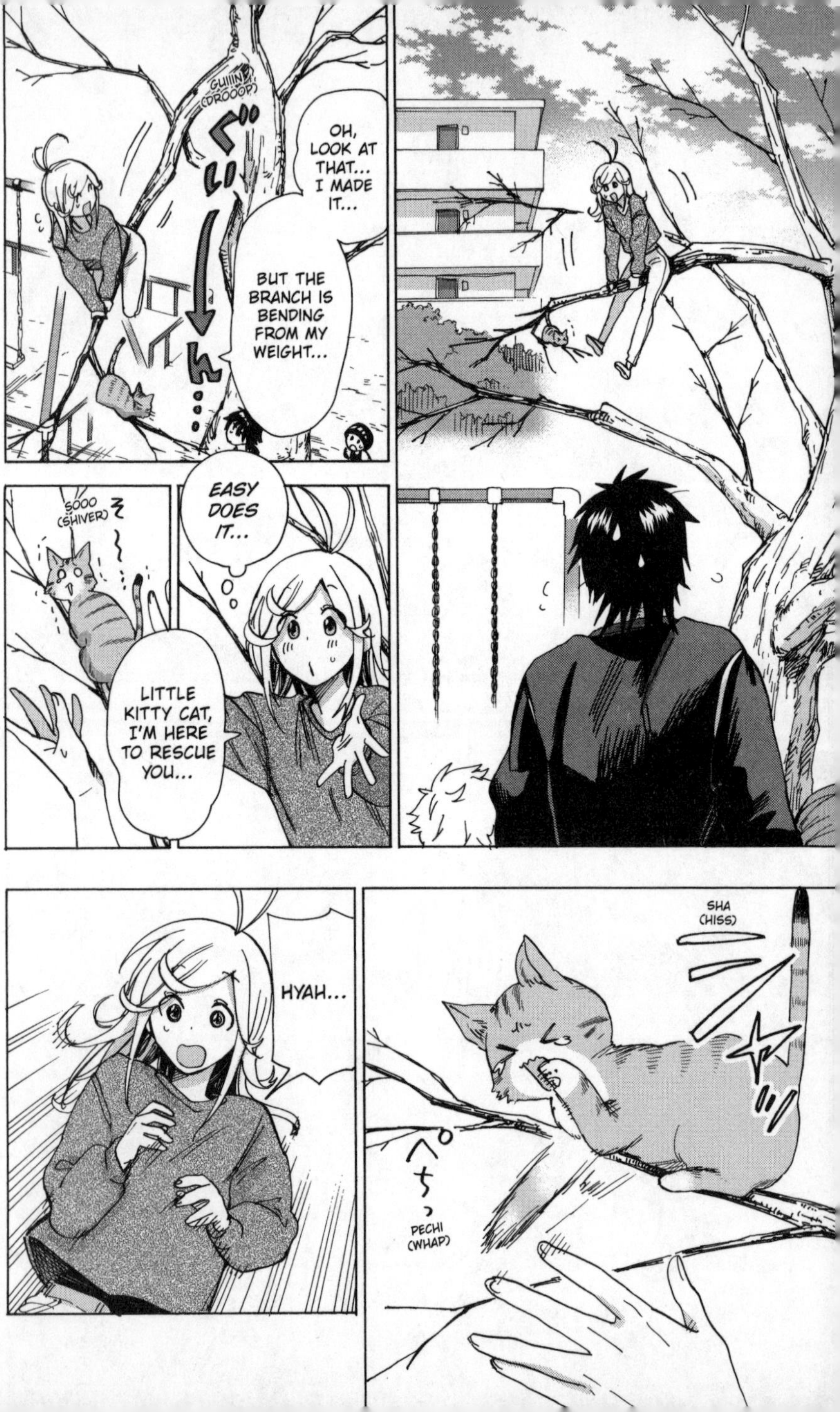
GUIIIN (DROOOP)
OH, LOOK AT THAT... I MADE IT...
BUT THE BRANCH IS BENDING FROM MY WEIGHT...
EASY DOES IT...
LITTLE KITTY CAT, I'M HERE TO RESCUE YOU...
SOOO (SHIVER)
SHA (HISS)
PECHI (WHAP)
HYAH...

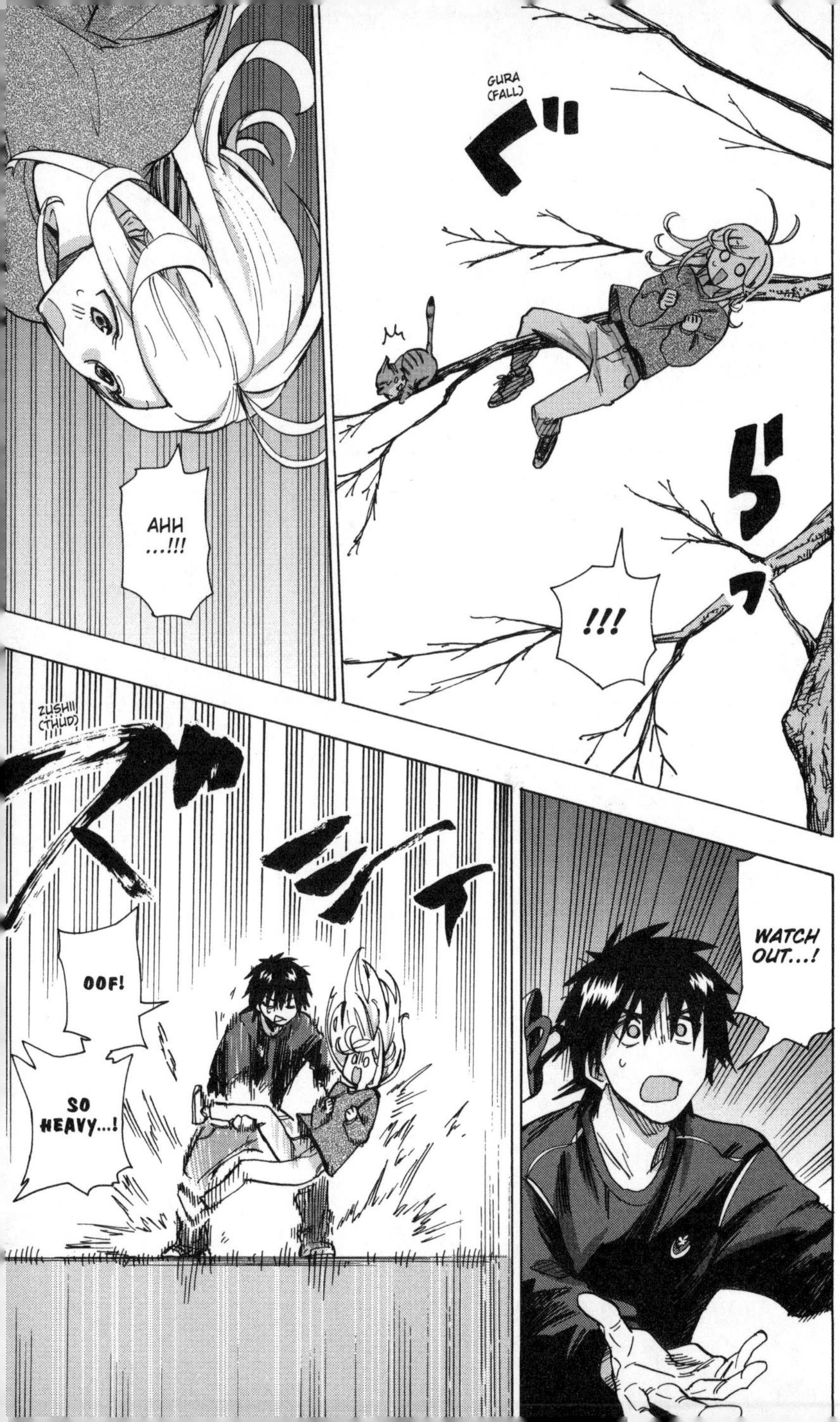
GURA (FALL)
!!!
AHH ...!!!
WATCH OUT...!
ZUSHI!! (THUD)
OOF!
SO HEAVY...!

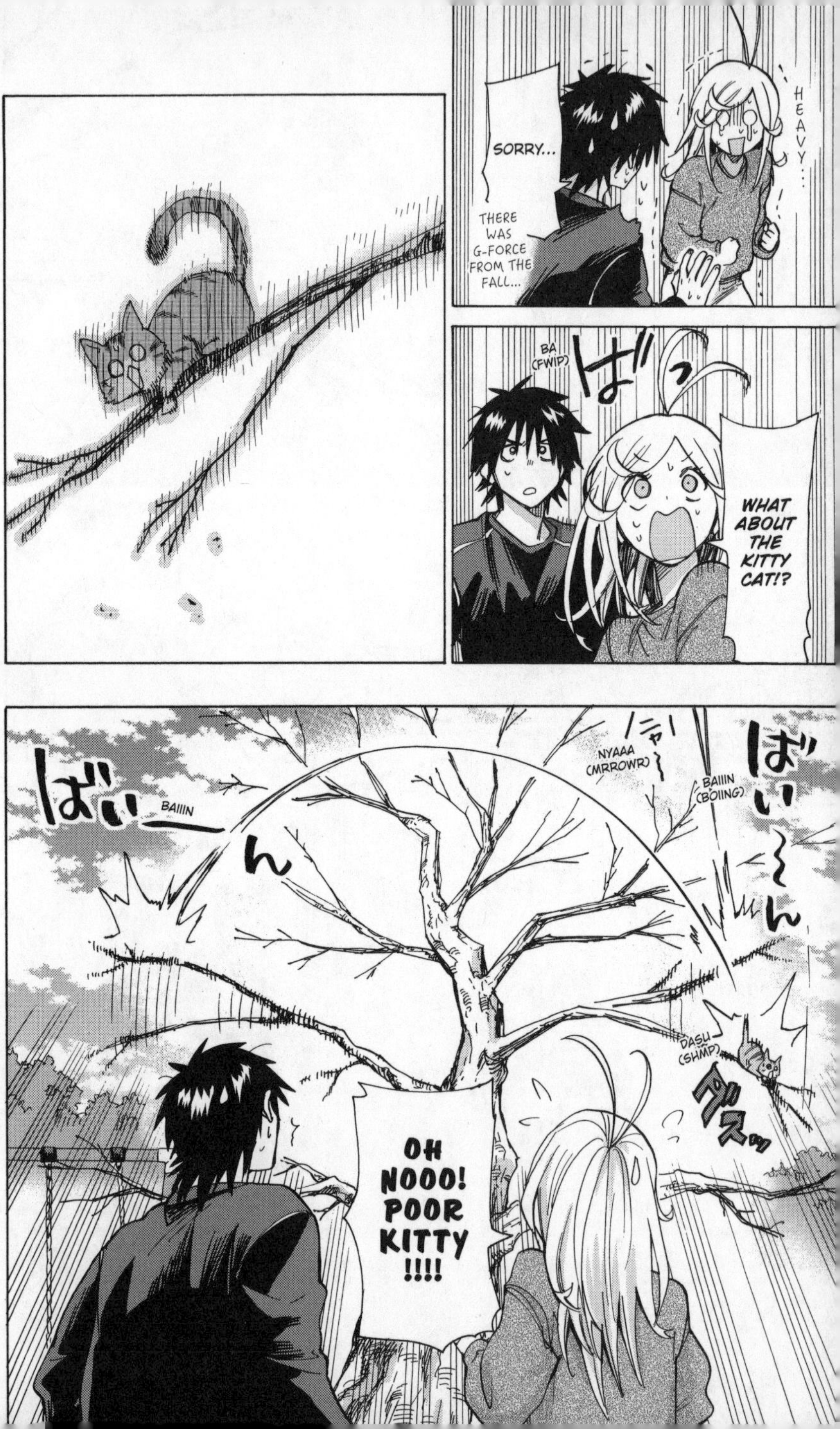
HEAVY...
SORRY...
THERE WAS G-FORCE FROM THE FALL...
ばっ
BA (FWIP)
WHAT ABOUT THE KITTY CAT!?
ばい~ん
BAIIIN (BOIING)
ニャ~
NYAAA (MRROWR)
グスッ
DASU (SHMP)
ばい—ん
BAIIIN
OH NOOO! POOR KITTY !!!!

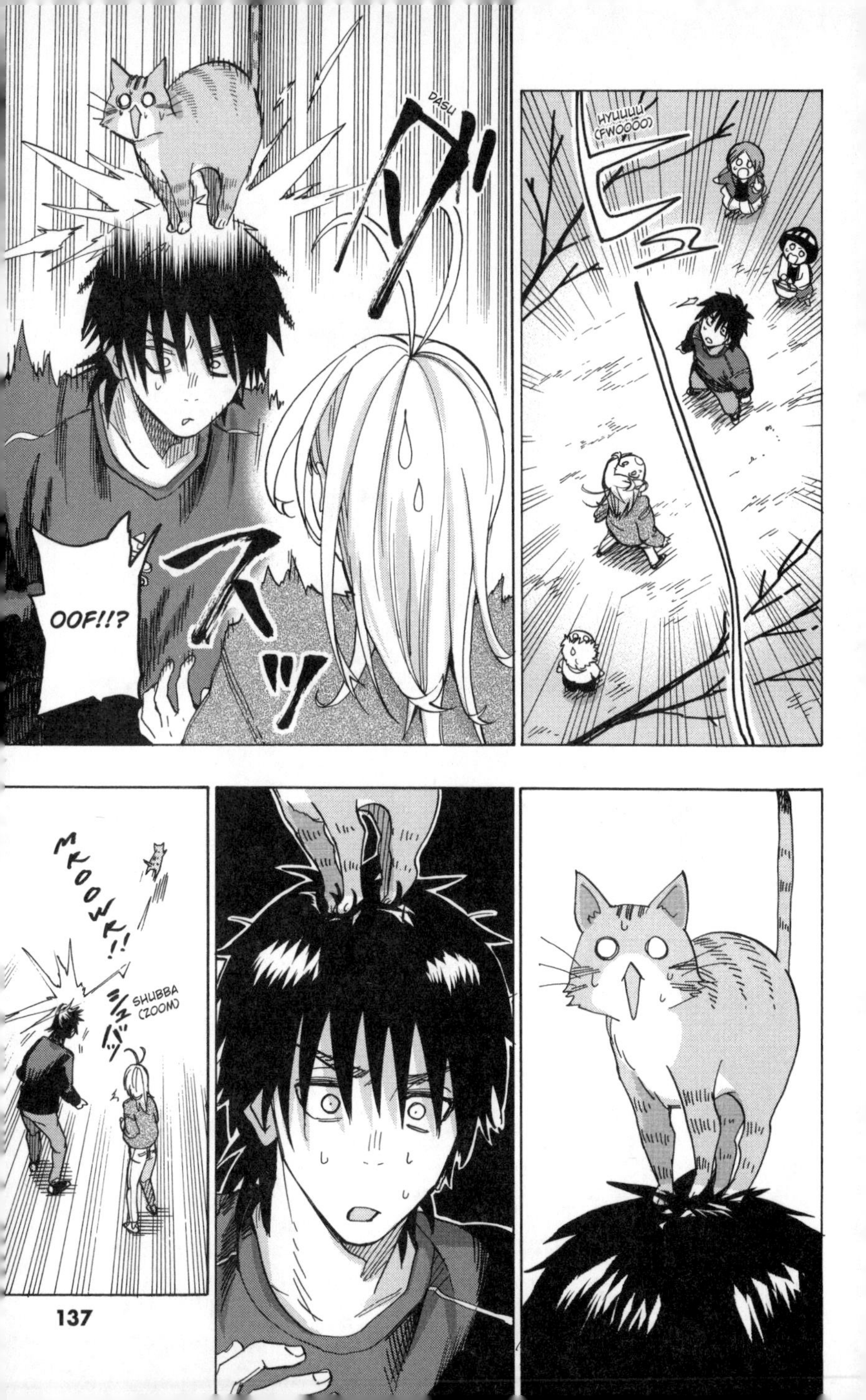

HYUUUU (FWOOOO)
DASU
OOF!!?
MKOOWK!!
SHUBBA (ZOOM)

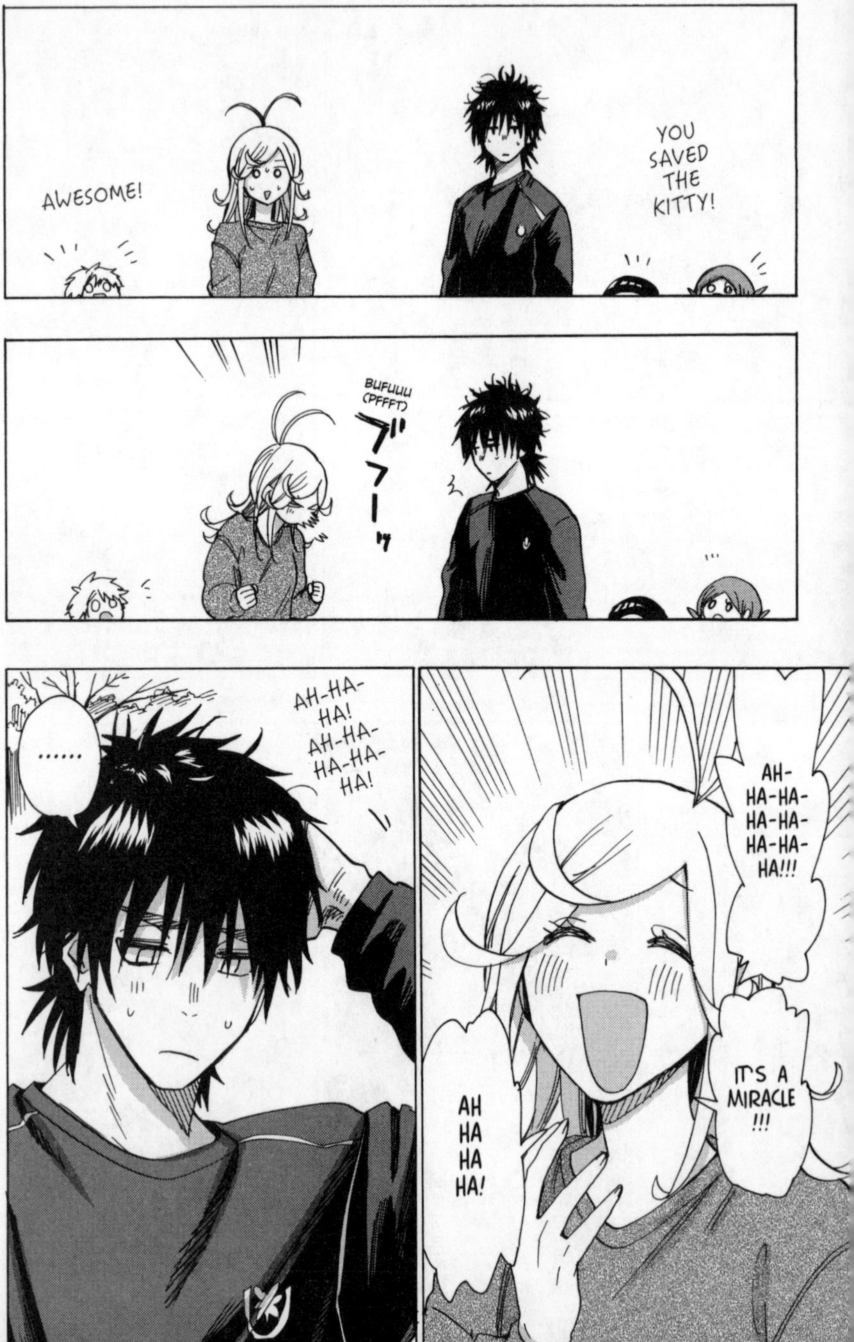
YOU SAVED THE KITTY!
AWESOME!
BUFUUU (PFFFT)
ブフーッ
AH-HA-HA-HA-HA-HA-HA-HA!!!
IT'S A MIRACLE!!!
AH HA HA HA HA!
AH-HA-HA! AH-HA-HA-HA-HA!
……

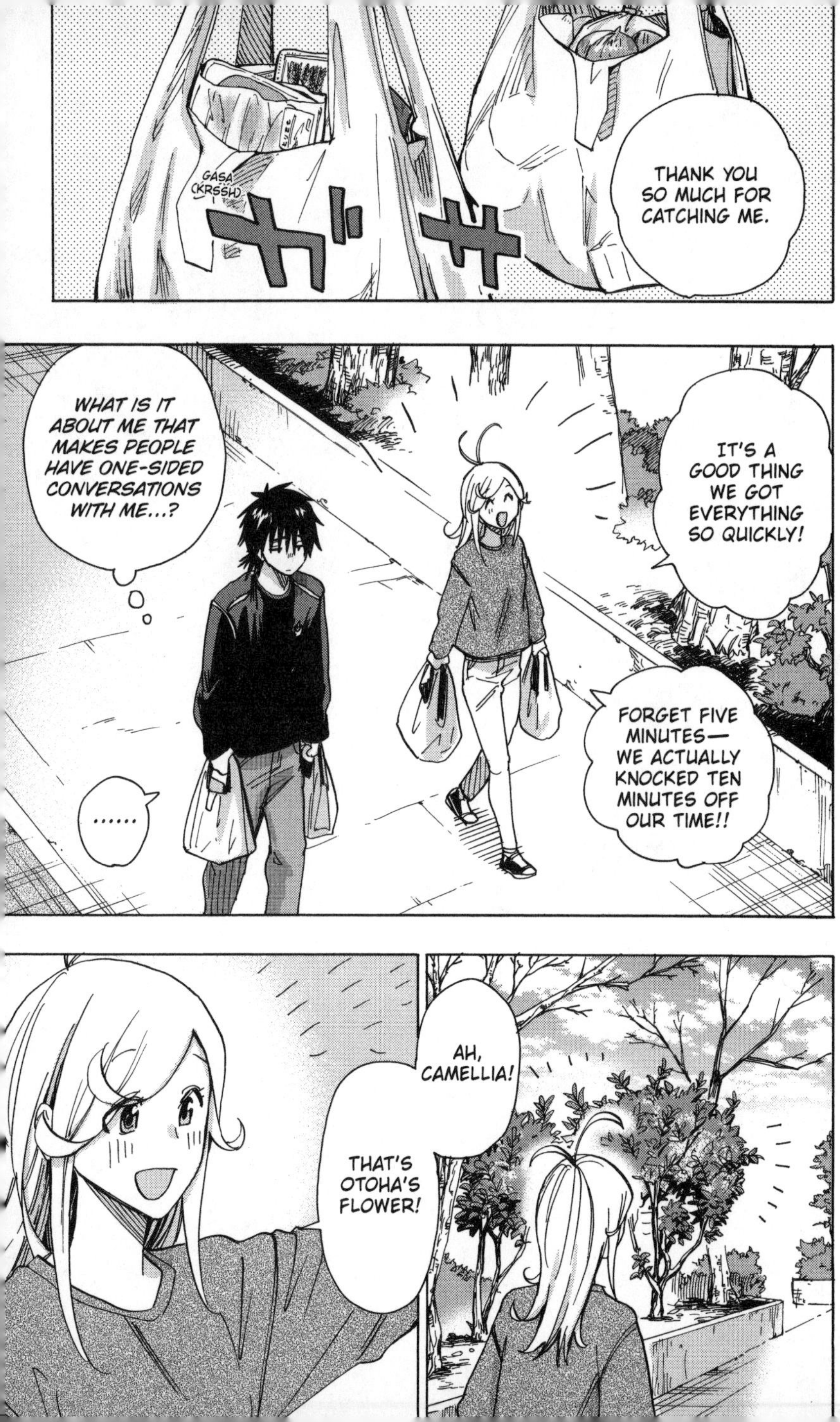
THANK YOU SO MUCH FOR CATCHING ME.
GASA (KRSSH)
IT'S A GOOD THING WE GOT EVERYTHING SO QUICKLY!
FORGET FIVE MINUTES— WE ACTUALLY KNOCKED TEN MINUTES OFF OUR TIME!!
WHAT IS IT ABOUT ME THAT MAKES PEOPLE HAVE ONE-SIDED CONVERSATIONS WITH ME...?
......
AH, CAMELLIA!
THAT'S OTOHA'S FLOWER!

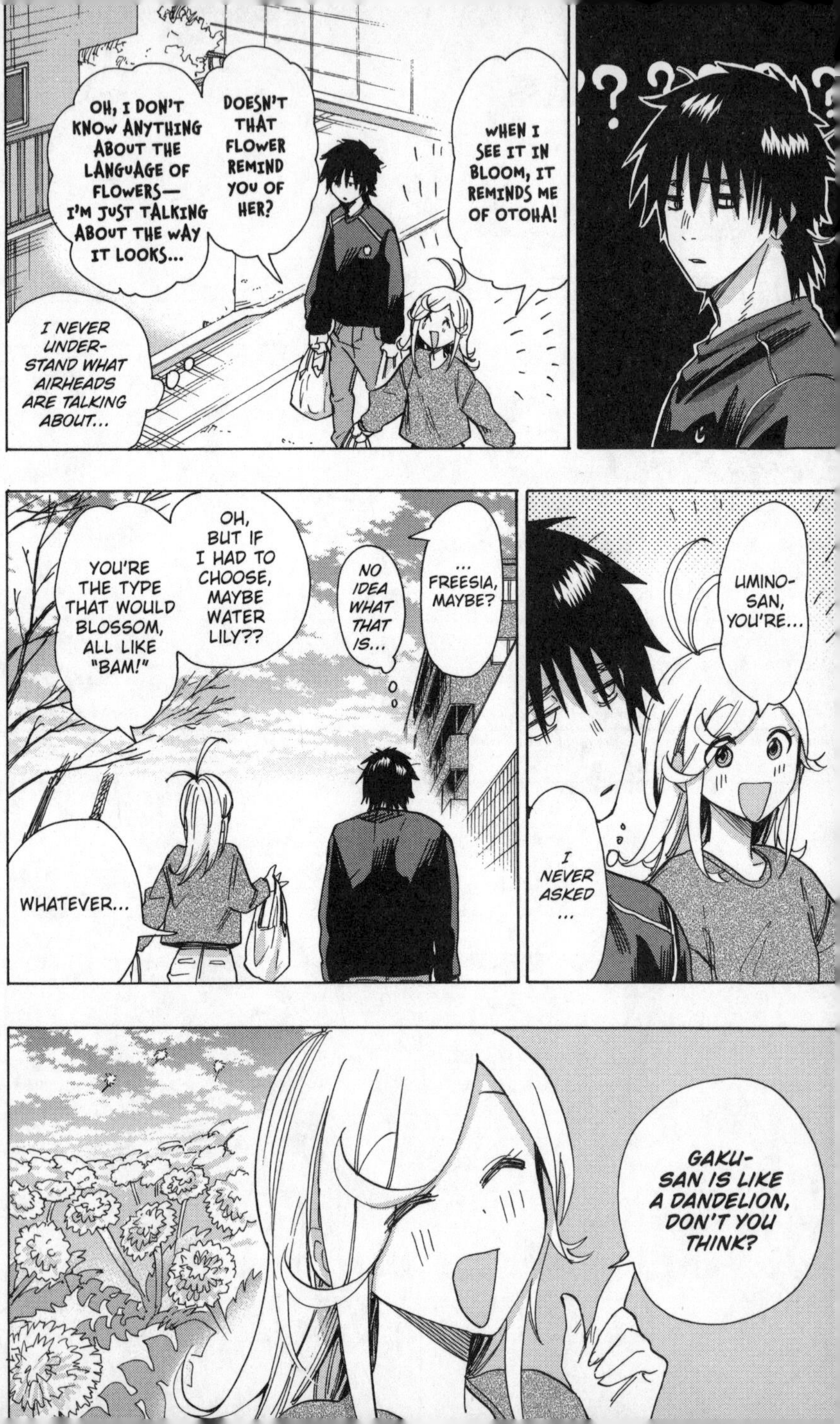
??
WHEN I SEE IT IN BLOOM, IT REMINDS ME OF OTOHA!
DOESN'T THAT FLOWER REMIND YOU OF HER?
OH, I DON'T KNOW ANYTHING ABOUT THE LANGUAGE OF FLOWERS— I'M JUST TALKING ABOUT THE WAY IT LOOKS...
I NEVER UNDERSTAND WHAT AIRHEADS ARE TALKING ABOUT...
UMINO-SAN, YOU'RE...
I NEVER ASKED...
...FREESIA, MAYBE?
NO IDEA WHAT THAT IS...
OH, BUT IF I HAD TO CHOOSE, MAYBE WATER LILY??
YOU'RE THE TYPE THAT WOULD BLOSSOM, ALL LIKE "BAM!"
WHATEVER...
GAKU-SAN IS LIKE A DANDELION, DON'T YOU THINK?

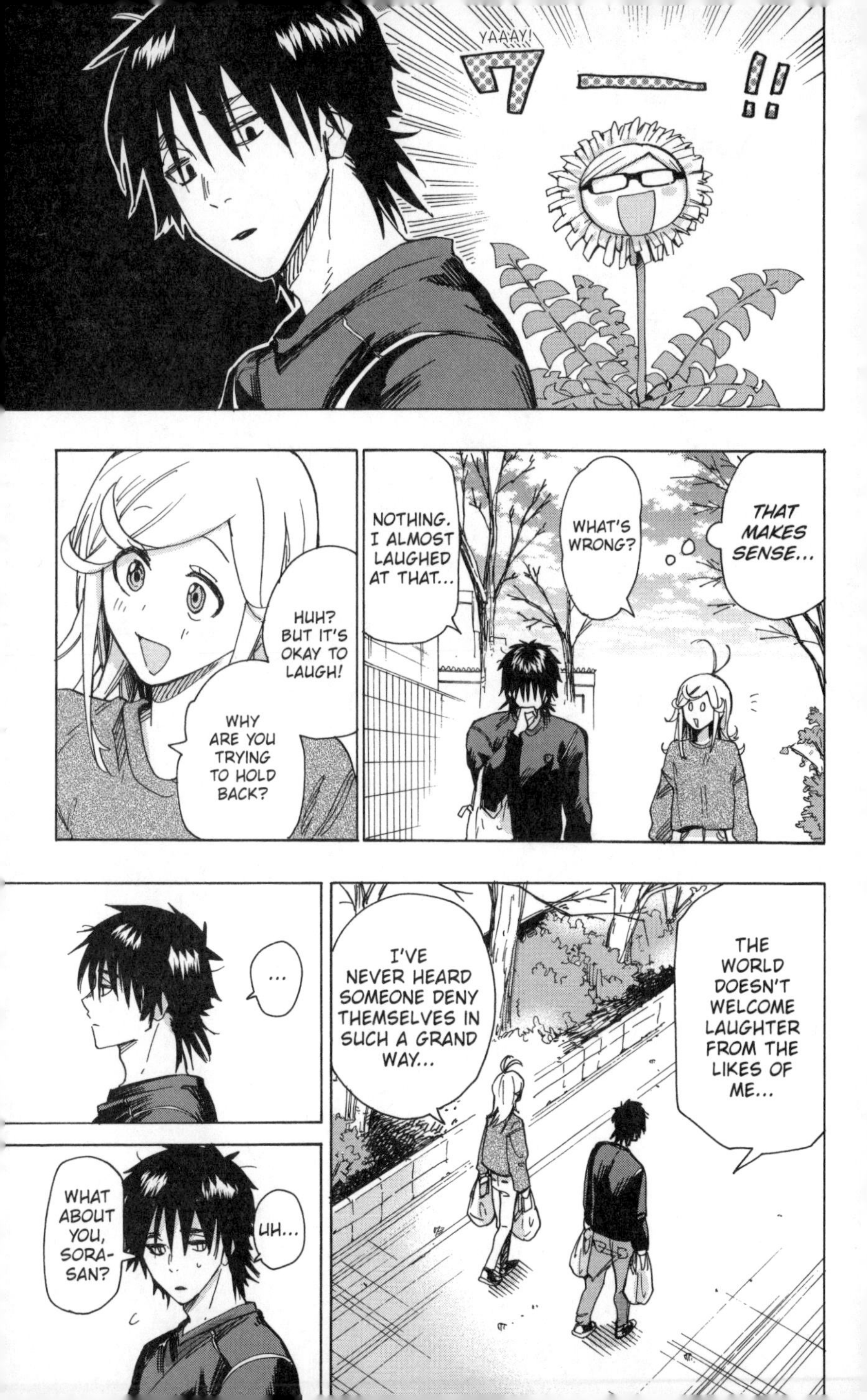
YAAAY!
THAT MAKES SENSE...
WHAT'S WRONG?
NOTHING. I ALMOST LAUGHED AT THAT...
HUH? BUT IT'S OKAY TO LAUGH!
WHY ARE YOU TRYING TO HOLD BACK?
THE WORLD DOESN'T WELCOME LAUGHTER FROM THE LIKES OF ME...
I'VE NEVER HEARD SOMEONE DENY THEMSELVES IN SUCH A GRAND WAY...
...
UH...
WHAT ABOUT YOU, SORA-SAN?

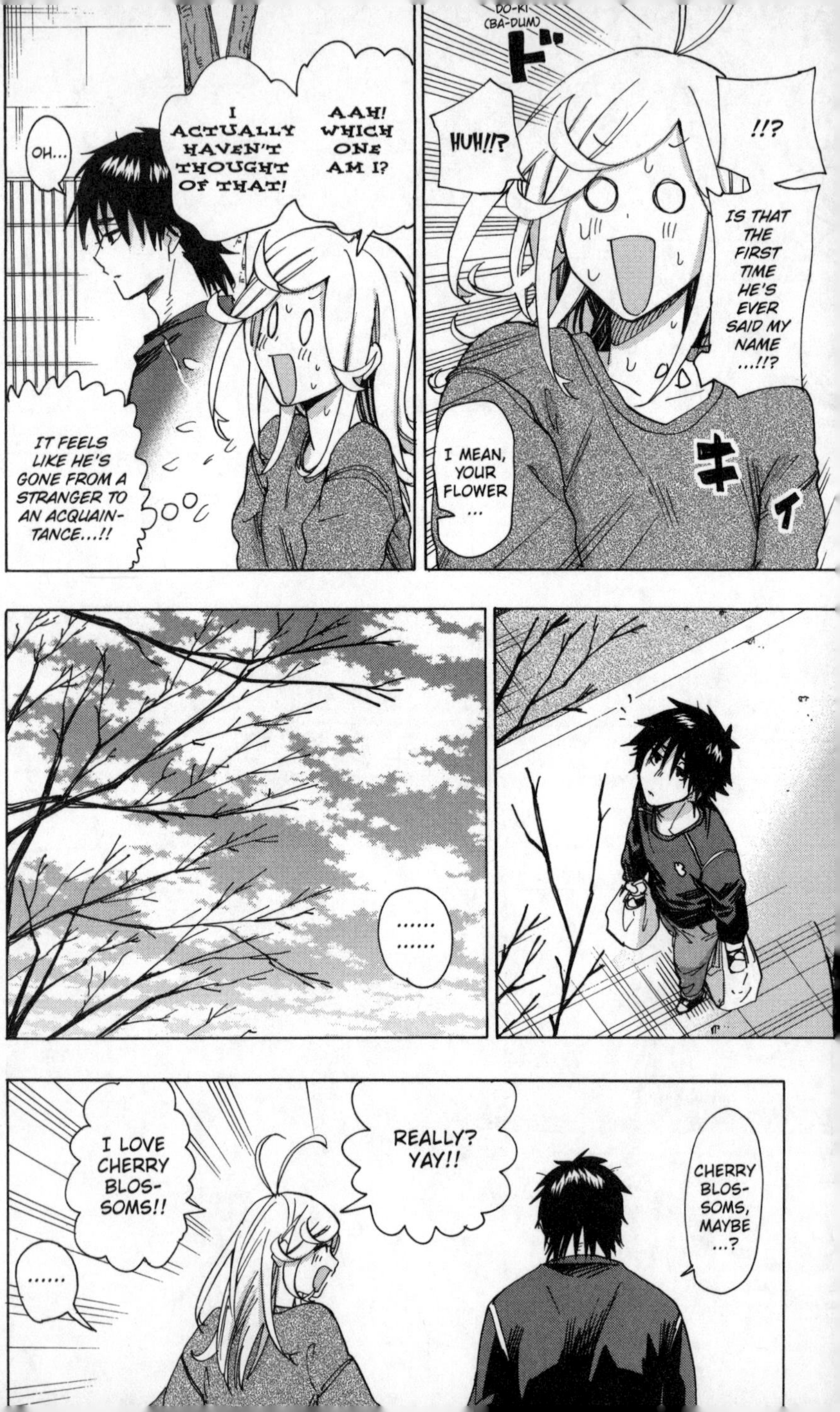
DO-KI (BA-DUM)
ド
!!?
HUH!!?
IS THAT THE FIRST TIME HE'S EVER SAID MY NAME ...!?
キイ
I MEAN, YOUR FLOWER ...
AAH! WHICH ONE AM I?
I ACTUALLY HAVEN'T THOUGHT OF THAT!
OH...
IT FEELS LIKE HE'S GONE FROM A STRANGER TO AN ACQUAIN-TANCE...!!
....
CHERRY BLOS-SOMS, MAYBE ...?
REALLY? YAY!!
I LOVE CHERRY BLOS-SOMS!!
......

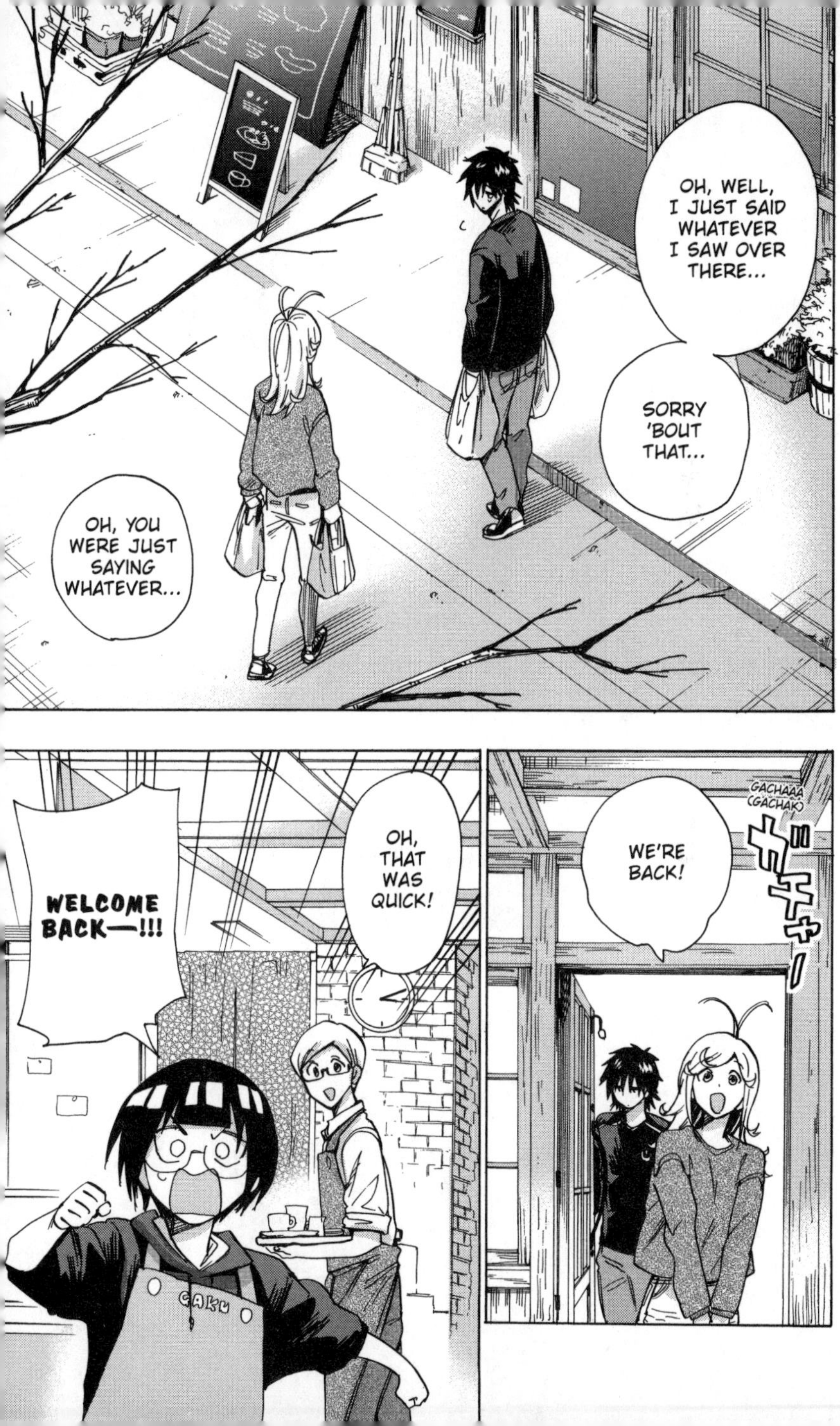
OH, WELL, I JUST SAID WHATEVER I SAW OVER THERE...
SORRY 'BOUT THAT...
OH, YOU WERE JUST SAYING WHATEVER...
GACHAAA (GACHAK)
WE'RE BACK!
OH, THAT WAS QUICK!
WELCOME BACK—!!!
GAKU

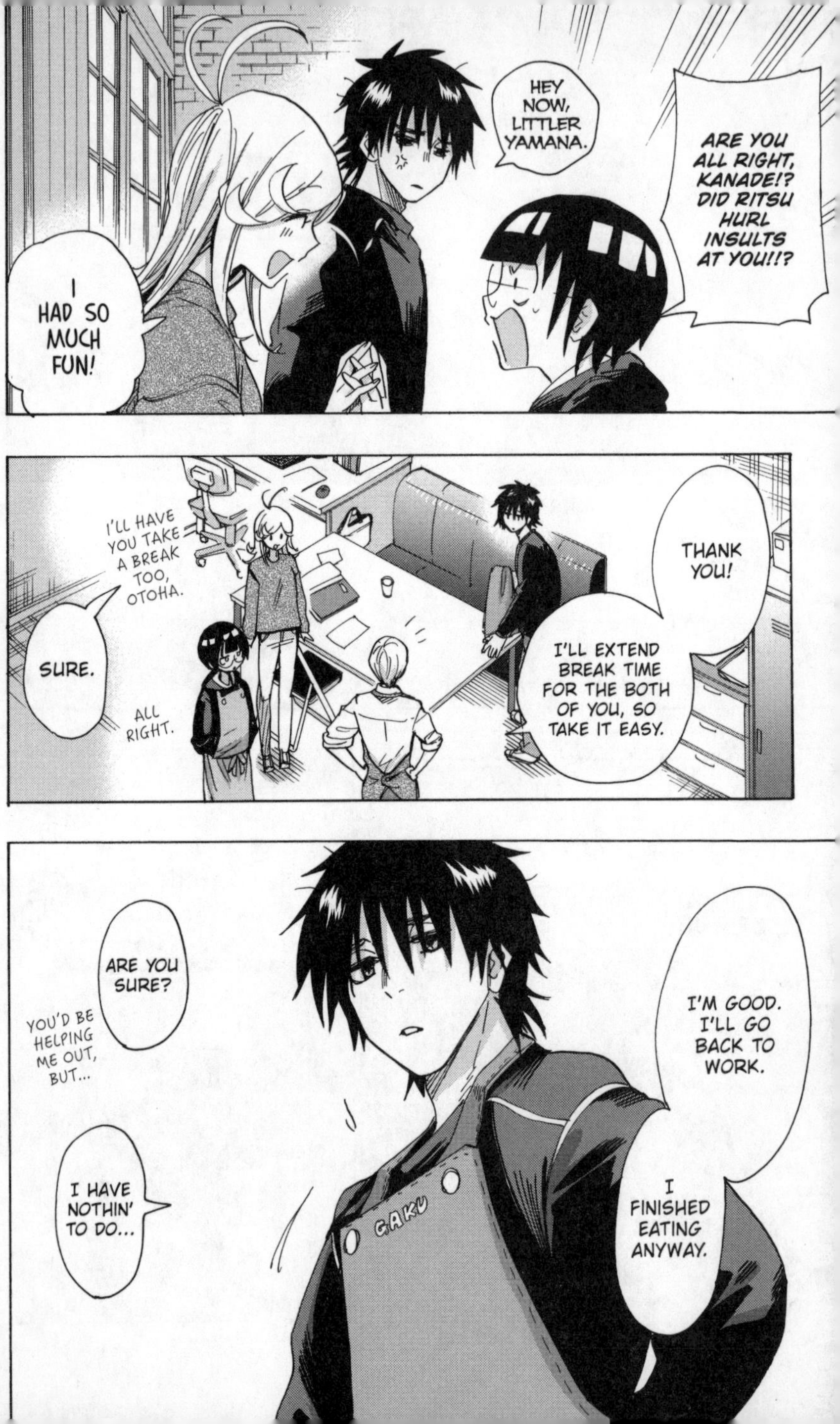
ARE YOU ALL RIGHT, KANADE!? DID RITSU HURL INSULTS AT YOU!!?
HEY NOW, LITTLER YAMANA.
I HAD SO MUCH FUN!
THANK YOU!
I'LL EXTEND BREAK TIME FOR THE BOTH OF YOU, SO TAKE IT EASY.
I'LL HAVE YOU TAKE A BREAK TOO, OTOHA.
SURE.
ALL RIGHT.
I'M GOOD. I'LL GO BACK TO WORK.
I FINISHED EATING ANYWAY.
ARE YOU SURE?
YOU'D BE HELPING ME OUT, BUT...
GAKU
I HAVE NOTHIN' TO DO...

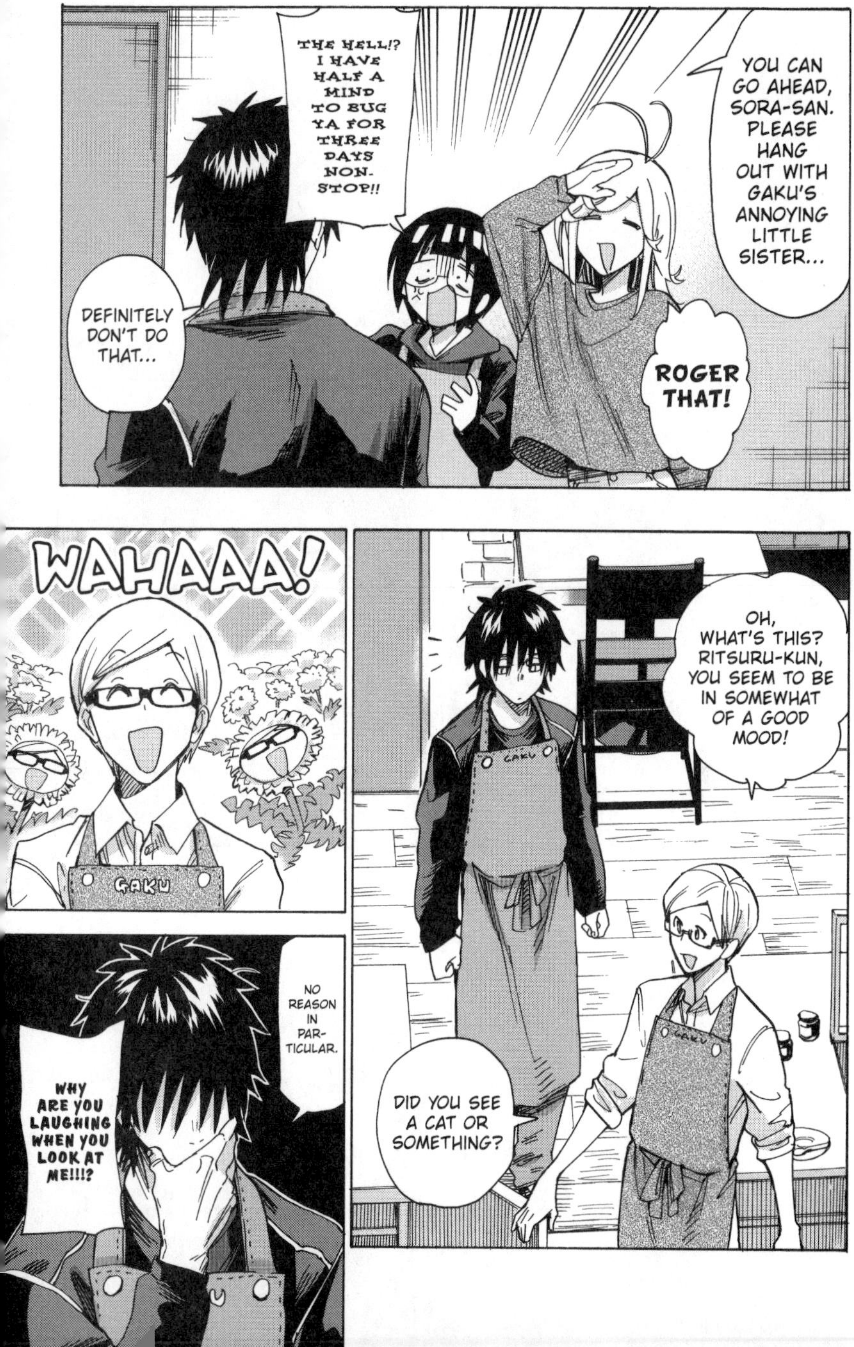
YOU CAN GO AHEAD, SORA-SAN. PLEASE HANG OUT WITH GAKU'S ANNOYING LITTLE SISTER...
ROGER THAT!
THE HELL!? I HAVE HALF A MIND TO BUG YA FOR THREE DAYS NON-STOP!!
DEFINITELY DON'T DO THAT...
OH, WHAT'S THIS? RITSURU-KUN, YOU SEEM TO BE IN SOMEWHAT OF A GOOD MOOD!
GAKU
DID YOU SEE A CAT OR SOMETHING?
WAHAAA!
GAKU
NO REASON IN PAR-TICULAR.
WHY ARE YOU LAUGHING WHEN YOU LOOK AT ME!!!?

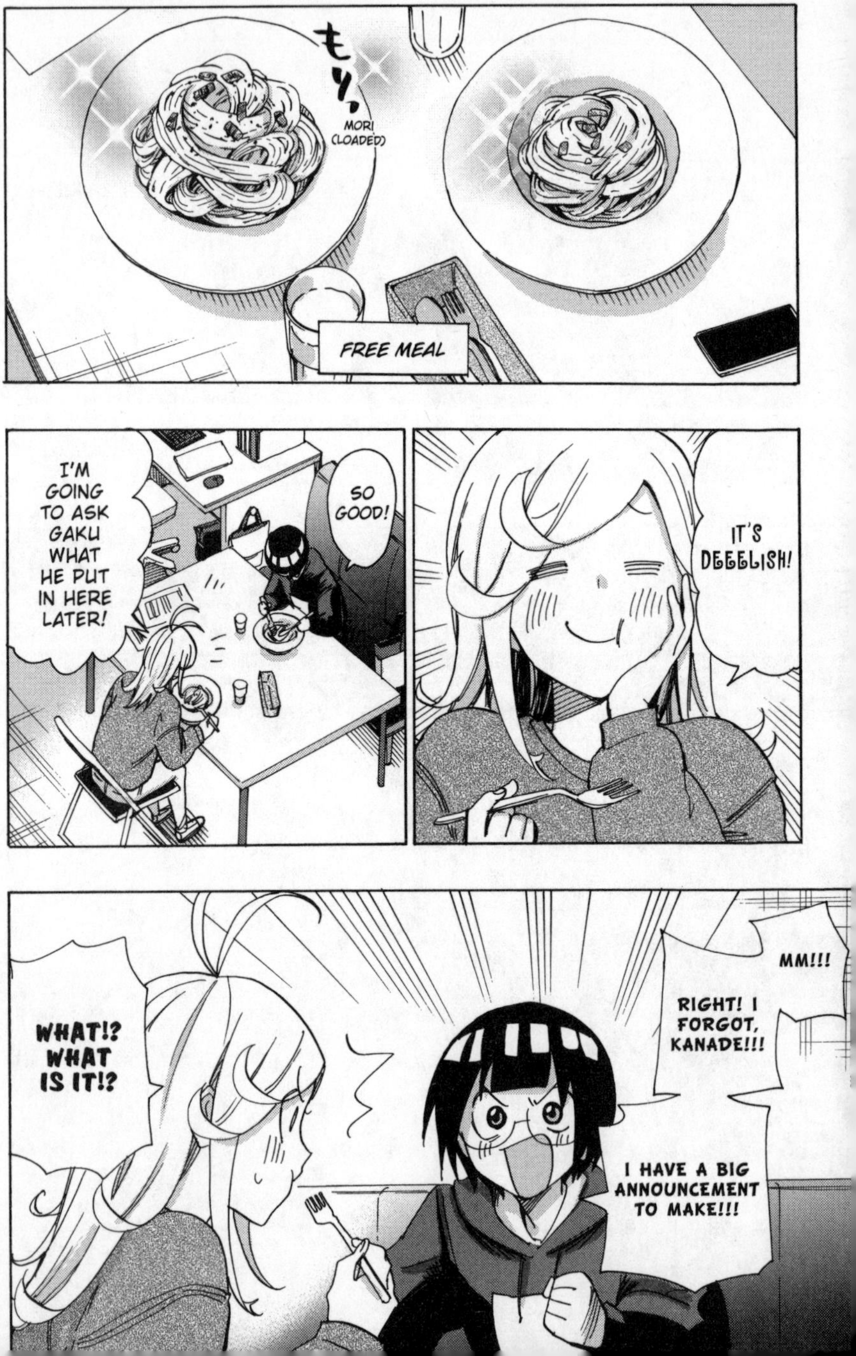
もり
MORI (LOADED)
FREE MEAL
IT'S DEEELISH!
SO GOOD!
I'M GOING TO ASK GAKU WHAT HE PUT IN HERE LATER!
MM!!!
RIGHT! I FORGOT, KANADE!!!
I HAVE A BIG ANNOUNCEMENT TO MAKE!!!
WHAT!? WHAT IS IT!?

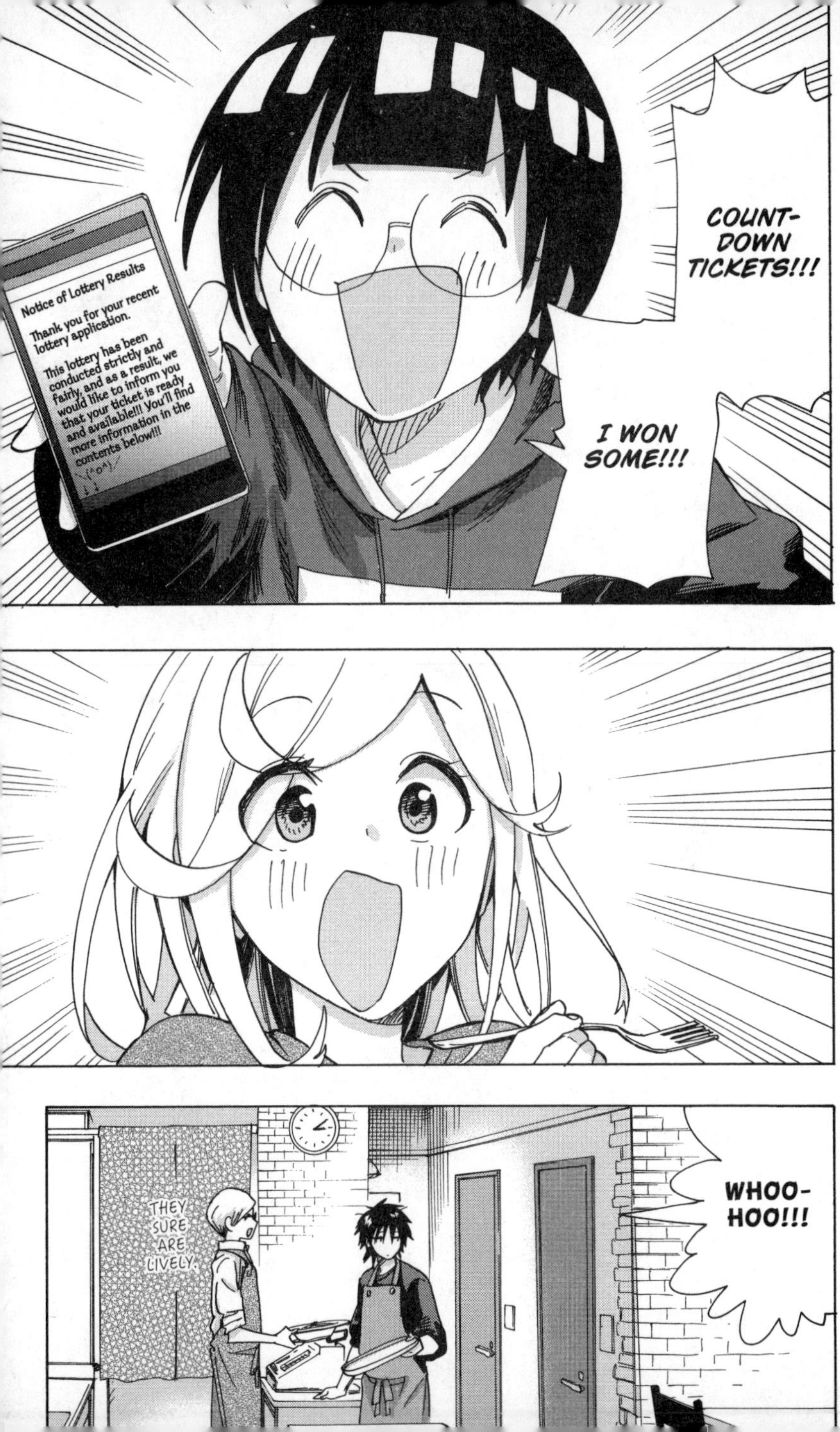
COUNT-DOWN TICKETS!!!
I WON SOME!!!
Notice of Lottery Results
Thank you for your recent lottery application.
This lottery has been conducted strictly and fairly, and as a result, we would like to inform you that your ticket is ready and available!!! You'll find more information in the contents below!!!
WHOO-HOO!!!
THEY SURE ARE LIVELY.

Days on Fes

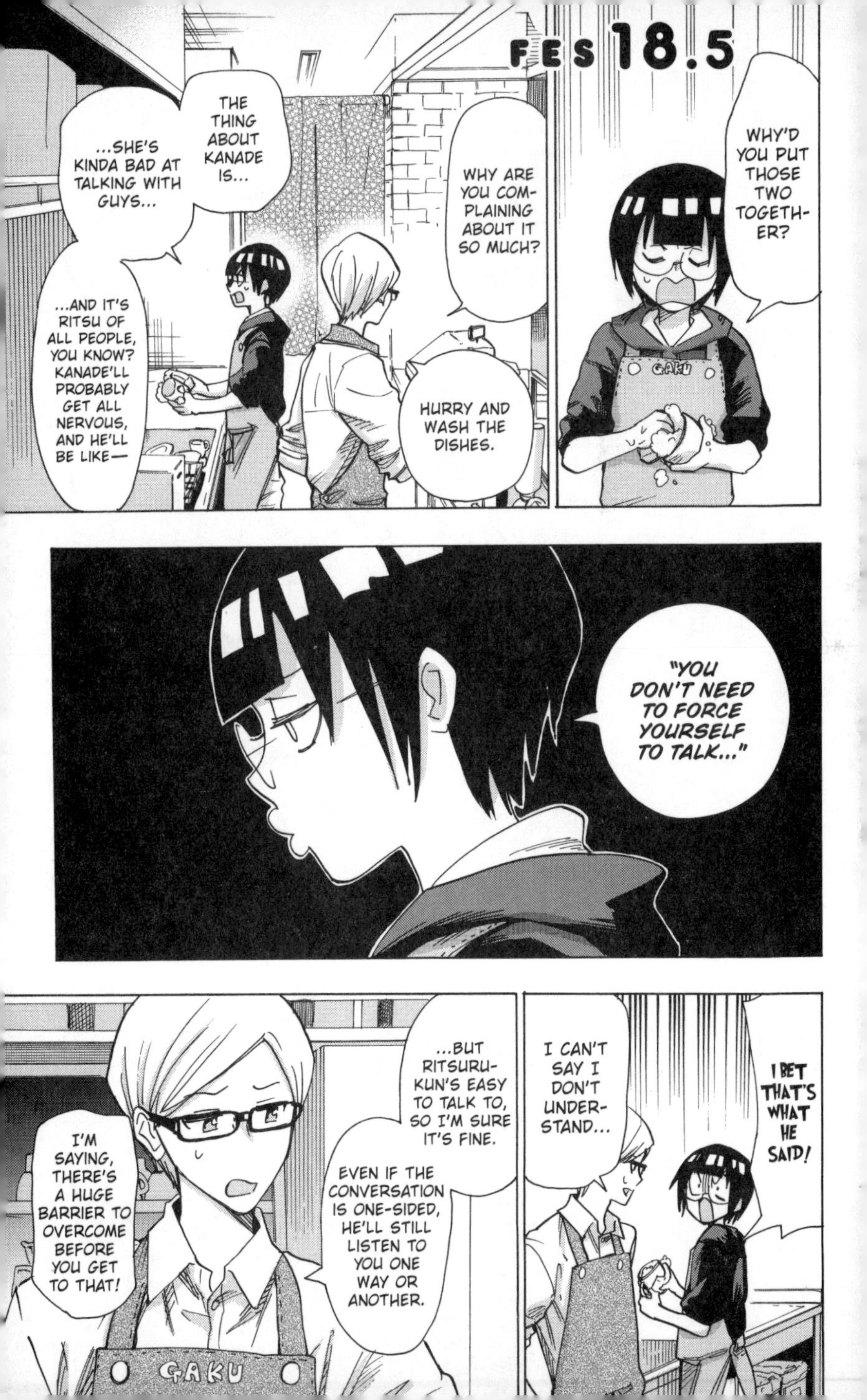
FES 18.5
WHY'D YOU PUT THOSE TWO TOGETH-ER?
WHY ARE YOU COM-PLAINING ABOUT IT SO MUCH?
HURRY AND WASH THE DISHES.
THE THING ABOUT KANADE IS...
...SHE'S KINDA BAD AT TALKING WITH GUYS...
...AND IT'S RITSU OF ALL PEOPLE, YOU KNOW? KANADE'LL PROBABLY GET ALL NERVOUS, AND HE'LL BE LIKE—
"YOU DON'T NEED TO FORCE YOURSELF TO TALK..."
I BET THAT'S WHAT HE SAID!
I CAN'T SAY I DON'T UNDER-STAND...
...BUT RITSURU-KUN'S EASY TO TALK TO, SO I'M SURE IT'S FINE.
EVEN IF THE CONVERSATION IS ONE-SIDED, HE'LL STILL LISTEN TO YOU ONE WAY OR ANOTHER.
I'M SAYING, THERE'S A HUGE BARRIER TO OVERCOME BEFORE YOU GET TO THAT!
GAKU

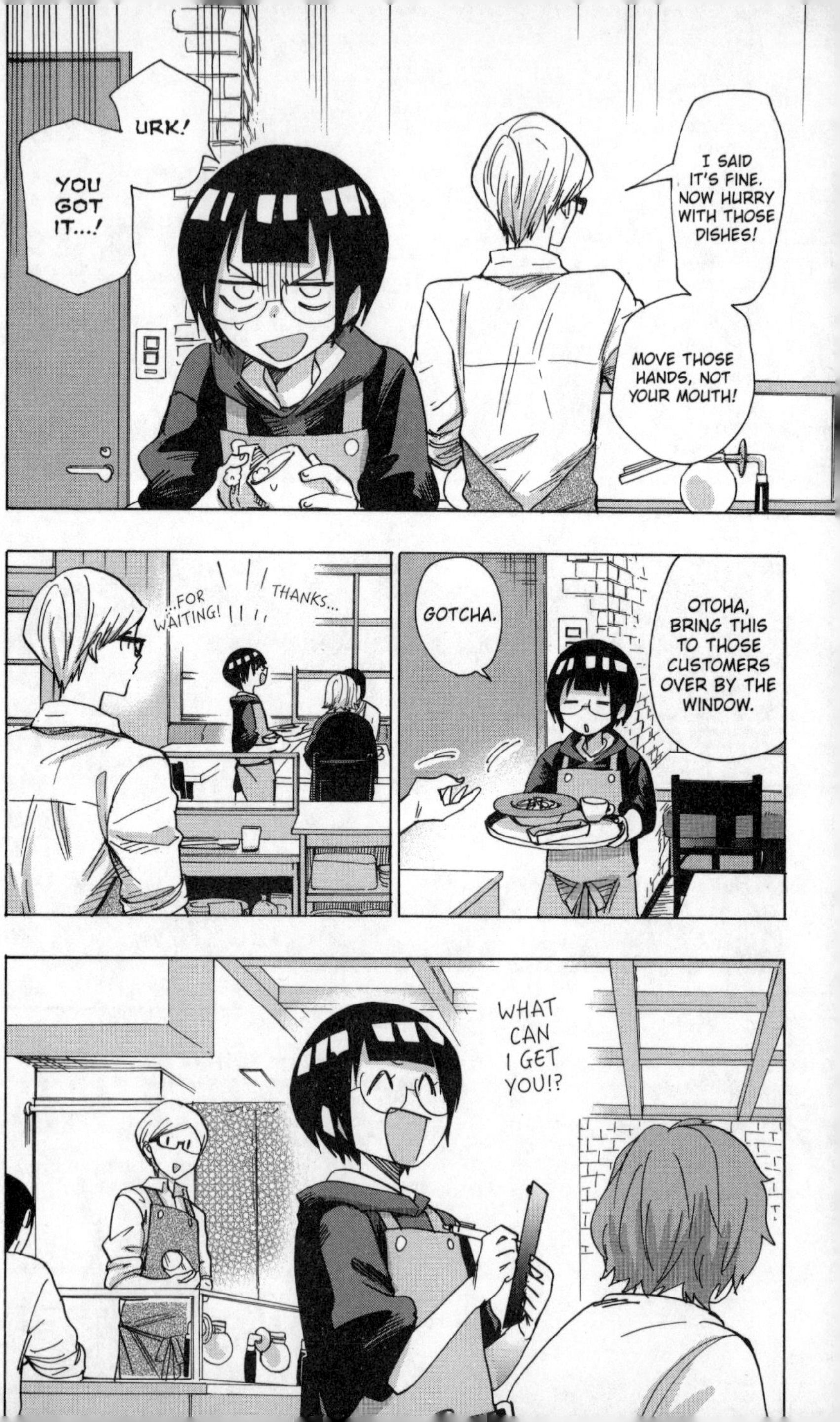
I SAID IT'S FINE. NOW HURRY WITH THOSE DISHES!
MOVE THOSE HANDS, NOT YOUR MOUTH!
URK!
YOU GOT IT...!
OTOHA, BRING THIS TO THOSE CUSTOMERS OVER BY THE WINDOW.
GOTCHA.
THANKS...
...FOR WAITING!
WHAT CAN I GET YOU!?

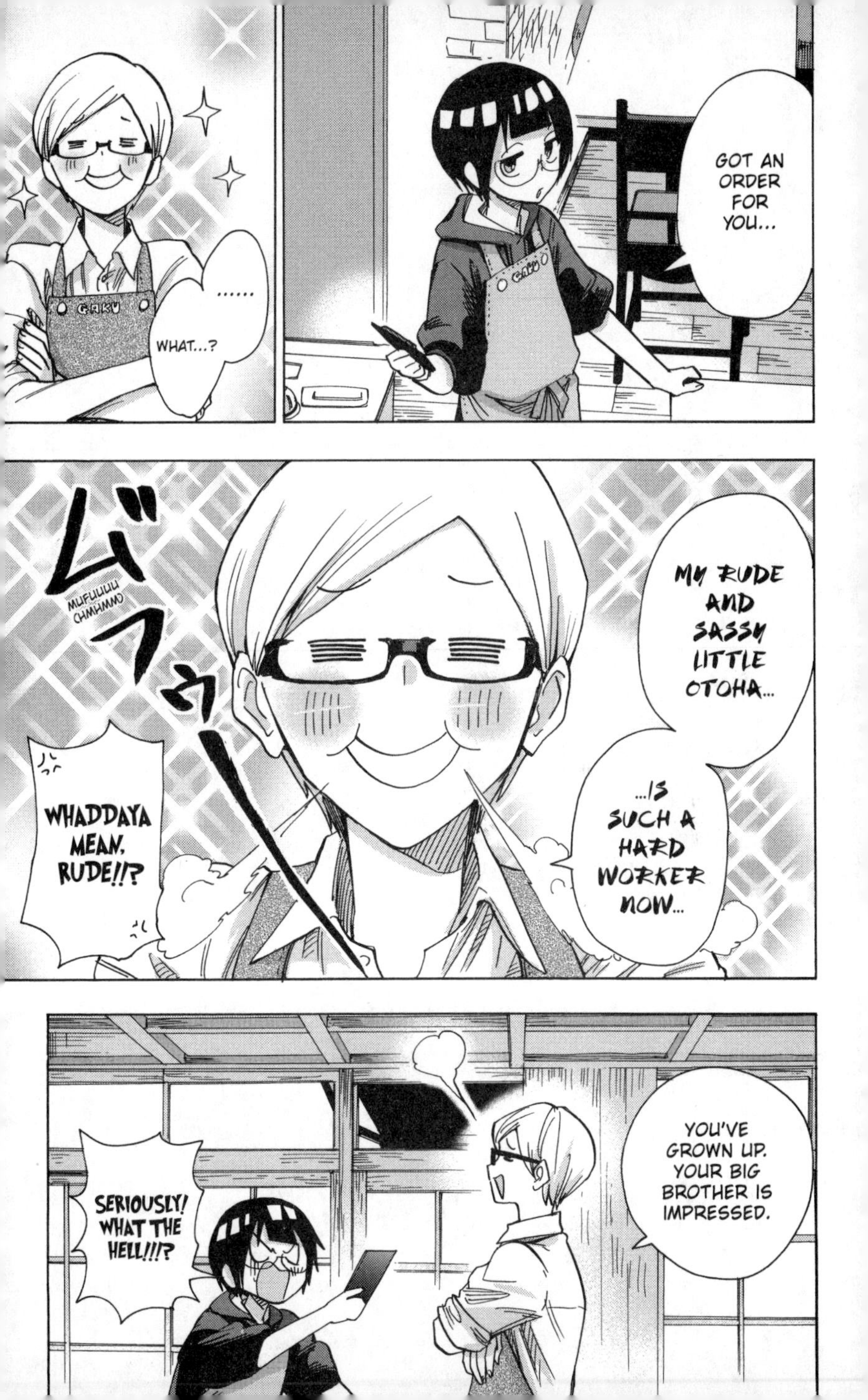
GOT AN ORDER FOR YOU...
......
WHAT...?
MY RUDE AND SASSY LITTLE OTOHA...
...IS SUCH A HARD WORKER NOW...
MUFUUUUU (HMHMM)
WHADDAYA MEAN, RUDE!!?
YOU'VE GROWN UP. YOUR BIG BROTHER IS IMPRESSED.
SERIOUSLY! WHAT THE HELL!!!?

Days on Fes

SP 5

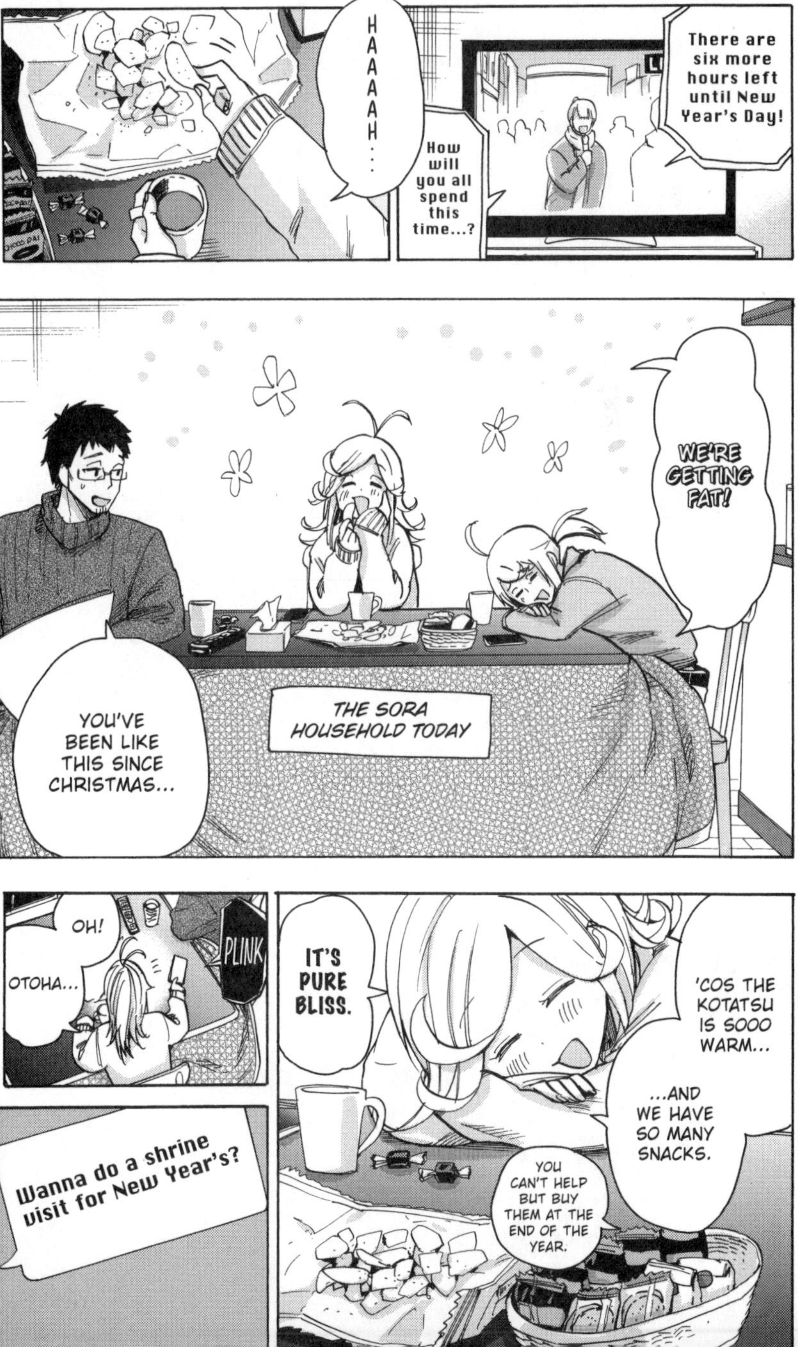
There are six more hours left until New Year's Day!
How will you all spend this time...?
HAAAAH...
WE'RE GETTING FAT!
THE SORA HOUSEHOLD TODAY
YOU'VE BEEN LIKE THIS SINCE CHRISTMAS...
'COS THE KOTATSU IS SOOO WARM...
...AND WE HAVE SO MANY SNACKS.
YOU CAN'T HELP BUT BUY THEM AT THE END OF THE YEAR.
IT'S PURE BLISS.
PLINK
OH!
OTOHA...
Wanna do a shrine visit for New Year's?

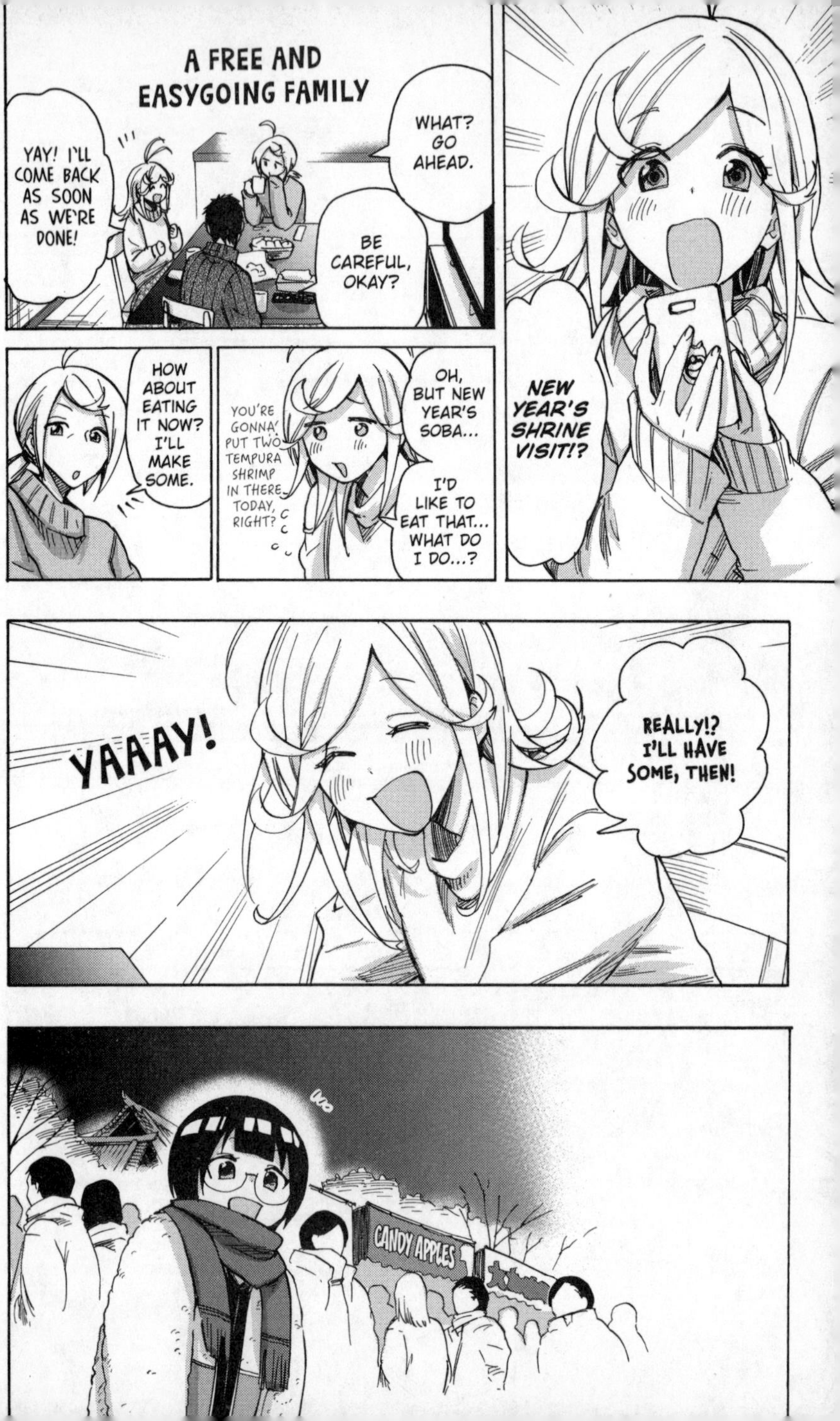
NEW YEAR'S SHRINE VISIT!?
A FREE AND EASYGOING FAMILY
WHAT? GO AHEAD.
BE CAREFUL, OKAY?
YAY! I'LL COME BACK AS SOON AS WE'RE DONE!
OH, BUT NEW YEAR'S SOBA...
I'D LIKE TO EAT THAT... WHAT DO I DO...?
YOU'RE GONNA PUT TWO TEMPURA SHRIMP IN THERE TODAY, RIGHT?
HOW ABOUT EATING IT NOW? I'LL MAKE SOME.
REALLY!? I'LL HAVE SOME, THEN!
YAAAY!
CANDY APPLES

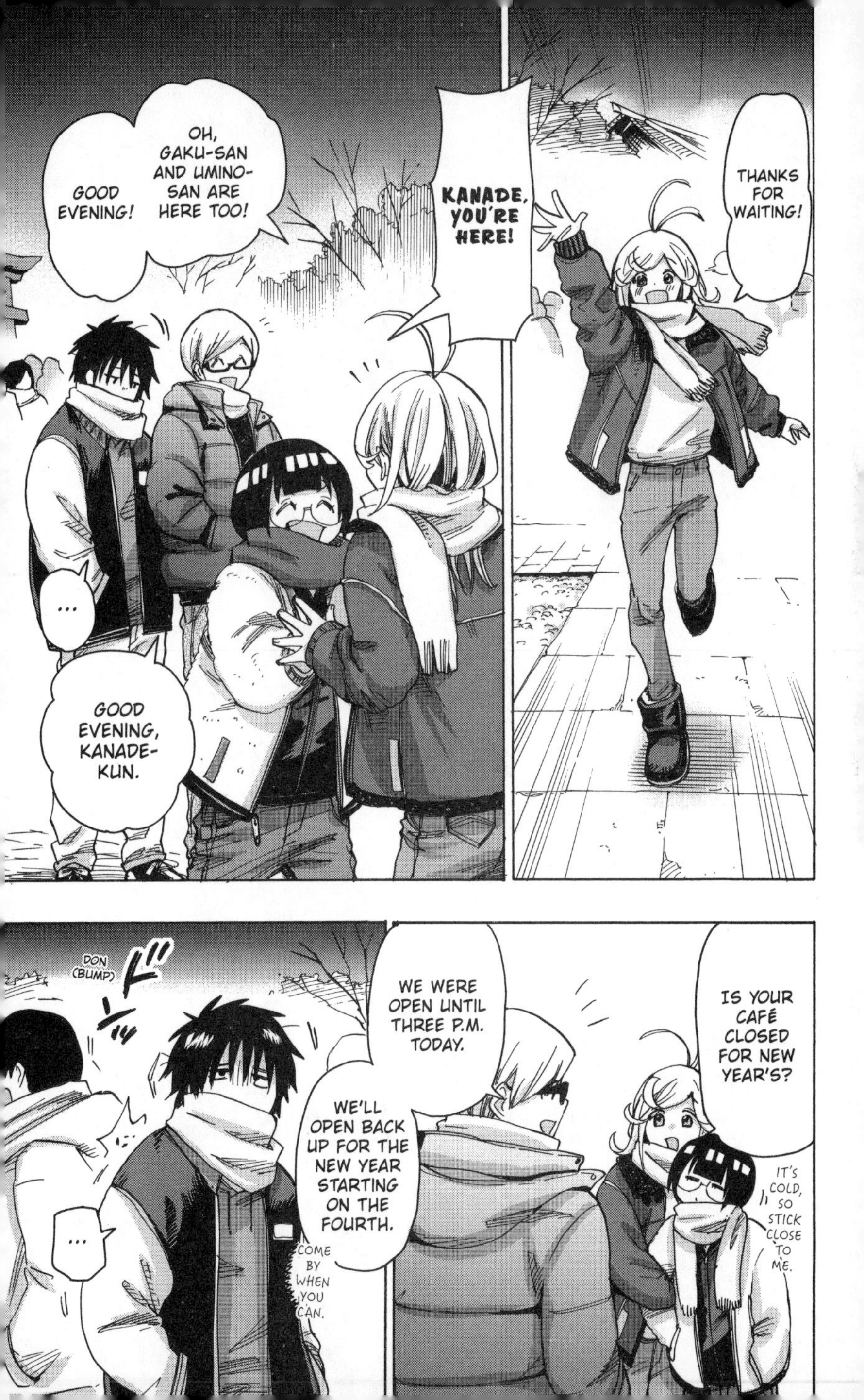
THANKS FOR WAITING!
KANADE, YOU'RE HERE!
OH, GAKU-SAN AND UMINO-SAN ARE HERE TOO!
GOOD EVENING!
...
GOOD EVENING, KANADE-KUN.
IS YOUR CAFÉ CLOSED FOR NEW YEAR'S?
IT'S COLD, SO STICK CLOSE TO ME.
WE WERE OPEN UNTIL THREE P.M. TODAY.
WE'LL OPEN BACK UP FOR THE NEW YEAR STARTING ON THE FOURTH.
COME BY WHEN YOU CAN.
DON (BUMP)
...

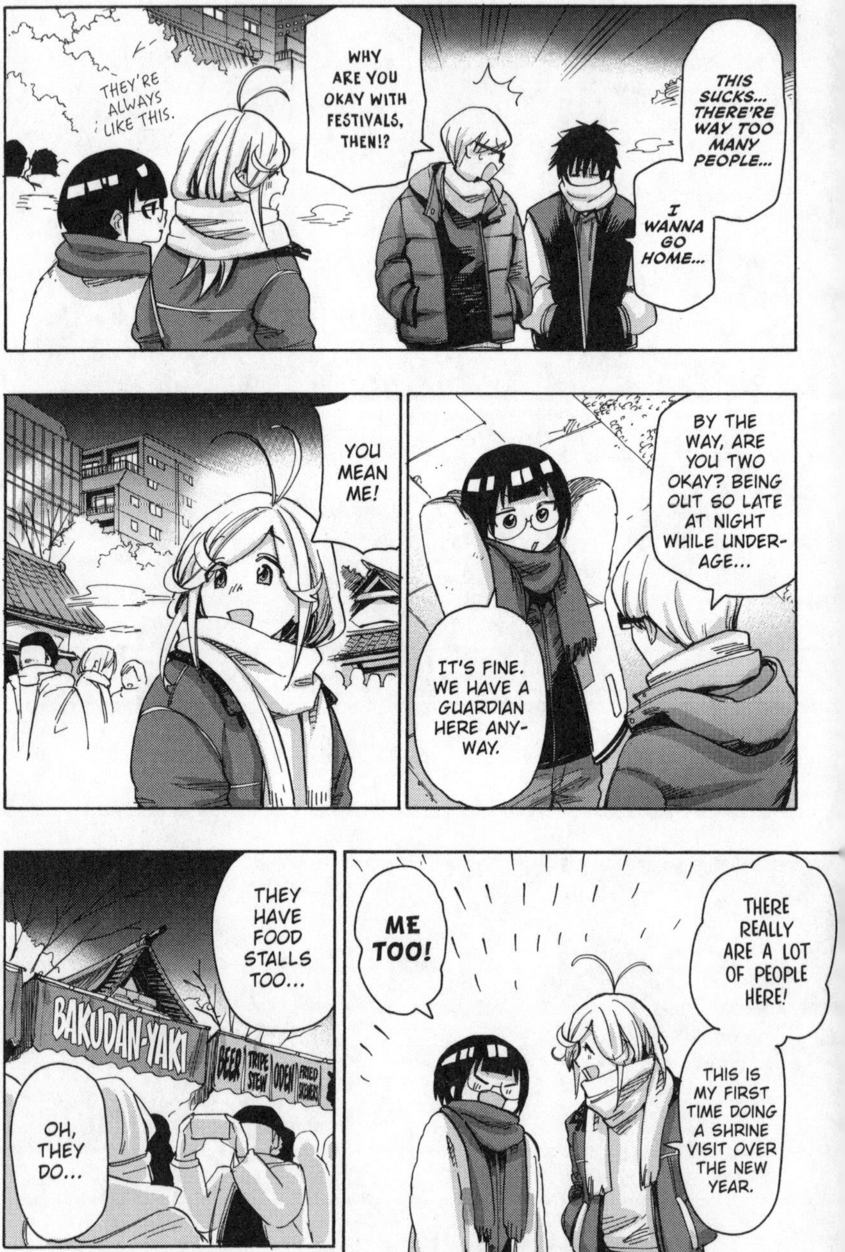
THIS SUCKS... THERE'RE WAY TOO MANY PEOPLE...
I WANNA GO HOME...
WHY ARE YOU OKAY WITH FESTIVALS, THEN!?
THEY'RE ALWAYS LIKE THIS.
BY THE WAY, ARE YOU TWO OKAY? BEING OUT SO LATE AT NIGHT WHILE UNDERAGE...
IT'S FINE. WE HAVE A GUARDIAN HERE ANYWAY.
YOU MEAN ME!
THERE REALLY ARE A LOT OF PEOPLE HERE!
THIS IS MY FIRST TIME DOING A SHRINE VISIT OVER THE NEW YEAR.
ME TOO!
THEY HAVE FOOD STALLS TOO...
BAKUDAN-YAKI
BEER
TRIPE STEW
ODEN
OH, THEY DO...

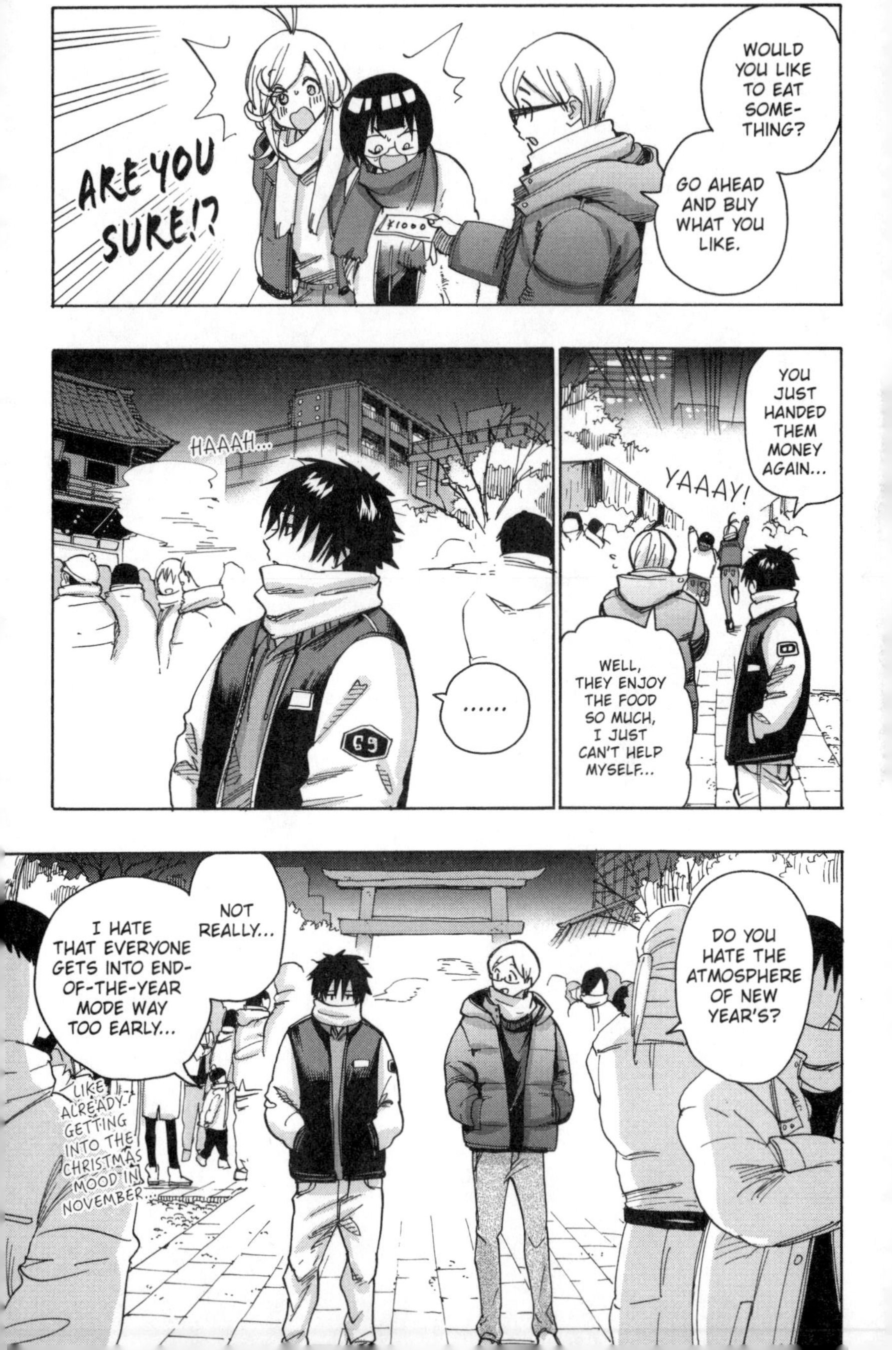
WOULD YOU LIKE TO EAT SOMETHING?
GO AHEAD AND BUY WHAT YOU LIKE.
¥1000
ARE YOU SURE!?
YOU JUST HANDED THEM MONEY AGAIN...
YAAAY!
WELL, THEY ENJOY THE FOOD SO MUCH, I JUST CAN'T HELP MYSELF...
HAAAH...
......
DO YOU HATE THE ATMOSPHERE OF NEW YEAR'S?
NOT REALLY...
I HATE THAT EVERYONE GETS INTO END-OF-THE-YEAR MODE WAY TOO EARLY...
LIKE ALREADY GETTING INTO THE CHRISTMAS MOOD IN NOVEMBER...

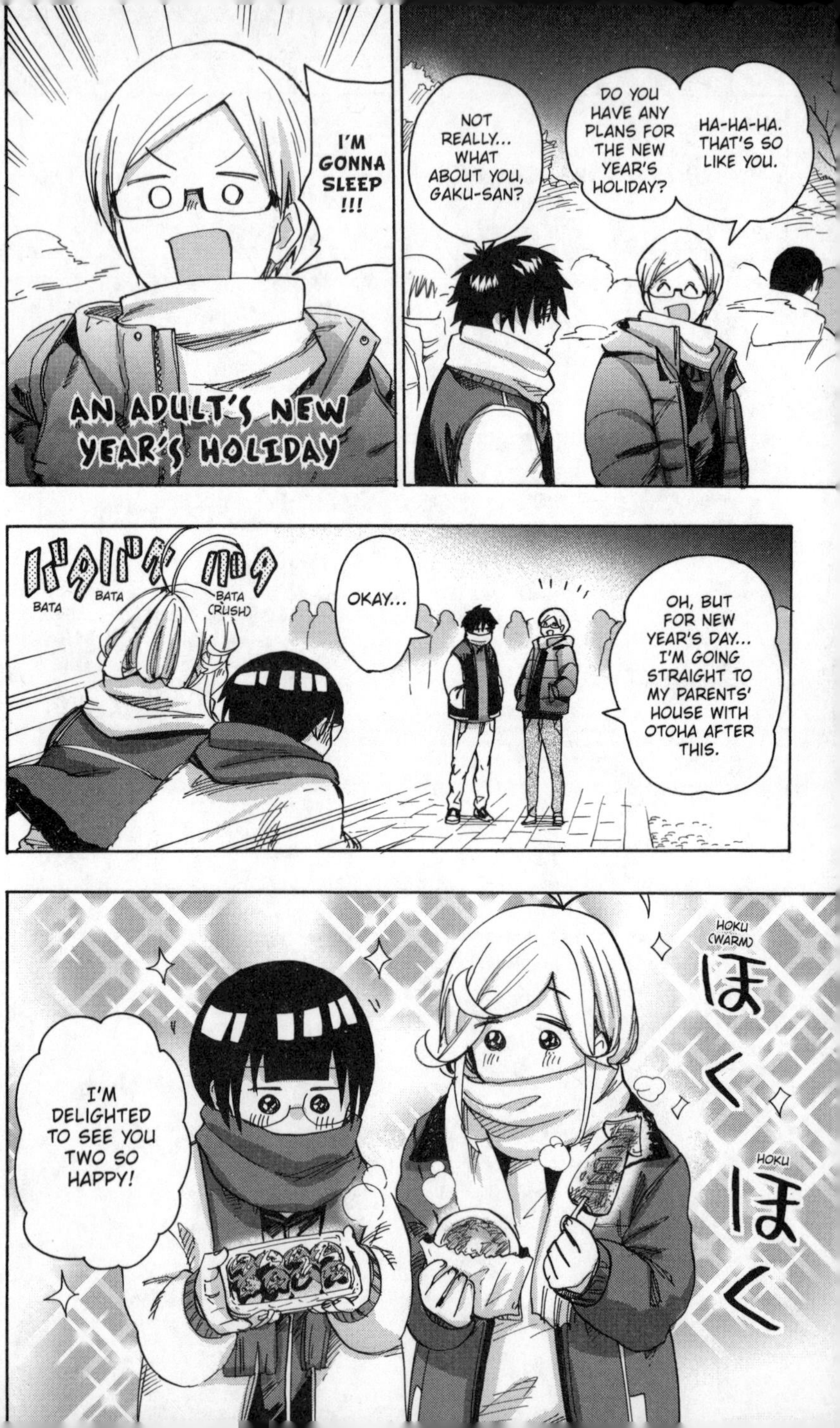
HA-HA-HA. THAT'S SO LIKE YOU.
DO YOU HAVE ANY PLANS FOR THE NEW YEAR'S HOLIDAY?
NOT REALLY... WHAT ABOUT YOU, GAKU-SAN?
I'M GONNA SLEEP !!!
AN ADULT'S NEW YEAR'S HOLIDAY
OH, BUT FOR NEW YEAR'S DAY... I'M GOING STRAIGHT TO MY PARENTS' HOUSE WITH OTOHA AFTER THIS.
OKAY...
バタ
BATA (RUSH)
バタバタ
BATA
BATA
ほく
HOKU (WARM)
ほく
HOKU
I'M DELIGHTED TO SEE YOU TWO SO HAPPY!

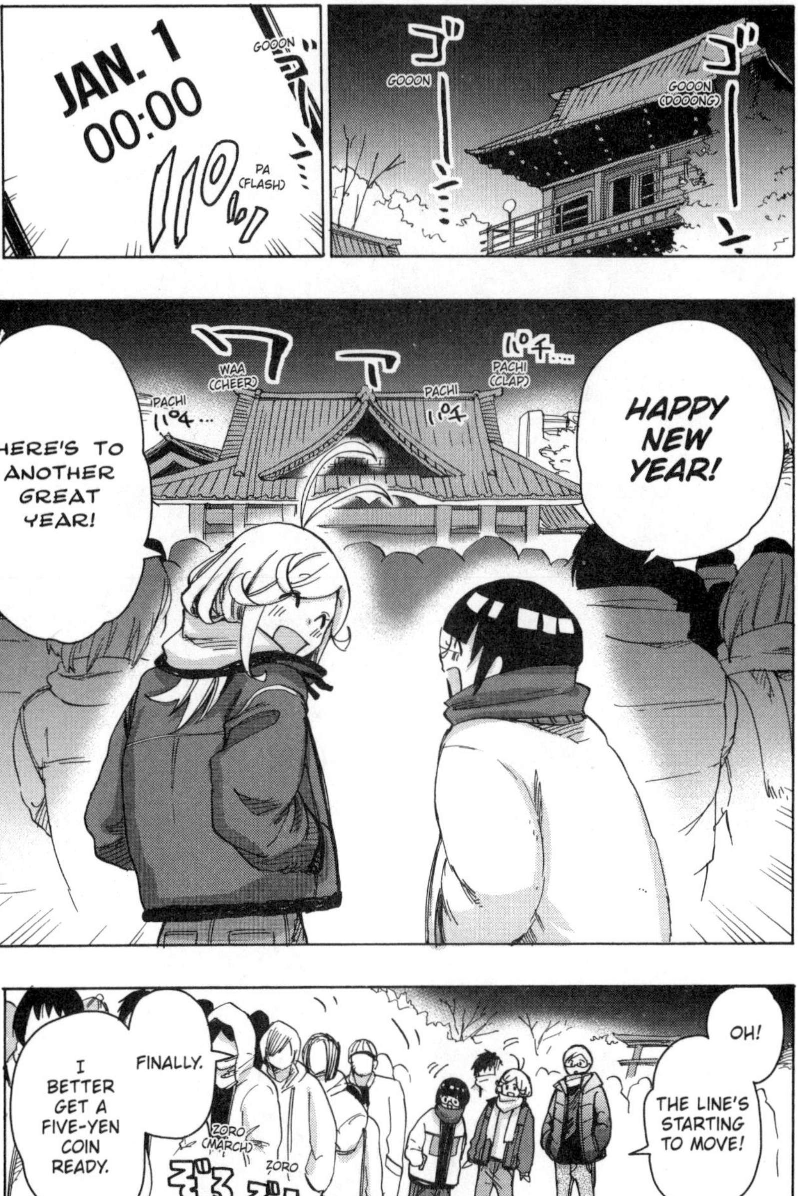
GOOON
GOOON (DOOONG)
JAN. 1 00:00
GOOON
PA (FLASH)
PACHI (CLAP)
PACHI
WAA (CHEER)
PACHI
HAPPY NEW YEAR!
HERE'S TO ANOTHER GREAT YEAR!
OH!
THE LINE'S STARTING TO MOVE!
FINALLY.
I BETTER GET A FIVE-YEN COIN READY.
ZORO (MARCH)
ZORO

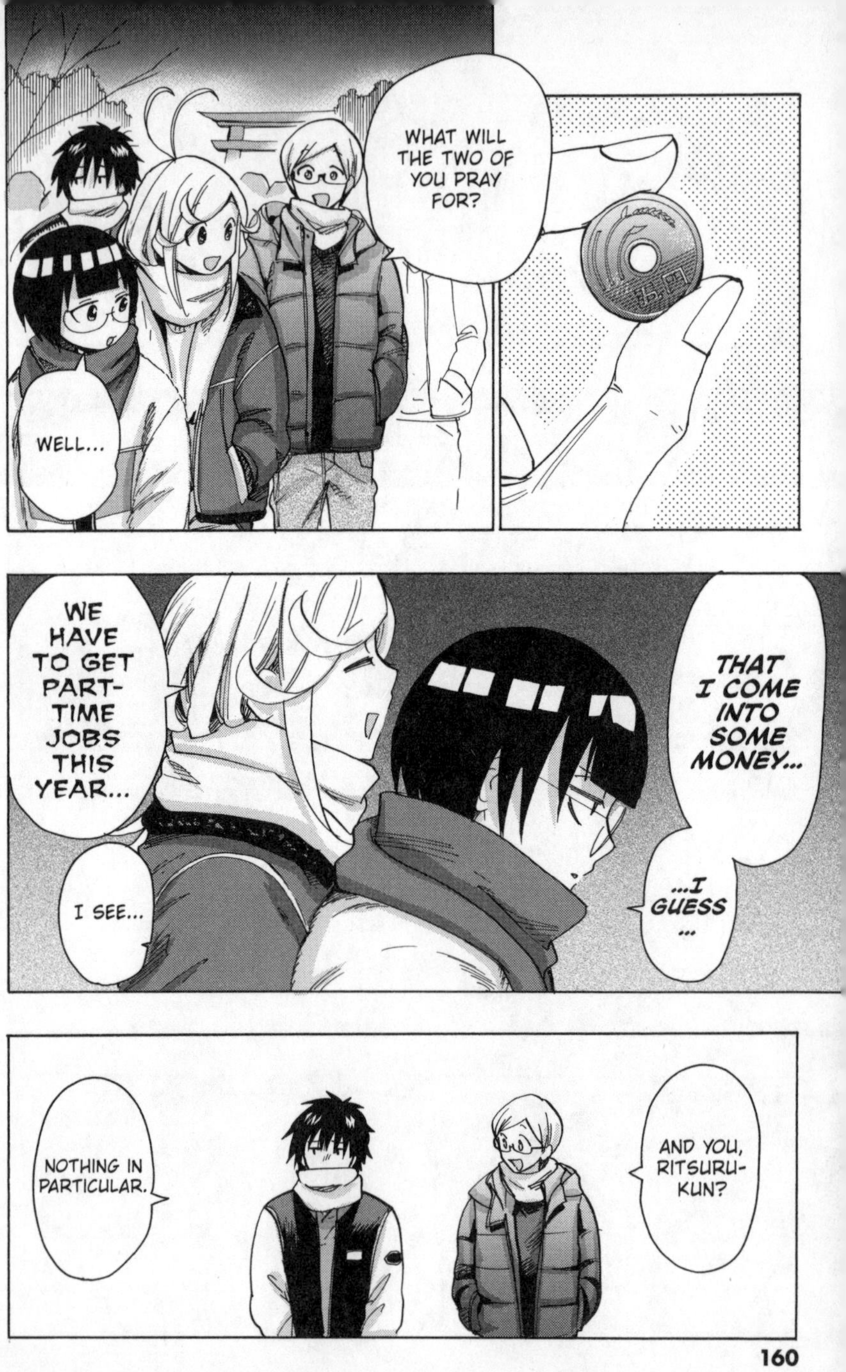
WHAT WILL THE TWO OF YOU PRAY FOR?
WELL...
THAT I COME INTO SOME MONEY...
...I GUESS...
WE HAVE TO GET PART-TIME JOBS THIS YEAR...
I SEE...
AND YOU, RITSURU-KUN?
NOTHING IN PARTICULAR.

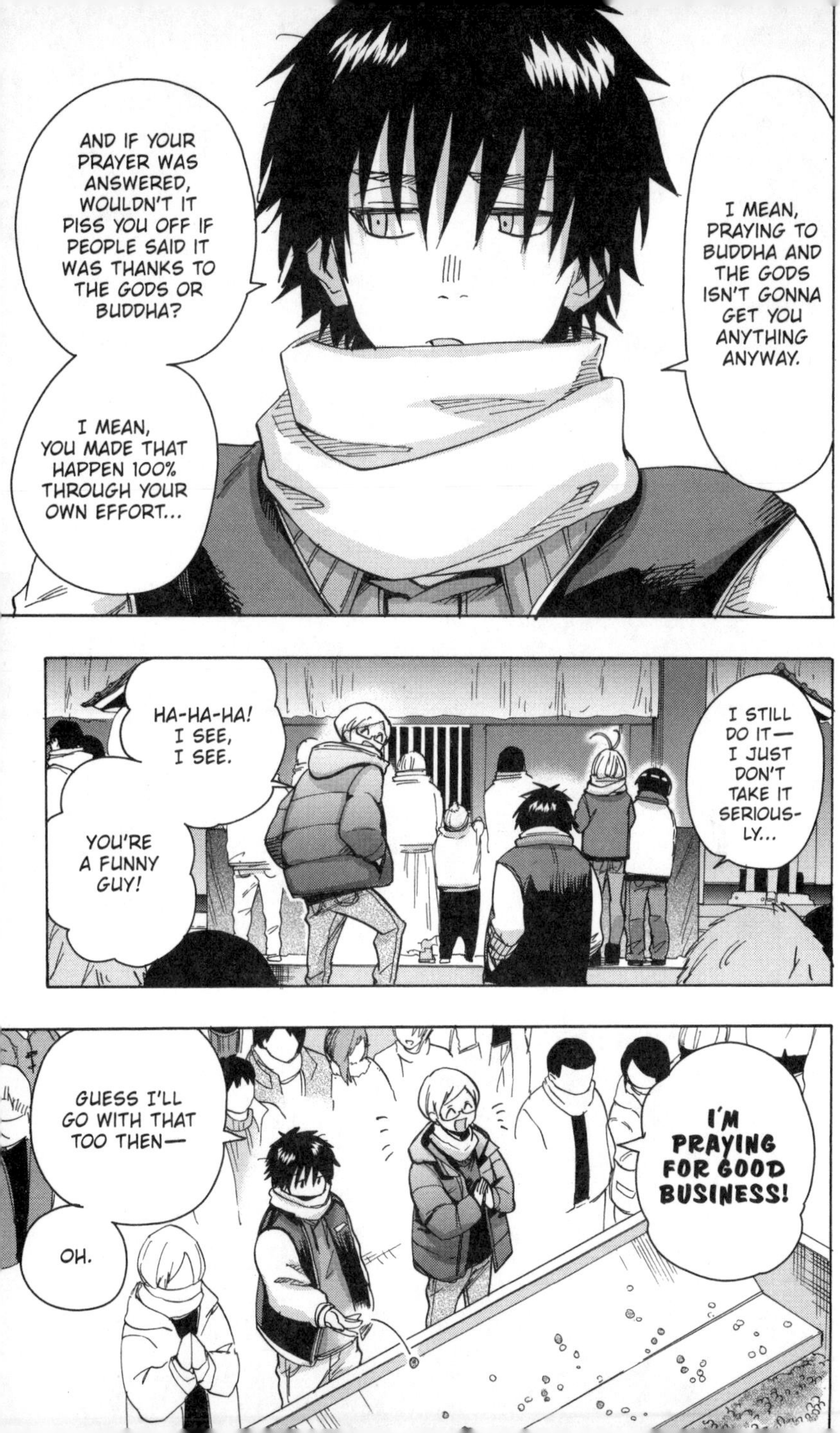
I MEAN, PRAYING TO BUDDHA AND THE GODS ISN'T GONNA GET YOU ANYTHING ANYWAY.
AND IF YOUR PRAYER WAS ANSWERED, WOULDN'T IT PISS YOU OFF IF PEOPLE SAID IT WAS THANKS TO THE GODS OR BUDDHA?
I MEAN, YOU MADE THAT HAPPEN 100% THROUGH YOUR OWN EFFORT...
I STILL DO IT— I JUST DON'T TAKE IT SERIOUSLY...
HA-HA-HA! I SEE, I SEE.
YOU'RE A FUNNY GUY!
I'M PRAYING FOR GOOD BUSINESS!
GUESS I'LL GO WITH THAT TOO THEN—
OH.

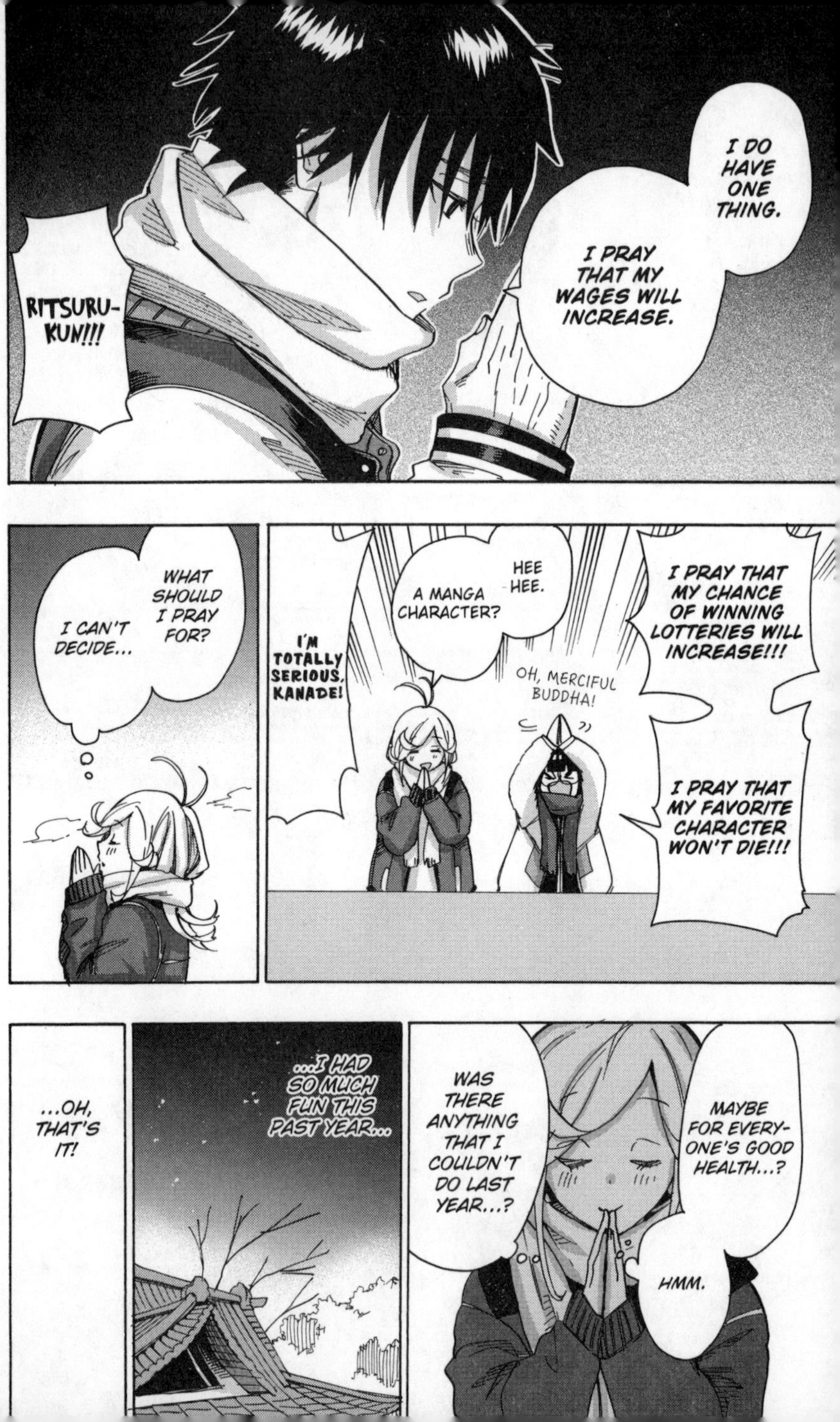
I DO HAVE ONE THING.
I PRAY THAT MY WAGES WILL INCREASE.
RITSURU-KUN!!!
I PRAY THAT MY CHANCE OF WINNING LOTTERIES WILL INCREASE!!!
HEE HEE.
A MANGA CHARACTER?
I'M TOTALLY SERIOUS, KANADE!
OH, MERCIFUL BUDDHA!
I PRAY THAT MY FAVORITE CHARACTER WON'T DIE!!!
WHAT SHOULD I PRAY FOR?
I CAN'T DECIDE...
MAYBE FOR EVERY-ONE'S GOOD HEALTH...?
HMM.
WAS THERE ANYTHING THAT I COULDN'T DO LAST YEAR...?
...I HAD SO MUCH FUN THIS PAST YEAR...
...OH, THAT'S IT!

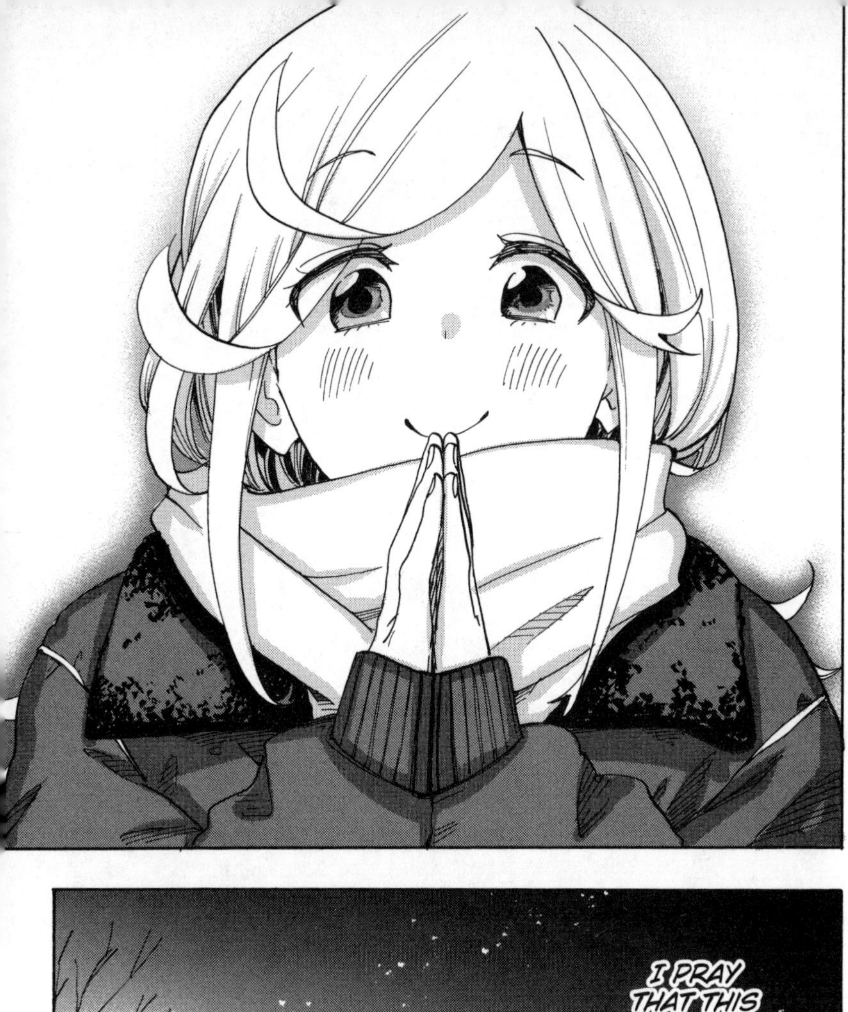

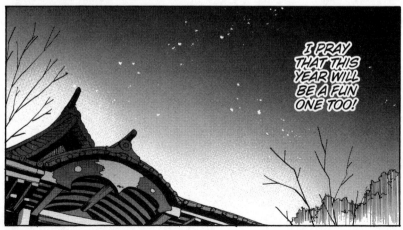

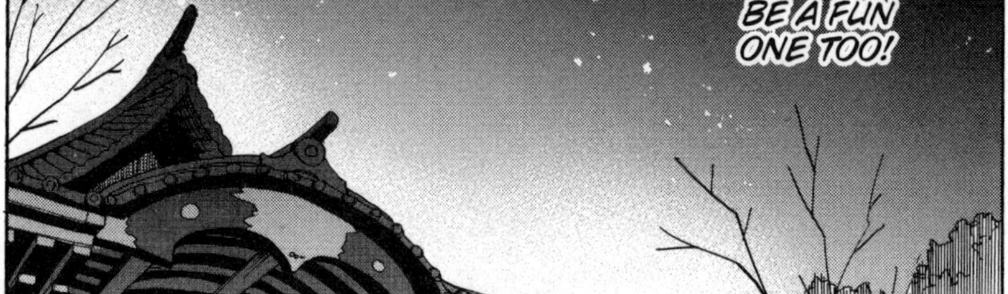
I PRAY THAT THIS YEAR WILL BE A FUN ONE TOO!

Days on Fes

SP 6

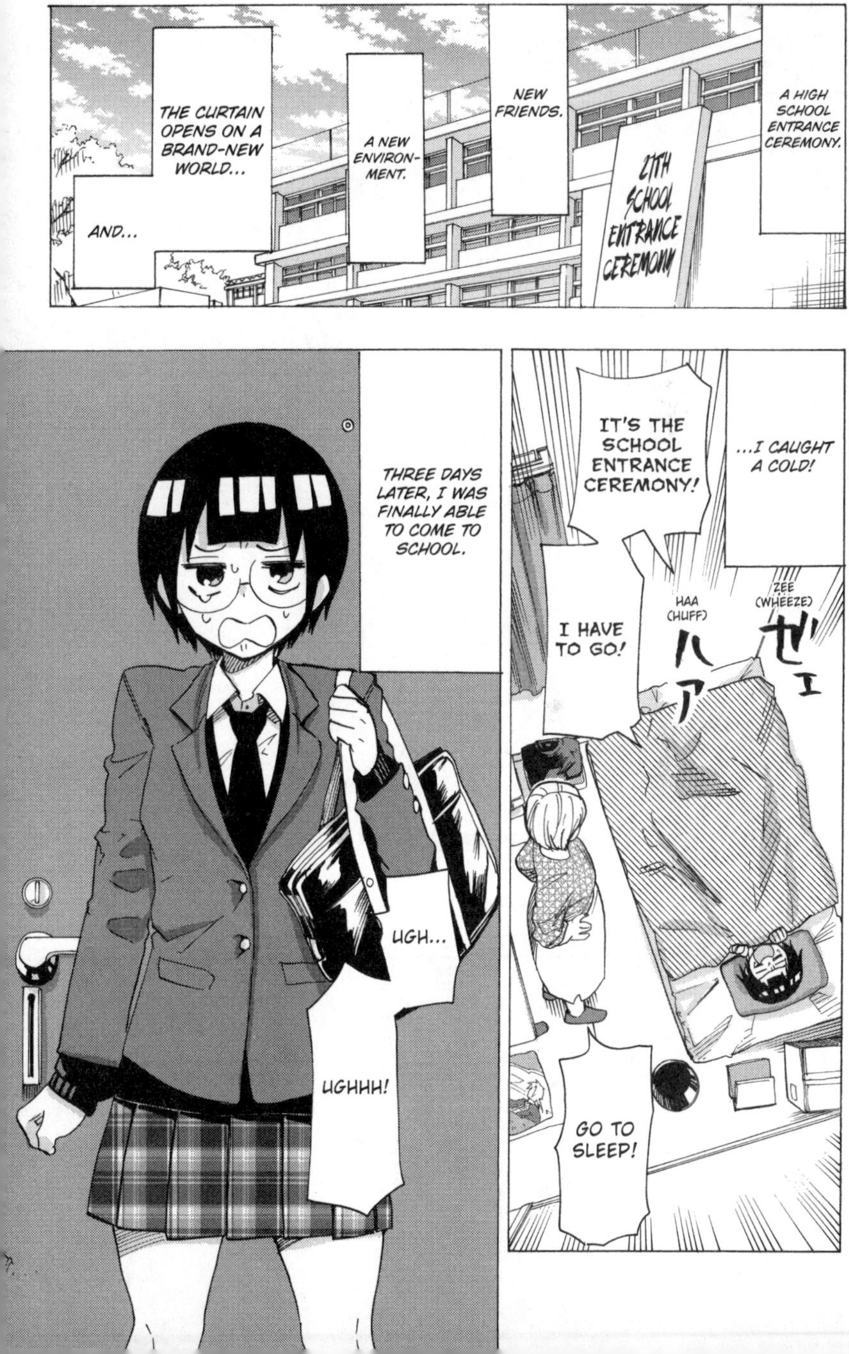
A HIGH SCHOOL ENTRANCE CEREMONY.
27TH SCHOOL ENTRANCE CEREMONY
NEW FRIENDS.
A NEW ENVIRONMENT.
THE CURTAIN OPENS ON A BRAND-NEW WORLD...
AND...
...I CAUGHT A COLD!
IT'S THE SCHOOL ENTRANCE CEREMONY!
ZEE (WHEEZE)
ゼェ
HAA (HUFF)
ハア
I HAVE TO GO!
GO TO SLEEP!
THREE DAYS LATER, I WAS FINALLY ABLE TO COME TO SCHOOL.
UGH...
UGHHH!

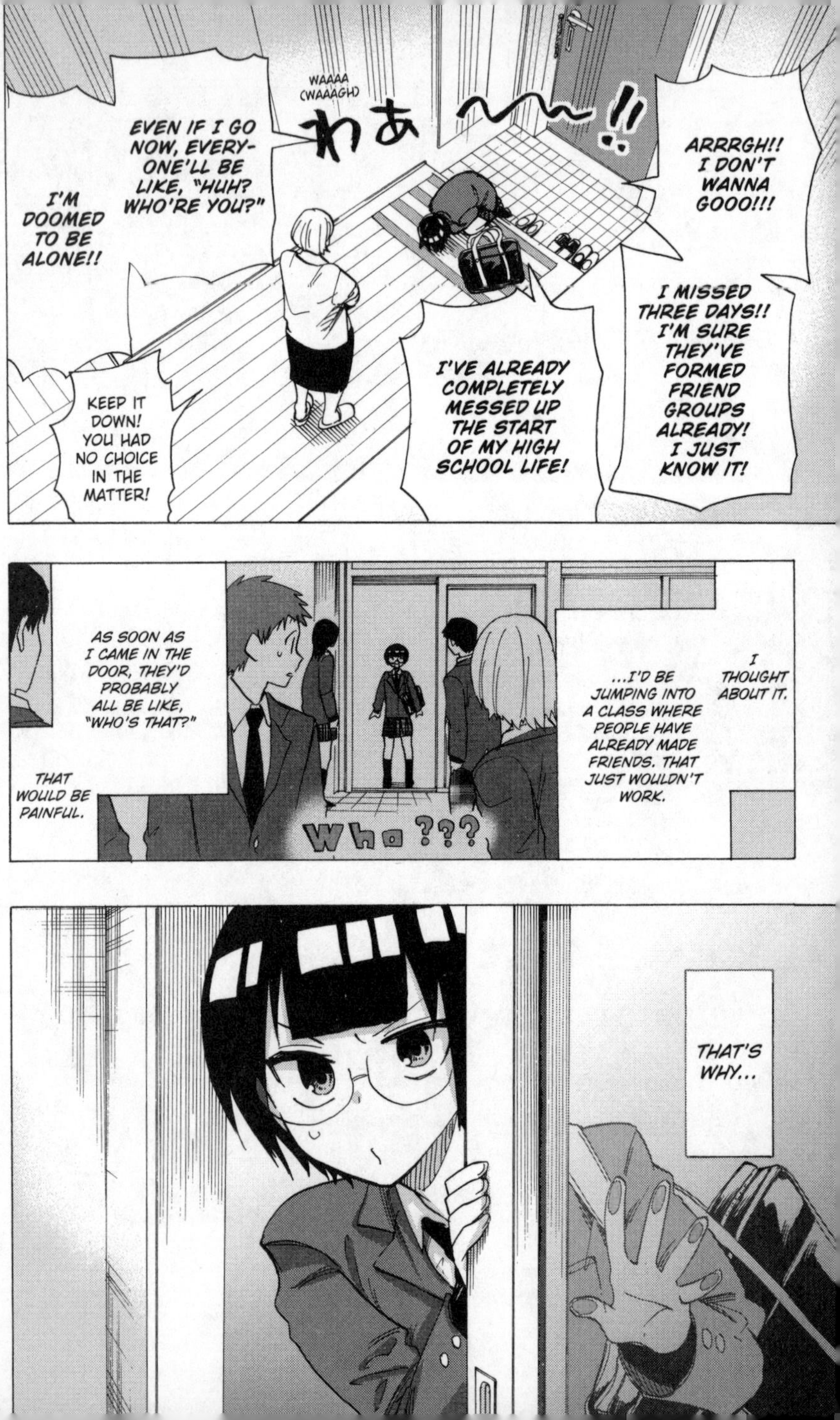
ARRRGH!! I DON'T WANNA GOOO!!!
I MISSED THREE DAYS!! I'M SURE THEY'VE FORMED FRIEND GROUPS ALREADY! I JUST KNOW IT!
I'VE ALREADY COMPLETELY MESSED UP THE START OF MY HIGH SCHOOL LIFE!
わあ~~!!
WAAAA (WAAAGH)
EVEN IF I GO NOW, EVERY-ONE'LL BE LIKE, "HUH? WHO'RE YOU?"
I'M DOOMED TO BE ALONE!!
KEEP IT DOWN! YOU HAD NO CHOICE IN THE MATTER!
I THOUGHT ABOUT IT.
...I'D BE JUMPING INTO A CLASS WHERE PEOPLE HAVE ALREADY MADE FRIENDS. THAT JUST WOULDN'T WORK.
Who ???
AS SOON AS I CAME IN THE DOOR, THEY'D PROBABLY ALL BE LIKE, "WHO'S THAT?"
THAT WOULD BE PAINFUL.
THAT'S WHY...

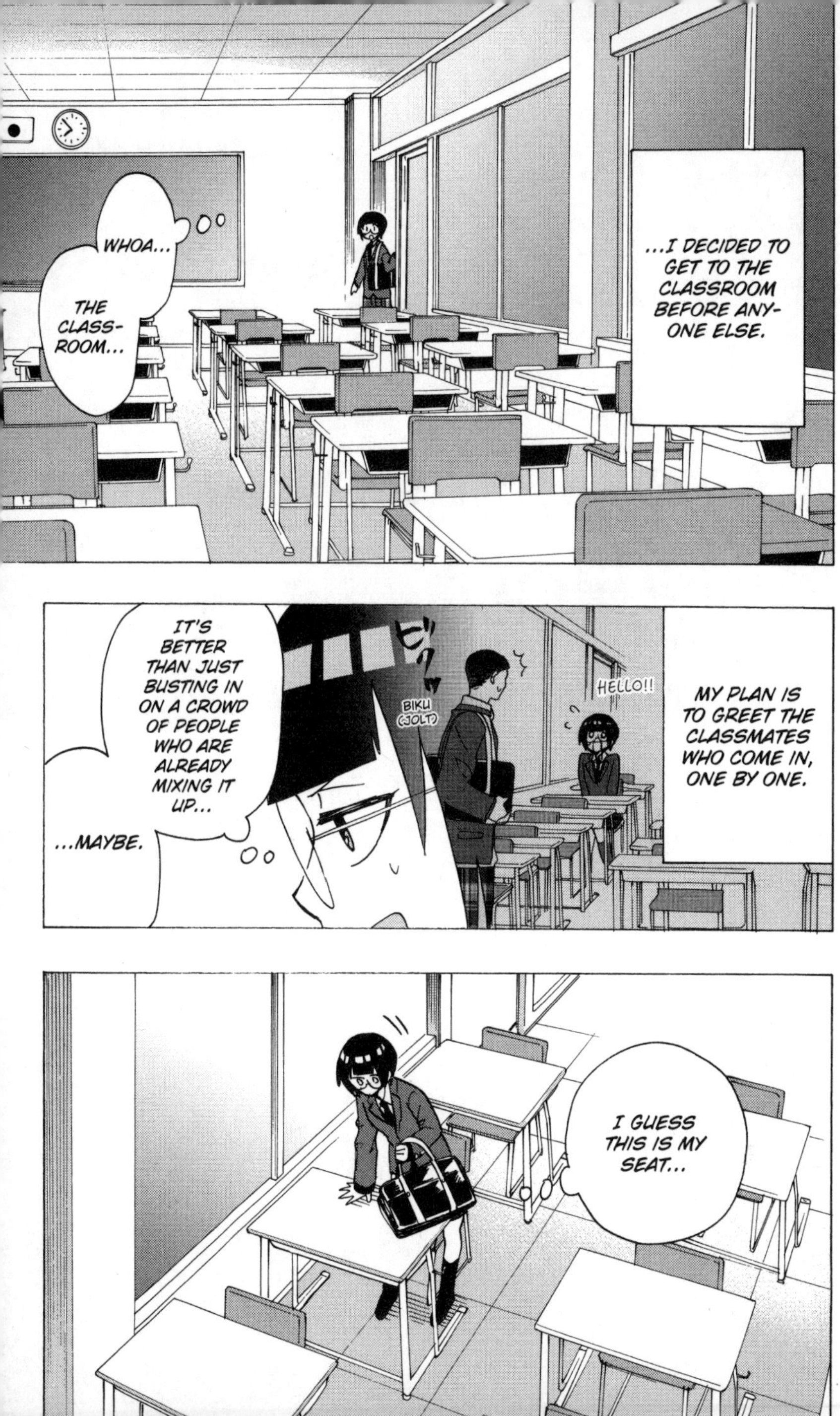
...I DECIDED TO GET TO THE CLASSROOM BEFORE ANY-ONE ELSE.
WHOA...
THE CLASS-ROOM...
MY PLAN IS TO GREET THE CLASSMATES WHO COME IN, ONE BY ONE.
HELLO!!
BIKU (JOLT)
IT'S BETTER THAN JUST BUSTING IN ON A CROWD OF PEOPLE WHO ARE ALREADY MIXING IT UP...
...MAYBE.
I GUESS THIS IS MY SEAT...

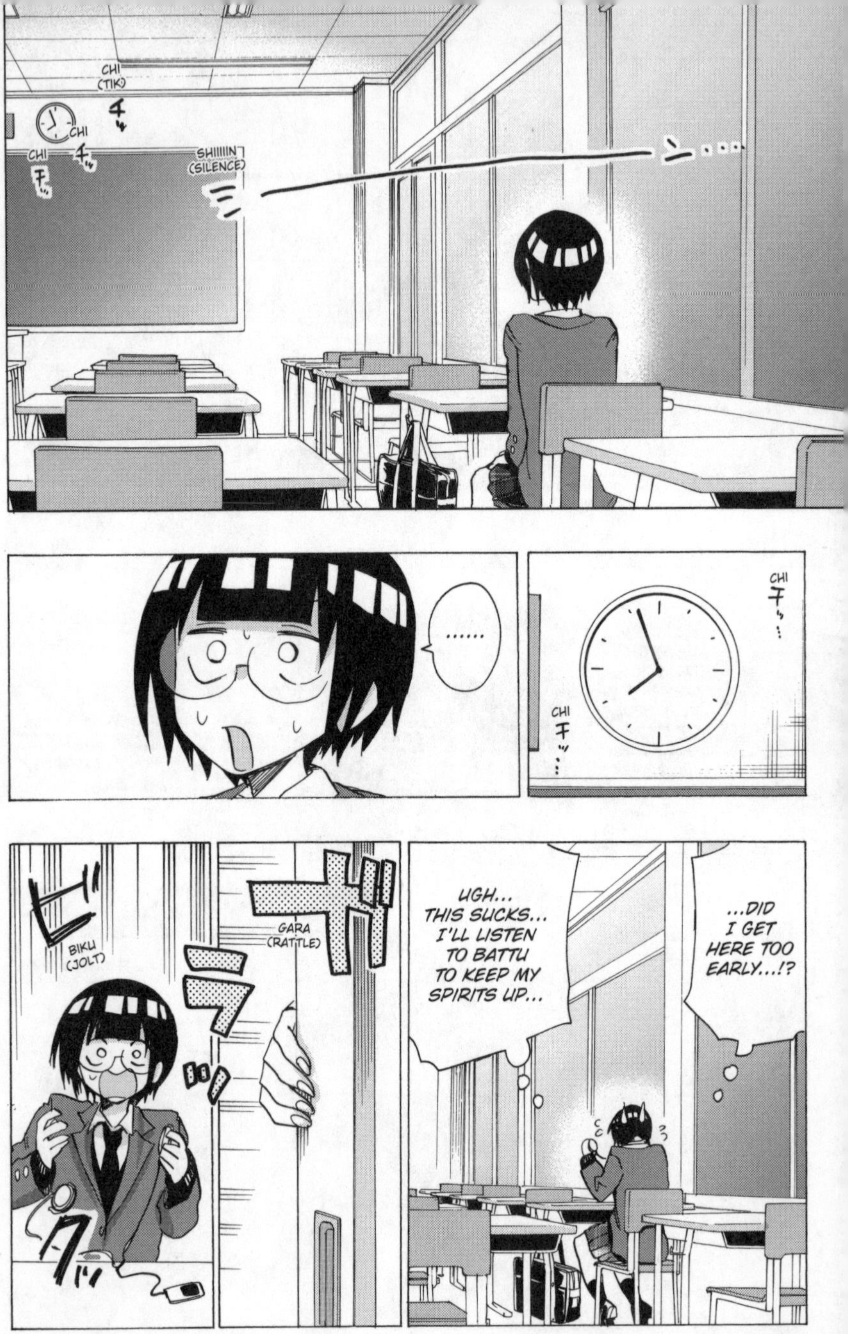
CHI (TIK)
CHI
CHI
SHIIIIN (SILENCE)
CHI
CHI
......
...DID I GET HERE TOO EARLY...!?
UGH... THIS SUCKS... I'LL LISTEN TO BATTU TO KEEP MY SPIRITS UP...
GARA (RATTLE)
BIKU (JOLT)

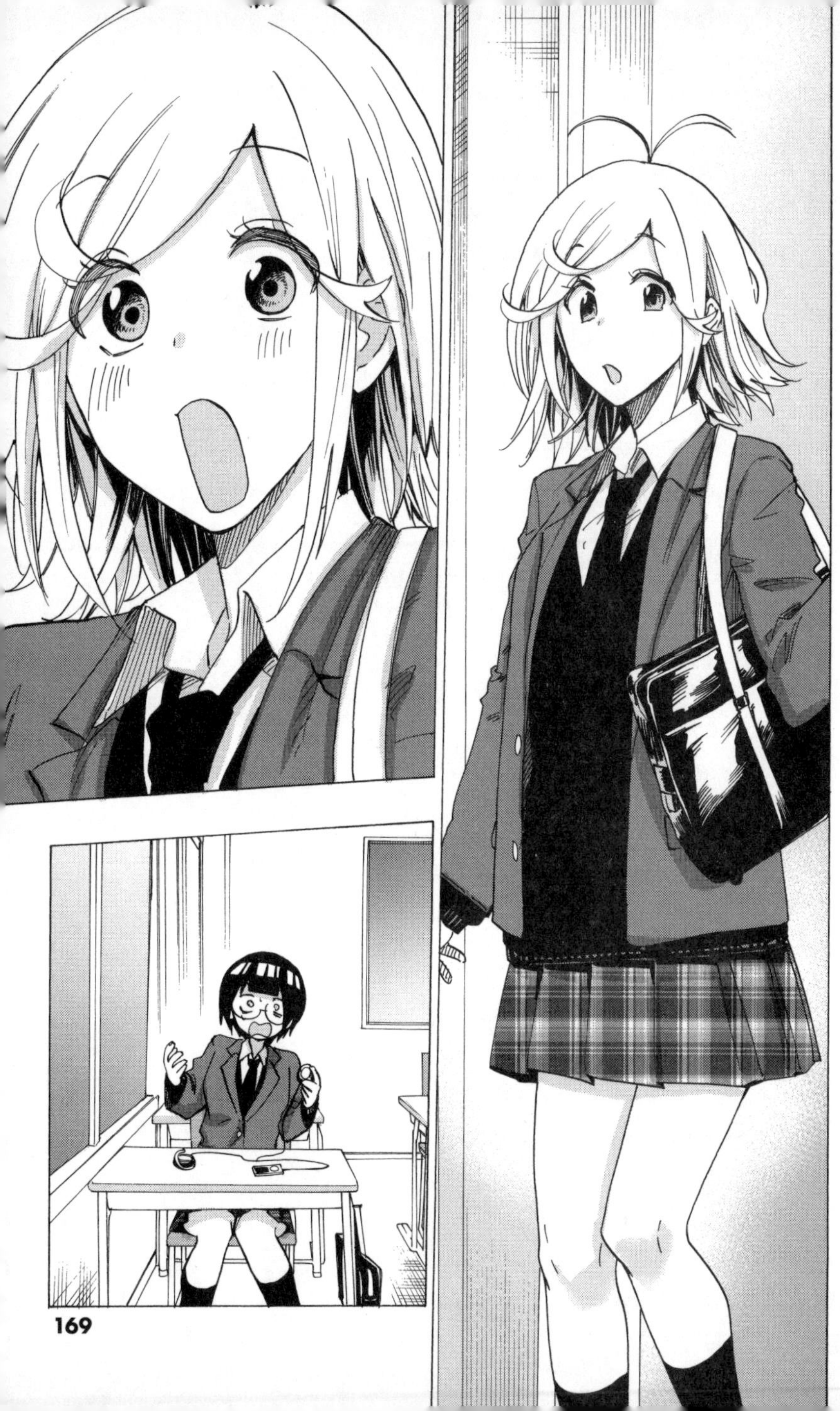

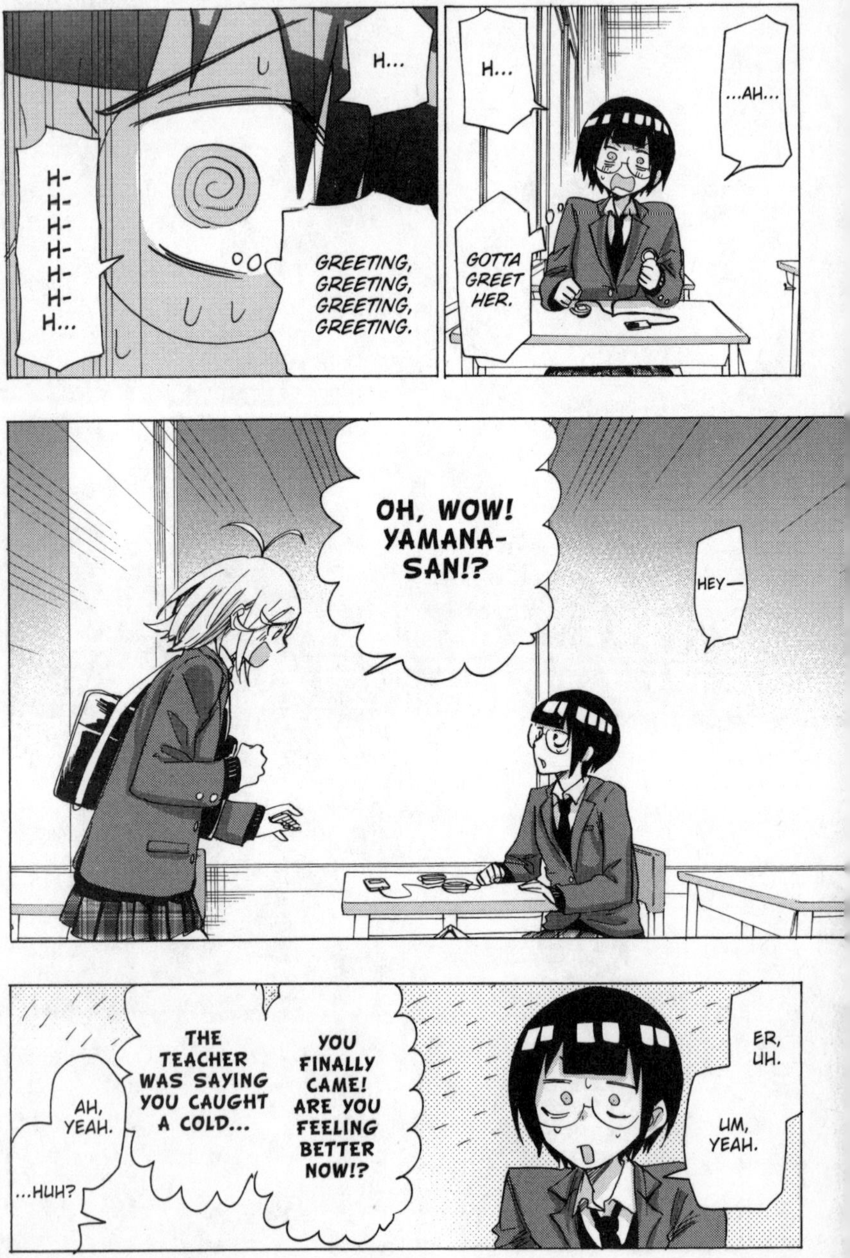
...AH...
H...
GOTTA GREET HER.
H...
GREETING, GREETING, GREETING, GREETING.
H-H-H-H-H-H-H...
HEY—
OH, WOW! YAMANA-SAN!?
ER, UH.
UM, YEAH.
YOU FINALLY CAME! ARE YOU FEELING BETTER NOW!?
THE TEACHER WAS SAYING YOU CAUGHT A COLD...
AH, YEAH.
...HUH?

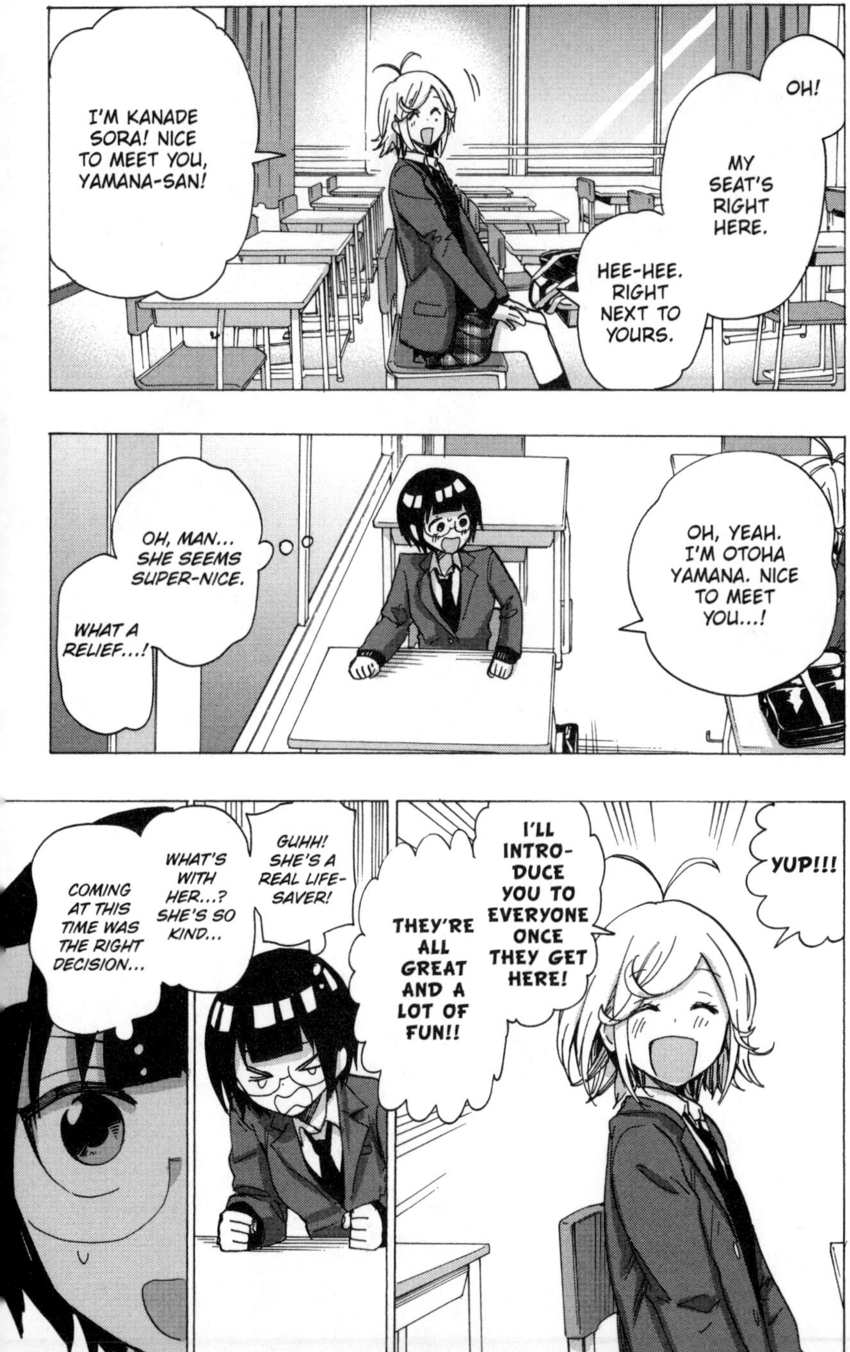
OH!
MY SEAT'S RIGHT HERE.
HEE-HEE. RIGHT NEXT TO YOURS.
I'M KANADE SORA! NICE TO MEET YOU, YAMANA-SAN!
OH, YEAH. I'M OTOHA YAMANA. NICE TO MEET YOU...!
OH, MAN... SHE SEEMS SUPER-NICE.
WHAT A RELIEF...!
YUP!!!
I'LL INTRO-DUCE YOU TO EVERYONE ONCE THEY GET HERE!
THEY'RE ALL GREAT AND A LOT OF FUN!!
GUHH! SHE'S A REAL LIFE-SAVER!
WHAT'S WITH HER...? SHE'S SO KIND...
COMING AT THIS TIME WAS THE RIGHT DECISION...

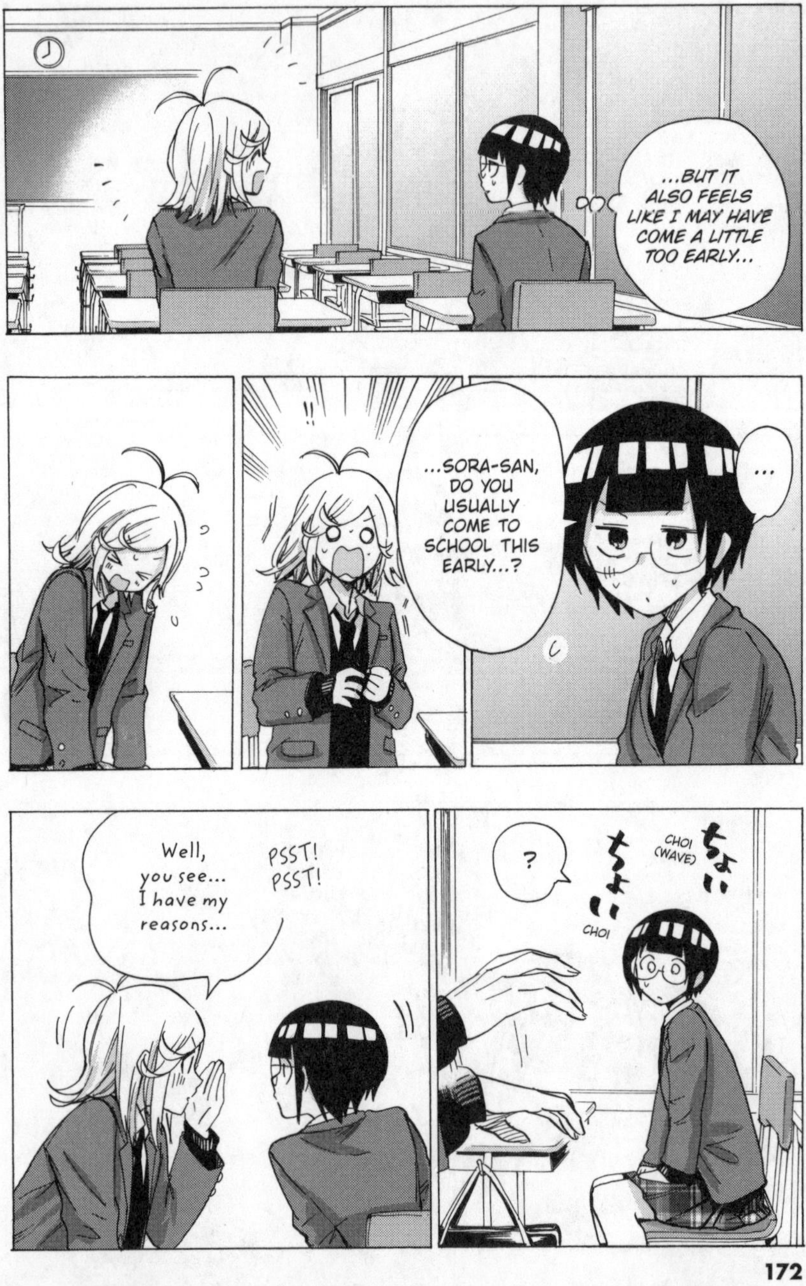
...BUT IT ALSO FEELS LIKE I MAY HAVE COME A LITTLE TOO EARLY...
...
...SORA-SAN, DO YOU USUALLY COME TO SCHOOL THIS EARLY...?
!!
ちょい
CHOI (WAVE)
ちょい
CHOI
?
PSST! PSST!
Well, you see... I have my reasons...

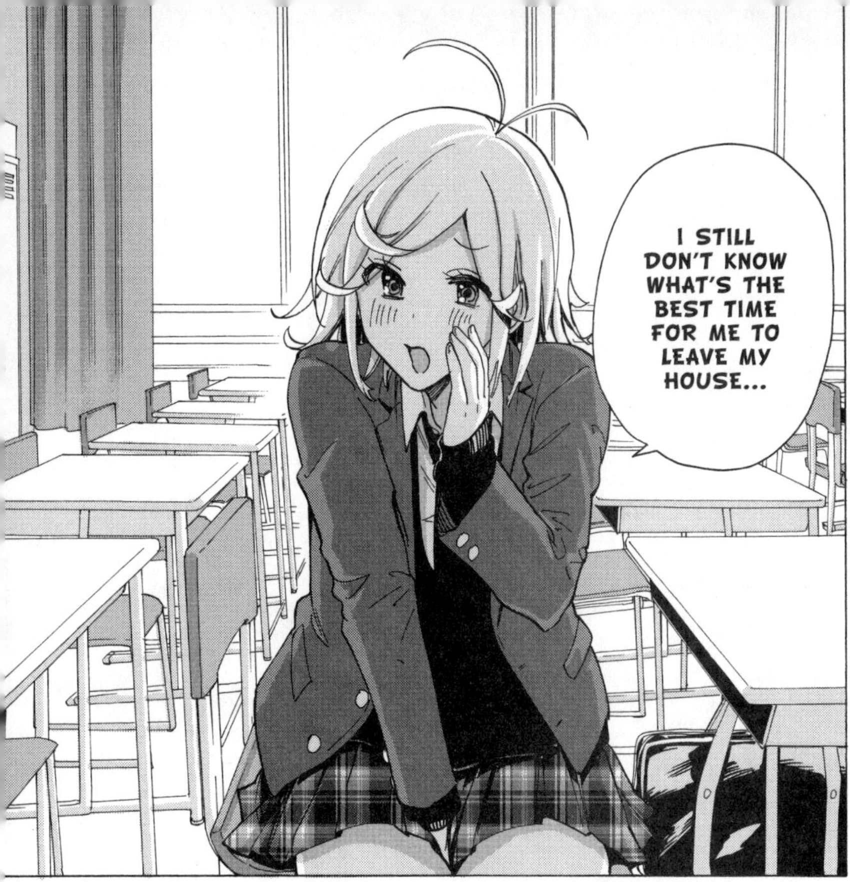
I STILL DON'T KNOW WHAT'S THE BEST TIME FOR ME TO LEAVE MY HOUSE...

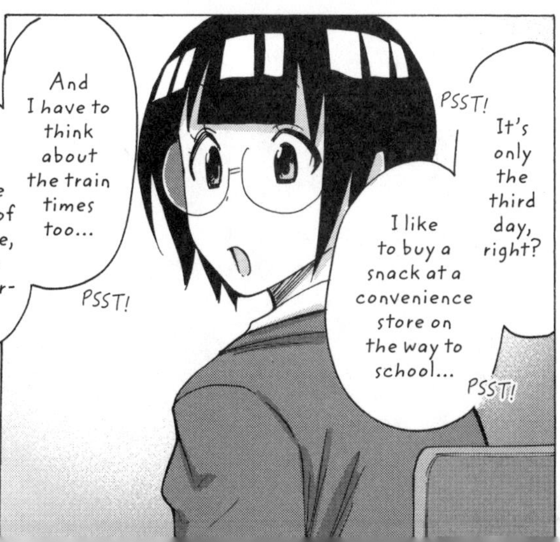
PSST!
It's only the third day, right?
I like to buy a snack at a convenience store on the way to school...
PSST!
And I have to think about the train times too...
PSST!

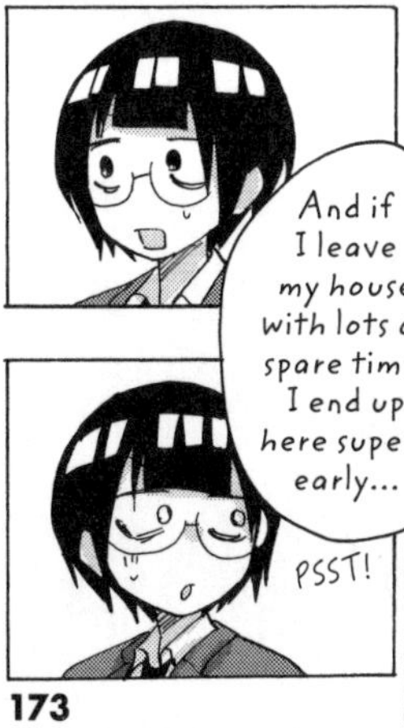
And if I leave my house with lots of spare time, I end up here super-early...
PSST!

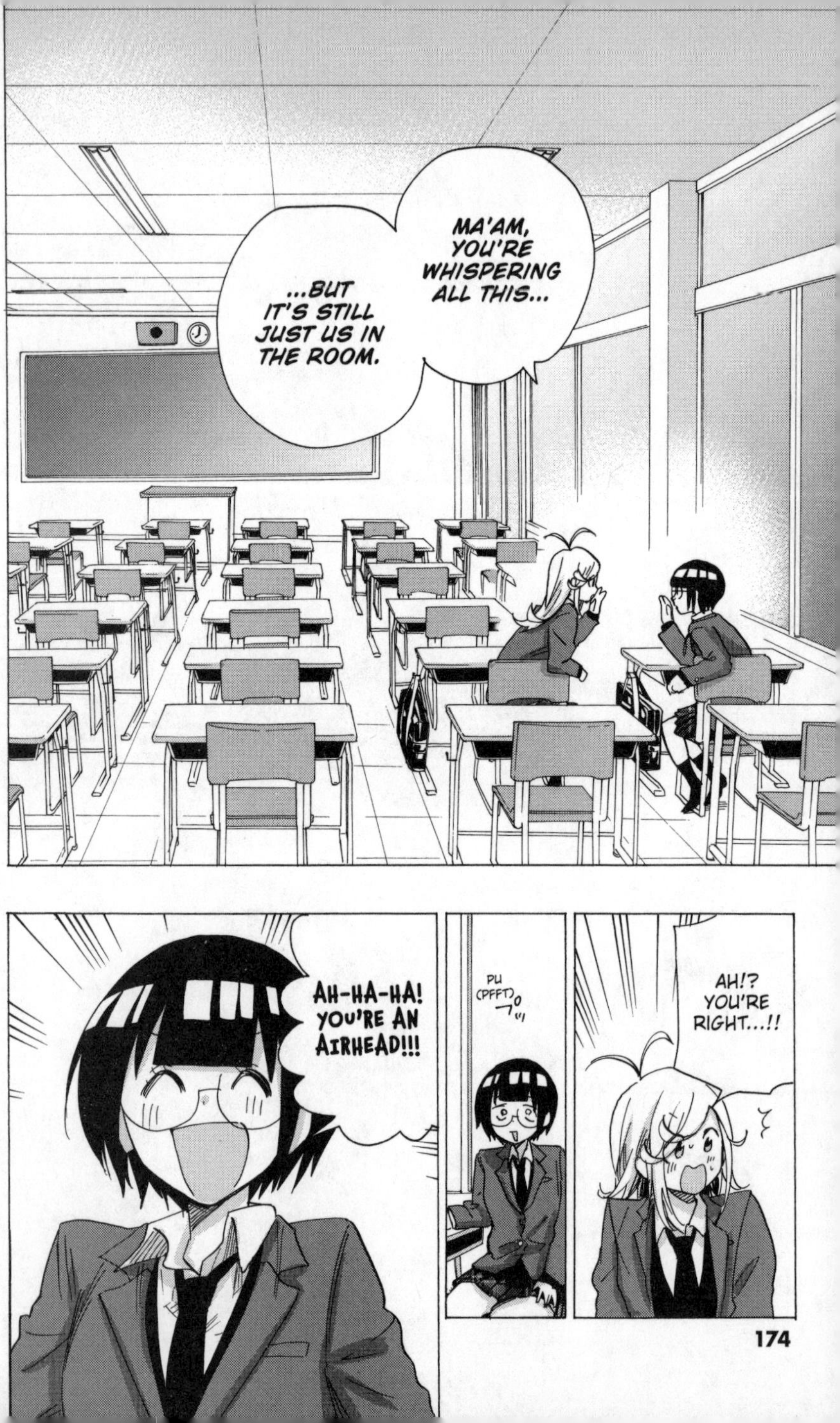
MA'AM, YOU'RE WHISPERING ALL THIS...
...BUT IT'S STILL JUST US IN THE ROOM.
AH!? YOU'RE RIGHT...!!
PU (PFFFT)
AH-HA-HA! YOU'RE AN AIRHEAD!!!

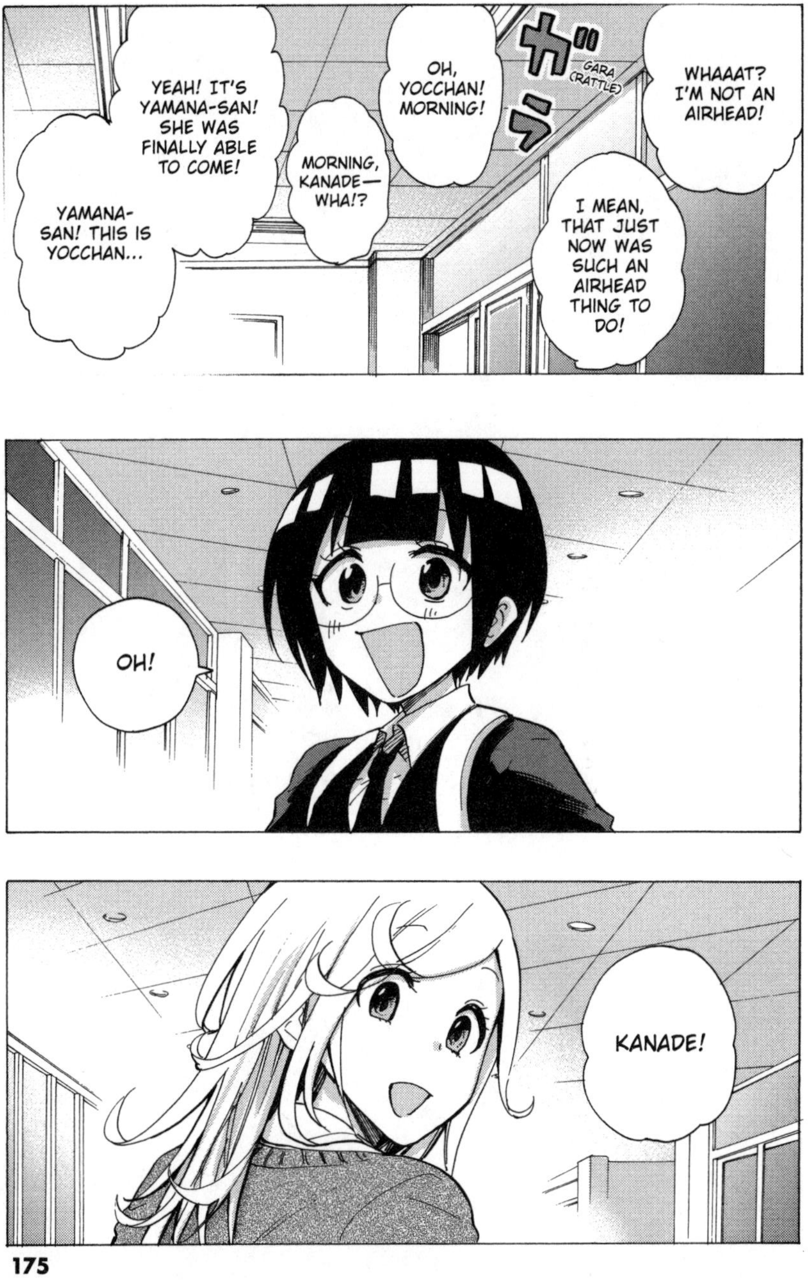
WHAAAT? I'M NOT AN AIRHEAD!
I MEAN, THAT JUST NOW WAS SUCH AN AIRHEAD THING TO DO!
GARA (RATTLE)
OH, YOCCHAN! MORNING!
MORNING, KANADE—WHA!?
YEAH! IT'S YAMANA-SAN! SHE WAS FINALLY ABLE TO COME!
YAMANA-SAN! THIS IS YOCCHAN...
OH!
KANADE!

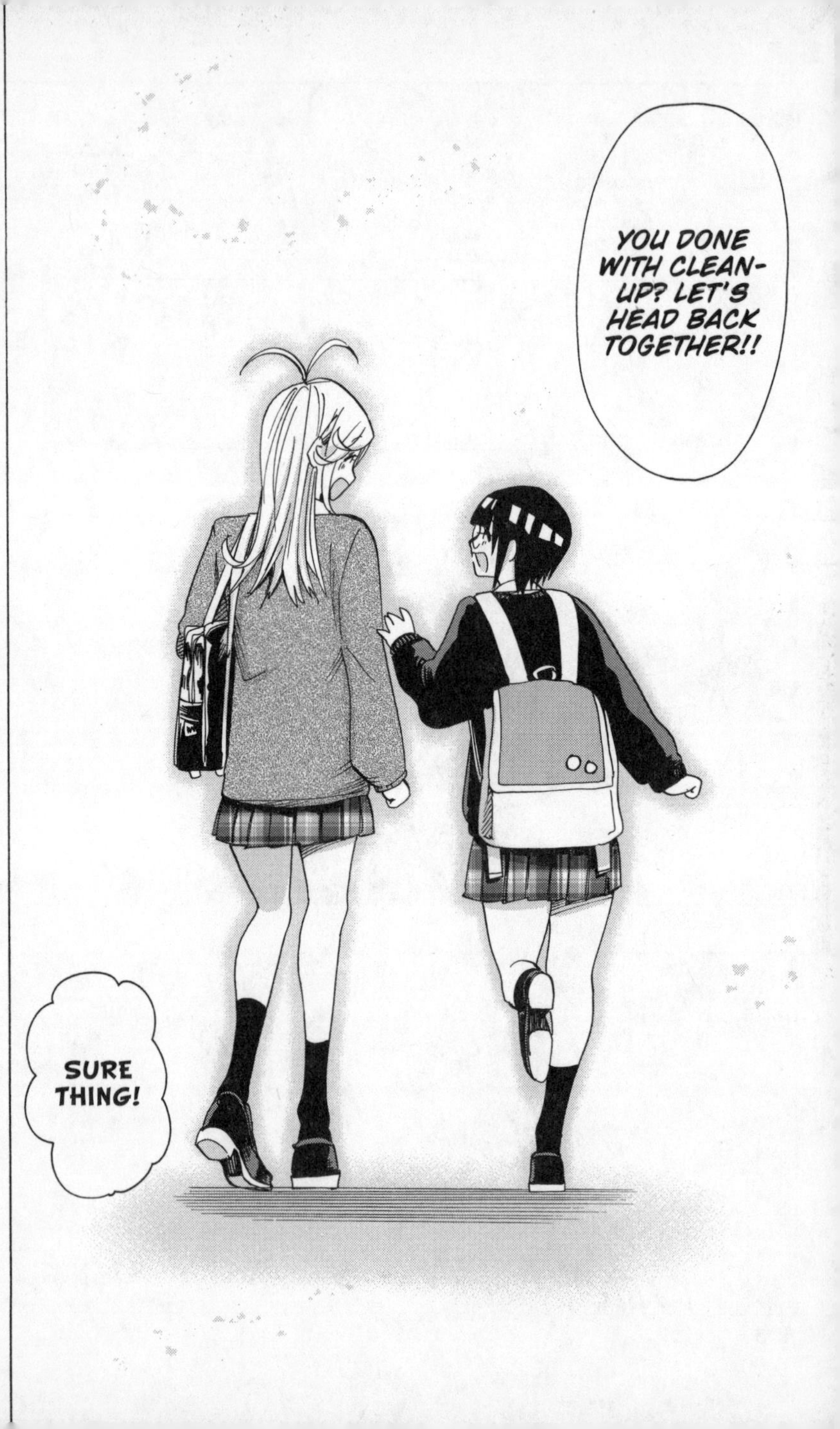
YOU DONE WITH CLEAN-UP? LET'S HEAD BACK TOGETHER!!
SURE THING!

SP 7

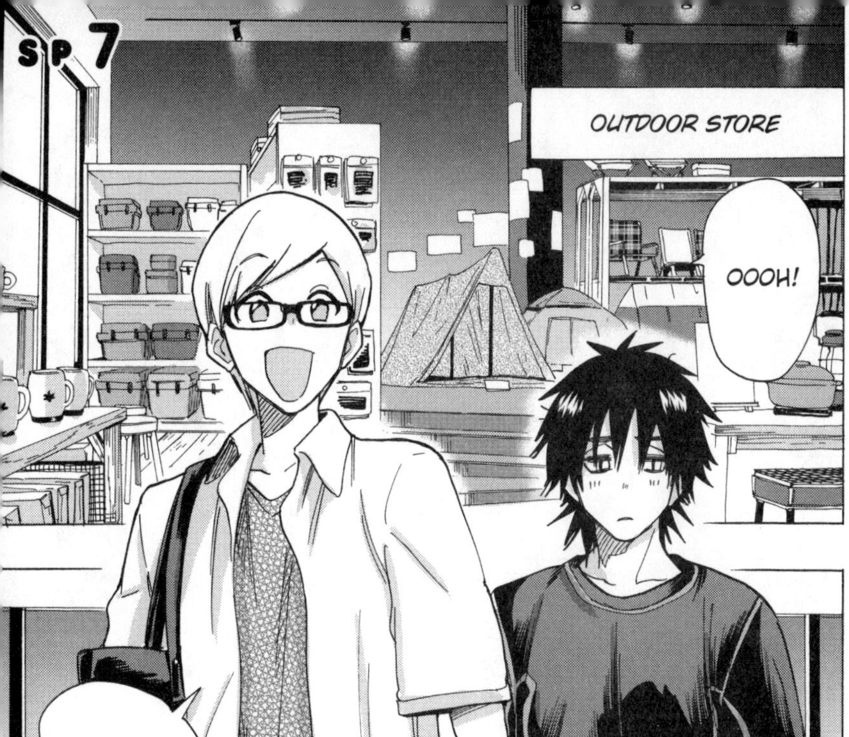
OUTDOOR STORE
OOOH!
A SHOP LIKE THIS REALLY GETS YOU EXCITED, HUH!!?

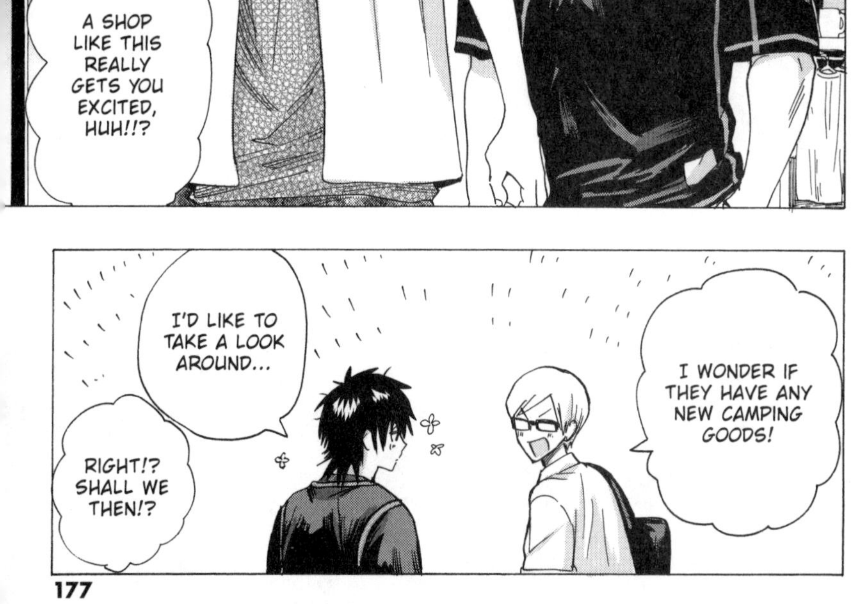
I WONDER IF THEY HAVE ANY NEW CAMPING GOODS!
I'D LIKE TO TAKE A LOOK AROUND...
RIGHT!? SHALL WE THEN!?

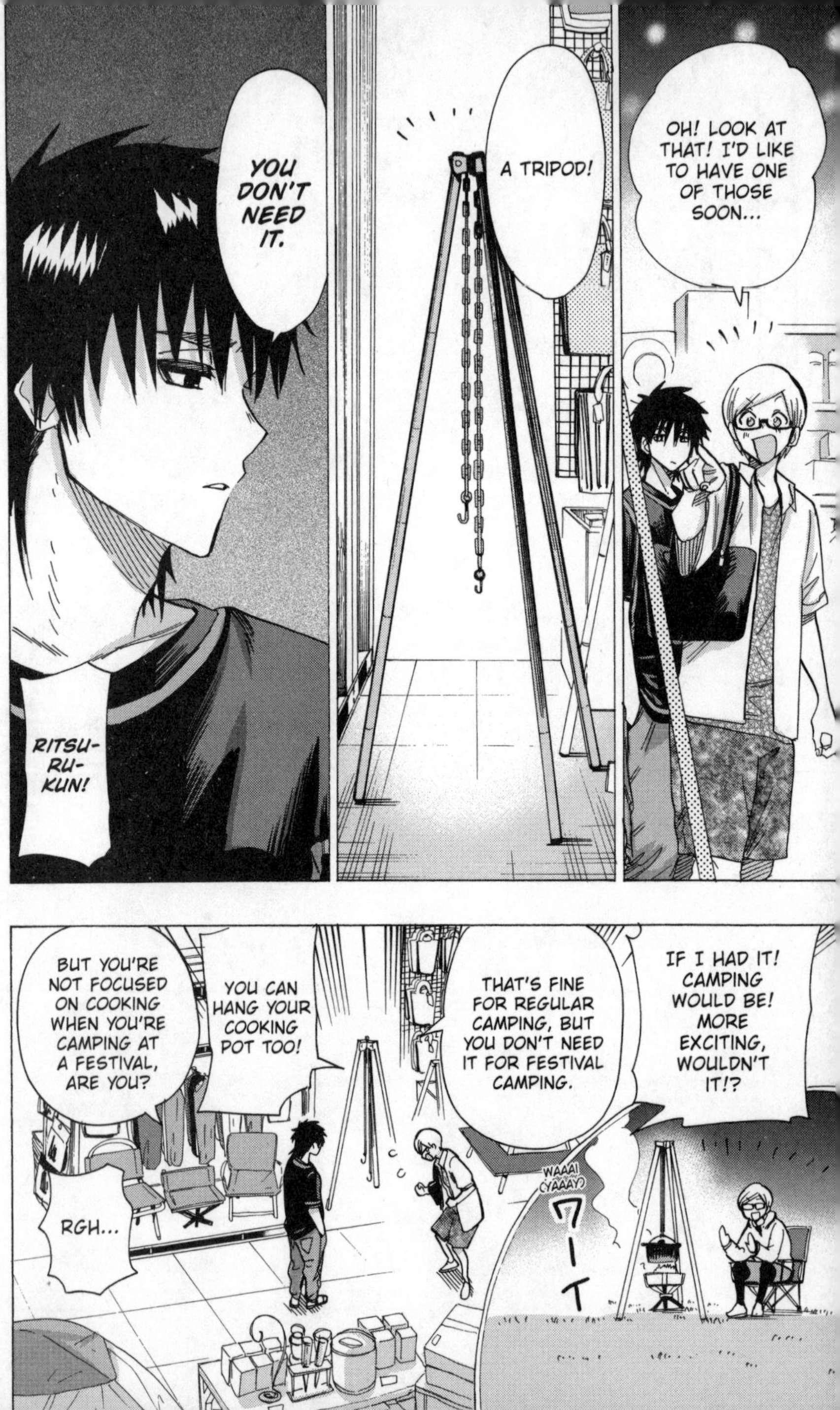
OH! LOOK AT THAT! I'D LIKE TO HAVE ONE OF THOSE SOON...
A TRIPOD!
YOU DON'T NEED IT.
RITSU-RU-KUN!
IF I HAD IT! CAMPING WOULD BE! MORE EXCITING, WOULDN'T IT!?
WAAAI (YAAAY)
ワーイ
THAT'S FINE FOR REGULAR CAMPING, BUT YOU DON'T NEED IT FOR FESTIVAL CAMPING.
YOU CAN HANG YOUR COOKING POT TOO!
BUT YOU'RE NOT FOCUSED ON COOKING WHEN YOU'RE CAMPING AT A FESTIVAL, ARE YOU?
RGH...

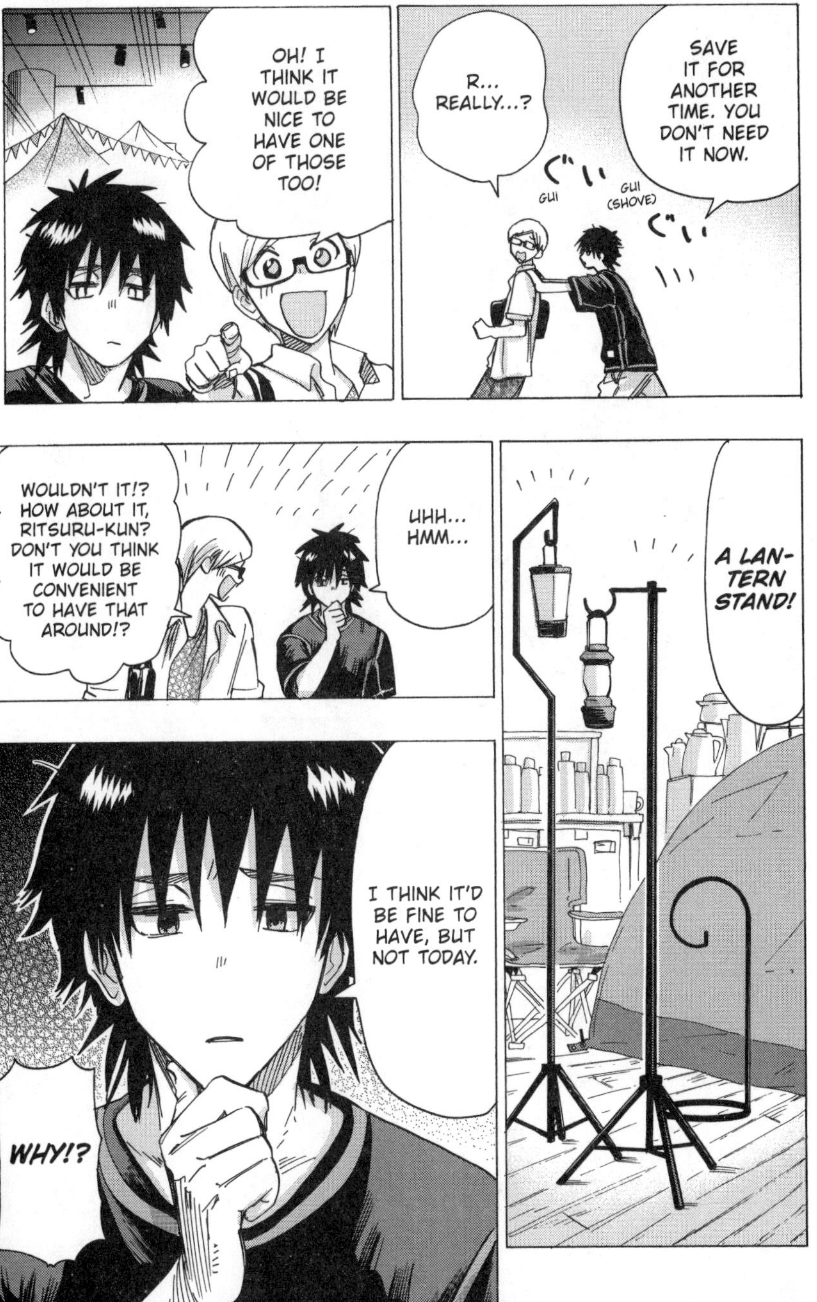

SAVE IT FOR ANOTHER TIME. YOU DON'T NEED IT NOW.
GUI (SHOVE)
GUI
R... REALLY...?
OH! I THINK IT WOULD BE NICE TO HAVE ONE OF THOSE TOO!
A LAN-TERN STAND!
UHH... HMM...
WOULDN'T IT!? HOW ABOUT IT, RITSURU-KUN? DON'T YOU THINK IT WOULD BE CONVENIENT TO HAVE THAT AROUND!?
I THINK IT'D BE FINE TO HAVE, BUT NOT TODAY.
WHY!?

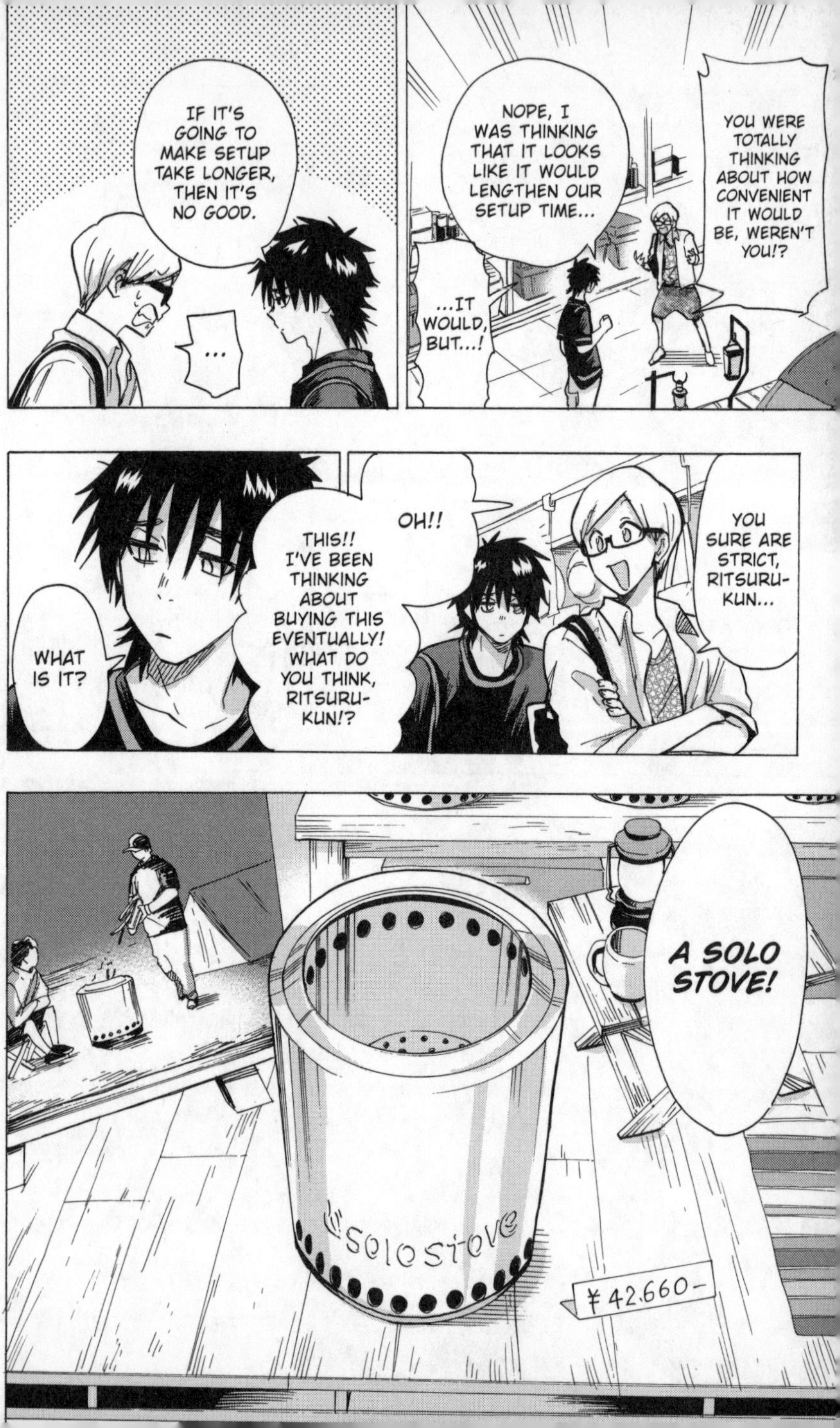

YOU WERE TOTALLY THINKING ABOUT HOW CONVENIENT IT WOULD BE, WEREN'T YOU!?
NOPE, I WAS THINKING THAT IT LOOKS LIKE IT WOULD LENGTHEN OUR SETUP TIME...
...IT WOULD, BUT...!
IF IT'S GOING TO MAKE SETUP TAKE LONGER, THEN IT'S NO GOOD.
...
YOU SURE ARE STRICT, RITSURU-KUN...
OH!!
THIS!! I'VE BEEN THINKING ABOUT BUYING THIS EVENTUALLY! WHAT DO YOU THINK, RITSURU-KUN!?
WHAT IS IT?
A SOLO STOVE!
solo stove
¥42.660-

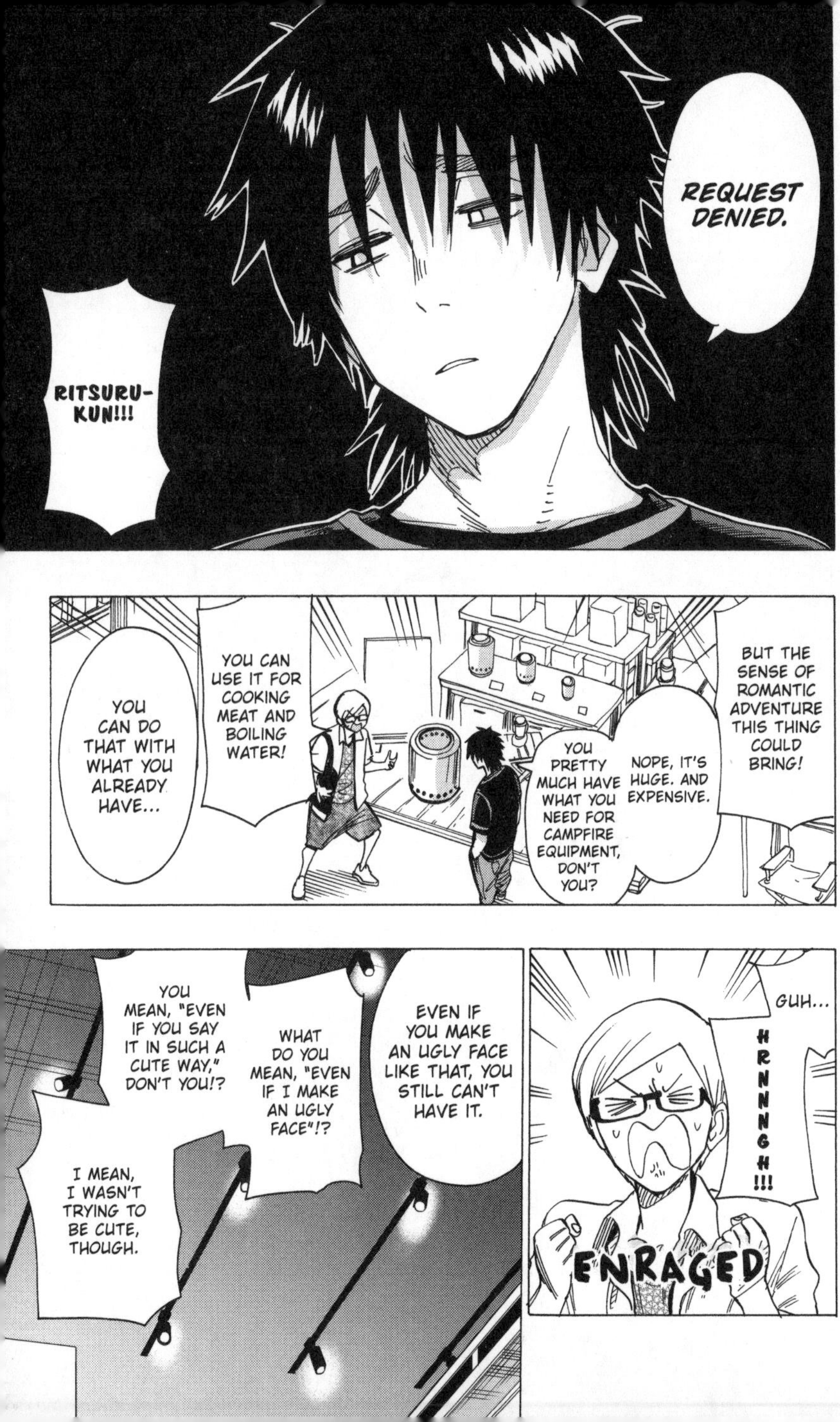
REQUEST DENIED.
RITSURU-KUN!!!
BUT THE SENSE OF ROMANTIC ADVENTURE THIS THING COULD BRING!
NOPE, IT'S HUGE. AND EXPENSIVE.
YOU PRETTY MUCH HAVE WHAT YOU NEED FOR CAMPFIRE EQUIPMENT, DON'T YOU?
YOU CAN USE IT FOR COOKING MEAT AND BOILING WATER!
YOU CAN DO THAT WITH WHAT YOU ALREADY HAVE...
GUH...
HRNNNGH!!!
ENRAGED
EVEN IF YOU MAKE AN UGLY FACE LIKE THAT, YOU STILL CAN'T HAVE IT.
WHAT DO YOU MEAN, "EVEN IF I MAKE AN UGLY FACE"!?
YOU MEAN, "EVEN IF YOU SAY IT IN SUCH A CUTE WAY," DON'T YOU!?
I MEAN, I WASN'T TRYING TO BE CUTE, THOUGH.

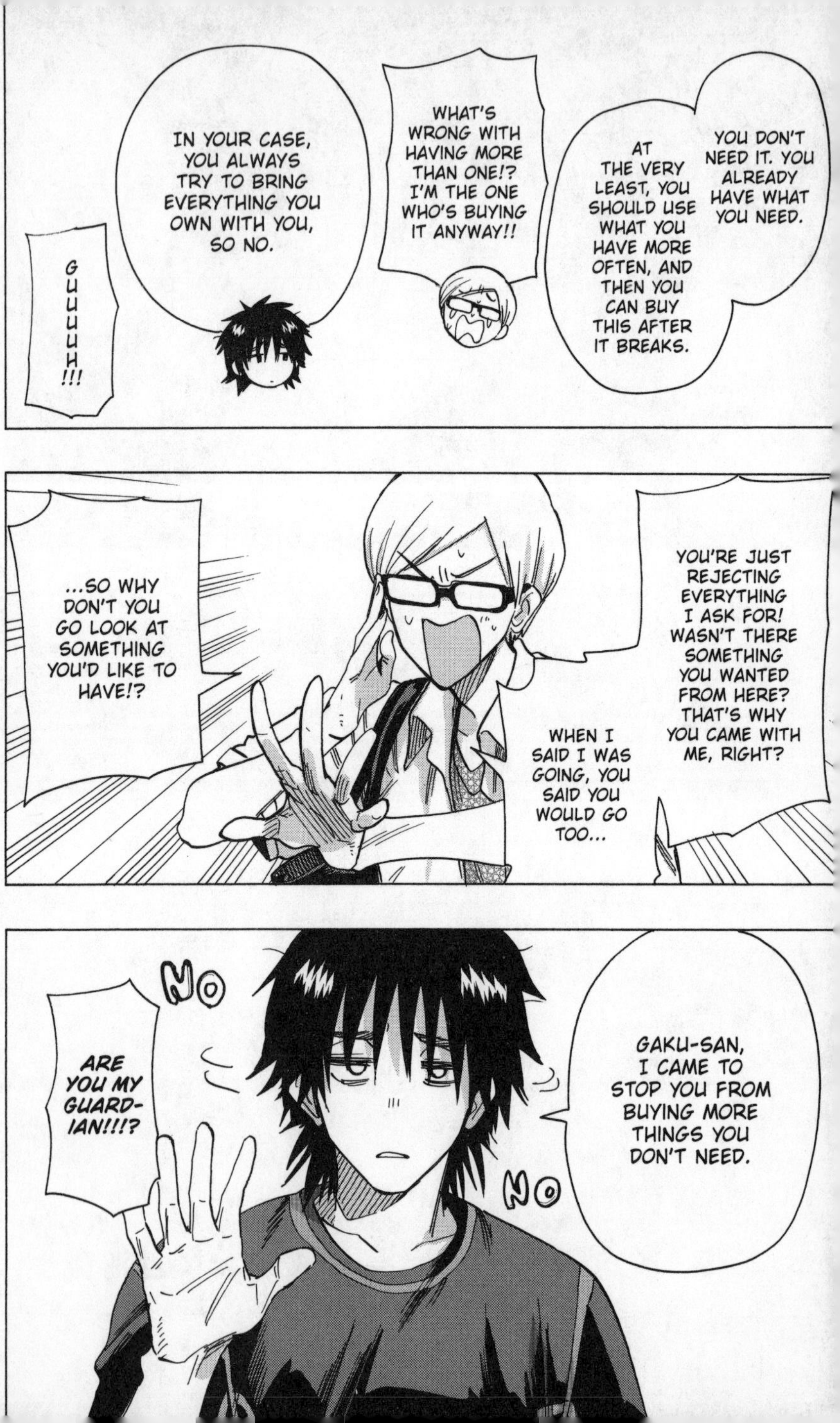
YOU DON'T NEED IT. YOU ALREADY HAVE WHAT YOU NEED.
AT THE VERY LEAST, YOU SHOULD USE WHAT YOU HAVE MORE OFTEN, AND THEN YOU CAN BUY THIS AFTER IT BREAKS.
WHAT'S WRONG WITH HAVING MORE THAN ONE!? I'M THE ONE WHO'S BUYING IT ANYWAY!!
IN YOUR CASE, YOU ALWAYS TRY TO BRING EVERYTHING YOU OWN WITH YOU, SO NO.
GUUUUUH!!!
YOU'RE JUST REJECTING EVERYTHING I ASK FOR! WASN'T THERE SOMETHING YOU WANTED FROM HERE? THAT'S WHY YOU CAME WITH ME, RIGHT?
WHEN I SAID I WAS GOING, YOU SAID YOU WOULD GO TOO...
...SO WHY DON'T YOU GO LOOK AT SOMETHING YOU'D LIKE TO HAVE!?
GAKU-SAN, I CAME TO STOP YOU FROM BUYING MORE THINGS YOU DON'T NEED.
NO
NO
ARE YOU MY GUARDIAN!!!?

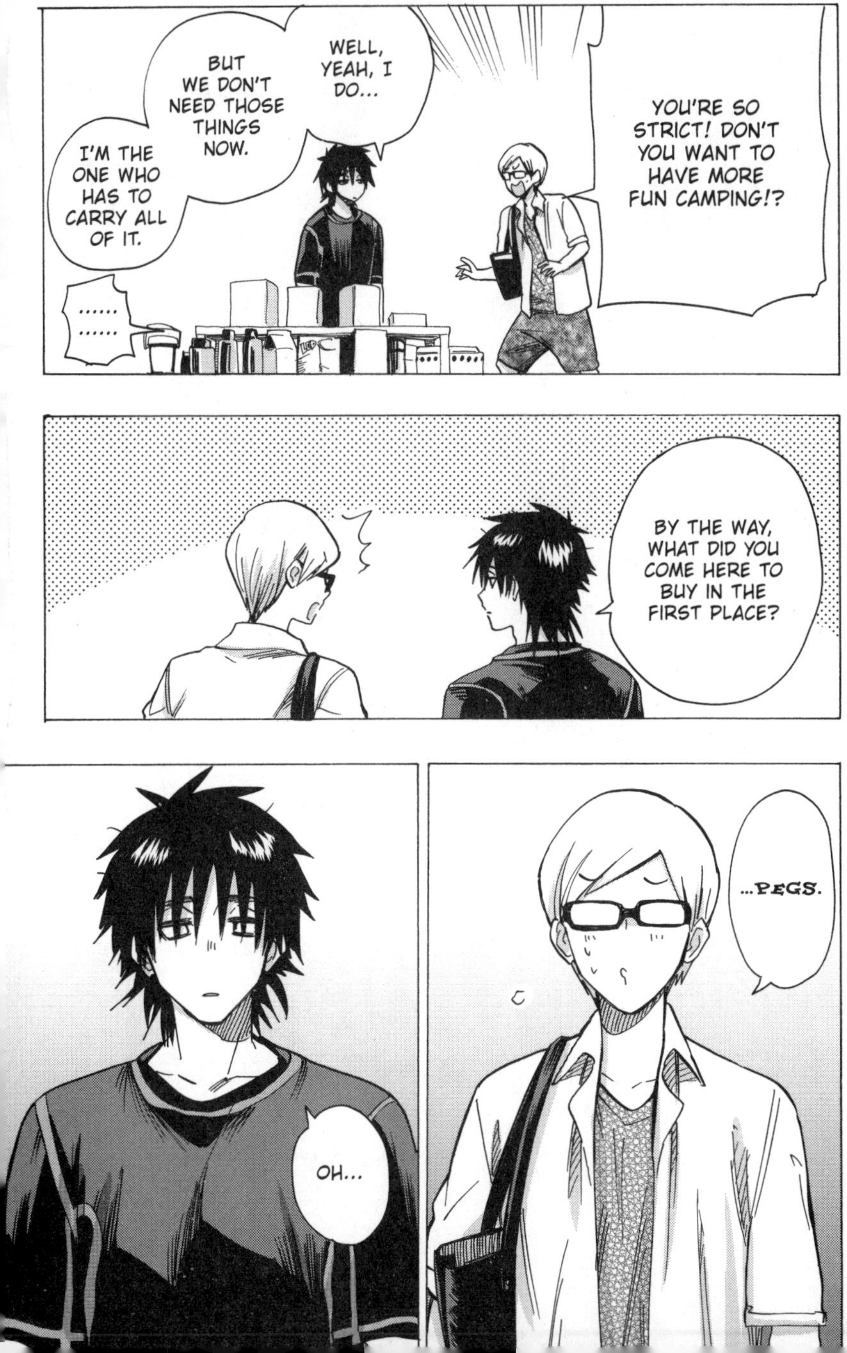
YOU'RE SO STRICT! DON'T YOU WANT TO HAVE MORE FUN CAMPING!?
WELL, YEAH, I DO...
BUT WE DON'T NEED THOSE THINGS NOW.
I'M THE ONE WHO HAS TO CARRY ALL OF IT.
....
BY THE WAY, WHAT DID YOU COME HERE TO BUY IN THE FIRST PLACE?
...PEGS.
OH...

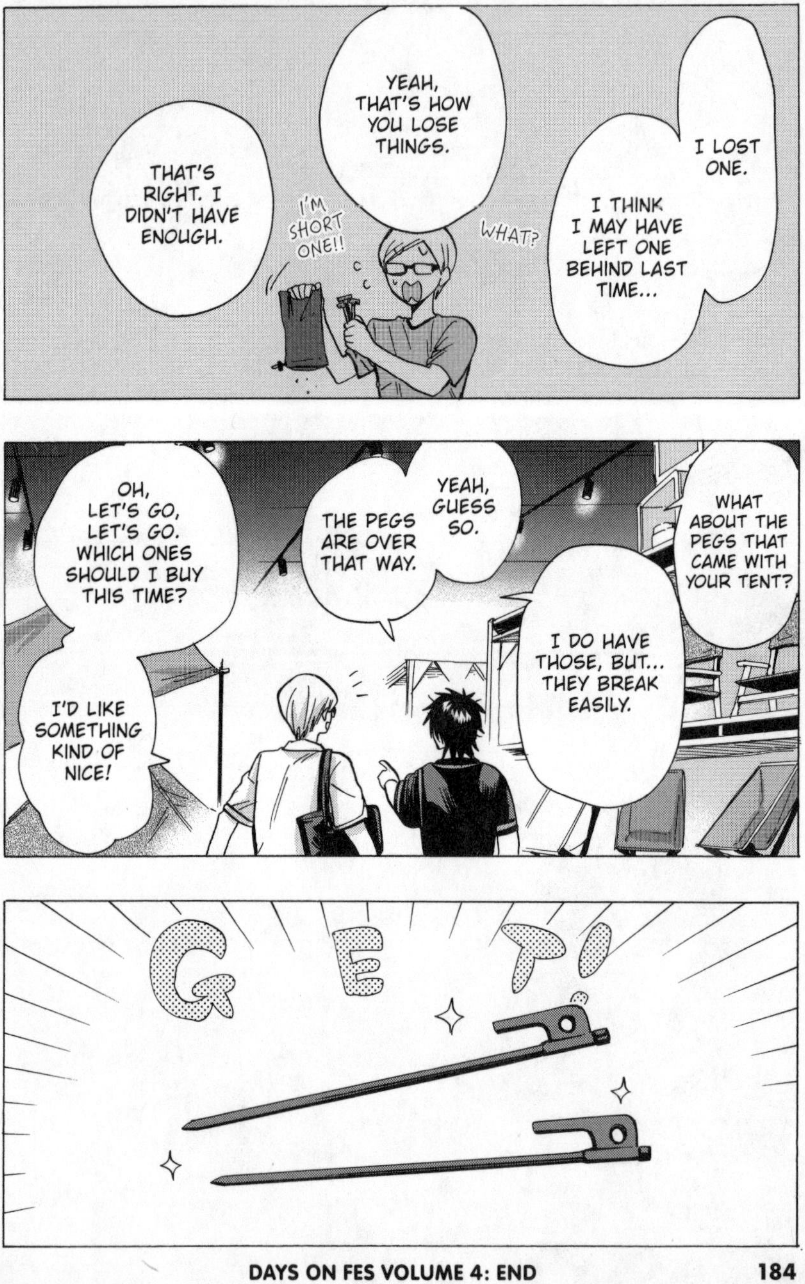
I LOST ONE.
I THINK I MAY HAVE LEFT ONE BEHIND LAST TIME...
WHAT?
YEAH, THAT'S HOW YOU LOSE THINGS.
I'M SHORT ONE!!
THAT'S RIGHT. I DIDN'T HAVE ENOUGH.
WHAT ABOUT THE PEGS THAT CAME WITH YOUR TENT?
I DO HAVE THOSE, BUT... THEY BREAK EASILY.
YEAH, GUESS SO.
THE PEGS ARE OVER THAT WAY.
OH, LET'S GO, LET'S GO. WHICH ONES SHOULD I BUY THIS TIME?
I'D LIKE SOMETHING KIND OF NICE!
GET!

DAYS ON FES VOLUME 4: END

Days on Fes

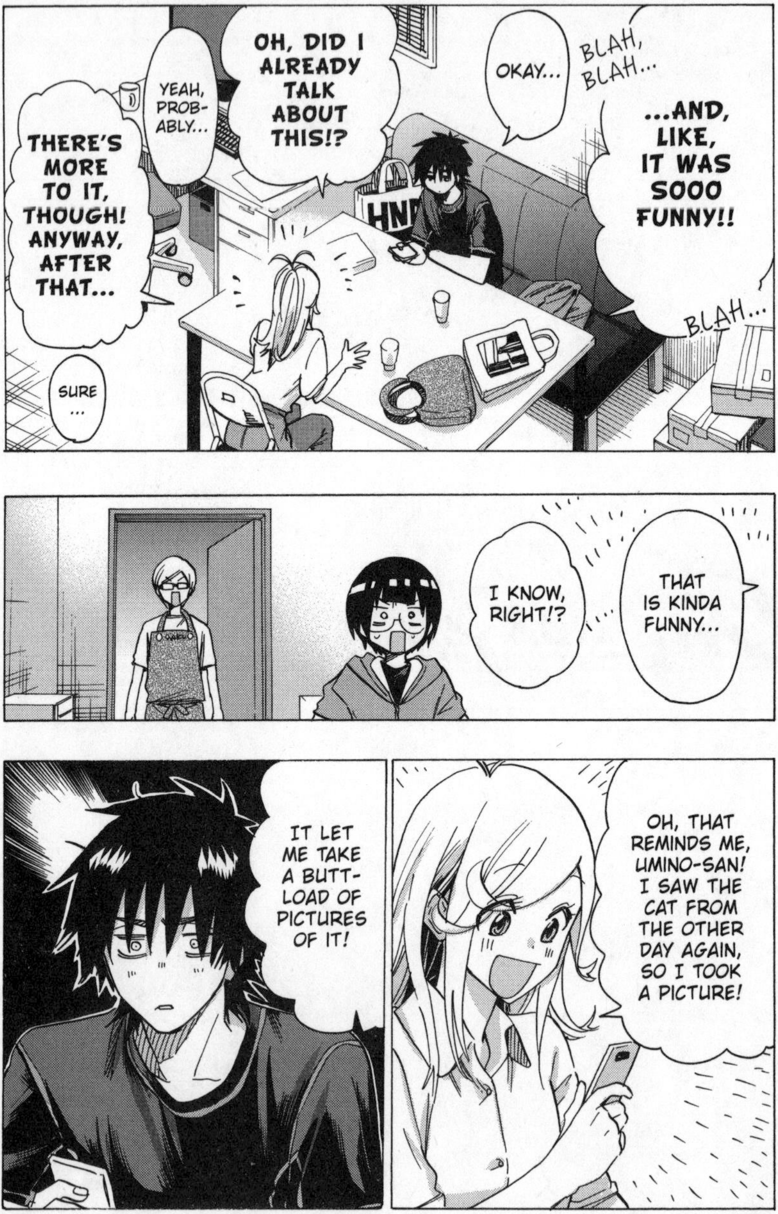
BLAH, BLAH...
...AND, LIKE, IT WAS SOOO FUNNY!!
BLAH...
OKAY...
OH, DID I ALREADY TALK ABOUT THIS!?
YEAH, PROBABLY...
THERE'S MORE TO IT, THOUGH! ANYWAY, AFTER THAT...
SURE ...
THAT IS KINDA FUNNY...
I KNOW, RIGHT!?
OH, THAT REMINDS ME, UMINO-SAN! I SAW THE CAT FROM THE OTHER DAY AGAIN, SO I TOOK A PICTURE!
IT LET ME TAKE A BUTT-LOAD OF PICTURES OF IT!

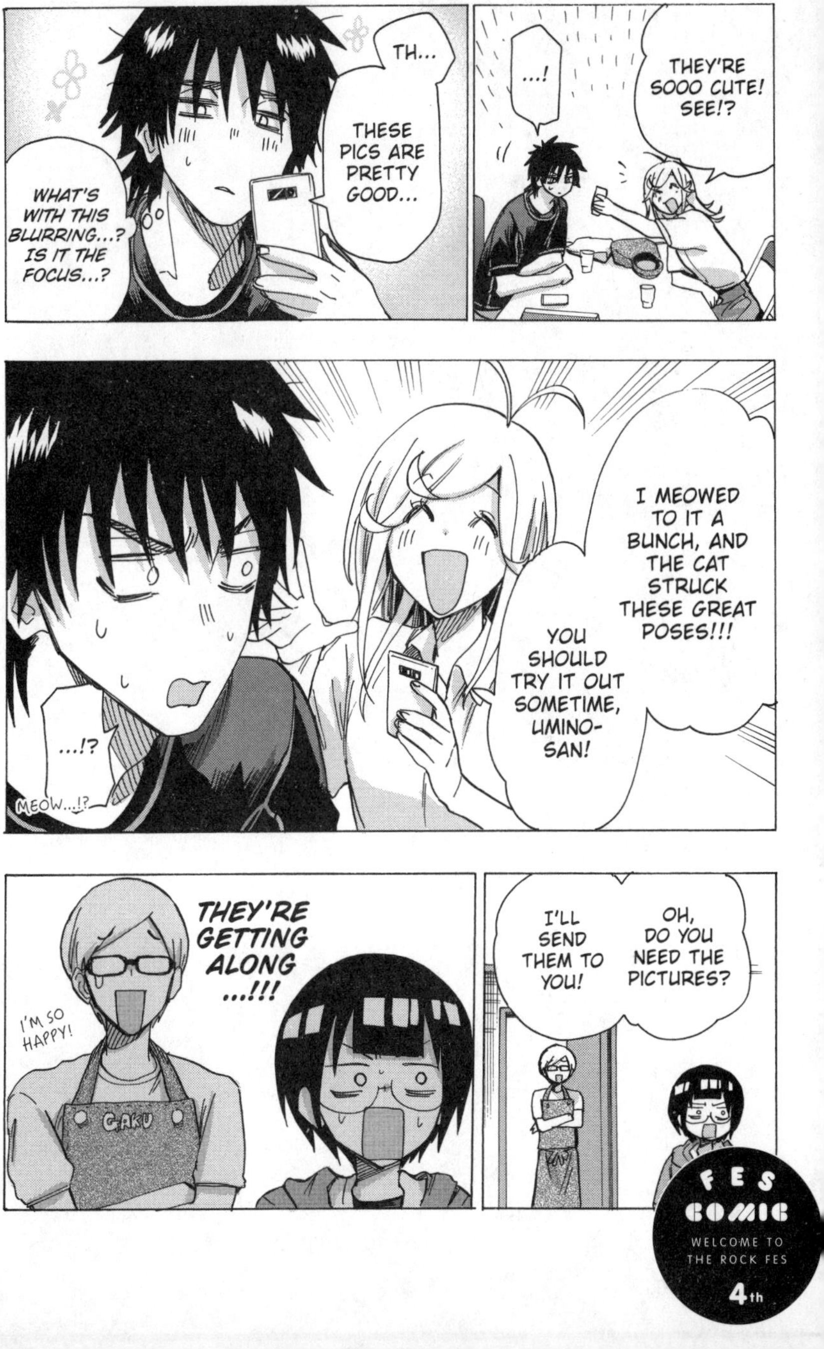
...!
THEY'RE SOOO CUTE! SEE!?
TH...
THESE PICS ARE PRETTY GOOD...
WHAT'S WITH THIS BLURRING...? IS IT THE FOCUS...?
I MEOWED TO IT A BUNCH, AND THE CAT STRUCK THESE GREAT POSES!!!
YOU SHOULD TRY IT OUT SOMETIME, UMINO-SAN!
...!?
MEOW...!?
OH, DO YOU NEED THE PICTURES?
I'LL SEND THEM TO YOU!
THEY'RE GETTING ALONG ...!!!
I'M SO HAPPY!
GAKU
FES COMIC
WELCOME TO THE ROCK FES
4th

Days on Fes

Translation Notes

GENERAL

no honorific: Indicates familiarity or closeness; if used without permission or reason, addressing someone in this manner would constitute an insult.

-san: The Japanese equivalent of Mr./Mrs./Miss. If a situation calls for politeness, this is the fail-safe honorific.

-sama: Conveys great respect; may also indicate that the social status of the speaker is lower than that of the addressee.

-kun: Used most often when referring to boys, this indicates affection or familiarity. Occasionally used by older men among their peers, but it may also be used by anyone referring to a person of lower standing.

-chan: An affectionate honorific indicating familiarity used mostly in reference to girls; also used in reference to cute persons or animals of either gender.

-(o)nii/(o)nee: Meaning "big brother"/"big sister," it can also refer to those older but relatively close in age to the speaker. It can be combined with other honorifics, such as -san, -chan, or -sama.

PAGE 6

A Japanese **police box**, or *koban*, is a small neighborhood police station, usually consisting of only a couple of rooms and a handful of officers. They tend to focus on low-level community policing, as well as operating lost and found services and providing directions.

PAGE 32

Elementary school students in Japan are traditionally given a distinctive leather **backpack** called *randoseru*, whose name and design both stem from Dutch "*ransel*" knapsacks that were utilized by the military in the late 19th century. Today, such backpacks are made by designer brands and can be an expensive purchase for parents.

PAGE 50

Oyakodon, whose name roughly translates to "parent-and-child rice bowl," is a dish featuring chicken, egg, and scallions simmered into a thick soup and served over a bowl of rice. The name refers to both chicken and egg being served together.

Soboro-ni is a dish made with vegetables and *soboro*—soy-simmered ground meat and beaten eggs.

PAGE 57

Despite the name, **melon bread** contains no melon, but is rather a round sweet bread with an outer crust formed from cookie dough. Its name is said to originate from the grooved skin looking similar to that of a muskmelon.

PAGE 104

A "**rain girl**" (*ameonna*) or the male equivalent, "rain guy" (*ameotoko*), are unlucky people who seem to have rain follow them about, spoiling every event they attend. Their opposite is the sunshine girl/guy, who bring good weather.

PAGE 153

A *kotatsu* is a self-heated table common in Japanese households. It's frequently portrayed as being so comfortable that it can lull any users to complete relaxation and induce laziness.

One popular Japanese tradition on New Year's day is to make a **shrine visit**, to wish for good luck for the coming year.

PAGE 154

Because **soba** noodles are easier to cut than other varieties, they're traditionally eaten on New Year's to symbolize ending the hardship of the last year and leaving it behind.

PAGE 156

Bakudan-yaki (fried bomb) are a powered-up version of the popular street food, *takoyaki*. While ordinary *takoyaki* consist of bite-sized balls of octopus wrapped in batter, *bakudan-yaki* are much larger and filled with a wider variety of ingredients.

PAGE 159

The Japanese word for "five yen," *go-en*, is a homophone for *goen*, meaning fate, opportunity, or relationship. The subtle pun means that many shrine-goers will offer a **five-yen coin** in hopes of having good fortune.

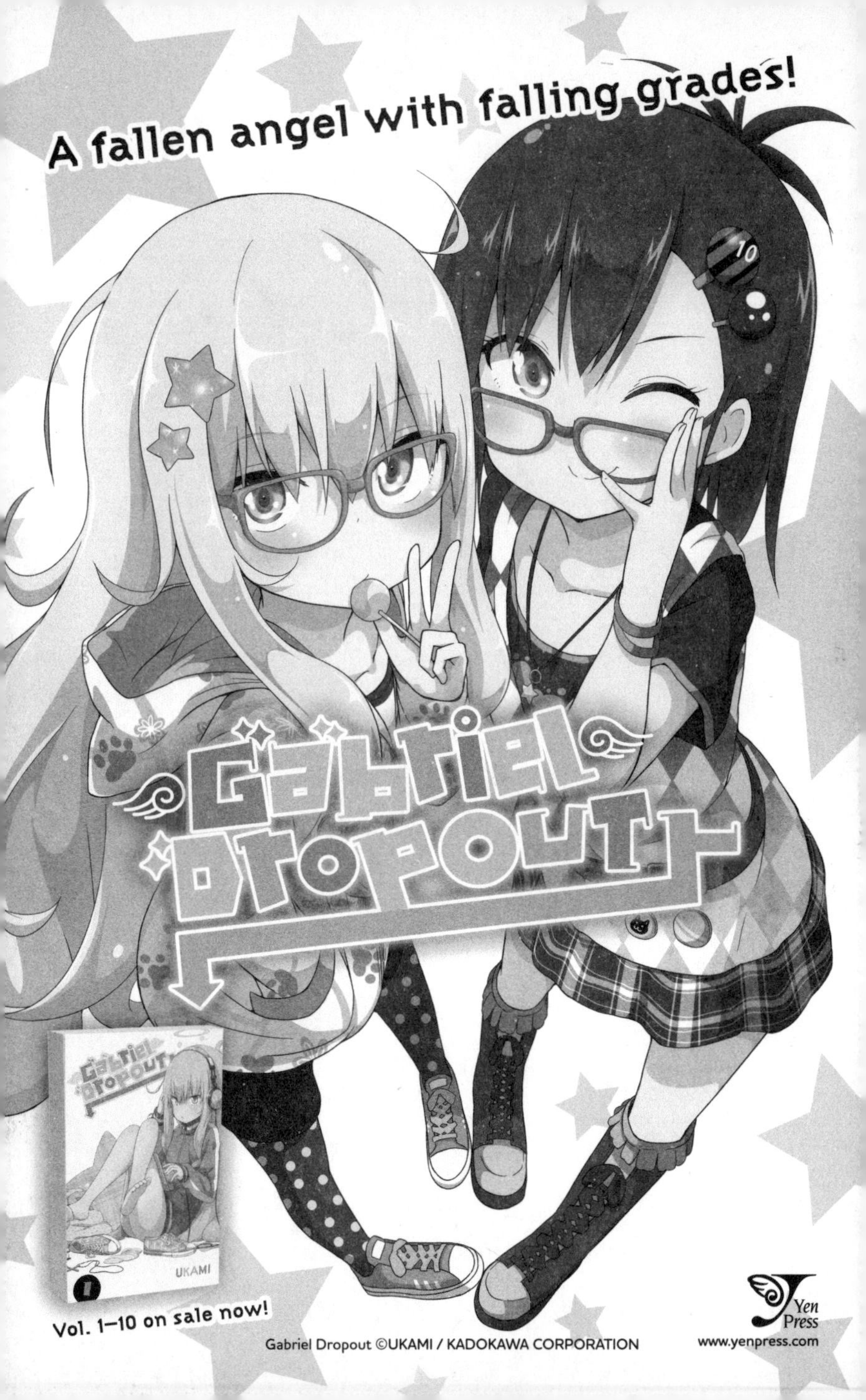
A fallen angel with falling grades!
Gabriel Dropout
UKAMI
1
Vol. 1–10 on sale now!
Gabriel Dropout ©UKAMI / KADOKAWA CORPORATION
Yen Press
www.yenpress.com

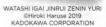

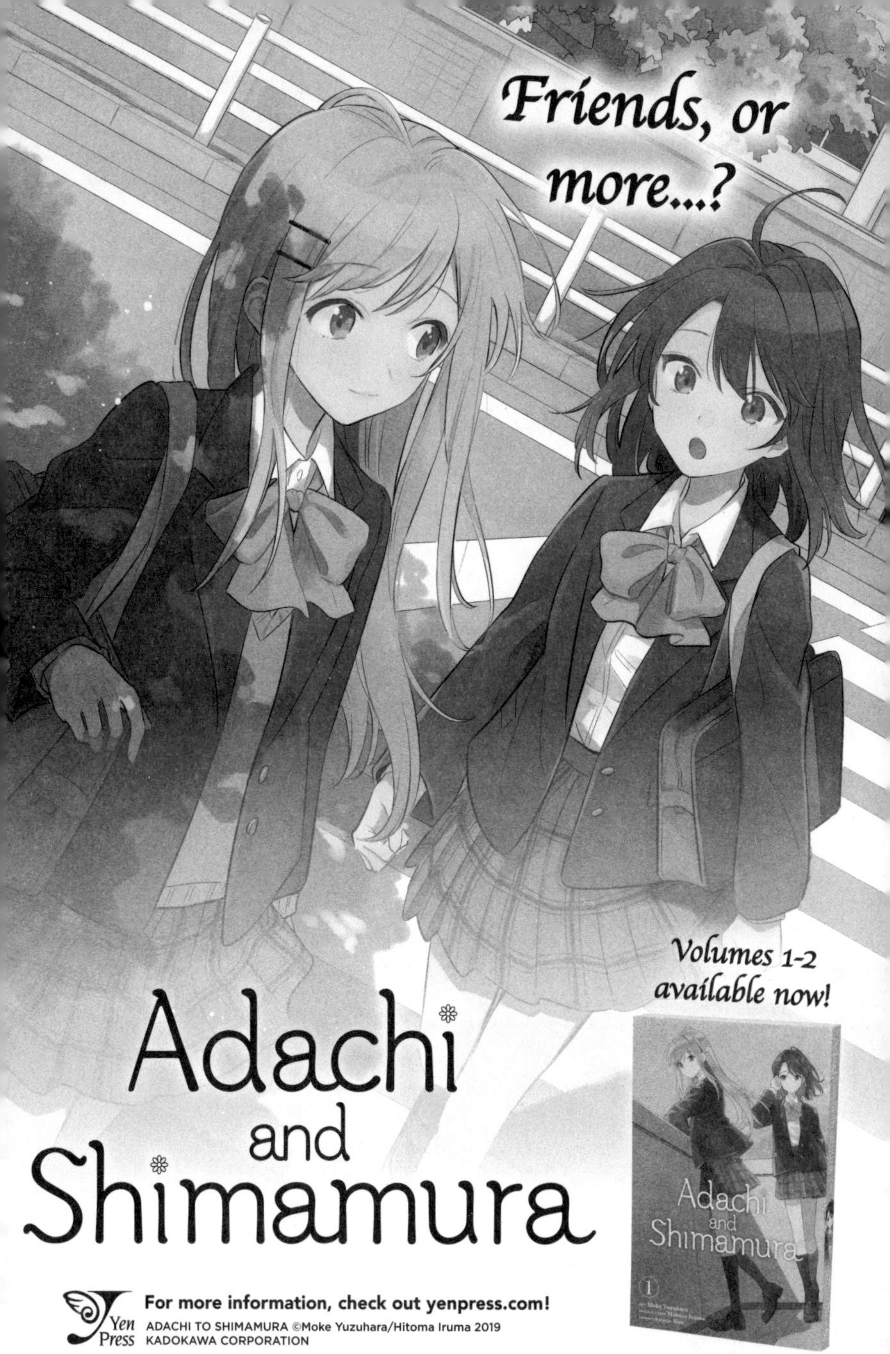
Friends, or more...?
Volumes 1-2 available now!
Adachi and Shimamura
Adachi and Shimamura
1

Days on Fes

vol. 4

KANATO OKA

TRANSLATION: AJANI OLOYE | LETTERING: KAI KYOU

DAYS ON FES Vol. 4
©Kanato Oka 2020
First published in Japan in 2020 by KADOKAWA CORPORATION, Tokyo.
English translation rights arranged with KADOKAWA CORPORATION, Tokyo
through Tuttle-Mori Agency, Inc., Tokyo.

English translation © 2022 by Yen Press, LLC

Yen Press
150 West 30th Street, 19th Floor
New York, NY 10001

Visit us at yenpress.com ♪ facebook.com/yenpress ♪ twitter.com/yenpress
yenpress.tumblr.com ♪ instagram.com/yenpress

First Yen Press Edition: January 2022

Yen Press is an imprint of Yen Press, LLC.
The Yen Press name and logo are trademarks of Yen Press, LLC.

Library of Congress Control Number: 2020950221

ISBNs: 978-1-9753-3977-7 (paperback)
978-1-9753-3978-4 (ebook)

10 9 8 7 6 5 4 3 2 1

WOR

Printed in the United States of America